Treatment of Drug Offenders

Policies and Issues

Carl G. Leukefeld, DSW, is Professor of Behavioral Science and Psychiatry and Director of the Drug and Alcohol Research Center at the University of Kentucky. He was a commissioned officer and Chief Health Services Officer in the U.S. Public Health Service, and for much of that time he was assigned to the National Institute on Drug Abuse in various management and scientific capacities. He has given presentations and has written articles on treatment, criminal justice, prevention, and AIDS. His current research interests include the use of judicial sanctions, drug-abuse treatment, the delivery of rural services, and the impact of HIV on the drug abuser.

Frank M. Tims, PhD, is a Professor in the Department of Psychiatry and Behavioral Medicine, College of Medicine, University of South Florida, and Courtesy Professor in the College of Public Health, USF. He is also Science Advisor to Operation PAR, one of the largest addiction treatment provider organizations in the United States, as well as consultant to the Portage Programs for Dependencies in Canada. He serves on the Scientific Advisory Board of the Center for Therapeutic Community Research, NDRI, New York, NY, and is a member of the Board of Directors of the Education and Mental Health Fund for Eastern Europe, Inc. He was previously Chief of the Services Research Branch, and Deputy Chief, Treatment Research Branch, National Institute on Drug Abuse, National Institutes of Health.

David Farabee, PhD, is Associate Research Psychologist at the UCLA Drug Abuse Research Center. Prior to this he served as lead analyst for criminal justice research at the Texas Commission on Alcohol and Drug Abuse (1992–1995), and as Assistant Professor of Psychiatry and Research Scientist at the University of Kentucky Center on Drug and Alcohol Research (1995–1997). He is presently Research Director of a 5-year evaluation of the California Substance-Abuse Treatment Facility (funded by the California Department of Corrections), Principal Investigator for a multisite evaluation of three residential substance-abuse treatment facilities for youth offenders (funded by the California Youth Authority), and Principal Investigator for a study of substance abuse, medication adherence, and criminality among mentally ill parolees (funded by the National Institute of Justice). He has published in the areas of substance misuse, crime, and offender treatment.

Treatment of Drug Offenders

Policies and Issues

Carl G. Leukefeld, DSW,
Frank Tims, PhD, and
David Farabee, PhD, Editors

 Springer Publishing Company

Springer Publishing Company, Inc.
536 Broadway
New York, NY 10012-3955

Acquisitions Editor: Sheri W. Sussman
Production Editor: Pamela Lankas
Cover design by Susan Hauley

02 03 04 05 06/ 5 4 3 2 1

Treatment of drug offenders : policies and issues / Carl G. Leukefeld . . .   [et al.].
    p.   cm.
    Includes bibliographical references and index.
    ISBN 0-8261-2303-1
    1. Drug abuse—Treatment—United States.   2. Drug abuse—Research—United States.
3. Involuntary treatment—United States.   4. Prisoners—Drug use—United States.
5. Narcotic addicts—Rehabilitation—United States.   6. Drug abuse and crime—United States.
Leukefeld, Carl G.
RC564.T738 2001
362.29'18'0973—dc21   2001042044
                                                     CIP

Printed in the United States of America by Maple-Vail Book Manufacturing Group.

Contents

Acknowledgments

W e would like to thank the many individuals who contributed to this volume. In particular, we are indebted to our colleagues, friends, and the drug users who consented to participate in the studies that are the foundation for this book. We specifically would like to thank chapter authors for their contributions and for their timely modifications. We are grateful to Ann Christianson for her help in editing, formatting, and working with our editor at Springer, Sheri Sussman. Finally, we would like to thank our families for their support in this undertaking as well as our other adventures.

Contributors

M. Douglas Anglin, PhD
University of California at Los
    Angeles
Los Angeles, CA

Robert J. Battjes, DSW
Friends Research Institute
Baltimore, MD

Steven Belenko, PhD
Columbia University
New York City, NY

William M. Burdon, PhD
University of California at Los
    Angeles
Los Angeles, CA

Susie Carleton, RN
University of California
Los Angeles, CA

Steven B. Carswell, MS
Friends Research Institute
Baltimore, MD

Jamie F. Chriqui, MA
Andrews University
Berrin Springs
Michigan

Foster Cook, MA
University of Alabama
Birmingham, AL

David A. Deitch, PhD
University of California
Los Angeles, CA

George De Leon, PhD
National Development and
    Research Institutes, Inc.
New York, NY

Richard Dembo, PhD
University of South Florida
Tampa, FL

John T. Dignam, PhD
Federal Bureau of Prisons
Washington, D.C.

Robert L. DuPont, MD
Du Pont Associates
Rockville, MD

Gary D. Field, PhD
Oregon Dept. of Corrections
Eugene, OR

Robert Fiorentine, PhD
University of California at Los
Angeles
Los Angeles, CA

Michael T. French, PhD
University of Miami
Miami, FL

Thomas E. Hanlon, PhD
Friends Research Institute and
University of Maryland
Baltimore, MD

Adele Harrell, PhD
The Urban Institute
Washington, D.C.

Angela Hegamin, PhD, MSPH
University of California at Los
Angeles
Los Angeles, CA

Matthew L. Hiller, PhD
University of Kentucky
Lexington, KY

Maureen P. Hillhouse, PhD
University of California at Los
Angeles
Los Angeles, CA

Robert M. Hooper, PhD
University of Delaware
Newark, DE

James A. Inciardi, PhD
University of Delaware
Newark, DE

Timothy W. Kinlock, PhD
Friends Research Institute, Inc.
and University of Baltimore
Baltimore, MD

Mark Kleiman, PhD
University of California at Los
Angeles
Los Angeles, CA

Kevin Knight, PhD
Texas Christian University
Ft. Worth, TX

Igor B. Koutsenok, MD
University of California at
Los Angeles, CA

D. Timothy Lane, MEd
Wright State University
Dayton, OH

Stephen Livingston, BA
University of South Florida
Tampa, FL

T. K. Logan, PhD
University of Kentucky
Lexington, KY

Douglas Longshore, PhD
University of California at Los
Angeles
Los Angeles, CA

Karin Marsolais, BA
University of California at Los
Angeles
Los Angeles, CA

Steven S. Martin, MA
University of Delaware
Newark, DE

Charles O. Matthews, PhD
University of South Florida
Tampa, FL

Duane C. McBride, PhD
Andrews University
Berrin Springs, MI

Kathryn E. McCollister, PhD
University of Miami
Miami, FL

Nina P. Messina, PhD
University of Maryland,
College Park
College Park, MD

Genevieve Monahan, PhD, RN
University of California at Los
Angeles, California State
University, Long Beach
Los Angeles, CA

Rosalie L. Pacula, MA
Andrews University
Berrin Springs, MI

Roger H. Peters, PhD
University of South Florida
Tampa, FL

Michael L. Prendergast, PhD
University of California at Los
Angeles
Los Angeles, CA

Sandyha R. Rao, PhD
Texas Christian University
Ft. Worth, TX

Richard C. Rapp, MSW
Wright State University
Dayton, OH

Stanley Sacks, PhD
National Development and
Research Institutes, Inc.
New York, NY

James Schmeidler, PhD
Mount Sinai School of Medicine
New York, NY

Harvey A. Siegal, PhD
Wright State University
Dayton, OH

D. Dwayne Simpson, PhD
Texas Christian University
Ft. Worth, TX

Michele Staton, MSW
University of Kentucky
Lexington, KY

Hilary L. Surratt, MA
University of Delaware
Newark, DE

Faye S. Taxman, PhD
University of Maryland, College
Park
College Park, MD

Yvonne Terry-McElrath, MA
Andrews University
Berrin Springs, MI

Curtis J. VanderWaal, MSW
Andrews University
Berrin Springs, MI

Robert Walker, MSW
University of Kentucky
Lexington, KY

Beth A. Weinman, MSW
Federal Bureau of Prisons
Washington, DC

Harry K. Wexler, PhD
National Development and
   Research Institutes, Inc.
New York, NY

I

Background

Clinical and Policy Opportunities

Carl G. Leukefeld, David Farabee, and Frank Tims

The growing interest in treatment, clinical interventions, and rehabilitation activities of drug abuse and criminal offenders has been attributed to the burgeoning U.S. criminal justice population, currently at more than six million people under criminal justice supervision (Bureau of Justice Statistics [BJS], 1998) with increasing costs. For example, about $40 billion a year is needed to pay for the incarceration of these 2 million people in U.S. prisons and jails (BJS, 1998). Most of the increase in the criminal justice population is related to the number of drug-involved offenders—estimated at about four million drug abusers in the U.S. criminal justice system, which is larger than the almost one million drug and alcohol users receiving community drug abuse treatment (Department of Health and Human Services, 1999).

The purpose of this book is to examine current approaches, update information, and focus on clinical interventions. Research findings on drug abuse interventions in criminal justice settings that have shown promise include the *Stay'n Out Program* in New York (Wexler, Falkin, Lipton, & Rosenblum, 1992), the *Cornerstone Program* in Oregon (Field, 1985), and the *Key Crest Program* in Delaware (Inciardi, Surratt, Martin, & Hooper, this volume). Recent studies by Wexler, Melnick, Lowe, and Peters (1999) on prison treatment, as well as drug court studies summarized by Belenko (1998) have also shown promising results.

This book explores opportunities to go beyond incarceration without interventions, particularly for drug abuse. It focuses on the most recent interventions and research in the area of offender drug treatments, including strategies and alternatives to incarceration across criminal justice settings. It also addresses related issues, such as drug courts and clinical implications. This volume was developed for practitioners working with drug-abusing offenders, students, and policy makers. It highlights the current situation the U.S. criminal justice system faces with expanded capacities and needs, largely fueled by drug-abusing offenders. This chapter also introduces selected clinical and policy issues. What is most interesting to those involved with drug-abusing offenders is the number of consistent issues. For example, most policymakers want "instant cures for addiction," and many practitioners shun research and approach interventions without considering theory. We hope this changes as information expands our understanding of drug addiction.

THE CHRONICITY OF DRUG ABUSE

Practitioners and policymakers need to be constantly reminded that drug addiction is a chronic and relapsing disorder (Institute of Medicine, 1996). This chronic and relapsing nature is important for practitioners to keep in mind, but is complicated by the way different people conceptualize drug use (Leukefeld & Leukefeld, 1999). For example, community-treatment providers are concerned with helping alcohol and drug abusers stop using these drugs. Criminal justice officials may look at the drug problem differently, focusing on crimes and eliminating drug sales. From a school's perspective, the focus is on behavior problems and developing/delivering drug education and prevention programs.

Policy approaches usually parallel public opinion polls. For example, as the public's attitudes toward drug use have become more conservative, policymakers change emphasis from treating drug abusers to law enforcement strategies, and are now moving to treatment in jails and prisons as well as drug courts. At the same time, public health officials, responding to the spread of HIV/AIDS, advocate distributing needles and condoms, together with giving advice on the importance of sexual abstinence, since injecting accounts for approximately one third of all persons with AIDS.

Practitioners are becoming more aware of current thinking among many scientists that drug abuse is an addiction and a brain disorder/disease. This has been summarized by Alan Leshner (1997), Director of the National Institute on Drug Abuse, as:

> Scientists have identified neural circuits that are involved in the actions of every known drug of abuse, and they have specified common pathways that are affected by almost all such drugs. Research has also begun to reveal major differences between the brains of addicted and non-addicted individuals and to indicate some common elements of addiction, regardless of the substance. (p. 46)

Understanding drug abuse as a brain disease can moderate a moralistic view of addiction. One consequence of disease-model research is to focus treatment on reversing or "compensating for" these changes in brain function using medications or behavioral treatments (Leshner, 1997). The relapsing nature of drug abuse can complicate the general public's understanding about the effectiveness of drug abuse treatment. Viewed from a correctional perspective, recidivism should be reduced as a direct function of reducing drug use. Viewed from a treatment perspective, treatment should be followed by "cure" and no drug abuse. These goals are compatible, but are frequently implemented differently, often causing tension. There is also criticism about the limitations of drug abuse treatment in spite of the research, which has generally supported the effectiveness of treatment (Institute of Medicine, 1996; Simpson, Joe, Fletcher, Hubbard, & Anglin, 1999), particularly when treatment is combined with criminal justice sanctions (Leukefeld & Tims, 1988).

TREATMENT

Offender drug treatment has been separated into Civil Commitment (supervision with urine testing), Criminal Justice Authority (community corrections), Urine testing, Offender Community Treatment Services (community drug abuse treatment), and Treatment Services in Prisons and Jails (Leukefeld & Tims, 1988). Many programs are not theoretically grounded. Although drug and alcohol community practitioners have used a bio/psycho/social model with alcohol treatment, this approach is less articulated in criminal justice settings. This approach is used to bridge the disease model, the 12-Step or self-help group approach, including Alcoholics Anonymous

(AA) and Narcotics Anonymous (NA), with behavioral-based and learning theory-based approaches. This approach incorporates the interaction of brain, behavior, and environment, and can be used as a framework for criminal justice practitioners.

The bio/psycho/social/spiritual model (Leukefeld & Leukefeld, 1999) is theoretically grounded and related to possible pathways for addiction as an interaction of behavior, social factors, spirituality, and biology (brain). It provides an approach to think about the advantages of treatment in criminal justice settings—emphases on therapeutic communities/residential treatment, talking therapies, skills training, disease concepts, and spirituality. It also provides a way to target limitations, including the limited use of pharmacological interventions in criminal justice settings.

A bio/psycho/social/spiritual approach includes four possible theories or pathways to drug abuse that are interwoven throughout this volume. Biological or *genetic* pathways include heritability and biologically conditioned aspects of addiction (Cloninger, 1999). This foundation for the disease model has been criticized because it is "used" by alcoholics and drug users to refuse to take responsibility for their addictive behaviors since a disease cannot be "controlled." *Psychological* pathways incorporate individual characteristics that contribute to motivation to use and abuse drugs, expectancies to use, and personality factors that can be assessed. Research has focused on identifying individual "risk" and "protective" factors (Hawkins, Catalano, & Miller, 1992). However, it is important for practitioners to keep in mind that a risk factor for one person may be a protective factor for another. *Social and environment* pathways include laws, culture, familial norms, customs, peer association, and moral consequences that have been associated in the literature with social learning (Bandura, 1977). *Spirituality* pathways incorporate research and anecdotal information that indicates that spirituality (Benson, 1997) and religiosity (Gorsuch, 1995) are related and protective. Although the literature is fairly consistent that spirituality is related to recovery, it is not without controversy.

There are three issues that are not fully covered in this book. The first is nationwide prison overcrowding (Becker, 1997). Private prisons have been identified as a partial solution (Logan & Rausch, 1985). Prison privatization services range from entire prisons to purchasing services, such as medical services. A major argument for privatization is the reduced costs (James, Bottomley, Liebling, & Clare, 1997), as well as flexibility (Logan & Rausch, 1985). Since efficacy is central to privatization for construction as well as services, it is logical that prison privatization includes drug treatment. Along with an increase in the number of private prisons is the concern that cost, particularly a need for corporate profits, has an effect on all services, including drug treatment and effectiveness. However, there is little research that compares private and public drug abuse treatment to help make informed decisions about the privatization of drug abuse treatment clinical services.

A second issue that impacts drug abuse treatment is the aging of U.S. prisoners and the associated and increased health problems (Hegamin, Longshore, & Monahan, this volume). McCorkel, Butzin, Martin, and Inciardi (1998) support this finding, and add that drug-involved offenders are likely to have chronic health problems. Health problems will increase, for example, since HIV prevalence is considerably higher in criminal justice settings than the general U.S. population (Farabee & Leukefeld, this volume).

A third issue is the limited number of research-grounded intervention approaches. For example, one approach is cognitive criminal thinking, developed by Yochelson and Samenow (1976). Criminal thinking is incorporated into criminal justice interventions, including drug treatment (Krueger, 1997). Criminal thinking emphasizes "thinking errors," and helps prisoners identify and change thinking errors to improve interactions and to change behaviors. Practitioners give positive feedback, however, there is limited research.

CLINICAL AND POLICY ISSUES

This volume is organized into five areas. The first area provides background information about drug abuse interventions in criminal justice settings. The second focuses on selected clinical issues in criminal justice settings. The third area presents interventions for drug abusers involved in criminal justice settings. The fourth focuses on effectiveness of criminal justice interventions. The fifth presents areas for future consideration.

It is important to note that the sustained research findings over the past years support the clinical activities of criminal justice practitioners who treat drug abusers. It is also most encouraging that criminal justice practitioners are refining treatment and adding to research. For example, therapeutic communities can be successful in treating drug-involved offenders. Additionally, continued aftercare and consistent follow-up treatment after prison therapeutic-community treatment is most successful (see Inciardi et al., this volume; Wexler et al., 1999). However, a number of drug abusers do not become involved in prison therapeutic communities, given finite capacities and resources. Consequently, other initiatives, such as drug courts and community-diversion programs, have increased.

As we look to the future, issues such as privatization and the need for expanded capacities will continue if statutes and guidelines are unchanged, as will the examination of treatment and control. Increasingly, special populations such as dually diagnosed substance abusers and women are receiving attention (see DeLeon, Sacks, & Wexler, this volume; Staton, Leukefeld, & Logan, this volume). Clearly, screening/assessment, matching treatment to drug-abuser needs, and prioritizing treatment are challenges within limited resources. In fact, we need to target drug abuse treatment on drug abusers who commit crimes as a result of their drug use, rather than for criminals who use drugs.

2

Historical Trends of Drug Treatment in the Criminal Justice System

Gary D. Field

This chapter reviews the trends and themes of drug treatment in the criminal justice system of the United States over the past 200 years. After an overview chronology, major themes are identified and explored. The chapter concludes with a review of the current state of major themes and recommendations for the future.

OVERVIEW CHRONOLOGY OF THE DEVELOPMENT OF CORRECTIONAL DRUG TREATMENT IN THE UNITED STATES

Three themes run through the early eras of drug treatment, leading up to current efforts in the criminal justice system in the United States. They are: (a) drug use patterns within the general population, (b) policy ambivalence over control and punishment versus treatment, and (c) the resulting federal initiatives arising out of that policy ambivalence.

Initial Recognition of Widespread Drug Problems
(1800–1880)

Problems with opiate addiction in the United States became widespread with the broad use of patient medicines in the 1800s. Morphine was discovered in 1806, and became so extensively used during the Civil War that addiction to morphine was called the "army disease." In the middle to late 1800s, private sanitariums that claimed to cure addiction were the primary source of available treatment.

The First Cocaine Epidemic (1880–1920)

In the 1880s, coca became widely available in the United States as a broad remedy and health tonic. By 1900, with an estimated 250,000 addicts, the dangers of addiction became part of the public agenda. The first cocaine epidemic in this country is generally seen as lasting until around 1920. The hypodermic syringe, and thus the possibility of an even more dangerous injectable drug use, was perfected about 1900. The Harrison Act of 1914 is the best known of several early legislative initiatives that regulated sale and distribution of narcotics (Bureau of Justice Statistics [BJS], 1992). Interestingly, the extent of the drug problem within the population at this time was roughly proportional to the drug explosion that occurred again in the 1960s (Musto, 1987).

Legal–Medical Conflicts (1914–1935)

The Harrison Act was administered by Treasury agents. From the beginning, Treasury Department officials held that medical maintenance (treatment through declining usage) was unacceptable. Physicians opposed this view, but lost in the courts, and initial enforcement activities even included arrests of physicians and pharmacists. Beginning in 1919, in response to a growing need for treatment, 44 cities opened municipal clinics to provide temporary maintenance for addicts, but the Treasury Department objected to these clinics and pushed for their closure. All of the clinics were closed by 1925. By the early 1920s, most early, federal, antidrug control measures of the 1920s to the 1960s were in place (BJS, 1992).

Early Federal Treatment Initiatives (1930–1975)

In 1929, the Porter Narcotic Farm Act authorized the Public Health Service to open federal hospitals for the treatment of incarcerated addicts. One facility opened in Lexington, Kentucky, in 1935, and a second facility opened in Fort Worth, Texas, in 1938. Both were essentially modified prisons, although voluntary patients were accepted, and both utilized detoxification as their primary treatment modality (Holden, Wakefield, & Shapiro, 1990). However, treatment also included counseling, vocational training, and community re-entry (Leukefeld, 1985). Little changed from this time until the mid-1960s, when the focus moved to community-based treatment and to civil commitment approaches.

In 1963 the President's Advisory Commission on Narcotics and Drug Abuse judged the Lexington and Fort Worth programs to be inadequate and marginally effective, and called for a larger federal role in treatment of narcotic addicts. The 1968 amendments to the 1963 Community Mental Health Centers Act established specialized addict-treatment grants for local areas that rapidly expanded in the early 1970s.

In 1966 the Narcotic Addict Rehabilitation Act (NARA) initiated a federal, compulsory treatment program using the California and New York civil commitment programs as models (Leukefeld, 1990). Initially provided at Lexington and Fort Worth, NARA inpatient-treatment facilities were opened in several cities. Individuals were sent to NARA programs in lieu of prosecution or sentencing. This legislation also created a linkage between the criminal justice system and the health care system through federal substance abuse and mental health agencies. The NARA facilities were transferred to the Federal Bureau of Prisons when NARA was phased out in the mid-1970s. Also in the 1960s and early 1970s, several other correctional treatment programs were tried and failed. In particular, prison programs in Nevada, New York, and the federal prison system opened and closed during this time.

In 1972 the Special Action Office for Drug Abuse Prevention and the National Institute for Drug Abuse were created, in part to attempt to create greater emphasis on treatment and rehabilitation of offenders. An important connection was made in initiatives during this time between community corrections and local drug-treatment programs with the creation of the Treatment Alternative to Street Crime Program (TASC) in 1972 by the Law Enforcement Assistance Administration and other agencies (Cook & Weinman, 1988). TASC was designed as a diversion and case-management program to coordinate community corrections and local drug treatment

(Leukefeld, 1990). It is one of the early federal drug-treatment initiatives that continues today.

Illegal Drug Use Rate and Pattern Changes (1960–1990)

During the 1960s, hallucinogens became popular. Additionally, heroin, cocaine, and marijuana all showed resurgent use (Johnson, Williams, Dei, & Sanabria, 1990). Hallucinogen use grew in the 1960s, but waned in the 1970s. Heroin addiction exploded in the inner cities between 1965 and 1973, as did the development of methadone maintenance programs (Holden et al., 1990). Cocaine use increased as heroin use faded between 1974 and 1984. Crack then emerged in 1984, again as primarily an inner-city drug (Johnson et al., 1990).

The "Nothing Works" Phenomena (1974–1990)

In 1974, at a time in which few correctional treatment programs had been tried and many of the more innovative programs had just begun, Robert Martinson published an article asserting that most of these programs proved to be unsuccessful (Martinson, 1974). Although his conclusions were over-stated in the popular media, his work was disputed by his colleagues, and Martinson himself reversed his position (Martinson, 1979); the perception of futility of correctional treatment continued to greatly influence popular and professional thinking (Holden et al., 1990). Despite continuously growing evidence to the contrary, the Nothing Works belief phenomena continued into the 1990s as an argument point for those who did not want to invest public resources into rehabilitating offenders.

Rapid Prison Growth (1980–Current)

In the 1980s, prison populations began increasing rapidly, with an increase of 2.5 times between 1980 and 1993. Just over 300,000 individuals were incarcerated in state and federal prisons in 1980, and that number topped 1 million in 1994. Most of these offenders were recidivists, and three of four were drug users (Reuter, 1992). The number of state correctional inmates in custody for drug offenses specifically increased ninefold between 1980 and 1992 (BJS, 1994). By the end of the 1990s, the prison population had continued to grow, stood at 1.8 million, and was expected to break 2 million by 2002 (Office of National Drug Control Policy, 1999).

The Nothing-Works Rebound (1980–1995)

Almost immediately following the Nothing-Works phenomena of the mid-1970s, scholarly works documented the positive effects of rehabilitation. A group of Canadian researchers had been particularly prolific (Gendreau & Ross, 1979; Andrews et al., 1990), as had a research group from New York that included one of Martinson's colleagues (Wexler, Lipton, & Johnson, 1988; Lipton, 1994, 1995). Also in the 1980s, national studies of general, community drug treatment found consistent and substantial positive results of drug treatment in reducing crime (Simpson, 1984; Hubbard, Rachal, Craddock, & Cavanaugh, 1984). Around this same time, the National Institute of Drug Abuse became active in providing knowledge development, technology transfer, and consultation services to enhance drug-treatment efforts with offenders (Leukefeld, 1990).

Public Awareness of the Drug–Crime Connection (1985–1995)

Earlier studies had shown that many addicts had criminal histories prior to their addiction, and that addiction increased criminal behavior to support the addiction (Gandossy, Williams, Cohen, & Harwood, 1980). In the mid-1980s, more thorough studies into the drug–crime connection were widely reported, partly in response to rapid prison growth. These newer studies showed that career criminals and violent predators had a tendency toward long histories of drug abuse (Chaiken, 1986; Chaiken & Chaiken, 1990). Moreover, crime days by groups of offenders were found to rise in relationship to drug-use days, and crime by these same offenders dropped as their drug use decreased (Anglin, 1988; Ball, Shaffer, & Nurco, 1983). With the introduction of crack cocaine in the mid-1980s, the already strong relationship between drugs and crime heightened. Cocaine use doubled in several cities (Lipton, 1995). Also in the 1980s, the first national program to test individuals for drug use at the time of arrest, the Drug Use Forecasting System (DUF), found that 50% to 75% of those arrested tested positive for recent illegal drug use (Wish & O'Neil, 1989).

The War on Drugs (1985–Current)

Because of the widely documented increase in drug use and its attendant increase in crime, as well as its impact on the criminal justice system, federal initiatives grew during the 1980s into an enhanced war on drugs. These initiatives included more aggressive strategies by local law enforcement, leading to more arrests, tougher mandatory sentencing policies creating longer sentences, and creation of new offenses specifically targeting drug dealers. In the late 1980s, federal interest shifted somewhat from supply reduction to demand reduction. Demand-reduction strategies surfaced in 1986 and 1988 laws, as well as in the 1989–1990 Drug Control Strategies. The 1986 Act authorized expanded drug-treatment grants to the states.

New Treatment Modalities (1988–Current)

Therapeutic Community Programs in Correctional Institutions

Building on the research cited above and a few contemporary studies of the effectiveness of prison-based treatment (Field, 1989; Wexler, Falkin, & Lipton, 1990), the Bureau of Justice Assistance launched Project Reform in 1987. This initiative was later transferred to the Center for Substance-Abuse Treatment as Project Recovery in 1991. These projects developed drug-treatment programs in 22 state prison systems, primarily using the therapeutic community-program model (Lipton, 1995). While institution therapeutic community programs had been attempted in the 1960s and 1970s with limited success, the systematic approach of Projects Reform and Recovery in the late 1980s and early 1990s yielded a great deal of program development. Projects Reform and Recovery had a major impact on U.S. prisons from the prison-as-drug-treatment-facility model from Alabama, to the prison system-wide treatment concepts in Florida, Oregon, and Wisconsin, to the several thousand prison-treatment beds developed in Texas. Projects Reform and Recovery efforts have most recently been continued and expanded to jails and prisons by the Residential Substance-Abuse Treatment for State Prisoners grants, which are from the Corrections Program Office of the U.S. Department of Justice.

Drug Treatment in Parole and Probation

While drug treatment had been an integral part of community corrections in many jurisdictions going back to the LEAA initiation of the TASC programs (now called Treatment Accountability for Safer Communities) and before, the renewed interest in demand reduction in the late 1980s influenced parole and probation, as well as prisons and jails. TASC programs re-emerged (Cook & Weinman, 1988). Drug treatment became an integral part of or an adjunct to the concept of "intermediate sanctions" to hold drug offenders accountable without using prison. Many parole and probation agencies established close and formal working relationships with local drug-treatment providers (Taxman, 1999). In some instances, parole and probation contracted with drug-treatment providers, while in other circumstances, community corrections' staff directly provided drug treatment.

Leveraged Treatment

Since the evaluations of the California Civil Addict Program in the 1970s, interest has been strong in finding better ways to engage offenders in their treatment by applying the leverage of incentives and sanctions to encourage treatment compliance (Anglin, 1988). Beyond the poor outcomes associated with offenders who do not participate in drug treatment, literature has generally shown treatment outcomes improve with time in treatment (Simpson, Chatham, & Knight, 1997), and that leverage is successful at getting offenders both to try treatment and to stay with it. Leukefeld and Tims' (1988) publication on "Compulsory Treatment" brought these themes together, and demonstrated the importance of incentives and sanctions for treatment to both institutional and community corrections, including as examples the programs from Lexington and Fort Worth.

Day Reporting Centers

The concept of Day Reporting centers for offenders originated in Britain in the early 1970s. British officials found that individual casework was not effective for the more chronic but less serious offenders (Parent, 1990). In 1986, Day Reporting centers began in the United States. Day Reporting centers typically provide drug treatment in a structure comparable to a halfway house, but without residential facilities citing problems. Some centers provide contact levels equal to or greater than intensive supervision programs (Parent, 1990). Therefore, much of treatment-positive structure and behavioral oversight can be provided in these settings. Day Reporting centers became an important level of intermediate sanctions for drug offenders, and, in some jurisdictions, they also serve as a transitional program from institution treatment.

Boot Camps

Boot camps began in 1983 in Georgia, and have enjoyed considerable popular support. These programs have a core of modeling after military training, including military drill and ceremony, physical training, and hard labor. However, the military-style regime is also usually supported by drug treatment, as well as general education services (MacKenzie & Hebert, 1996). Boot camps have generally been designed for young male offenders convicted of nonviolent offenses. Some boot camps, most notably the Lakeland program in New York, are structured as a therapeutic community and provide a high level of drug treatment (MacKenzie & Souryal, 1994).

Drug Courts

Drug courts were first implemented in Miami, Florida, in the late 1980s. They utilized expedited drug case-management systems to reduce the time between arrest and conviction and to speed up drug case processing. It was soon discovered that the initial efforts did little to address the problems of habitual drug use (Cooper & Trotter, 1994). Drug courts were formed by making drug treatment a central component, establishing a collaborative approach by all parties, and making the offender directly accountable to the court for treatment compliance. These programs have their roots in TASC treatment-based partnerships. In exchange for successful treatment completion, the court may dismiss the charge, reduce or set aside a sentence, require a lesser penalty, or some combination (Drug Courts Program Office, 1997). Drug courts formed an innovative approach to diverting offenders from deeper involvement in the criminal justice system. They utilize the established behavior-modification principles of punishment (certainty of sanctions, swiftly applied, repetitively utilizing modest punishers) with drug treatment. Drug courts experienced a high degree of growth in the last half of the 1990s. In 1994, there were 12 drug courts. By 1999, 380 drug courts existed across the county (Office of National Drug Control Policy, 1999).

Focusing on Special Populations, Especially Co-Occurring Disorders

The national GAINS Center, which began in the mid-1990s for individuals with co-occurring disorders in the criminal justice system, is the first formal recognition that many drug offenders also have mental health problems, and that most mentally ill inmates are drug involved (Peters & Hills, 1997). Drug use is the most critical factor for people with mental illness who have become violent, and it is the critical factor that often undermines successful mental health treatment. The GAINS center currently has projects to train staff, develop partnerships, provide consultation services for program development, study particular aspects of the problem (e.g., the special needs of women), and to evaluate programs. As identified by the GAINS Center, integrated treatment of these co-occurring disorders has the potential to make treatment more effective while saving on individual treatment costs.

MAJOR THEMES IN THE CHRONOLOGY OF CORRECTIONAL DRUG TREATMENT

Public Perception of Drug Use

Following widespread morphine addiction during the Civil War, the first identified "epidemic" of drug use was cocaine use in the late 1800s to early 1900s. In 1910, President Taft called cocaine the most threatening drug introduced to the country. The federal government reacted with a series of control strategies, but drug use was already on the decline by that time. Anger and fear toward both the drug and its user dominated public opinion from 1900 to 1920. Drug use had always been closely attached to the social issues of the time, including race relations. This was clearly the case during the first two decades of the 1900s (Musto, 1987).

As illegal drug use waned in the 1930s through the 1950s, naive attitudes toward both drug use and control strategies emerged. By the 1960s, part of the population had unrealistic expectations regarding the effectiveness of control strategies, whereas another part was naive about drug-use risk.

With the explosion of drug use from 1960 to 1990, the public and their representatives again responded with control strategies, this time emphasizing incarceration. As prison populations increased, the phrase, "we can't build our way out of this problem," emerged in public policy discussions, causing a search for other options. Little seems resolved at the end of the century relative to public perception of drug use and drug users. Drug legalization and decriminalization proposals have some popularity, while high rates of incarceration for drug law violations continue.

Public Perception of Treatment Value

Drug treatment efforts prior to the 1960s relied heavily on short- or long-term detoxification. Little drug treatment had been conducted in corrections settings when the 1970s "nothing works" phenomena came forward. Minimal drug treatment experience in corrections, and even less evaluation of these drug treatment programs, coupled with the public's fear and anger toward drug users gave the nothing-works perception endurance that was not easily overcome. Clear evidence of the effectiveness of correctional drug treatment did not become clear until the late 1980s. As the number, type, and sophistication of studies have increased, general acceptance of the value of correctional drug treatment has developed within the scientific community (Leshner, 1997). However, public perceptions continue to vary. The support for correctional drug treatment is often offset by continuing skepticism. Additionally, there is public ambivalence about the growth of correctional drug treatment at a time of decreasing public-sector drug treatment availability outside the criminal justice system.

Control Versus Treatment

Attempts to deal with this duality is probably the major variable weaving throughout the history and themes of correctional drug treatment. Beginning around the time of the Harrison Act of 1914, control (including punishment) or treatment of drug addicts developed into direct conflicts between medical practitioners and government treasury agents. One issue was that, unlike Europe, pharmacists in the United States were unlicensed. The larger issue, however, was societal ambivalence regarding whether to punish addicts or to provide them with treatment. Because so little was known about treatment during this time, as well as the public's fear and anger toward addicts, control and punishment dominated. Another factor was the unrealistic expectations of the efficacy of control strategies of the time.

The federal 1929 Porter Narcotic Farm Act and its resulting programs were largely discredited by 1960. The 1968 addition of addictions treatment to the Community Mental Health Centers Act, and the following early 1970s corrections treatment initiatives by the federal government, made marginal inroads to unseating the more pervasive control measures of their time.

Continuing today, control and punishment approaches have a great deal of public support. The phrase, "war on drugs," implies much more orientation toward control than it does an orientation to rehabilitation. However, the failed experiment of large-scale incarceration of drug-involved offenders has led to a more recent "second look" at treatment. The turning point probably occurred between 1986 and 1988, when demand for reduction strategies began surfacing, with increasing strength in federal planning documents.

While many during the last 100 years have been compelled to choose between control and treatment strategies, control and treatment are not polarities. Good drug-treatment programs offer enhanced security with institutions and improved control in community corrections. Strong control measures (offender accountability) are likewise needed in correctional drug-treatment programs. Drug testing, for example, is almost universally employed in correctional drug-treatment programs, and functions both as a control measure and as an aid to treatment. Control and treatment are interdependent, and better thought of as different sides of the same coin, rather than as opposite ends of a polarity.

Changing Treatment Modalities and Settings

Treatment approaches barely changed between the 1800s and the middle 1900s. Much has changed, however, over the past 40 years. Institution-based therapeutic community programs, after largely failed efforts in the 1960s and 1970s, have been refined, greatly expanded, and now widely studied. Drug treatment in community corrections has developed closer working relationships between local corrections and community alcohol and drug providers. Community corrections has also added technologies, such as day-reporting centers and relapse-prevention strategies. Both institution and community settings have made use of coercive strategies to enhance offender participation and treatment completion. Both institution and community corrections have improved offender accountability requirements, as best represented by the pervasiveness of urinalysis and other drug-testing methodologies used by these programs.

As another step in balancing control and treatment strategies, several programs have been developed that implicitly involve some level of diversion of the offender from the criminal justice system into treatment alternatives. Boot camps, while projecting an emphasis on military drill, almost always employ a great deal of rehabilitation efforts, including drug treatment, and usually significantly reduce the offender's sentence. Drug courts divert the individual from penetrating far into the criminal justice system earlier and more directly. Drug courts are the most prominent example of utilizing swift and certain sanctions at the local level, while continuing to encourage (leverage) the offender into rehabilitation and prosocial choices.

CONCLUSIONS: CURRENT TRENDS—HOPEFUL FUTURE

It is always a suspect endeavor to make assumptions involving current trends continuing into the future. As should be evident from the preceding sections, America's attempts at addressing the nexus of drugs and crime, including drug-treatment efforts with criminal justice clients, are replete with fits, starts, and reversals. However, the current trends that will hopefully continue into the future are the recognized value of treatment, the integration of control and treatment approaches, and the building on what we have learned.

During this century, correctional drug treatment has gone from being subjugated to early control strategies, to minimal efforts in mid-century, to being rejected as useful at the three-quarters point, to coming into its own over the last 12 years. The professional and research communities clearly see the value of correctional drug treatment (Leshner, 1997). Federal policy also supports drug treatment with criminal justice populations (Office of National Drug Control Policy, 1999). Yet, public support continues to be ambivalent. Members of the public will usually support control strategies in response to general questions, but favor treatment when given case studies. Perhaps public sentiment is still catching up with research and policy, or perhaps drug treatment will take the back seat to punishment as long as the American public continues to see prison as the only genuine, societal limit-setting response to drug addiction.

The best marketing strategy for further enhancement of the value of correctional drug treatment is probably alignment with control strategies into comprehensive responses. The control versus treatment duality needs to come together into a unified approach. The Breaking the Cycle programs represent one of the best of system-wide interventions to date at the community level. Breaking the Cycle, which began in Birmingham in 1997 and has now expanded to four other cities, is a community-wide initiative to address the drug offender in a comprehensive and systematic way in the community.

Certainly, fragmentation of services and sanctions serves neither the offender nor the community well. From a distance, drug-involved offenders can be seen simply as individuals whose lives are out of control. Many started drug use in pre-adolescence, and did not experience the growth and maturity during their teenage years that most nondrug users have experienced. At times, this population needs both some external controls along with direct training and assistance to mature into responsible adults. Tight coordination of services at the community level is one of the best ways to aid this process.

As with all history, the idea is to build on what we have learned and avoid the mistakes of the past. For example, we know that duration of treatment, aftercare, peer accountability and support, and cognitive behavioral approaches improve outcomes (Simpson & Knight, 1999). While much remains to be learned about drug treatment with offenders, we cannot afford to lose what has been gained over the past few years.

Twenty years ago, a little more than 300,000 individuals were incarcerated in this country. This year, more than 500,000 of the 1.8 million incarcerated offenders, most of whom have drug problems, will be released back to their home communities. Without treatment, the problem will only get worse.

3

The Economic Cost
of Substance-Abuse Treatment
in Criminal Justice Settings

Kathryn E. McCollister
and Michael T. French

Society is increasingly challenged to absorb the costs imposed by criminal activity and an expanding prison population. The relationship between criminal activity and drug and alcohol use has been extensively researched (e.g., Chaiken & Chaiken, 1990; Inciardi, Martin, Butzin, Hooper, & Harrison, 1997; Inciardi & Pottegier, 1998; French et al., 2000c; Anglin & Speckart, 1986; Gandossy, Williams, & Harwood, 1980; Nurco, Hanlon, Kinlock, & Duszynski, 1988; Tonry, 1990). Although the direction of causality between drug use and crime remains unconfirmed, the complementarity between these behaviors implies that there are important substance-dependence issues to address within the criminal justice population. For many criminal offenders, effective rehabilitation must incorporate substance-abuse treatment.

The prison population in the United States has expanded rapidly over the past 20 years. Drug-law violators accounted for more than 30% of the increase in incarceration at the state level and 68% of the increase in the federal population (Farabee et al., 1999). Recent reports estimate that 1,825,000 U.S. residents were incarcerated by the end of 1998 (Simpson, Wexler, & Inciardi, 1999; Beck & Mumola, 1999). Furthermore, the U.S. Department of Justice and the National Center on Addiction and Substance Abuse (CASA) determined that 60% to 80% of all criminal offenders have used drugs at some point during their lifetime. According to reports for correctional expenditures in 1996, approximately 80% ($30 billion) of a $38 billion budget was spent incarcerating individuals who had a history of substance abuse, were convicted of drug-law violations, tested positive for drugs when arrested, or perpetrated the crime for which they were incarcerated to be able to purchase drugs (CASA, 1998).

The social cost of crime is much higher than reflected in these expenditure reports. Rajkumar and French (1997) divided the social costs of crime into four principle categories: victim costs; costs of crime protection and law enforcement; crime career/productivity losses; and other external costs. They estimated both the tangible and intangible costs of crime, by specific criminal act. The most costly crimes, excluding murder, are aggravated assault (total social cost of $50,743 per assault) and robbery ($21,890 per act), followed by burglary ($1,304 per act) and auto theft ($1,138 per act) (in 1992 dollars).

A study by French et al. (2000c) compared the types of crimes committed in a sample of chronic drug users (CDUs) and nondrug users (NDUs), separating acts by predatory crime and property crime. Their results showed that CDUs had a higher probability of committing both predatory and property crimes relative to NDUs. In an earlier study, Chaiken and Chaiken (1990) found that rates of predatory crime were positively and significantly related to the quantity and frequency of illicit drug use among adults. Specifically, frequent heroin use or use of multiple drugs appeared to be the most directly linked to the prevalence of committing predatory crimes relative to NDUs.

While the need for substance-abuse treatment in correctional settings appears significant, an important challenge in providing effective treatment is low inmate demand for these services. The U.S. Department of Justice estimated that while some form of treatment was available in 90% of the facilities examined, only 10% to 20% of inmates utilized the services (Office of National Drug Control Policy [ONDCP], 1998). Within state correctional facilities, 70% to 85% of inmates were classified as needing some level of intervention, yet only 13% were involved in any form of treatment (Camp & Camp, 1997).

This study offers an important perspective on prison-based substance-abuse treatment. Economic cost analyses were performed on four in-prison treatment programs located in different parts of the United States. The results highlight the modest incremental cost of providing substance-abuse treatment in criminal justice settings.

RECENT FINDINGS

Short-run outcomes from in-prison treatment have been highlighted recently in several reports. Lower rates of drug use and recidivism for inmates receiving some form of treatment compared with nontreated inmates are common themes. The Bureau of Prisons reviewed treatment outcomes from existing reports and found that inmates who completed residential drug-abuse treatment reported both reduced recidivism and reduced substance use. Only 3.3% of treatment completers were likely to be rearrested within 6 months of release from a treatment program, compared with 12.1% of nontreated inmates. Moreover, 36.7% of untreated parolees were likely to relapse into drug use, compared with 20.5% of treatment completers (ONDCP, 1998).

Longer postrelease evaluation timelines were considered in a series of articles published in *The Prison Journal* (September, 1999). Wexler, Melnick, Lowe, and Peters (1999b) reported on the incidence of reincarceration three years postparole for clients that received treatment in the Amity therapeutic community (TC) and aftercare programs in California. Those clients participating in both the prison TC and aftercare showed the best results in terms of reduced recidivism: 27% of clients receiving in-prison treatment plus aftercare recidivated versus 75% for those receiving prison treatment only or no treatment.

This result resonated in other programs as well. In a study of a Texas in-prison TC (ITC), Knight, Simpson, and Hiller (1999) found that 25% of offenders who completed both in-prison treatment plus aftercare were reincarcerated at some point during the 3-year follow-up period, whereas 42% of untreated offenders and 64% of aftercare dropouts had been reincarcerated. Martin, Butzin, Saum, and Inciardi (1999) reported on Delaware's Key-Crest program. Among these inmates, prison plus aftercare completers also showed the lowest rates of recidivism at 3 years postrelease.

Based on these reports, the long-term returns to prison-based treatment and aftercare programs appear promising. To further clarify these returns to society, rigorous economic analyses that estimate the costs and benefits of these programs are necessary. Initial work has been completed in this area, providing impetus for additional evaluations. Griffith, Hiller, Knight, and Simpson (1999) performed a cost-effectiveness analysis (CEA) of an ITC and aftercare in Texas. Treatment effectiveness in terms of lower recidivism was measured for high-risk parolees and low-risk parolees who participated in treatment and aftercare relative to nontreated parolees. In addition, a criterion for treatment completion was factored into the effectiveness assessment. Treatment proved most cost-effective for the high-risk parolees who completed treatment and aftercare relative to low-risk parolees who completed treatment and aftercare, high-risk and low-risk noncompleters, and the nontreated comparison group.

Mauser, Van Stelle, and Moberg (1994) examined the benefits and costs of the Treatment Alternative Programs (TAP) for criminal offenders in Wisconsin. Three pilot projects were funded to examine the effectiveness of diverting offenders into treatment instead of jail using a case management model. To measure benefits, criminal justice cost reductions, avoided cost of medical care, and productivity improvements were considered. There was no control group for this study, so the authors assumed that accrued benefits were the result of treatment. The results of their benefit-cost analysis (BCA) showed that for every dollar invested in TAP, the societal benefit amounted to between $1.40 and $3.30.

A detailed and comprehensive review of the costs and benefits of programs to reduce crime and substance abuse—from childhood interventions to adult offender programs—is presented in Aos, Phipps, Barnoski, and Lieb (1999). Among the programs examined, five ITCs were evaluated. Results of the BCA of these ITCs showed that, from a societal perspective, the average program generated $1.07 in benefits (in terms of reduced crime) per dollar invested in treatment. The authors emphasized that additional research must be performed on similar programs to better understand the social value of prison-based treatment.

The following section describes the economic cost analysis performed on four prison-based treatment programs from disparate regions of the United States. The methods of the analyses are carefully outlined, with particular attention paid to the components of total cost and the various perspectives that guide a cost analysis.

METHODS

The foundation for economic evaluations of healthcare or addiction-treatment programs is a comprehensive economic cost analysis. Ultimately, health economists are interested in measuring and comparing the costs and outcomes of different treatment approaches (Drummond, O'Brien, Stoddart, & Torrance, 1997). Economists generally prefer to examine program costs from a societal perspective. This entails examining both direct and indirect costs associated with addiction treatment. Direct costs, often referred to as accounting costs, represent out-of-pocket expenditures for items such as start-up and operating costs, fixed costs, and overhead costs (French, 2000). Indirect costs include the value of donated resources, transportation costs to/from treatment, lost wages, and time/resources involved in caretaking by family members or others (French, 2000).

The theoretical basis for an economic cost analysis is the concept of opportunity cost. Opportunity cost implies that all resources employed in a particular use have value. The value is captured by the forgone opportunity (income) to employ a resource in its best alternative use. Assuming a competitive resource market, a resource will be employed where it is valued most highly, in which case the opportunity cost and the market price are equal. However, in situations where resources are donated or partially subsidized, the opportunity cost will generally be higher than the accounting cost. For example, the opportunity cost of a donated building is equal to the amount of rental income the building would generate in a competitive real estate market. Similarly, volunteer support has an opportunity cost equal to the market salary that would have to be paid to hire a worker to perform the volunteered services.

It is important to note that there are often several perspectives of interest when estimating the costs of treatment. The different points of view in an economic evaluation of public or private investment in healthcare include society, the government or one of its agencies (e.g., a department of corrections), the patient, the treatment provider, or the employer (Drummond et al., 1997). A state corrections department, for example, is interested in the direct costs (i.e., accounting costs) associated with providing treatment described on expenditure reports. Society, however, is concerned with all tangible and intangible costs associated with treatment (i.e., the economic or opportunity cost of treatment). Further discussion on the distinction between accounting and economic cost follows.

Significant improvement in the approach to performing a cost analysis is offered by the Drug Abuse Treatment Cost Analysis Program (DATCAP). The DATCAP is a structured data-collection instrument developed by French and colleagues, which outlines both program revenues and costs (French, 1999a, 1999b). The instrument is used to collect resource use and other data to estimate total annual cost, distinguishing between economic and accounting cost. Client caseflow data is incorporated to determine the average annual cost per client. Other useful computations include average cost per treatment episode and marginal cost per enhancement (French, Dunlap, Zarkin, McGeary, & McLellan, 1997; Salomé & French, in press). The DATCAP has been applied to a variety of treatment interventions, such as methadone maintenance, outpatient drug-free, adolescent outpatient, short- and long-term residential, prison-based programs, and employee-assistance programs (e.g., French et al., 1997; French, Zarkin, Bray, & Hartwell, 1999; Salomé & French, in press; French et al., in press).

Accounting costs were obtained from program expenditure reports, which outline the direct costs of treatment. Economic cost, as described above, was calculated using the competitive market value of all treatment resources, whether they were explicitly purchased or not. Resource value represents the forgone compensation (the opportunity cost) had the resource been employed in its best alternative use. In many cases, the economic cost and the accounting cost will be the same, but differences will occur when programs are using donated or subsidized resources or when resources are obtained below market rates. Economic costs are calculated using market rates of compensation (e.g., wages, prices) multiplied by the share of the resource used by the program.

Finally, estimating the economic or accounting costs of prison-based treatment requires an incremental analysis of resource use because common resources in the prison (e.g., housing, food, security) are not attributable to the treatment program. The costs of treatment are the additional costs above the costs of housing an inmate, thus are expressed by the total costs associated with incarceration and treatment minus the standard cost of resources provided to the general prison population.

PROGRAM DESCRIPTIONS AND COST RESULTS

Four prison-based treatment programs in California, Colorado, Delaware, and Kentucky were analyzed. For each program, the results of the cost analyses were divided according to accounting costs and economic costs, by resource category. The four prison-based programs are referred to as program 1, program 2, program 3, and program 4 to protect anonymity of potentially sensitive cost information. A brief description of each program is followed by the summary results of the cost analyses. A full presentation of the cost analysis for each program is available upon request. Following this, each program is considered in the context of a hypothetical cost-effectiveness analysis. This exercise illustrates how to apply cost information in more complex economic evaluations.

Program 1: California

Program 1 is a residential ITC that operates within a medium-security prison for male offenders located in California. Program participants are housed in one of the prison's five cellblocks that is designated for the program's use. A separate area next to the housing unit contains two trailers where most program activities are held.

To be eligible for participation in the program, prisoners must be within 9 to 14 months of parole, be free from psychosis or other serious mental disorders, and have a history of substance abuse (Graham & Wexler, 1997). Openings in the program are filled by a random selection process (Wexler, De Leon, Thomas, Kressel, & Peters, 1999a). The average daily census in fiscal year 1993 was 200 inmates (program capacity) and the average length of stay was 47 weeks.

The costs of treatment for program 1 are summarized in Table 3.1. Coincidentally, the economic costs are equal to the accounting costs for this particular program, as all resources were purchased at market value. Based on information collected for fiscal year 1993, the total annual cost of treatment (expressed in 1999 dollars—the comparison year for all programs) was $708,918. This amount represents the incremental cost above standard incarceration costs for inmates receiving treatment in the program. The largest component of treatment cost was labor ($580,500). This program had 20 full-time employees, including a program director, administrative assistant, four consultants/trainers, a community services liaison, and several counselors. In addition, inmates who were serving life sentences ("Lifers") provided counseling and guidance services. The Lifers represented an important addition to the program and were compensated with a modest stipend. Miscellaneous costs, the second largest component of total cost, included staff training, travel, insurance, and utilities.

The annual economic cost per client was $3,545, translating into a weekly cost per client of $68. Since the average length of stay in treatment was slightly less than a full year (47 weeks), the average economic cost per treatment episode was $3,196.

Program 2: Colorado

Program 2 is a 32-bed TC program located within a 250-bed medium-security prison facility for male offenders in Colorado. This program was designed to address the special needs of chronically, mentally ill inmates.

TABLE 3.1 Cost Comparisons for Four Prison-Based Treatment Programs and One Aftercare Facility (1999 Dollars)

Cost measure	Program 1 (CA)	Program 2 (CO)	Program 3 (DE)	Program 4 (KY)	Aftercare (CA)
Total accounting cost ($)*	708,918	85,910	343,112	239,069	243,308
Total economic cost ($)*	708,918	86,055	346,170	246,036	320,352
Weekly cost per client ($) (Accounting method)	68	51	62	36	137
Weekly cost per client ($) (Economic method)	68	52	62	37	181
Cost per episode ($) (Accounting method)	3,196	969	2,406	998	3,483
Cost per episode ($) (Economic method)	3,196	988	2,427	1,027	5,060
Average daily census	200	32	107	129	34
Average length of stay (Weeks)	47	19	39	28	28

*These are the total annual costs for each program.

Program eligibility criteria are based on Colorado Department of Correction guidelines for mental illness, substance abuse, and criminal risk. In addition, to be eligible for the treatment study on which the cost analysis is based, inmates had to be within 18 to 24 months of parole subsequent to program admission. The program is a modified TC that addresses criminal behavior and thinking, mental illness, and substance-abuse disorders.

Inmates were sequentially assigned to the program on a bed-available basis from a list of eligible inmates that were referred from the correctional institution. The average daily census in fiscal year 1999 was 32 inmates and the average length of stay was 19 weeks.

The costs of program 2 are summarized in Table 3.1. Again, all costs are expressed in 1999 dollars. A modest cost differential was present between accounting and economic costs due to valuation differences in the equipment-resource category. This program used office furniture, computers, and electrical equipment, all of which were purchased prior to 1999. The accounting cost of this equipment was $764, but the economic cost was slightly higher at $909.

The total economic cost of treatment in fiscal year 1999 was $86,055 and the total accounting cost was $85,910, which reflects the slight cost differential for equipment described above. The cost of labor was the largest component of total cost ($64,781). Given an average caseload of 32 inmates, the annual opportunity cost per client was $2,689, or $52 per week. The economic cost per treatment episode (19 weeks) was $988.

Program 3: Delaware

Program 3 is a prison-based TC for male inmates in Delaware. A large section of the prison facility is dedicated to housing program residents and running the daily program activities. Participants are segregated from the general inmate population while they are in the program.

Eligibility for the program was based on the following factors: Inmates had to be within 18 months of work-release eligibility, be free from mental disorders, and have a history of chronic substance abuse (Inciardi et al., 1997). The average daily census in fiscal year 1997 was 107 inmates and the average length of stay was 39 weeks.

Treatment costs in 1999 dollars are summarized in Table 3.1. In total, the accounting cost and economic cost for program 3 differed by $3,058, resulting from valuation differences for labor costs and equipment costs. Program 3 had volunteer support from AA members (to run meetings for program participants), as well as volunteers to teach parenting classes. Volunteer support had an estimated opportunity cost of $1,950. In addition, program 3 used office furniture and electrical equipment that were purchased prior to 1997. The accounting cost of the equipment in 1997 was $3,759, but the economic cost was higher at $4,867.

The total economic cost of treatment in fiscal year 1997 was $346,170 and the total accounting cost was $343,112. As with the other programs, the economic cost of labor was the largest component of total treatment cost ($320,899). The annual opportunity cost per client was $3,224, or $62 per week. Given that the average length of stay in the program was 39 weeks, the economic cost per treatment episode was $2,427.

Program 4: Kentucky

Program 4 is a three-phase treatment program designed to focus on criminal tendencies and relapse prevention. The program operates in a dormitory on the grounds of a medium-security prison for male offenders in Kentucky. Inmates from all medium-security facilities in the state of Kentucky are eligible for the program if they have self-admitted problems with drugs and/or alcohol (Staton, Leukefeld, Logan, & Purvis, 2000). Inmates that are referred by the parole board have a priority admission status. The average daily census in fiscal year 1999 was 129 inmates and the average length of stay was 28 weeks.

Table 3.1 presents the results of the cost analysis for program 4. The economic cost exceeded the accounting cost for labor (again, the largest component of total cost) and equipment resources. The estimated opportunity cost of volunteer support and the equipment the facility had "on hand" (i.e., equipment that was purchased prior to 1999) was $6,967. The total accounting cost for the program was $239,069 and the total economic cost was $246,036.

The average annual economic cost per client (given an average caseload of 129 individuals in 1998) was $1,907, or $37 per week. The average treatment episode was 28 weeks, generating an economic cost per treatment episode of $1,027.

Program Differences

Table 3.1 presents a summary of the key cost estimates for each of the four programs considered in this analysis.[1] One notable issue is the fact that there are modest differences between the accounting costs and economic costs for these treatment programs, indicating that most program resources were purchased at fair market values. From society's perspective, this finding is important because it implies that minimal (or zero) additional opportunity cost was associated with the use of these resources in the prison-treatment programs.

Program 1 had the greatest number of inmate participants (200), the most full-time employees (20), and the highest total cost ($708,918). The

---

[1]Table 3.1 also includes cost estimates for an aftercare program for parolees in California. These estimates are discussed in the Discussion and Conclusions section.

average weekly cost for program 1 was $68. Program 2 had 32 inmate participants, four full-time TC staff, and a slightly lower complement of correctional staff than other non-TC units. Program 2 had the third highest weekly cost ($52), although it had the lowest total cost ($86,055). Program 3 had the second highest weekly cost ($62) and total cost ($346,170), but was third in terms of program size (average daily census of 107 inmates). Program 4 had a total economic cost of $246,036, but with 129 participants, its average weekly cost was the lowest of the four ($37).

Another measure of significant interest is the cost per treatment episode. The weekly cost per client depends on the annual cost of treatment and the average daily census in the program. The cost per treatment episode uses the weekly cost per client estimate and the reported average length of stay. The average episode cost is a program-specific cost estimate for treating the average client. Program 1 had the longest average length of stay (47 weeks), resulting in an economic cost per episode of $3,196. Program 3 had the second longest average length of stay (39 weeks) and a cost per treatment episode of $2,427. Program 4 had an average length of stay of 28 weeks and a cost per treatment episode of $1,027, followed by program 2, which had an average length of stay of 19 weeks, leading to the lowest cost estimate per treatment episode ($988).

The cost estimates permit interesting comparisons across programs and services, but it is important to emphasize that evaluators should not make inferences about the advantages of one program over another based on the cost information alone. The pivotal economic question is whether higher treatment costs (i.e., larger treatment programs with more staff, services, and clients) translate into better treatment outcomes. This important question can be addressed with more complex economic evaluation techniques, such as CEA or BCA. The policy simulation that follows provides an example of a CEA applied to prison-based treatment.

HYPOTHETICAL CASE STUDY: COST-EFFECTIVENESS ANALYSIS

A CEA compares the opportunity cost of providing treatment with a common desired outcome (Drummond et al., 1997). The results of the analysis are expressed as a cost-effectiveness ratio—typically with cost in the numerator and the effectiveness measure in the denominator (a lower cost-effectiveness ratio is viewed as desirable). Effectiveness can either be described as a specific treatment outcome (e.g., reduced number of arrests or increased hours employed) or as a combination of outcomes using a common scale (e.g., change in quality-adjusted life-years) (French, 2000). Cost-effectiveness analysis is an incremental procedure when comparing across two or more programs. Alternatively, the ratio of cost and effectiveness can be derived for a single program and then compared to an established benchmark ratio in the literature (Kenkel, 1997; Gold, Siegel, Russell, & Weinstein, 1996; Sindelar, Jofre-Bonet, French, & McLellan, 2000).

Table 3.2 reports the cost-effectiveness results for a hypothetical case study of four prison-based, substance-abuse treatment interventions. Information on number of treatment clients (column [1]), average weekly cost (column [2]), average length of stay (column [3]), and total treatment cost (column [4]) was taken from the cost analyses presented earlier. Following a recent study by Griffith et al. (1999), we measure effectiveness by a *hypothetical* percentage of paroled inmates who completed treatment and were not reincarcerated by follow-up, relative to a comparison group of paroled inmates who did not participate in treatment. The chosen effectiveness values represent a variety of scenarios possible when comparing in-prison treatment clients with an untreated control group. (See Griffith et al., 1999, Wexler et al., 1999b, and Martin et al., 1999, for recent outcome data on rates of drug use and recidivism for clients in prison-based treatment programs.)

The focus of the analysis is on columns [4] through [8]. Program 1 has the highest total treatment cost ($639,200 in column [4]), followed by program 3 ($258,726), program 4 ($133,644), and program 2 ($31,616). In this example, greater effectiveness (i.e., highest percentage of parolees not reincarcerated by follow-up) is reported by program 4 (78% in column [5]). The second most effective program is program 1 (74% not reincarcerated) followed by program 3 (65% not reincarcerated) and program 2 (34% not reincarcerated). Relative to an untreated control group, program 1 has the highest incremental treatment effectiveness (26 in column [7]). The control group for program 4 reports a total effectiveness of 71 (column [6]), thus the incremental difference in effectiveness for program 4 is only 7 (column [7]). Treatment effectiveness for program 3 is 65, versus 50 for its control group. The incremental effectiveness for program 3 is, therefore, the second highest (15 in column [7]). Program 2 has a negative incremental effectiveness value (−8 in column [7]), indicating that for this example, the control group actually had a lower rate of reincarceration.

The last column in Table 3.2 presents the hypothetical cost-effectiveness ratios for the example. One can immediately conclude that program 2 is

TABLE 3.2 Hypothetical Cost-Effectiveness Analysis of Four Prison-Based Treatment Programs (1999 Dollars)

Program	Treatment clients[a] [1]	Average weekly cost ($) [2]	Average length of stay (weeks) [3]	Total treatment cost ($)[b] [1] × [2] × [3] = [4]	Treatment outcome[c] (clients/year) [5]	Comparison outcome[d] (clients/year) [6]	Incremental treatment effectiveness (clients/year) [5] − [6] = [7]	Cost-effectiveness ratio ($) [4] ÷ [7] = [8]
Program 1	200	68	47	639,200	74	48	26	24,585
Program 2	32	52	19	31,616	34	42	−8	N/A
Program 3	107	62	39	258,726	65	50	15	17,248
Program 4	129	37	28	133,644	78	71	7	19,092

[a]The same number of clients are in the treatment and comparison groups.
[b]These estimates are based on the average length of stay and number of treatment clients. Therefore, they are less than the total annual cost of treatment reported in Table 3.1.
[c]The percentage of paroled inmates who participated in treatment that were not reincarcerated during the follow-up period.
[d]The percentage of paroled inmates who did not receive treatment that were not reincarcerated during the follow-up period.
NA = not applicable.

not an optimal choice for treatment—it has the lowest, overall effectiveness value, and is ineffective relative to a hypothetical control group of untreated parolees (negative incremental effectiveness value in column [7]). Although program 1 is the most effective relative to its control group (26 in column [7]), it is also the most costly program, yielding the highest cost-effectiveness ratio of 24,585 (column [8]). Program 4 is less costly, but with an incremental effectiveness of only 7 (column [7]), it has the second highest cost-effectiveness ratio (19,092). The conclusion of this exercise is that program 3 offers the most cost-effective treatment approach relative to the other programs, evidenced by the fact that it has the lowest cost-effectiveness ratio of the four (17,248 in column [8]).

Other evaluation approaches, such as a BCA, can offer additional and somewhat different information on treatment interventions. Benefit-cost analysis compares the cost of providing treatment with the dollar value of positive outcomes (i.e., the monetary benefits resulting from treatment). Benefit-cost analysis allows for more direct comparisons than CEA, since the latter only focuses on the cost of achieving a single outcome (French, 2000). To perform a BCA, unit cost estimates are applied to data on treatment outcomes so that disparate outcomes can be translated into monetary terms. For example "reduced number of criminal acts," "increased number of days employed," and "reduced number of visits to the emergency room," are all potential treatment outcomes for the economic benefit analysis. Examples of BCAs applied to healthcare interventions can be found in French, McCollister, Sacks, McKendrick, and De Leon, 2000a; French, Salomè, Sindelar, and McLellan, 2000b; Harwood, Hubbard, Collins, and Rachal, 1988; and Aos et al., 1999.

DISCUSSION AND CONCLUSIONS

The most important and unique contribution of this analysis is the actual documentation of the relatively low cost of treating drug-abusing prisoners, especially when compared with community-based treatment programs. For example, an evaluation of a residential-modified TC program in New York found the average annual cost of treatment to be $31,970 ($1999) (French et al., 2000a). At $3,536 (1999 dollars), the highest average annual cost[2] among the four prison-based treatment programs was considerably smaller. It is important to note, however, that inmates participating in treatment are

---

[2]Calculated using average weekly economic cost ($68) times 52 weeks.

II

Clinical Issues

4

Assessing and Evaluating Mandated Correctional Substance-Abuse Treatment

Matthew L. Hiller, Kevin Knight, Sandhya R. Rao, and D. Dwayne Simpson

Research has shown that intensive rehabilitation services provided to offenders in correctional settings can reduce criminality and drug use following incarceration (Gendreau, 1996). Particularly within prisons, long-term residential treatment programs (such as therapeutic communities [TCs]) have been found to reduce postincarceration involvement in illicit drugs and crime. These findings are highlighted in numerous primary studies (Field, 1989; Inciardi, Martin, Butzin, Hooper, & Harrison, 1997; Knight, Simpson, Chatham, & Camacho, 1997; Wexler, De Leon, Thomas, Kressel, & Peters, 1999; Wexler, Falkin, & Lipton, 1990; Inciardi, Surratt, Martin, & Hooper, this volume), in a congressionally mandated review completed by the University of Maryland (MacKenzie, 1997), in the National Institute for Drug Abuse (NIDA)-funded Correctional Drug

Abuse Treatment Effectiveness meta-analysis (CDATE; Pearson & Lipton, 1999), and in a recent series of studies on 3-year posttreatment reincarceration rates presented in two special issues of *The Prison Journal* (Simpson, Wexler, & Inciardi, 1999a, 1999b).

However, comparatively little is known about the impact of TCs when used within the context of correctional supervision in the community. Examination of community-based treatment has shown that many enter these programs with a legal status, which is a trend that has been surprisingly consistent across the last several decades. For example, data from three major, national, multisite evaluations spanning from 1969 to 1993 showed that about two thirds of treatment intakes were under probation or parole supervision, and one third were directly referred by criminal justice authorities (Craddock, Rounds-Bryant, Flynn, & Hubbard, 1997). This pressure from legal authorities improves retention in community-based programs and increases the likelihood of favorable outcomes (Hiller, Knight, Broome, & Simpson, 1998). Nevertheless, probation and parole populations continue to expand, and most of these individuals have a drug or alcohol problem (Bureau of Justice Statistics, 1997, 1998). This has forced a continued reliance on community-based treatment resources, the development of additional facilities within correctional agencies, and the creation of models to coordinate and amplify the linkages between treatment and correctional resources, like treatment-based drug courts.

With these issues comes the need to assess and appropriately classify the individuals' problems and to monitor service delivery, as well as therapeutic progress to help ensure effective treatment. Figure 4.1 describes a conceptual model of the treatment process for residential programs, adapted from research in outpatient settings (see Simpson, Joe, Greener, & Rowan-Szal, in press; Simpson, Joe, Rowan-Szal, & Greener, 1995, 1997). It provides the theoretical foundation for an evaluation system we use for assessing, classifying, and tracking individuals as they receive TC-based treatment as a condition of their probation. This model represents the treatment episode as a series of interrelated events, each presenting an opportunity to collect data. For example, the therapeutic experience begins when the individual undergoes clinical-records processing at admission to the program. At this point, a comprehensive baseline assessment of offender risks, needs, and problems is completed. This includes constructing detailed social histories, classifying drug problems, assessing mental health and abuse histories, determining the level of behavioral risks for contracting HIV/AIDS, and detailing criminality and criminal involvement. Collecting these types of data helps program administrators and staff to understand

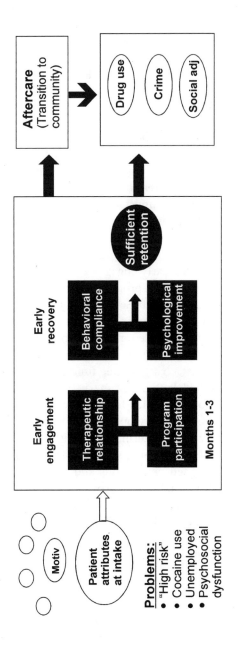

FIGURE 4.1   TCU treatment process model.

43

who is being placed in their facility and whether these placements are appropriate for the prescribed level of services provided (Knight & Hiller, 1997; Knight, Simpson, & Hiller, this volume).

The problems that offenders present at intake, in turn, can influence the therapeutic process as individualized treatment plans are developed to address the most serious and immediate needs. As shown in the "early engagement" phase of the central box of the model presented in Figure 4.1, these background characteristics also may influence how probationers perceive their peers, program staff, and their own willingness to become involved in and commit to their recovery during the first few months of the treatment episode (Broome, Knight, Knight, Hiller, & Simpson, 1997; Hiller, Knight, & Simpson, 2000). Pretreatment levels of motivation, for example, have been shown to play an important role in the development of therapeutic relationships with counselors and to indirectly determine the likelihood of rearrest following treatment in a 4-month, modified TC for probationers (Broome et al., 1997). Therapeutic activities and feelings of personal progress made during the early engagement phase also impact the "early recovery" stage of the treatment process, when the probationers are making important behavioral and psychosocial changes that will facilitate long-term recovery upon return to the community. Prospective data collection (based on both probationer self-report and on formal documentation of treatment contact) is made throughout the treatment episode, thus providing the opportunity to track changes over time and to determine who will be retained the expected length of time in the program. This evaluation system, therefore, promotes quick feedback to treatment-delivery staff and administrators who then develop targeted therapeutic interventions intended to improve short-term outcomes (Blankenship, Dansereau, & Simpson, 1999; Farabee, Simpson, Dansereau, & Knight, 1995). Also, monitoring offender self-perceptions and their appraisals of the therapeutic intervention is essential to this process because remaining in correctional substance-abuse treatment has been shown to be related both to offender motivation (De Leon, Melnick, Thomas, Kressel, & Wexler, 2000) and to their satisfaction with the programming they received (Hiller, Knight, & Simpson, 1999).

The goal of this chapter, therefore, will be to provide a broader description of the baseline and during-treatment assessments that we use with probationers in a "real-world" treatment setting. Special emphasis will be placed on describing the data-collection instruments, as well as on their potential for narrowing the feedback loop between stakeholders, program staff, and probationers to help improve selection, classification, and the treatment process. Because administrators often use correctional substance-abuse programs as a stopgap measure to address a variety of issues only tangentially related to substance abuse (Farabee et al., 1999), we begin with a functional assessment of the risks and needs the offenders present at treatment intake (including classification of drug-dependence problems). We next examine the short-term impact of the TC on improvements in psychosocial functioning and treatment motivation. Finally, a series of analyses will be conducted to determine if we can predict who will drop out of treatment prematurely.

METHOD

Sample

Data were collected from 429 felony probationers admitted to the Dallas County Judicial Treatment Center (DCJTC), a 6-month modified TC, between January and December 1998, but data analyses are limited to 417 cases (97% of the total sample) who completed all of the baseline assessments. The sample was predominantly male (70%), African American (48%) or Caucasian (39%), and had never been married (43%). Most (60%) were between the ages of 17 and 34 (average age was 32).

Data System Overview

Written, informed consent was obtained from each resident prior to the collection of the assessments. During their first week of treatment, residents received a comprehensive intake battery that included the (a) Initial Assessment, (b) Self-Rating Form (SRF), and (c) Intake Interview questionnaires (Simpson, Knight, & Hiller, 1997). The Initial Assessment, a brief, structured, counselor-led interview, was done within 24 hours of treatment entry, and it recorded sociodemographic background information and drug-use history. Immediately following this, residents also completed the SRF, a 95-item, self-report instrument designed to assess psychosocial functioning and treatment motivation at intake. Finally, a counselor administered the Intake Interview approximately 2 to 7 days after the Initial Assessment, after residents had time to become acquainted with the program and staff. It included detailed questions on the resident's social background, family and peer relations, health and psychological status, criminal involvement and history, and drug-use problems. Indicators of the treatment process were based on the Resident Evaluation of Self and Treatment (REST). It was collected prospectively at the end of treatment months 1, 3, and 6, which linked it to major landmarks in the resident's therapeutic episode (end of orientation, 90-day treatment plan, and discharge plan, respectively). The REST contained a reassessment of the psychosocial and treatment-motivation scales originally collected in the SRF.

Measures

Social History

Sociodemographic information was collected during the Initial Assessment and Intake Interview. This included employment history, education level, insurance coverage, and sources of financial support.

Classification of Drug Problems

Four independent sections in the Initial Assessment were used to assess Diagnostic and Statistical Manual IV (DSM-IV; American Psychiatric Association, 1994) criteria for dependence and abuse for *Alcohol, Cannabis, Cocaine, and Opioids*. Wording of these items closely followed those found in the DSM-IV, and scoring was identical (i.e., three or more criteria met for classification of dependence, one or more for corresponding abuse items).

Psychological Problems

Similar to Joe, Brown, and Simpson (1995), two brief measures were created from responses to items on the Intake Interview that elicited indicators of psychological dysfunction (e.g., "Not counting the effects from alcohol or drug use, have you ever experienced serious depression?"). The *pathology index* (coefficient alpha = .65; range 0–5) was comprised of a set of symptoms that included depression, serious anxiety or tension, hallucinations, trouble understanding, concentrating, or remembering, and trouble controlling violent behavior. The majority of the probationers (73%) scored a 1 or more on this measure; and the average numbers of symptoms reported was 1.7 (SD = 1.45). The *suicidal ideation* composite (coefficient alpha = .81) focused on two questions that asked probationers if they had ever had "serious thoughts of suicide" or "attempts at suicide."

Abuse History

Reports of previous physical, emotional, and sexual abuse were recorded during the Intake Interview, with questions like "Have you ever been physically abused (hit, slapped, beaten)?" A composite *abuse index* (coefficient alpha = .75) was created to summarize the total number of types of abuse (range 0–3) the probationer had experienced during his/her lifetime.

Behavioral Risks for HIV/AIDS

Based on work by Simpson et al. (1994), two measures were constructed from information in the Intake Interview to quantify behaviors shown to be associated with an increased probability of contracting the virus that causes HIV/AIDS. The *risky needle exposure index* (coefficient alpha = .67) was formed by adding two separate items reflecting the number of times nonsterilized drug-injection equipment had been shared. We attempted to replicate a *risky sex exposure index* to describe the number of times an individual had had sex without using a condom with someone who was not their spouse or primary sexual partner, with someone who was an injection drug user, or in exchange for drugs, money, or gifts in the preceding 6 months (see Simpson et al., 1994). Internal consistency reliability, however, was relatively low (coefficient alpha = .54), so we analyzed the individual items separately.

Criminality and Criminal History

Criminal involvement was gauged through self-reports made during the Intake Interview about previous arrests and incarcerations. Also, a composite measure for classifying risk for recidivism among the probationers, modeled after the Lifestyle Criminality Screening Form (LCSF; Walters, White, & Denny, 1991), was constructed from information collected in the Initial Assessment, Intake Interview, and the SRF. Conceptually, the *criminality classification index* emphasized four behavioral dimensions related to having a criminal lifestyle, including *irresponsibility, self-indulgence, interpersonal intrusiveness,* and *social rule breaking* (Walters, 1990), and Walters (1998) recommends clinical interpretations based on a total composite score to define "high" (values of 10 and above), "moderate" (7 to

9), and "low" (6 and below) risk categories (also see Hiller et al., 1999, for a complete description of the development of this measure).

Psychological Functioning

Current levels of psychological functioning were assessed at intake, months 1, 3, and 6 through the SRF and REST, and included scales for depression and anxiety (coefficient alphas = .67 and .74, respectively), and ratings of self-esteem and decision-making confidence (coefficient alphas = .66 and .71, respectively). Sample items for the anxiety scale included, "You feel anxious or nervous," "You have trouble sleeping," and "You have trouble sitting still for long." The SRF and REST both included the *Pearlin Mastery Scale* (Pearlin & Schooler, 1978) to assess general feelings of self-efficacy (coefficient alpha = .72). For this, residents indicated their agreement with statements such as, "You have little control over the things that happen to you" and "There is little you can do to change many of the important things in your life."

Social Functioning

Social-functioning indicators also were measured four times during treatment using the SRF and REST. This included scales for hostility and risk-taking (coefficient alphas = .79 and .77, respectively). Ratings for hostility, for example, were made on items like, "You have urges to fight or hurt other," "You get mad at other people easily," and "You like others to feel afraid of you."

Treatment Motivation

Finally, motivation for treatment was based on the problem recognition, desire for help, and treatment-readiness scales (coefficient alphas = .82, .67, and .72, respectively; see also Joe, Knezek, Watson, & Simpson, 1991; Simpson & Joe, 1993), collected at intake by the SRF and during treatment by the REST. As discussed by Simpson and Joe (1993), these scales represent conceptually distinct "stages" of treatment motivation, beginning with problem recognition and culminating with treatment readiness.

Treatment Dropout

The outcome criterion used for the third set of analyses was a dichotomously scored measure (0 = "completer"; 1 = "dropout"), based on the treatment-discharge information that was abstracted from facility records. Like community-based TCs (see De Leon, 1984, 1991; De Leon & Schwartz, 1984), many residents left the program before they had completed the expected treatment duration of 6 months. About 5% of the total sample dropped out each month, and examination of the reasons for treatment discharge showed that 69% of offenders completed treatment, 15% quit against staff advice (ASA), 13% were discharged for rules' violations, and 3% left for other reasons (e.g., medical problems, incarcerated in another county for an outstanding arrest warrant). However, because the "other" discharge group was small ($n = 16$) and represented a set of offenders "not appropriate" for treatment at the DCJTC, it was excluded from analyses. Comparisons, therefore, were made between those who had the opportunity to and completed treatment ($n = 287$) and those who dropped out early (ASA) or were removed for violation of program rules ($n = 114$).

Analytic Strategy

To meet the first goal of the study, an assessment of the probationers' needs on treatment entry, a series of descriptive statistics were calculated for the major assessment domains, including social history, drug dependence, psychological problems, abuse history, behavioral risks for HIV/AIDS, and criminality and criminal history. Next, individual response to treatment was tested through a series of growth curve models, which examined changes in psychosocial functioning and treatment motivation. This analytic method was used because it represents "change" in terms of individual trajectories over time. In contrast, traditional methods (e.g., analysis of variance) test differences between group means and treat individual variation as error. The strength of growth curve analysis, therefore, is its ability to summarize the overall pattern of change while accommodating individual differences. Finally, based in part on findings presented in Hiller et al. (1999), a series of Pearson correlations (r) were performed to explore the simple relationships between treatment-discharge status (i.e., dropout or completer), and the variables used during the needs' assessment analyses. After this, factors found to be significantly related to treatment dropout during the bivariate analyses were loaded into a stepwise logistic regression model. Hosmer and Lemeshow (1989) present a detailed description of a similar model-building strategy.

RESULTS

Needs' Assessment

Social History

Serious social history deficits were evident among this sample at program entry. Many of the probationers presented to treatment with problems in their employment history (50% were unemployed, an additional 11% had less than a full-time job) and education level (36% did not have the equivalent of a high school diploma).

Classification of Drug Problems

A total of 56% of the probationers were clinically dependent on alcohol (15% met criteria for abuse), 70% were dependent on cocaine (3% more for abuse), 36% on marijuana (14% for abuse), and 16% on opiates (an additional 1% for abuse). Additional analysis of drug patterns indicated the most common profiles were concurrent alcohol and cocaine ($n = 91$; 22%), and alcohol, cocaine, and marijuana problems ($n = 79$; 19%). Interestingly, 10 (2%) of the probationers reported no clinically problematic drug use, and 21 (5%) had problems only with marijuana.

Psychological Problems

Symptoms indicative of a history of psychiatric problems were commonly reported, including serious depression (47%), anxiety (42%), hallucinations (9%), attention and memory deficits (49%), violent impulses (26%), and suicide ideation (20%) and attempts (16%). Examination of the pathology index showed the majority of the probationers (51%) had multiple problems, and 28% indicated that they had received formal treatment for psychiatric problems during their lifetime.

Abuse History

Like psychological problems, most probationers (59%) indicated they had been abused during their lifetime, either physically (43%), emotionally (54%), or sexually (21%). Many (42%) were victims of multiple types of abuse. A strong correlation ($r = .35$, $p < .001$) between psychological problems and abuse history also was evident.

Behavioral Risks for HIV/AIDS

Overall, injection drug use was uncommon, but 14% of the sample did exhibit behavior that could result in exposure to the virus that causes HIV/ AIDS (i.e., shared nonsterilized needles or equipment). Risks associated with sexual behavior were more common. Forty percent indicated that they had recently had unprotected (i.e., no latex condom was used) sex with someone who was not their spouse or primary partner, 11% with an injection drug user, and 18% had traded unprotected sex for either money or drugs.

Criminality and Criminal History

Criminal careers for this sample were serious and extensive. The majority had been arrested and incarcerated at least six times (54% and 52%, respectively), and many (42%) had been arrested as juveniles. Seventy percent scored a 7 or higher on the criminality classification index, which indicated they were a moderate-to-high risk for recidivism.

Response to Treatment

The probationers generally showed significant improvements during treatment in both their psychological and social functioning, but not in their motivation for treatment (see Table 4.1). For example, the probationers entered the program with an average score of 4.01 ($SD = 0.92$, which varied significantly across individuals) on the self-esteem scale, and this improved significantly over the course of time ($b = .37$, $t = 13.39$, $p < .0001$). Decision-making confidence levels also increased ($b = .19$, $t = 8.40$, $p < .0001$), and depression scores decreased ($b = -.18$, $t = -6.68$, $p < .0001$) significantly over time. Examination of the two social-functioning scales revealed that risk taking decreased ($b = -.13$, $t = -4.17$, $p < .0001$), while hostility increased ($b = .11$, $t = 4.19$, $p < .0001$) during treatment. Finally, although there was substantial variation in baseline scores, readiness for treatment decreased significantly over time ($b = -.10$, $t = -3.98$, $p < .0001$), which probably should be expected because they were near the end of their treatment episode when the final assessment of motivation was collected. No change was observed in the scores for the problem recognition and desire for help scales.

TABLE 4.1   Summary of Growth Curve Models for Changes in Psychosocial
Functioning and Treatment Motivation

Measures	Initial status	Rate of change
Psychological functioning		
Self-esteem	4.01 (0.92)*	0.37 (0.29)*
Depression	3.46 (0.97)*	−0.18 (0.32)*
Anxiety	3.69 (1.09)*	−0.03 (0.33)
Decision-making	4.76 (0.79)*	0.19 (0.31)*
confidence		
Self-efficacy	5.25 (0.91)*	0.02 (0.25)
Social functioning		
Risk taking	4.14 (1.10)*	−0.13 (0.41)*
Hostility	3.06 (1.09)*	0.11 (0.33)*
Treatment motivation		
Problem recognition	5.58 (0.95)*	−0.03 (0.35)
Desire for help	6.08 (0.66)*	0.00 (0.19)
Treatment readiness	5.61 (0.77)*	−0.10 (0.26)*

Note. Standard deviations appear in parentheses.
*$p < .05$.

Treatment Dropout

Several factors identified as "needs" at admission to treatment were related
significantly to early attrition from the program. For example, women were
more likely than men to drop out early ($r = .12$, $p < .05$), as were those
who were unemployed in the 30 days prior to admission ($r = .17$, $p <
.001$) and those who received financial support from illegal activities ($r =
.16$, $p < .001$). Older probationers and those who reported income from a
job were less likely to leave prematurely ($r = −.15$ and $−.17$, $p < .01$,
respectively). Mental health problems also were associated with dropout,
including reports of serious depression ($r = .16$, $p < .001$), problems
controlling violent impulses ($r = .11$, $p < .05$), and a previous psychiatric
treatment episode ($r = .10$, $p < .05$). Higher scores on the pathology ($r =
.14$, $p < .01$), suicide ($r = .15$, $p < .01$), and abuse ($r = .18$, $p < .001$) indices
were associated with higher dropout rates. When criminal background was
considered, we found that more extensive arrest ($r = .12$, $p < .05$) and
incarceration histories ($r = .12$, $p < .05$) were related to a greater probability
of attrition, and those who scored "low" on the criminality index were
less likely to drop out ($r = −.17$, $p < .001$). Finally, higher self-ratings on

the risk-taking ($r = .13$, $p < .01$) and hostility ($r = .17$, $p < .001$) scales taken at intake were related to not remaining for the expected 6-month treatment duration, but higher self-efficacy acted as a protective factor ($r = -.11$, $p < .05$). As shown in Table 4.2, when all of the needs that were significantly related to dropout were simultaneously considered in a stepwise logistic regression model, the most efficient set of predictors that emerged were unemployment ($b = .69$, $p < .01$), younger age ($b = .62$, $p < .01$), abuse history ($b = .34$, $p < .01$), lifetime incarcerations ($b = .62$, $p < .05$), and not being classified as a low risk on the criminality index ($b = .60$, $p < .05$).

DISCUSSION

As probation populations continue to expand, community corrections agencies need to develop and implement good assessment procedures designed to make appropriate referrals to limited program slots, to track the offenders' therapeutic progress, and to determine who remains in treatment long enough to benefit from the services provided (Petersilia, 1995, 1997). The current study presents a theory-driven evaluation system designed to do this for correctional substance-abuse programs. It includes a comprehensive battery of intake measures, as well as prospective during treatment assessments. The information taken during admission processing using these intake questionnaires can help to determine if an offender was referred to the right treatment type and intensity level. For example, 10 probationers in our sample did not meet clinical criteria for drug dependence or abuse,

TABLE 4.2 Summary of Stepwise Logistic Regression Model Predicting Treatment Dropout

Predictor	B	SE	χ^2	Odds ratio
Intercept	−1.63	0.30		
Unemployed prior 30 days*	0.69	0.24	8.21	2.0
Less than 32 years old*	0.62	0.24	6.65	1.6
Abuse history*	0.34	0.10	10.59	1.4
6+ Lifetime incarcerations**	0.62	0.25	6.19	1.9
Not a low recidivism risk**	0.60	0.30	4.15	1.7

*$p < .01$; **$p < .05$.

and another 21 had problems only with marijuana (7% of the total). Recent research from community-based programs (see Simpson, Joe, Fletcher, Hubbard, & Anglin, 1999) indicates that intensive services are best saved for the cases with the most severe problems. Likewise, inmates with the most serious profiles of problems showed the most improvements after in-prison TC treatment that was followed by community-based transitional services (Knight, Simpson, & Hiller, 1999). The 31 probationers in our sample who had no or only minor drug problems, therefore, probably should have been sent to outpatient services instead of residential treatment so that the more intensive slots could have been reserved for referrals with more problematic profiles. This finding underscores the importance of using early screening for substance-abuse problems when making treatment decisions for correctional settings (Peters, Greenbaum, Edens, Carter, & Ortiz, 1998).

The intake battery also was designed to help practitioners to know what types of issues the offenders bring to treatment with them, thus focusing attention during individual diagnostic plans and guiding program development. Our sample reported extensive problems in their social background, drug use, mental health, abuse history, and criminality. For example, most (88%) of the probationers did not have either private or public medical insurance, so corrections-based or publicly funded treatment appeared to represent the best and, perhaps, only opportunities for them to get formal interventions targeted at their addiction. Moreover, most had serious problems with their drug use, 70% were dependent on cocaine, 56% on alcohol, and 16% on opioids, and many used multiple drugs—a factor that usually indicates a poor prognosis for an individual's treatment episode, especially when alcohol is used in combination with cocaine or opioids (see Rowan-Szal, Chatham, & Simpson, 2000). An alarming number also reported extensive histories of being victims of physical, emotional, and sexual abuse, and this was associated with early dropout from treatment. Increasing recognition is being placed on the interaction between addiction and prior abuse (e.g., Langeland & Hartgers, 1998), and as an emerging issue, the interplay between abuse history and retention and outcomes deserves serious attention in future evaluations of correctional substance-abuse treatment.

In spite of the many problems they presented at admission to the program, most of the probationers did show improvement in psychosocial functioning across the course of their treatment. This included enhanced feelings of psychological well-being (self-esteem, decision-making confidence), as well as reduced ratings of depression. Surprisingly, hostility scores increased significantly over time, suggesting that additional therapeutic focus should be placed on anger and stress management. Hostility has been shown to be related to early treatment dropout from both community-based (Broome, Flynn, & Simpson, 1999) and correctional TCs (Broome, Hiller, & Simpson, 2000), and modifying program content to more fully address issues, including engagement, anger management, and stress-reduction techniques, will likely improve treatment-retention rates.

When we examined the relationship between other probationer-background characteristics and whether they left treatment early (i.e., either ASA or because they were expelled for breaking cardinal rules), several attributes were found to be associated with higher attrition rates. For example, being unemployed and reporting income from illegal sources both were predictive of leaving treatment prematurely. These individuals appear to need vocational training earlier in their treatment episode to help them to become more fully involved in the treatment process, and to learn how to support themselves through legitimate means once they leave the program (Platt, 1995).

When we examined the probationer needs concurrently in a multivariate model, we found that criminal classification level (i.e., not scoring in the "low risk" range) was a strong predictor of early treatment attrition—and this measure probably represents an efficient means for integrating several relevant dimensions into a single factor to be used in treatment referrals and planning. This finding complements previous work showing these types of risk indices to be robust correlates of recidivism, poor in-prison behavioral adjustment, and early treatment dropout (see Gendreau, Goggin, & Law, 1996; Gendreau, Little, & Goggin, 1996; Hiller et al., 1999). Although this correctional-treatment program addresses criminal attitudes and thinking patterns during the standard treatment regimen (e.g., through behavioral modification and confrontation of antisocial behavior), it appears that even more directed attention should be focused on these factors to help improve retention and subsequent outcomes.

In conclusion, implications from these findings may be of interest to several types of professionals who work in corrections-based substance-abuse treatment. Correctional managers should be aware of the need to do up-front screening and assessment of substance abuse and criminality problems to make better use of limited intensive resources for "high-needs" drug-involved probationers (see also Knight et al., 1999). These findings also provide program administrators with empirically derived information for making practical decisions about what types of services they may need to add or augment. It appears that program modifications should include a greater emphasis on anxiety and anger management, trauma and victimization, and mental health issues. For those not yet "ready" for treatment, an "induction" intervention also could be used to increase early engagement and involvement (see Blankenship et al., 1999; Dees, Dansereau, & Simpson, 1999; Farabee et al., 1995). Finally, practitioners should note that their work has both short-term (i.e., improved psychosocial functioning) and long-term effects (reduced recidivism), but knowing which offender attributes need to be assessed and therapeutically addressed to reduce dropout is only a prelude to more detailed research on what occurs during the metaphorical "black box" of the treatment process. Promising areas of study include (a) treatment satisfaction (Hiller et al., 1999), (b) treatment expectations (McCorkel, Harrison, & Inciardi, 1998), (c) the peer environment within the TC (Broome, Knight, Hiller, & Simpson, 1996; Hiller et al., 1999), (d) the offender-counselor relationship (Broome et al., 1996, 1997), and (e) procriminal thinking and attitudes (Walters, 1996; Walters & Elliott, 1999). Improved posttreatment outcomes likely will be realized only through serious efforts to understand and to improve the processes underlying therapeutic progress in correctional-treatment settings.

ACKNOWLEDGMENTS

This project was funded by Grant No. 98-RTVXK00496-IJ-CX-0024 awarded by the National Institute of Justice, Office of Justice Programs, U.S. Department of Justice. Points of view in this document are those of the authors and do not necessarily represent the official position or policies of the U.S. Department of Justice. Special appreciation is extended to Ron Goethals, Director of the Dallas County Community Supervision and Corrections Department, and to Julien Devereux, Bill Hornyak, Barbara Jiles-Smith, and the clinical staff at the Dallas County Judicial Treatment Center who assisted in conducting this study. Special appreciation also is extended to Kirk Broome at the Institute of Behavioral Research for his assistance in planning the data analyses presented here.

5

Clinical Approaches for Drug Offenders

Robert L. DuPont

American state, federal, and local prisons and jails hold about 2 million people at any one time at a cost of about $40 billion a year. A recent Justice Department study showed that 62% of released offenders will be charged with a new crime after release, and that 41% will be returned to incarceration within 3 years of release (Bureau of Justice Statistics [BJS], 1998). After a decade in which the U.S. prison population doubled with lengthening sentences and falling crime rates, the major challenge for the 21st century is life after prison, in which the current lack of effective services and meaningful supervision produce a high cost in terms of repeat criminal offenses and reimprisonment (BJS, 1998).

The U.S. criminal justice system is bigger than the prisons and jails. There are now more than 6 million Americans under the supervision of agencies of the criminal justice system (CJS) (BJS, 1998). More than two thirds of these men, women, and children have significant problems as a result of their use of alcohol and/or other drugs (National Institute of Justice, 1998). Within the criminal justice system are included not only probation and parole along with jails and prisons, but also the large number of people in preadjudication status who are under court supervision. This broad definition of the CJS includes the local, state, and federal levels of jurisdiction for both adults and juveniles. Within this definition of the CJS are the modern drug courts, which deal with an increasingly broad range of offenders.

Not only does the definition of a "crime" change over time, as does the societal response to crimes, but so does the definition of "treatment" for the users of alcohol and other drugs (White, 1998). In this chapter, a "drug" is defined as an intoxicating or an impairing substance that is used nonmedically in ways that create personal and social harm (DuPont, 1998). The term "drug" refers to chemicals, the use of which is illegal for everyone, such as marijuana, cocaine, heroin, as well as to alcohol, the use of which is legal for adults but illegal for minors. This definition of a drug does not include nicotine although there is an evolution taking place in American thought that defines nicotine as a drug. This movement holds the potential for making tobacco smoking not only illegal for minors as alcohol is now, but illegal for everyone as marijuana smoking is now.

A "treatment" for alcohol and other drug use is broadly defined as all organized efforts to stop the use of alcohol and other drugs by individuals whose use of these substances has created personal or social problems (Carlson, 1998). Treatment could also include efforts to moderate the use of these substances or to promote the responsible use of alcohol or other drugs, but in this chapter, these efforts that, in any case, remain marginal in society in general, and in the CJS in particular, are not considered to be treatment. The 12-step fellowships (Alcoholics Anonymous [AA], Narcotics Anonymous [NA], and the myriad of other fellowships that are derived from AA) are not defined as treatment, although many substance-abuse treatment programs not only use the principles of the 12-step fellowships, but they also encourage (or even require) participation in these programs. The 12-step fellowships lack the structure of an alcohol- or drug-treatment program, including a paid staff, an organized intake and case-management system, and individualized records that characterize alcohol- and other drug-treatment programs (DuPont, 1997; DuPont & McGovern, 1994).

The treatment of drug offenders within the CJS fits within the larger context of compulsory treatment of drug abuse, which was comprehensively reviewed 10 years ago by the National Institute on Drug Abuse (NIDA; 1988). The rationale for the use of the CJS to enforce abstinence and to promote treatment participation has been explored from both the legal and humanitarian perspectives in the development of the new concept of "therapeutic jurisprudence." This term was coined by David Wexler in a paper delivered to the National Institute of Mental Health in 1987. Therapeutic jurisprudence is defined as "the use of social science to study the extent to which a legal role or practice promotes the psychological and physical well-being of the people it affects" (Slobogin, 1995).

The CJS now holds more alcohol and other drug users (about four million) than the total number involved in addiction treatment for alcohol and other drugs at all levels, including both public and private treatment (a bit less than one million) (Department of Health and Human Services [DHHS], 1999). This makes the CJS potentially the nation's largest environment for addiction treatment. There are many important commonalities between alcohol and other drug offenders within the CJS and alcohol and other drug users outside the CJS. All of the drug-involved offenders in the CJS were previously using alcohol and other drugs outside the CJS, often for long periods of time prior to their arrests. Most of them will be using alcohol and other drugs outside the CJS after release from supervision. A large proportion of alcohol and other drug users find their way into the CJS, but many alcohol and other drug users, including some problem-generating heavy users, never get caught in the CJS.

Despite substantial overlap, the drug offenders in the CJS are, on the average, different in important ways from the alcohol and other drug users outside the CJS. Drug offenders are more likely to be male, more likely to be members of minority groups, less educated, poorer, and heavier users. The alcohol and other drug use of criminal offenders creates more social harm than is created by nonoffender users. Drug offenders have higher levels of comorbidity for both medical and psychiatric disorders (NIDA, 1997). This is not to say, however, that there are not many disadvantaged, heavy drug users outside of the CJS, nor that everyone in the CJS fits this picture as a minority-group member who is a disadvantaged, heavy user, with multiple psychiatric and medical disorders. The alcohol- and other drug-user population within the CJS, and the population outside the CJS, are both heterogeneous, defying simple characterizations. The modal drug-involved prison inmate is an employed (prior to imprisonment), 25- to 29-year-old, White, non-Hispanic, male high school graduate who has never married. The modal nondrug involved prison inmate in America today shares all these demographic characteristics (National Center on Addiction and Substance Abuse at Columbia University, 1998).

This chapter reviews what is known about the provision of treatment services for drug offenders in the CJS and explores future opportunities.

Past Work

The modern linkage of the CJS and the alcohol and other drug user goes back to the late 1960s and early 1970s. At that time, civil commitment was a dominant form of addiction treatment, particularly in California and New York, the two states with the largest addict populations and with the largest public responses to the then-emerging illegal drug-abuse epidemic. That was when methadone maintenance (MM) and the therapeutic communities (TCs) emerged as promising new forms of addiction treatment. In the early 1970s, these two often mutually hostile treatment approaches came to dominate public-sector addiction treatment as civil commitment was virtually abandoned (DuPont & Mackenzie, 1994; White, 1998).

From the beginning of modern public-sector drug treatment in the early 1970s, drug-free outpatient (DFOP) treatment has been a major component of the drug-treatment system, although far less visible and more varied that either MM or TCs. The CJS showed a continuing preference for TCs and an aversion for MM. DATOS intake data showed that 50% of TC referrals suffered from antisocial personality disorder (ASP), whereas about one third of referrals to DFOP and MM had this diagnosis. Only about 2% of MM referrals were from the courts. Methadone maintenance patients were also older than patients in either TCs or DFOP, with averages in the mid-30s, suggesting that they may have been less prone to violent crime than the younger referrals to TCs. These data also suggest that pharmacological treatments, including MM, may be underused by the CJS. With the high prevalence of co-occurring disorders in the offender population, greater use of routine screening for mental disorders and pharmacotherapy appear indicated within the CJS.

The first universal, court-based, drug-testing program in the United States started when the D.C. Superior Court began drug testing of all defendants in 1970. That pioneering program, which has been operating without interruption ever since, involved continuing urine drug testing of criminal offenders released to the community, combined with referral to the city's large drug-treatment program, as well as to a variety of private addiction-treatment programs. The D.C. Superior Court-testing program was not a diversion program but a supervision and referral-to-treatment program (DuPont, in press). In 1972, the White House Special Action Office for Drug Abuse Prevention (SAODAP) adopted this model to create the Treatment Alternatives to Street Crime (TASC) program, which included a diversion component. This meant that participation in TASC was for some participants an alternative to incarceration.

From the origins of the California and the New York civil commitment programs in the 1960s, there has been an enduring close relationship between prisons and TCs. This has included the use of TC programs and TC ideas in prisons (Mahon, 1997). Most TC programs have a high percentage of residents referred from the CJS. All community-based addiction treatment, particularly public-sector addiction treatment, has, from its origins 30 years ago, had a large percentage of patients under the supervision of an agency of the CJS. For example, between its beginning in 1970 and 1973, the Narcotics Treatment Administration (NTA), the large DC heroin-addiction treatment program, went from a patient population that contained about one-third referrals from the CJS to two-thirds referrals from the CJS (DuPont, in press).

In the early years of the buildup of the state and federal public-sector drug treatment, there was an intensive focus on the problem of heroin addiction and the connection of heroin addiction and crime (Massing, 1998; DuPont & Katon, 1971). This early, heroin-addiction orientation and the success of the D.C. Superior Court-testing program led to a proposal in 1978 for universal drug testing within the CJS, with release to the community being conditioned on offenders maintaining abstinence from heroin use as shown by random drug tests (DuPont & Wish, 1992).

In the early 1990s, the first Drug courts were established. They differed from TASC because the Drug court programs were run by judges using the staff of the courts. They were not external, addiction-treatment referral programs affiliated with the courts, but they were integrated parts of the courts themselves. Drug courts had characteristics of the driving while intoxicated (DWI) programs that were not found in most addiction-treatment programs or in TASC (Ross, 1993). Drug courts typically included intensive educational programs about addiction (based on the "disease concept" of AA) and court-based drug testing linked to tough consequences, which were progressively more severe for any positive drug tests indicating continued illegal drug use. Drug courts usually mandated attendance at one or more of the 12-step programs, and used the principles of AA in their activities.

Drug courts typically required some payment from the offender for the services they received. This was not common in public-sector addiction treatment outside a few privately run methadone-treatment programs. Drug courts had lower levels of professional counseling services and, therefore, lower costs than characterized many addiction-treatment programs. The drug court staff functioned as case managers, using the persuasive powers of the court to help clients access other services in the community, including addiction treatment and such services as mental health, vocational, and medical and other specialized care. The direct, repeated, and highly personal role of drug court judges with drug offenders under supervision and the use of large-group support were different from more traditional drug-treatment programs or TASC (see Balenko, this volume).

Today, there are a multitude of alcohol- and other drug-treatment services for drug offenders in all parts of the CJS, from parole and probation to jails and prisons. These addiction-treatment programs include services provided within the CJS, as well as referral to community treatment services. The treatment services for drug offenders in the CJS, while varied and widespread, are fragmented and not comprehensive. CJS services for drug offenders seldom reach more than a small percentage of the total number of drug offenders under supervision of any CJS agency. Fragmentation and lack of comprehensiveness of services have been characteristic of drug treatment generally, and have not been unique to the CJS. The CJS appears to offer the best opportunity for fully integrated and comprehensive addiction-treatment services because there is a relative abundance of resources in the CJS and because these are among the most severe and needy of all addicted people. Additionally, the use of coercion in this population is possible to insure that addicted people participate in a full range of the most effective services for a prolonged period of time.

In the early days of civil commitment, TCs, and MM, there was a generous mixture of skepticism that anything worked at all, along with a boundless optimism about the benefits of treatment for addicts (DuPont, Goldstein, & O'Donnel, 1978). Since then, a robust industry has developed studying the costs and benefits of addiction treatment, with the single, most consistent finding being that the length of stay in treatment is positively correlated with improvement (Hubbard et al., 1989).

Drug-abuse treatment-outcome research has focused on four variables: retention in treatment, drug use, crime, and employment. When alcohol use was studied, it was found that alcohol use was not reduced to the extent that drug use was reduced in addiction treatment, even though about one fifth of drug-addiction treatment patients reported excessive alcohol consumption. The most dramatic benefits of drug treatment have been reduced drug use and reduced crime. When other variables were studied, including alcohol abuse and employment, it became clear that most addiction treatment undertreats the patient's needs. Drug-treatment programs do not routinely use "best practices" for the full range of problems the patients experience. There is an important opportunity for the CJS to set a higher standard for drug-addiction treatment that can be applied to other addicted populations, including non-CJS public-sector drug treatment, as well as to private-sector drug treatment.

The benefits of addiction treatment have been substantially less than miraculous, leading to a rethinking of the nature of addiction. Addiction is increasingly seen as "chronic and relapsing brain disease," more similar to asthma or coronary artery disease, and less like an acute infectious disease that, once "treated," seldom recurred. Having said that addiction treatment works and that it is cost-effective—on a scale similar to that for chronic medical conditions that also have better prognoses when behavior change is made—it is important to acknowledge that many alcohol and other drug abusers fail in all forms of treatment, not once but many times. Substantial costs, including further criminality, are a common finding of addiction treatment-outcome research.

Major Issues

There are three primary deficiencies in the CJS response to drug offenders today. The first is conceptual. There needs to be a clear distinction made between addiction treatment on the one hand and CJS programs aimed at enforcing abstinence. These latter efforts include the detection of continuing alcohol and other drug use and the sanctions imposed for that continued use. Often, these two roles, "treatment and enforced abstinence," are blurred in both policy and in practice. In the CJS, testing and the responses to continued drug use are commonly transferred from the CJS to addiction treatment. Similarly, it can be too easily assumed that every illegal drug user needs (or wants) addiction treatment. Some criminal offenders just need a reason to stop using drugs and a referral to the 12-step programs. When these two roles are confused, addiction-treatment programs have an inherent conflict of interest as they attempt to be understanding and tolerant of the chronic, relapsing nature of addiction, at the same time that they enforce the mandates of the CJS that the offender remain drug free. Treatment resources can be wasted on offenders who do not want or need treatment. A much better policy is to separate these two functions, with the CJS agencies retaining the responsibility for drug testing and for the imposition of whatever consequences are appropriate for failure to adhere to the no-use standard of the CJS. Drug testing and supervision should be universal and unitary in the CJS. Treatment should be selective and highly varied as it is used by the heterogeneous population of drug-involved criminal offenders. A similar conflict of interest can be seen in workplace-addiction programs, where the transferring of the testing to addiction treatment can be associated with a more relaxed attitude toward continuing drug use than the employer's policy permits.

The second deficiency that limits the benefits of addiction treatment in the CJS is the lack of comprehensiveness for drug testing and addiction treatment. There is a plethora of relatively small and highly diverse programs dealing with drug offenders throughout the CJS. There is no overall standard of care to identify all drug-involved offenders, and to provide each with an individualized treatment plan using specialized services while the offenders are incarcerated and with prolonged supervision with community release.

The third deficiency of the CJS's approach to alcohol and other drug abuse is the failure to recognize that addiction treatment is highly varied in the settings in which it occurs and the services addiction treatment provides. The CJS needs to respect the varied needs of drug offenders and the local availability of specific forms of addiction treatments, as well as to some extent the preferences of the offenders themselves for diverse forms of addiction treatment. The policy of no use of illegal drugs while under the supervision of the CJS needs to be universally enforced with progressively escalating penalties for violations, regardless of the forms of alcohol and other drug treatments selected.

The explosive growth of the CJS population in the past decade has spawned a lively public debate about the most appropriate role of the CJS as it deals with alcohol- and other drug-involved offenders. In contrast to addiction treatment where, both within the public and private sectors, there has been relatively intense pressure for cost reductions leading to widespread curtailment of services during the past decade, there has been relatively little public resistance to spending more on jails and prisons, which now cost about $40 billion a year. This figure compares with less than $5 billion a year spent on alcohol treatment, and $7.5 billion spent on other drug-abuse treatment in all of its many forms, both public and private (NIDA, 1997). There is an urgent need to think creatively about how to best help all alcohol- and other drug-involved offenders, not only the nonviolent offenders most likely to find their ways into drug courts.

The positive future of CJS treatment of addicted people envisioned here can only be obtained with greater public and political education about the importance of the CJS, about the role of addiction in the crimes that lead offenders into the agencies of the CJS, and the vital importance of addiction treatment in reducing both addiction and crime. The comprehensive approach to addiction treatment proposed here is expensive, but it is not as expensive as the costs generated by untreated addicts in the CJS. There is a unique opportunity in the CJS at this time that can find favor with both hard-headed realists and soft-hearted humanitarians. This new perspective reaches across the political divisions that bedevil much of the modern public sector activities and most national drug policies. It is that common ground that needs to be cultivated for the CJS to fulfill its potential for the most disabled of all addicted people.

In the future, the management of drug offenders in the CJS needs to be based on these seven principles:

1. The CJS should enforce a no-use standard for alcohol and other drugs, while under any form of supervision, for all offenders regardless of their addiction status. *All criminal offenders need random drug tests*, with the frequency of testing being determined by the expectation of finding positive tests. Nondrug-involved offenders should be tested at least three times a year on a random basis—the frequency of testing in the U.S. military. Testing should be more intensive in community settings among offenders with a history of addiction to alcohol and other drugs. Testing should be less intense for offenders with no prior history who are in prisons, but these offenders should be subjected to some random drug testing as well. Even offenders in relatively low-risk categories need random drug testing because drug testing is a cost-effective way to prevent drug problems. Drug tests are essential for early intervention when drug use occurs.

2. Positive drug-test results should lead to increased frequency of drug testing and to the *imposition of progressively more severe consequences* up to and including reincarceration. Inmates of jails and prisons who test positive for recent drug use should lose valued privileges. The principle needs to be established throughout the CJS that community participation (and privileges in jails and prisons) are conditioned on nonuse of alcohol and other drugs, as demonstrated by regular, random drug testing. Positive drug tests should also lead to more services to help the drug users overcome their addictions.

3. The authority and responsibility for the *monitoring and supervision should be retained within a CJS agency,* and not delegated to an addiction-treatment program or other agency. This is important because treatment programs seldom have the sense of urgency of the CJS and often find reasons to overlook slips back to drug use.

4. *Supervision and drug testing should be prolonged after release from prison,* for at least 2 years, for all drug-involved offenders to help them

get back into their communities and to use appropriate resources, including the 12-step programs, to sustain recovery. The intensity of supervision should be calibrated to the needs of individual offenders, but it should generally not be less than one visit per week at the start in the community, and not less than one visit per 3 months during the final months of supervision.

5. An *individualized treatment plan* should be developed for every drug offender in the CJS, identifying special needs and seeking ways to help each offender meet those needs with available community resources. Systematic monitoring of adherence to the treatment plan is important to insure that other needs, such as mental disorders or vocational or educational deficiencies, are addressed as part of each offender-personalized, community release plan.

6. Drug offenders should be expected *to pay for some of the costs of their drug testing and treatment.* For example, a charge of $5 for a positive urine result is reasonable not only to create revenue for the CJS, but to establish an additional incentive to remaining drug free.

7. All drug-involved offenders should be required to *participate in one or more of the 12-step programs* on a regular and frequent basis. Generally, one meeting a day is a sound standard both in prison and in the community, but less than three meetings a week is seldom enough. For offenders who object to the 12-step programs, it is important that alternative community-support programs be identified that promote nonuse of alcohol and other drugs, as well as promoting other prosocial values.

Each of these seven principles are met today for some offenders. What is missing now is the universal application of all seven principles to all criminal offenders. The offender population is at high risk of addiction to alcohol and other drugs. These seven principles will reduce that risk. There are no other interventions that hold the promise of reducing criminal recidivism that these ideas hold for the six million criminal offenders now under supervision in the CJS in the United States.

If the sweeping reforms envisioned in this chapter are to earn support from both liberals and conservatives, a realistic balance must be maintained. Conservatives deserve to be reassured that criminal offenders will be closely supervised and that they will experience substantial negative consequences, including reincarceration, for failure to maintain abstinence. Liberals deserve to be reassured that good-faith efforts will be made to provide meaningful services and that those offenders who succeed in addiction treatment will be rewarded with increased time out of prison and in the community.

Both goals can be met with a consistent splitting of the functions of supervision and consequences from that of addiction treatment. The specifics of treatment need to be varied to reflect both the availability of resources in the community and the choices and the needs of the drug-involved offenders themselves.

Conclusions

The overlap of the CJS and addiction to alcohol and drugs is the most important frontier today for both the CJS and for addiction treatment. Not only are drug-involved offenders among the most needy and most socially costly of all drug abusers, but the drug-involved offenders are the most treatable of all criminal offenders. There is nothing else available that can compare to effective alcohol and other drug treatment as a crime-reduction intervention. In other words, within the CJS, the drug offenders are the most likely of all offenders to be helped by available interventions, including both drug testing and addiction treatment. Drug offenders are the most serious and the most problem-generating class of potential patients of addiction treatments. The use of the coercive power of the CJS provides the leverage to make addiction treatment more effective. In 1992, Mark Kleinman estimated that "a serious national program of drug testing and sanctions for offenders who are users of illicit drugs could be mounted for approximately $5 billion a year."

A recent review of opportunities for using substance-abuse treatment to reduce crime concluded:

> Crime and violence can be reduced to significant levels by addressing the problem of substance abuse. Empirical evidence shows that drug and alcohol abuse has had a fundamental effect on the criminal behavior of an overwhelming majority of inmates. Thus, it is necessary to introduce treatment-based substitutes for imprisonment to curb criminal and violent behavior. This approach, combined with intensive correctional treatment, support services and aftercare, has been proven effective in reducing criminal recidivism and relapse to drug and alcohol use. (Belenko & Peugh, 1998, p. 58)

Future Directions

One of the most striking features of both criminal justice and addiction treatment is the tremendous diversity of supervision and treatment in the

CJS. This diversity is matched by a lack of comprehensiveness with which CJS supervision and addiction treatment occur. The recent development of drug courts has revitalized the CJS to the issues of addiction and to the potential for interventions within the CJS. The National Institute of Justice (NIJ) has pioneered in this area for 20 years. Recently, the Department of Justice has become even more involved in the issue of postprison supervision and care for drug offenders (BJS, 1998). The NIDA held a major national meeting on the interface of addiction treatment and the CJS (NIDA, 2000). There is reason for optimism because of the growing interest of all levels in the CJS, as well as in addiction treatment and research.

Now we need to identify the best practices and to provide funding to extend them universally. We need more research into the costs and benefits of alternative approaches. The drug-treatment system offers a largely untapped resource for the CJS to use available knowledge to reduce drug use by offenders under supervision (NIDA, 1988). Community-based addiction treatment, both in the public and private sectors, has been hit by severe funding limitations in the past decade. For community-based treatment to play a larger role in the response of the CJS, substantial additional resources will be needed.

Relevant research on the range of approaches to alcohol and other drug offenders in the CJS needs to be a top priority for both the Department of Justice and the DHHS. The payoff will be large for the people involved.

There is reason for optimism today as the convergence of forces on the issue of drug use by criminal offenders holds the promise of dramatic improvements in the immediate future. There is a troubling prospect that may affect support for these efforts in the future. The currently falling crime rates in the United States may erode the public will to seize this unique opportunity. In the early days of the American illegal drug epidemic, there was a major outpouring of federal and local funding for a massive addiction-treatment program in Washington, D.C., which was seen at the time as a national model. When the rate of serious crimes in D.C. was cut in half between 1969 and 1973, the political will to pursue this promising beginning disappeared on a bipartisan basis (NIDA, 1988). There is a danger that the next decade will see this unfortunate history repeated nationally if the current significant decline in the rate of major crimes continues. It will be a tragedy if this opportunity to link the CJS to drug treatment is lost. Not only would the approaches recommended here, if implemented and sustained universally throughout the CJS, substantially cut the crime rate, but they could empty the prisons of the nation, since drug offenders are responsible for much of the growth of the nation's prison population.

6

Employment Rehabilitation

Robert Walker and Carl G. Leukefeld

Rehabilitation embraces a wide range of services, such as cognitive rehabilitation, speech therapy, occupational therapy, psychosocial rehabilitation, and vocational rehabilitation. It has been defined as a spectrum of interventions that seeks to normalize the individual's life or to achieve fulfillment in living (Corrigan, 1995; Englehart, Robinson, & Kates, 1997). This chapter focuses on the employment needs of drug offenders and the rehabilitation services that can contribute to drug offenders' employability. Vocationally oriented rehabilitation is designed to meet the employment needs of individuals with disabilities or conditions that impair their ability to find work. In fact, traditional vocational rehabilitation has been defined as a process that prepares individuals for employment by helping to select a vocational role and then prepare for functioning in that role (Deren & Randell, 1990).

Employment rehabilitation incorporates the spectrum of services that improve an offender's ability to get employment, maintain employment, and to upgrade employment. It also includes services that facilitate employer acceptance and accommodation of clients in the workplace. Employment rehabilitation for drug offenders includes assessment, training, work-related social skills building, and job-coaching services to address drug offenders' unemployment and underemployment throughout recovery

(Deren & Randell, 1990). In addition, the employment focus in rehabilitation can be integrated into treatment, as well as being an element of case-management services.

Employment has consistently been identified as an important indicator of positive substance-abuse treatment outcome (McLellan, 1983), and is a variable that is generally included as an outcome measure of substance-abuse treatment (Hubbard, 1997). However, drug users' employment needs are typically not the focus of substance-abuse treatment (Brown, 1997; Room, 1998). In fact, less than one third of substance-abuse treatment clients in community treatment reported receiving any vocational service within the first 6 months of treatment (Arella, Deren, Randell, & Brewington, 1990). More recently, fewer programs in the 1990s used employment-focused interventions than in the previous decade in spite of evidence of an even greater need (Brown, 1997; Room, 1998). It is interesting to note that the *American Psychiatric Association Practice Guidelines* do not address employment stability or employment problems, and do not include employment among the clinical features that influence treatment, such as parenting, culture, comorbid conditions, social milieu, and gender (American Psychiatric Association, 1996). The *ASAM Patient Placement Criteria for the Treatment of Substance-Related Disorder, 2nd ed.,* which is used to assess levels of impairment, only briefly mentions employment as one part of the patient's environment for recovery (American Society of Addiction Medicine, 1996) and does not address vocational or social skills.

In contrast with clinical areas of substance-abuse treatment, case management generally includes employment- and vocational rehabilitation-focused services to promote client independence (Siegal, 1998). Employment-focused interventions can be carried out by case managers either through referral to vocational programs or by including employment-focused services as a direct part of the case-management function. For example, Assertive Community Treatment, which is conceptually linked with strengths-based case management, places importance on employment services as one of the principal ways for clients to achieve independence and a higher degree of self-determination (Stein & Santos, 1998).

Employment Rehabilitation and Drug Offenders

Criminal justice treatment for substance abusers can be effective in reducing recidivism and drug use (Leukefeld & Tims, 1988; Martin, Butzin, Saum, & Inciardi, 1999). However, offender substance-abuse treatment involves more than just focusing on substance use. Psychosocial intervention that include rehabilitation may be as important as focusing on drug use (McLellan et al., 1994). Studies suggest that vocational and educational rehabilitation services are viewed as important by drug users, but that these services are generally unavailable in most community-treatment programs (Arella et al., 1990; Brewington, Arella, Deren, & Randell, 1987; Brown, 1997; Hubbard & Harwood, 1981; McLellan et al., 1994). This may, in part, be attributable to clinicians' focus on clients' substance-abuse recovery rather than focusing on what have been characterized as "ancillary" issues (McLellan et al., 1994).

Rehabilitation needs, including vocational needs, are typically seen as part of the case-management function (Liese & Najavits, 1997), and thus may be outside the direct interests of clinicians in treatment planning. Liese and Najavits (1997) stress the importance of including vocation- and employment-focused rehabilitation in clinical practice, and Inciardi (1994) includes employment issues in assessment, as well as treatment planning for criminal justice clients. In fact, the inclusion of employment rehabilitation might be more important for criminal justice substance abusers because work is related to reduced criminal activity (Inciardi, Surratt, Martin, & Hooper, this volume). Also, employment rehabilitation is related to post-treatment stability and sustained recovery (McLellan et al., 1994; Platt, Husband, Hermalin, Cater, & Metzger, 1993).

Platt (1997) concludes from a review of the literature that employment and employment-related interventions play important roles in substance-abuse recovery. In fact, various vocational-rehabilitation approaches have been reported as contributing to positive treatment outcomes (Hall, Loeb, Coyne, & Cooper, 1981; Platt et al., 1993). However, McLellan et al. (1994) found that only 24% of substance abusers received an individual or group discussion about employment problems during community treatment. DATOS findings indicate that less than 10% of residential drug-free clients and less than 3% of methadone clients reported receiving employment-related services during community treatment (Hubbard et al., 1989).

The employment rate of drug and alcohol abusers who enter treatment is dramatically lower than that of the general population (Platt, 1997). In fact, the unemployment of substance-abuse clients appears to be increasing in spite of improved economic circumstances (Brown, 1997), which suggests additional issues for recovering drug offenders. While there is limited employment rehabilitation in substance-abuse programs in general, the low availability of employment rehabilitation may be even more troubling for drug offenders.

For drug offenders, the concern about vocational rehabilitation may be more urgent given the relationship between employment and treatment retention (Platt, 1986). Longer stays in treatment have been associated with positive treatment outcomes for a wide range of substance abusers (Hubbard et al., 1989). Obtaining employment during treatment has also been related to reductions in drug use and related criminal activity (Joe, Chastain, & Simpson, 1990). Since employment is linked with decreased drug use and reduced criminality (Anglin & Fisher, 1987), programs for drug offenders should incorporate employment interventions in their services. Consequently, since many offenders have very limited job skills, limited work histories, little job-seeking experience and skills, and limited social skills (Finn, 1998), several programs have been developed to meet the specific employment needs of offenders. The need for these programs was recognized by the National Institute of Corrections in 1995 (National Institute of Justice [NIJ], 1998), which developed employment-services training for offender-treatment practitioners in community and correctional settings.

Offender Employment Rehabilitation and Vocational Adjustment

Four major elements are included in comprehensive drug-offender employment rehabilitation: a) assessing employment skills, history, interests, and clinical characteristics; b) training referrals; c) employment-focused interventions, including social skills' counseling to support clients in obtaining, maintaining, and upgrading employment; and d) job placement and coaching to bridge employment preparation with the actual workplace environment.

1. *Assessment*—Drug-offender employment history should be assessed to identify strengths that can be enhanced through rehabilitation. The offender's history should include the types of jobs, duration of each job, ways of relating to employers, circumstances of employment termination, successful school experiences, and vocational interests (Schottenfeld, Pascale, & Sokolowski, 1992). Determining the offender's percentage of adult years of employment is an important indicator of employment-rehabilitation needs. Studies suggesting that pretreatment employment may be a robust predictor not only of posttreatment employment, but also for positive treatment outcome, particularly for decreased drug use (Marsh &

Simpson, 1986), support the importance of a detailed work-history assessment. One way of looking at this finding is to target those offenders with poor work histories for intensive, employment-focused rehabilitation. In addition, detailed assessment of unemployment or underemployment factors may help target specific offender problems, such as limited social skills. For example, the lack of knowledge or skills that might have contributed to unemployment may be qualitatively different from a lack of desire to obtain employment (Hermalin, Steer, Platt, & Mettzger, 1990). Practitioners may be tempted to make negative inferences about poor employment histories when skill deficits are the issue, not a lack of offender motivation for self-improvement.

Assessment should identify offenders' specific work skills and the extent to which these skills were acquired in formal training programs or in on-the-job placements. Assessment should also include job-seeking attitudes and knowledge. For instance, methadone clients who lack knowledge about how to look for work have been reported as having a three-times greater likelihood of obtaining employment than those without the desire (Hermalin et al., 1990).

Assessment should include information from medical and clinical sources (Groah, Goodall, Kreutzer, Sherron, & Wehman, 1990). However, clinical findings may be less relevant than an employment history (Hermalin et al., 1990). The offender's level of risk for harm to self and others should be considered in providing employment rehabilitation. For example, drug offenders with higher levels of hostility or aggression may benefit from employment services, but their previous behavior should be considered in work placements, since hostile clients can potentially jeopardize job placements for other clients and damage program reputation. Assessment should also include cultural factors surrounding employment histories, since clients' employment problems are affected by their ethnic or racial minority status, as well as a lack of education (Leung, 1995). A drug offender's culture should be discussed to better differentiate antisocial personality from social factors.

2. *Training Referral*—Drug offenders need specific work skills to progress from entry-level, minimum wage jobs. The "strengths perspective" encourages assessment that focuses on client positives and growth potential rather than pathology and deficits (De Jong & Miller, 1995; Saleeby, 1996). Employment may be premature if the offender has significant deficits in work skills and accompanying social skills. Employment-focused rehabilitation can include referrals for job-skill development in vocational- or technical-training programs, supported employment, training in a sheltered

employment setting, or other onsite training. Drug offenders with clearly defined employment goals frequently need technical-skills training, such as plumbing or electrical work. Supported employment provides a job placement, accompanied by follow-along services that diminish as clients gain confidence and job success (Groah et al., 1990). Supportive employment also helps by monitoring work progress and skill development with feedback and emotional support. Sheltered employment is most applicable for more impaired offenders who need close supervision during their training.

3. *Employment Counseling and Pre-employment Counseling*— Employment counseling with offenders incorporates employment-assessment feedback, information about the local job market, available skill and training services, and counseling about realistic expectations and ways to achieve goals. Pre-employment counseling can establish job readiness and level of job-seeking interest. Programs may err in directing offenders too quickly into job placement or training without focusing on offenders' interests and/or readiness for employment. This may result in noncompliance with rehabilitation plans. When a drug offender has made choices about employment or training goals, practitioners should focus on problem-solving skills that promote those goals (Schottenfeld et al., 1992). It can be helpful to partition goals into short- and long-term goals in order to develop incremental steps to achieving successful employment (Rubin & Roessler, 1995). The approach should lead to an employment plan that is tailored to the drug offender's current employment needs for obtaining, maintaining, or upgrading their employment. Depending on the offender's needs, an individualized plan should be developed. The plan should focus on job-skills training, as well as social skills.

Schottenfeld et al. (1992) suggested two levels of employment activities with substance abusers: a) assistance with obtaining employment, and b) help in maintaining employment. Building on these two components, a strengths' perspective suggests at least a third level—helping the drug offender to upgrade employment. This third level of employment rehabilitation adds a future orientation and more goal-directed approach to a client's employability. The three levels of employment rehabilitation suggest a phased approach to meeting client need.

1. *Obtaining employment.* Drug offenders who have difficulty in obtaining employment typically need pre-employment services. These include exploring the offender's values pertaining to work, work history, work

interests, attitude about applying for work, and other basic skills associated with employment seeking. Basic job training and social skill development are also included in this phase. Service needs for drug offenders in this phase include: specific job-skill identification; exploring offenders' work interests; training in specific marketable skills; job-interviewing skill development, including résumé preparation, telephone etiquette, appropriate dress, and ability to present strengths realistically but positively; assistance in overcoming criminal-records issues; assistance with cultural and ethnic factors that can impede employment; motivational encouragement for continued drug-abuse treatment and mental health treatment that can support employment; and job referrals and placement for initial employment.

2. *Maintaining employment.* Drug offenders with a history of being able to obtain employment but with difficulty retaining jobs need a focus on social skills and interpersonal factors in the workplace. Other offenders may have progressed through the obtaining-employment phase, and can benefit from information and skill building for maintaining employment, which includes appropriate ways of managing workplace conflicts; understanding the business culture, including punctuality, work manners, and dress codes; attitudes about work; managing relapse risk and employment concerns; adapting to structure in lifestyle, including work habits; coping with frustration; maintaining self-worth in entry-level jobs; and exploring different job placements to create a better fit of client to environment.

3. *Upgrading employment.* The drug offender who can obtain employment and maintain jobs could benefit from information about how to improve their level of employment. Upgrading employment is associated with overall progress in treatment and recovery. Periods of economic growth provide opportunities for upgraded employment for those just entering employment with few job skills (Burtless, 1997). Upgrading employment also encourages clients to think about future goals, which include job goal setting; training for a more advanced career, including formal course work or on-the-job training; preparing updated résumés and job portfolios; coping with success and changes in self-image; incorporating the identity of a working person; capitalizing on experience; and focusing on longer-term personal and employment goals.

4. *Job placement and coaching.* Drug offenders who need jobs and have a job history may still need job-placement help at any phase in their rehabilitation (Rubin & Roessler, 1995). Practitioners can partner with welfare-to-work programs, since many welfare-to-work programs have recruited employers who are willing to hire individuals with uneven employment histories and limited skills. Job coaching may also be useful for drug

offenders to transition from unemployment to employment. Job coaching has two elements: (a) onsite visits to support and encourage adaptation to their jobs, and (b) consultation with the employers about drug-offender characteristics and realistic supervisory needs and accommodations. Job coaching is part of the National Institute of Corrections job-training program (NIJ, 1998). Practitioners should also consider recruiting employers who are open minded about hiring offenders. Employers can also benefit from training or coaching to learn more about offender behaviors and how to evaluate their work performance and behavior.

Current Status of Employment-Focused Rehabilitation

French, Dennis, McDougal, Karuntzos, and Hubbard (1992) studied four community-treatment sites, and reported numerous barriers and obstacles to successful employment and considerable complexity affecting employment for drug offenders. These barriers included lack of social skills, a criminal record, lack of specific job skills, lack of motivation, and many program-level barriers, such as a lack of vocational specialists and vocational programming (French et al., 1992). However, some programs have made an effort to specifically address vocational needs of substance abusers. The Wildcat experiment was the first large-scale effort to assess the impact of vocational rehabilitation among substance abusers and ex-offenders in New York City (Platt, 1997). Although there were difficulties in defining the intervention and sampling problems, the co-occurrence of positive employment outcomes with other positive treatment outcomes highlights the importance of vocational efforts (Anglin & Fisher, 1987). More recently, the Venus Project identified numerous barriers and problems associated with successful job placement of substance abusers, including environmental constraints and individual cognitive distortions about employment possibilities (Deren & Randell, 1990). In addition, McLellan et al. (1994) concluded from a study of 22 substance-abuse treatment sites that posttreatment social adjustment was significantly predicted by more employment-focused services during treatment. However, it should be noted that many of the studies of employment factors among substance abusers focused on methadone clients or opiate addicts, and these results may have limited generalizability to other drug-abusing populations.

Vocational-rehabilitation studies focused on substance abusers should be reevaluated in the light of welfare reform and the unparalleled, national economic growth in the past few years. The employment picture for many underemployed individuals has changed with unemployment rates being the lowest since they have been recorded. Also, the growth in the service industries may mean an increase in entry-level jobs. Problems in obtaining employment in the past were often related to overall economic factors such as high unemployment rates, but now they may be more related to individual factors.

Conclusions

Terkel (1972) opened his study of work by stating, "This book, being about work, is, by its very nature, about violence—to the spirit as well as to the body. . . . It is, above all (or beneath all), about daily humiliations. To survive the day is triumph enough for the walking wounded among the great many of us." The view of employment presented here is very different from Terkel's perspective. However, for many drug offenders, Terkel's description is more likely to capture their experience. For many drug offenders, like many persons in the welfare-to-work environment, the promise of employment may be very different from their desired lifestyle. Consequently, programs that incorporate employment-rehabilitation services should have a realistic understanding of the difficulties for many drug offenders to obtain, maintain, and upgrade their employment.

Future research on offender-employment rehabilitation should focus on identifying specific employment-problem typologies. It could more clearly define employment-focused interventions for different treatment settings. Furthermore, the overall effectiveness of employment-focused interventions has not been closely examined. While improved employment among drug abusers is linked to overall positive treatment outcomes, it is not clear how employment-related interventions improve employment outcomes. The robust predictive quality of pretreatment employment may act as a confound in outcome studies that examine posttreatment employment. Consequently, the science does not definitively support the idea that employment rehabilitation is related to greater post-treatment employment, reasonable though it might seem. Controlled studies with well-defined employment interventions for the experimental groups could help establish the relationship between employment-focused interventions and overall treatment outcomes. The clinical literature, however, suggests a need to continue to explore offenders' needs for vocational rehabilitation along with other psychosocial needs.

Drug offenders' specific employment problems need to be examined to determine which problems are amenable to change. These problems have multiple dimensions, including limited job skills, learning deficits, poor cognitive ability, poor socialization to work culture, race and ethnic biases as job barriers, criminal-thought patterns, criminal records, as well as co-occurring mental health problems such as depression. The literature does not offer a clear typology of employment problems or a widely endorsed framework for assessing offender-employment problems. After reviewing research over the past decade, Room (1998) observed that improved employment is associated with treatment, but does not suggest anything about the specific effects of employment-focused services on overall treatment outcome. Given the growing program emphasis on employment among drug offenders, controlled studies of employment interventions are needed to examine these interventions among offenders at different levels of employment. For example, most studies have focused on efforts to obtain client employment, while less attention has been given to understanding interventions focused on maintaining and upgrading employment.

Given the limitations in research on employment rehabilitation, practice recommendations remain guarded. However, there are issues to consider in developing employment services. Although it is not clear that employment-rehabilitation services contribute directly to positive substance-abuse treatment outcomes, an association between employment and treatment outcome has been reported (Anglin & Fisher, 1987; French et al., 1991; McLellan et al., 1994). Programs may overlook an important factor in drug offenders' recovery by not addressing employment needs.

Employment and reduced drug use are associated with decreased arrests, which is a goal of offender-treatment programs (Anglin & Fisher, 1987). Clearly, criminal justice practitioners should maintain interest in employment programming as part of reentry planning and community-based services for paroled offenders.

Offender-treatment programs should incorporate employment-focused interventions along with standard treatment approaches (Room, 1998). For example, motivational interviewing can be used to target employment and substance-abuse issues (Miller & Rollnick, 1991). Motivational interviewing can engage the drug offender in problem identification and in deciding to commit to specific employment-skill development along with other recovery activities. Likewise, social skills' training for drug offenders can focus on skills in the employment setting as a way of addressing general treatment needs along with employment needs (Monti, Abrams, Kadden, & Cooney, 1989). Most of the other cognitive or cognitive-behavioral substance-abuse treatment approaches can incorporate employment issues in the session content as a way to address employment and general recovery needs. Comerford (1999) suggests that employment should be included with other cognitive-behavioral approaches as a way of enhancing client self-efficacy and positive self-image. Practitioners who exclude employment and other psychosocial factors from treatment may miss important contributions to drug-offender recovery.

ACKNOWLEDGMENT

This project is supported by grant number RO1 D13076 from the National Institute on Drug Abuse. Opinions and points of view expressed are those of the authors and do not represent the official position of the National Institute on Drug Abuse.

7

Corrections-Based Case Management and Substance-Abuse Treatment Programming

Harvey A. Siegal, Richard C. Rapp, and D. Timothy Lane

W ith the increasing number of substance abusers involved with the criminal justice system, greater attention has been focused on rehabilitation. The scientific literature has suggested that "coerced treatment" does apparently produce positive results, even among those who do not initiate such treatment themselves (Hser & Anglin, 1991). Consequently, corrections-based drug-abuse treatment is gaining popularity as more simplistic approaches to behavior change, such as longer sentences and boot camps, fail to achieve the desired goals.

Although behavior change is not easily accomplished, it is important to acknowledge that chemical-dependent or substance-abusing offenders present with a range of problems and deficits that go well beyond their abuse or addiction to one or even several drugs. Long-term, extensive behavior change or rehabilitation should not be seen as an event, but is more meaningfully described as a process. To be successful, the individual will necessarily have to address becoming and remaining drug free, correcting errors in thinking, and learning how to function as an autonomous, productive individual. In doing so, the offender must not only acquire and master a range of social and psychological skills, but will have to address "real life" issues, such as obtaining housing, employment, education, along with the acquisition of other needed resources. Today, with the focus on community-based corrections and determinate sentencing, such concerns take on immediate needs for the offender and those providing rehabilitative services. Unless these real-life issues are adequately addressed, the goals of rehabilitation may be compromised, and/or therapeutic gains made while the individual was incarcerated may be set aside once release is secured. Traditionally, the task of supporting recovery by addressing these ancillary needs has been delegated to discipline loosely known as *case management*.

The goal of this chapter is to examine case management and its appropriate role in criminal justice programming. Case management has been a central part of many criminal justice–centered programs. For example, for more than 20 years, Treatment Alternatives for Street Crime (TASC)—now, Treatment Accountability for Safer Communities—has offered community-based case management to support diversion activities (see Cook, this volume). However, the nature of the services offered has varied widely, so much so that it would be impossible to typify "TASC case management." Rather than attempting to describe all, or even characterize the range, of case-management applications in a criminal justice setting, we will, instead, approach case management in a more generic fashion, first describing several popular models and examining functions that are common to all.

CASE MANAGEMENT: A BRIEF PRIMER

Like many of the other helping interventions, the conceptual and practical roots of case management can be traced to the early 20th century, with the emergence of the rudiments of a formal, organized welfare system, with the explosion of immigration to the United States, coupled with burgeoning urban areas, both sectarian and secular groups began offering increased assistance to those in need. Later, following the Great Depression and the recovery of the 1930s, the Social Security legislation created a very large number of governmental agencies, each offering numerous programs. The trend toward the bureaucratization of welfare or social service programs ultimately exploded during the 1960s with our nation's "War-On-Poverty" and "Great Society," which offered mega-initiatives such as the Office of Economic Opportunity, the Mental Health Act, and Model Cities.

Each provided resources that enabled people in need to obtain economic, housing, health care, and educational/vocational and other resources. Although the resources were ostensibly available, observers began using words such as "overly complex," "duplicative," and "un-coordinated and fragmented" to describe the delivery system. It was increasingly noted that people were falling between the bureaucratic cracks and actually receiving fewer needed benefits. The answer was simple: develop a human-services specialty that provided a process or method for ensuring that consumers are provided with whatever services they need in a coordinated, effective, and efficient manner (Intagliata, 1982).

Definitions and Functions

It is difficult to offer a single, comprehensive definition of case management. The service called "case management," instead, is frequently defined by the agency or organization providing it, the training and orientation of service providers, or even regulatory language. What the definitions have in common is a recognition that troubled people have needs, and that linking them to appropriate resources is a way to best address these needs.

A more productive way to approach case management is by identifying its core functions. Five *core functions* emerged as case-management services are delivered (National Association of Social Work, 1992). They are: (a) *assessment*—identifying an individual's current and potential deficits, weaknesses, strengths, and needs; (b) *planning*—developing a specific plan for each individual based upon an understanding of needs; (c) *linking*—referring or transferring individuals to all services needed to actualize the plan; (d) *monitoring*—continual evaluation of individual progress; and (e) *advocacy*—interceding on behalf of the client to assure that access to legitimate service is not denied.

In substance-abuse treatment, the value of case management is generally recognized. Case management is one of eight counseling skills identified by the National Association of Alcoholism and Drug Abuse Counselors (National Association of Alcoholism and Drug Abuse Counselors, 1986) and one of five performance domains developed in the Role Delineation Study (National Certification Reciprocity Consortium/Alcohol and Other Drug Abuse, 1993).

Models of Case Management with Substance Abusers

Case-management models, like the definitions of case management, vary extensively with the context in which the service is provided. Some models focus on delivering social services, others on coordinating the delivery of services by other providers, and some provide both. The models result as much from the needs of specific client populations and service settings as they do from distinct theoretical differences about what case management should be. Four models from the mental health field have been adapted for the field of substance-abuse treatment. Each of these models has proven valuable in treating substance abusers in a particular setting. These models are described and examples of their implementation offered.[1]

Brokerage/Generalist

Brokerage/generalist models of case management seek to identify clients' needs and help clients access resources. Assessment and referral planning may be limited to the client's initial contacts with the case manager, rather than an intensive long-term relationship. Ongoing monitoring, if provided at all, is relatively brief, and does not usually include active advocacy. Meetings between case manager and client are not frequent; typically, they occur on a monthly or ad hoc basis.

Brokerage/generalist models are frequently criticized because of the limited nature of the client-case manager relationship and the relative absence of advocacy. Nonetheless, this approach embodies the basic functions of case management, and has proven useful in selected situations. The relatively limited nature of the relationship allows a larger caseload. The model works best with clients who are not economically deprived, who are motivated, possess resources, and who are not dysfunctional.

Two creative uses of a brokerage model involved clients who were infected with HIV or who were at significant risk of acquiring HIV. In one program, case managers also served as educators, delivering cognitive, behaviorally oriented, educational sessions focusing on substance abuse and high-risk behaviors (Falck, Siegal, & Carlson, 1992). Another variation of the brokerage model focuses on case management with HIV-infected clients as a "quick response"-referral approach intended to provide immediate results to clients and to link them with agencies or services that would provide ongoing services (Lidz, Bux, Platt, & Iguchi, 1992).

Generalist approaches to working with substance-abusing clients have taken several forms. Case managers in the central-intake facility of a large

---

[1]This discussion draws heavily on CSAT's Treatment Improvement Protocol (TIP) Series 27, Comprehensive Case Management for Substance-Abuse Treatment, on which authors served as Consensus Panel Chair and Workgroup Leader.

metropolitan area performed the core functions of case management, linking clients with area substance-abuse treatment and other human-service providers. These case managers had access to funds for purchasing treatment services, thereby dramatically reducing waiting periods for these services (Mejta, Bokos, Maslar, Mickenberg, & Senay, 1997).

Assertive Community Treatment

The Program of Assertive Community Treatment (PACT) model was developed in Wisconsin to assist with deinstitutionalizing psychiatric patients (Stein & Test, 1980). It emphasizes: (a) making and maintaining contact with clients in their homes and natural settings; (b) resolving practical problems of daily living, and understanding that a long-term commitment to clients was likely necessary, and (c) advocating for clients in their communities. Martin and Scarpitti (1993) adapted PACT, so case managers provided direct-counseling services and worked with clients to develop the skills necessary to function successfully in the community. Case managers also provided family consultations and crisis-intervention services and functioned as group facilitators departing from the mental health origins of the PACT model however, ACT had time limits and pre-established success goals, rather than the long-term care envisioned for the mentally ill.

Strengths-Based Perspective

The strengths-based perspective of case management was developed at the University of Kansas to help a population of persons with persistent mental illness make the transition from institutionalized care to independent living (Modrcin, Rapp, & Chamberlain, 1985). The two principles on which the model rests are: (a) providing clients support for asserting direct control over their search for resources, such as housing and employment; and (b) using the clients' own strengths and assets as the vehicle for resource acquisition. This model of case management encourages the informal-helping networks (as opposed to institutional networks); promotes the primacy of the client-case manager relationship; and provides an active, assertive form of outreach to clients.

A strengths perspective of case management is useful for work with substance abusers for three reasons: (a) case management's usefulness in helping them access the resources they need to support recovery; (b) the strong advocacy component that characterized the strengths approach challenges the common belief that substance abusers are wholly in denial or morally deficient—perhaps even unworthy of needed services (Bander, Goldman, Schwartz, Rabinowitz, et al., 1987; Ross & Darke, 1992); and (c) the emphasis on helping clients identify their strengths, assets, and abilities supplements treatment models that focus on pathology and disease. Strengths-based case management has been implemented with both female (Brindis & Theidon, 1997) and male substance abusers (Siegal et al., 1995; Siegal, Rapp, Fisher, Cole, & Wagner, 1997).

Because of the strong advocacy component and client-driven goal planning, a strengths-based approach can, at times, cause tension between a case manager and other members of the treatment team (Rapp, Kelliher, Fisher, & Hall, 1994). Despite this, there is evidence that the approach can be integrated with the disease-model treatment, and that its use leads to improved outcomes for clients. The improved outcomes include employability, retention in treatment, and reduced drug use (Rapp, 1998; Siegal, Rapp, Li, Saha, & Kirk, 1997).

Clinical/Rehabilitation

Clinical/rehabilitation approaches to case management are those in which clinical- and resource-acquisition activities are integrated by the case manager. This case-management model argues that the separation of these two activities is not feasible over an extended period of time and that the case manager must be trained to respond to client-focused, as opposed to solely environmental, issues (Kanter, 1996). Client-focused services could include providing psychotherapy, teaching specific skills, and family therapy.

CASE MANAGEMENT AND THE CRIMINAL JUSTICE SYSTEM

One of the first adaptations of case management with substance-abusing offenders was the TASC program. As a central element of TASC, case management was designed to serve both *criminal justice* and *treatment-related* objectives (see Cook, this volume).

The Center for Interventions, Treatment and Addictions Research (at Wright State University), in collaboration with the Ohio Department of Rehabilitation and Correction (ODRC), implemented the Substance-Abuse

Treatment Continuum for Offenders (SATCO) Project. This project provides correctional institution-based substance-abuse treatment, followed by community-based case-management services to offenders. This treatment continuum begins at the inmates' admission to the Dayton Correctional Institution (DCI), a medium-security facility of inmates. SATCO occupies a unit of 120 beds. The involvement continues up to 6 months after the inmate has been released to the community for those offenders who are returning to five counties. SATCO admissions' criteria include a history of substance abuse/dependence, appropriate correctional status/classification, and an interest in treatment.

Institutional and Community-Treatment Continuum

SATCO provides treatment to address substance-abuse problems, errors in thinking, deficits in the basic skills, and resources needed in the community. Institutionally based treatment activities are organized under the four treatment components: (a) *Responsible living community*—a treatment milieu in which inmates acknowledge rules, accept confrontation, give/earn respect, and demonstrate progressive responsibility; (b) *cognitive behavioral therapy*—a structured program to challenge inmates to develop alternative thinking patterns, as well as learn self-correction techniques and empathy for others, using the approach developed by Wanberg and Milkman (1998); (c) *basic life skills*—skills development focuses on proficiencies, including developing employment interview skills, using computers, education, learning budgeting and personal financial skills, and acquiring problem-solving and goal-planning abilities. Substance-abuse education and anger management is also provided; (d) *strengths-based case management*—case managers engage inmates in a systematic process of identifying strengths and assets that will be used to help the inmate successfully reintegrate into the community and follow up.

Offenders move through four phases of treatment, three in the institution and one in both institution and community. Each phase incorporates changing motivational levels and treatment needs. Clients petition treatment and correctional staff to move to subsequent phases. While institutional phases are not time limited, 2 months is the average. The phases are designated as:

1. *Challenge*—During the first month, the inmates focus on learning how to function within the responsible living community. Emphasis is

placed on basic living skills. An on-going assessment is conducted on the areas of substance abuse, criminal behavior, and difficulties in cognitive functioning (both organic and functional). Privileges are limited in this phase.

2. *Commitment*—This phase is confrontational and frequently frustrating for the inmate. The commitment phase focuses on learning and practicing new skills.

3. *Ownership*—The inmate demonstrates prosocial values and constructive thinking, works in the larger prison community, and focuses on release planning. Plans are facilitated by the primary counselor and a community strengths-based case manager.

4. *Implementation*—Community reintegration activities include connecting the offender to substance-abuse aftercare services and needed community resources. Skills, behaviors, and cognition from the first three phases are reinforced.

CONCLUSIONS

By framing rehabilitation as a process, the need for case management is apparent. In the context of corrections-based programming, case management can support the offender as he or she makes the transition from institution to community or from one level of supervision to another. Given the experiences of those involved with the criminal justice system, employing the more intensive models of case management is more likely to produce superior outcomes. Assessment, linkage, advocacy modeling, and skills development are all compatible with substance-abuse treatment and can be effectively delivered by practitioners trained in their use. The challenge is learning how, when, and where to integrate effective interventions to initiative and support recovery.

ACKNOWLEDGMENT

The research was supported by the Ohio Department of Rehabilitation and Correction and the Bureau of Criminal Justice Services.

III

Interventions

8

Drug-Abuse Treatment Programs in the Federal Bureau of Prisons: Past, Present, and Future Directions

Beth A. Weinman and John T. Dignam[1]

The Federal Bureau of Prisons (BOP) is in the midst of an unprecedented period of expansion, which began about 10 years ago. This rapid growth is largely the result of an aggressive federalization of many drug crimes, one component of the so-called "war on drugs" initiated by the Nixon administration, and subsequent incarceration of offenders who previously would have been sentenced to state and local systems, if at all. The actual numbers are staggering: between April 1991 and March 2000, the population of incarcerated federal offenders has virtually doubled from 61,691 to 121,035. Of the many missions of the agency, one that has become of significantly greater importance (as a result) is the provision of quality, empirically based drug abuse treatment services to all inmates with a demonstrated need and interest in treatment.

---

[1]Opinions expressed in this chapter are those of the authors and do not necessarily represent the opinions of the Federal Bureau of Prisons or the Department of Justice.

In this chapter, we describe the history and current status of drug treatment programs in federal prisons; review existing research on the outcomes and effectiveness of programs; discuss a variety of organizational and clinical issues faced in developing and managing a drug treatment operation of such large scale; and point to future directions in assessment and treatment in corrections and elsewhere.

HISTORY AND CURRENT PRACTICE

The BOP's long history of providing drug-abuse treatment to its inmates began in 1919, when the Narcotics Unit of the Treasury Department urged Congress to establish federal "narcotics farms" to incarcerate and treat heroin users. The first of these farms did not open until 1935 at the U.S. Public Health Service (PHS) hospital in Lexington, Kentucky, with a second opening in Fort Worth, Texas, in 1938. The Lexington/Fort Worth approach was to treat drug users in an institutional setting sufficiently different from the urban communities thought to be fostering their drug addictions, to address their basic "immaturities" and personality disorders, and to return them to their communities to resume their lives free from their psychological dependence on drugs (Inciardi, 1988). Follow-up studies of the Lexington/Fort Worth program suggested that addicts treated under legal coercion had better outcomes than others, but prisoners without compulsory postinstitution supervision and treatment did no better than voluntary-community patients (Maddux, 1978).

The next formal effort to treat drug abusers in the BOP began with the passage of the Narcotic Addict Rehabilitation Act (NARA) in 1966. NARA consisted of four separate Titles, each designed to manage treatment for drug addicts. NARA, Title II, authorized treatment of certain addicts convicted of specific federal crimes and was administered by the BOP. NARA addicts could be sentenced for up to 10 years of institutional treatment, but were eligible for release to community supervision and aftercare earlier if judged to have completed treatment. The NARA experience demonstrated that civil commitment could be used successfully as a way to treat addicts who might not otherwise be treated. Compulsorily treated, drug-dependent inmates seemed to do as well as or better than inmates who received care in noncompulsory programs (Kitchener & Teitelbaum, 1986).

NARA mandates inspired a major shift in the way convicted addicts and others were managed in the BOP. In 1970, an experimental treatment program emerged at the Lexington facility. It was a therapeutic community where all but the most severe security infractions were managed by the inmates themselves (Conrad, 1972). Programs and services were later extended to addicted offenders not eligible for NARA. Drug Abusers Program (DAP) units were established in five federal prisons in 1971. These DAP units, generally staffed the same as the NARA units, used similar therapeutic-community processes and followed NARA policy and procedures. The success of these early programs, particularly in promoting more positive adjustments while incarcerated, led to the "functional unit management" approach to housing all BOP offenders, an innovation that remains the standard in the Bureau today.

In 1978, there were 33 DAP units in BOP institutions, but the programs varied widely in terms of quality and focus. In response to these program inconsistencies, then Director Norman Carlson appointed a task force, which published *The Drug Abuse Program Incare Manual*, a set of core standards for BOP drug-abuse programs, which led to program improvements. But in the early 1980s, drug-abuse treatment efforts regressed in response to new pressures of a burgeoning inmate population, diminishing resources, an absence of effective leadership and support for drug programs, and inadequately trained staff. The residential, unit-based treatment model that had emerged over time gave way to a reliance on less expensive, nonresidential treatment approaches across institutions (cf., Murray, 1992).

The Anti-Drug Abuse Acts of 1986 and 1988 led to renewed interest and resources for in-prison drug-treatment programs. In 1989, the BOP convened a group of drug-treatment and corrections professionals to develop a comprehensive drug-treatment strategy for the agency. The group's recommendations, which constitute the basic structure of the program to this day, included: (a) the creation of new treatment and administrative positions dedicated solely to implementing drug-abuse treatment initiatives across all agency sites; (b) thorough screening and assessment procedures to identify inmates in need of drug-abuse treatment on entry and throughout their incarceration; and (c) a multipronged, treatment-delivery strategy to accommodate the entire spectrum of inmate need and motivation, including drug-abuse education, nonresidential and residential (unit-based) treatment, and transitional, drug-abuse treatment on inmates' return to general population and/or to the community.

The core philosophy underlying all of the agency's drug-abuse programs is that individuals must assume personal responsibility for their behavior. Despite the influence of environmental conditions and circumstances, the primary target for change is the individual's conscious decision to engage in drug-taking and criminal behavior. Therefore, the principal goal of treatment is to equip the individual with the cognitive, emotional, and behavioral skills necessary to choose and maintain a drug-free and crime-free lifestyle.

The Bureau subscribes to a biopsychosocial model of treatment that guides interventions in all of its drug abuse programs. This holistic approach emphasizes comprehensive lifestyle change as the key to treatment success. Issues such as family relationships, criminality, and health promotion are targeted for change, in addition to traditional treatment goals of relapse prevention and abstinence. The acquisition of positive life skills is the means through which drug-abuse treatment-program participants can change the negative thinking and behavior patterns that led to their drug use and criminality in the past. Through individual and group counseling, participants can gain awareness of the negative consequences of their previous thinking/behavior patterns and can learn and develop alternative and prosocial skills.

The agency's residential drug-abuse treatment program is the flagship of its drug-abuse treatment strategy. Currently, 47 BOP institutions operate residential drug-abuse treatment programs, with a combined annual capacity of more than 12,000 inmates. The program lasts 9 months, and participants receive a minimum of 500 treatment hours; a basic curriculum exists to maintain some level of consistency throughout all residential treatment programs. The current curriculum has three phases of treatment: orientation to treatment; the intensive treatment phase; and the transitional treatment phase.

Typically, inmates are involved in treatment 4 to 5 hours a day, 5 days a week. The remainder of the day is spent in prosocial activities, such as work, school, religious services, and/or recreational activities. Each residential drug-abuse treatment program is staffed by a psychologist who supervises the drug-abuse treatment staff, each of whom carries a caseload of no more than 24 inmates. Treatment is voluntary. All inmates who complete a residential program are required to continue treatment on transfer to half-way houses, called Community Corrections Centers (CCCs), typically for the last 6 months of their custody. During this CCC placement, inmates are treated by community-based providers who are asked to follow the Bureau's treatment philosophy to enhance the continuity of care. Coordination with U.S. Probation also occurs to ensure a seamless transfer of information between the agencies, as inmates leave BOP custody and fall under their supervision.

OUTCOME EVALUATION RESULTS

The hallmark of any good drug-treatment program is the parallel application of a strong evaluation component to assess treatment effectiveness. Given the scale of the BOP's most recent drug-abuse treatment initiative, and the cost involved in launching and maintaining it, a quality-outcome evaluation process was considered essential to preserving the integrity and long-term success of the program. With funding and assistance from the National Institute of Drug Abuse (NIDA), the agency embarked on an ambitious outcome-evaluation program from the outset. Given the comprehensive nature and complexity of this longitudinal evaluation project, outcome results in their entirety are not yet available. However, promising preliminary results on the residential drug-abuse program component have been published in an interim report (Pelissier et al., 1998).

Original research plans presumed that random assignment of inmates into the residential drug-abuse treatment programs would occur. However, it was determined early in the process that inmates were not readily volunteering for treatment. New federal sentencing guidelines, implemented in November 1987, effectively eliminated federal parole, and inmates did not believe they received any "tangible" benefits for participating in residential drug treatment. This prevented true random assignment to treatment groups, so evaluators identified matched-comparison subjects for whom treatment was not readily available.

One of the first questions addressed by researchers was whether a significant increase in staffing resources and time in treatment had a more positive impact on treatment success for residential program participants. The original evaluation design called for two residential-program structures. The "pilot" sites had a staff-to-inmate ratio of 1:12 and provided a minimum of 1,000 treatment hours over a 1-year period. The "comprehensive" sites maintained a staff-to-inmate ratio of 1:24 and conducted treatment for a minimum of 500 hours over a 9-month period. Comparisons of inmates from the two types of programs on multiple indicators of treatment progress and success revealed no significant differences. Those findings ultimately led to an administrative decision to maintain all residential drug-abuse treatment programs in the agency at the treatment hours and staffing levels of the original comprehensive sites.

Other preliminary outcome results suggest early postrelease success on the part of residential drug-abuse program graduates. Evaluators tracked inmates 6 months following reentry into the community, and found that inmates who completed the residential drug-abuse treatment program were 73% less likely to be arrested for a new offense than those who did not participate in a residential drug-abuse program. Moreover, inmates who completed the residential drug-abuse treatment programs were 44% less likely to use drugs or alcohol than those who did not participate in a residential drug-abuse treatment program. These findings are particularly impressive given the rigorous design and methodology of the evaluation project, the large sample size (1,866 inmates), and the uniqueness of this multisite sample (20 programs at various institutions). The findings also are consistent with those of other prison-based programs (e.g., Inciardi, Martin, Butzin, Hooper, & Harrison, 1997).

In a separate study (Innes, 1997), researchers looked at in-prison functioning of inmates housed in high-security institutions who had completed a BOP residential drug-abuse program. Results indicated that in 2 years posttreatment, rates of institutional misconduct by inmates who completed the residential drug-abuse treatment dropped by 50%. This finding was replicated for minimum-, low-, and medium-security male inmates who completed residential drug-abuse treatment (25% average reduction in misconduct rates) and for minimum- and low-security female inmates who completed residential drug-abuse treatment (70% reduction in misconduct rates). These findings suggested that drug-abuse treatment in corrections-based settings, in addition to reducing the likelihood of relapse postrelease, also assists in the general management of inmates and may play a vital role in increasing safety and security within correctional institutions.

MAJOR ISSUES

The BOP has faced a number of challenges in developing, implementing, and managing effective drug-abuse treatment programs for inmates. Many of those challenges continue today, but much has been learned since this large-scale treatment initiative began. The following is a discussion of some of the more significant issues encountered in attempting to strike a necessary but delicate balance among administrative, political, research, and treatment concerns.

Rapid Program Implementation and Staffing

Key to sound program development is careful program implementation. In the early days of the BOP's latest drug-treatment initiative, there was significant pressure for a quick start-up of new drug-abuse programs. In just the first 3 years, the agency activated 3,100 residential-treatment beds at 31 different correctional institutions across the country. The most daunting task during this rapid implementation process was hiring a large treatment-staff complement. Funding was not an issue; Congress had appropriated sufficient resources for the program, and the agency subsequently created new positions. The problem was finding sufficient numbers of professional staff with the skills, experience, and motivation to work with drug-addicted offenders. Most new staff had good clinical experience generally, but many did not have much experience working specifically in drug-abuse treatment. Others had correctional experience and brought with them the knowledge and savvy essential to working with offenders, but had very little clinical experience, let alone drug-abuse treatment experience. Still others had excellent drug-counseling credentials, but had no experience working with incarcerated offenders and had some difficulty adjusting to a correctional-work environment.

Thus, the need for a comprehensive and intensive training effort was evident. This was quite challenging, given that it had to occur concomitantly with an aggressive agenda of new program development. But in 1993, a multitiered training strategy was implemented that addressed basic, advanced, specialty, and remedial training needs for all drug-abuse treatment staff. This system remains in place today, and, along with annual, continuing-education funding, insures quality professional training for the more than 400 treatment staff. Targets of training include not only the requisite clinical skills, but inmate management and interdepartmental coordination skills as well.

The latter is pertinent to another matter regarding rapid implementation. Although the BOP had managed drug-addicted offenders for years, the creation of many intensive residential drug-treatment units in a relatively short span of time at institutions with little experience managing such programs did raise certain organizational culture and climate issues. Due to funding and political imperatives, drug-program staff needed to focus exclusively on assessment and treatment as the residential units developed. At times, this clashed with the agency's long and successful tradition of expecting all staff, regardless of specialty, to be "correctional workers first." In contrast to many state and local prison systems, there is no firm distinction made between "custodial" and "professional" staff in the BOP. When it comes to inmate management and maintaining the security of work areas throughout a correctional facility, all employees are responsible and may need to fulfill multiple roles when practical or necessary. It took time at some facilities for new drug-treatment staff to be perceived (and perceive themselves) as part of the team, and for other staff to recognize that effective drug treatment contributed to institutional safety and security. Significant inroads have been made; more than 10 years later, there is wide acceptance of drug-treatment staff/programs and acknowledgment of the special expertise required to treat addicted offenders.

Inmate Recruitment

Recruiting inmates for residential treatment was more difficult than originally anticipated. With no paroling authority to consider treatment participation as a means to earn an early release, motivation for inmates to volunteer for treatment was low. Other incentives to engage in treatment were tested: for example, small, financial incentive awards for each quarter an inmate successfully participated in treatment; tangible goods such as tee shirts with the drug-program logo; and maximum consideration for half-way house placement. However, such incentives did little to motivate inmates to fill up the 3,100 treatment beds that were available between 1989 and 1991.

In September 1991, a report entitled, "Despite New Strategy, Few Federal Inmates Receive Treatment," was published by the General Accounting Office. The report outlined some of the challenges faced when implementing such a large-scale program, and emphasized the lack of incentives (i.e., early parole dates) as most responsible for difficulties recruiting inmates. In part, as a result of this report, the Violent Crime Control and Law Enforcement Act (VCCLEA) was passed in 1994 and had a significant impact on BOP drug-abuse treatment programs. This legislation required the agency to provide residential drug-abuse treatment, the most intensive and comprehensive component of the program, to 100% of all inmates needing and wanting treatment by the end of fiscal year 1997 and every year thereafter. In addition, the VCCLEA provided the Director of the BOP the discretion to provide up to 1 year off of a nonviolent inmate's incarceration upon his or her successful completion of the residential drug-abuse treatment program.

Not surprisingly, the number of inmates volunteering for the residential-treatment program increased dramatically. The residential-treatment units were filled, but a new administrative burden threatened to distract treatment staff from providing quality services. Significant paperwork was necessary to verify that inmates did, indeed, have a legitimate substance-abuse problem (many inmates attempted to malinger in an effort to obtain early release), that inmates could meet the nonviolent-eligibility criterion, and that inmates generally met all other stipulations in the VCCLEA. In addition, inmates became increasingly litigious, filing lawsuits because they believed they were unjustly refused treatment or expelled from a residential drug-abuse treatment program, or they argued that their offense(s), determined by the BOP to constitute a violent crime, was actually nonviolent.

In response to the VCCLEA and its sequelae, the agency embarked on an ambitious expansion plan that would become the largest drug-abuse program expansion in the history of corrections. Among the many components of this plan were a redoubling of efforts to recruit and develop new drug-abuse treatment staff, to redesign and test the most efficacious staff-training approaches, to refine and implement a standardized drug-treatment curriculum, and to expand the transitional-services component so that offenders stayed engaged in treatment as they returned to their home communities. By the close of fiscal year 1997, the BOP satisfied the requirement of providing treatment to all eligible inmates and has continued to meet that requirement each subsequent year. To date, more than 50,000 inmates have received residential drug abuse treatment in the BOP, and more than 9,000 of them have obtained early release from BOP custody as a result of their participation.

Despite those numbers, it is also true that there are inmates in BOP custody with drug abuse problems who remain reluctant to enter the program. In an effort to motivate them, the agency will soon implement a pilot program of new incentives and sanctions. Once identified as being in need of and eligible for treatment, inmates will be offered a choice: participate in the residential drug abuse program or experience the effects of nonparticipation. Inmates who choose the latter will lose the ability to receive pay increases in work assignments, will get less time in a half-way house, and will be ineligible for furloughs. Such sanctions are thought to be justified, given the proven cost and risk to the community when an offender who has not addressed his or her drug abuse problem is released from custody. It is believed that this plan will encourage recalcitrant inmates to participate in a course of treatment to help them overcome their substance-use difficulties.

Establishing Treatment Communities

Much time and effort have been expended from the start of this initiative in developing clear policy statements and comprehensive treatment curriculum to insure that drug-abuse treatment staff have the tools to provide quality drug abuse treatment in a prison setting. However, it was soon learned that policy guidance and curriculum content were not enough. While some residential-program staff expanded on that base by cultivating a strong sense of community on their units where the lessons of treatment permeate every aspect of inmates' lives, other programs merely "taught" the required curriculum content. At the latter programs, opportunities for communicating consistent therapeutic messages about the need for complete and congruent lifestyle and behavioral changes are often lost. Administrators and supervisors note this disconnect is easily perceived by inmates who exploit it and may "complete" treatment without truly engaging in meaningful attempts to change. Creating treatment communities in which inmates are held accountable for all behavior, in and out of treatment sessions, is an important but sometimes overlooked goal of all the residential programs.

There may be many reasons for the absence of a treatment community in some programs. One reason may be the prior training and orientation of many drug-abuse program coordinators who lead and supervise treatment operations. They are psychologists by training who, more often than not, have had good clinical training in areas other than traditional drug-abuse treatment. Developing a treatment community is generally not within their realm of experience or expertise. To remedy this and ensure that more residential units become models of true therapeutic communities, an aggressive training plan in this area for all treatment staff is in development.

When to Treat

From the earliest conception of the residential, drug-abuse treatment programs, it was recognized that transitional care in the community upon release from incarceration was essential. Originally, it was assumed that the optimal time for treatment was at the end of an inmate's sentence, to permit completion of the residential program and immediate transfer to a half-way house and concomitant transitional services. There is, however, a persuasive counterargument for providing treatment early in an inmate's sentence. Presumably, this is a time when many inmates are particularly vulnerable. The aversive consequences of their drug-abusing and criminal behavior are fresh, they may feel alienated and fearful, and they have not had time to settle into a comfortable or less stressful routine. This may be the right time for placement in an intensive residential program that, in addition to needed drug abuse treatment, offers support, positive structure, and opportunities to learn more prosocial and adaptive coping strategies. Of course, a major disadvantage is that, upon treatment completion, an inmate will return to the far less structured environment of a general population unit, where treatment gains are unlikely to be maintained or reinforced. An additional placement dose in intensive residential treatment prior to release would be helpful, but is unrealistic given available resources.

The model currently in place has inmates entering residential treatment near the end of their sentences, participating in a phase of institutional transitional services if they happen to return briefly to general population prior to release, and receiving aftercare upon placement in a half-way house or their home community. This is primarily due to a decision to design programs in accordance with the original timing assumption referred to above, but is, in part, driven by the congressional mandate to treat all eligible inmates prior to their release with available resources. Nonresidential, drug-abuse treatment services are made available to all inmates prior to eligibility for more intensive residential treatment, and may be sufficient to capitalize on stronger inmate motivation earlier in a sentence, but questions related to optimal timing of treatment remain open and require further examination and study.

Dual Disorders

Comorbidity is an unavoidable issue when planning treatment services for large numbers of incarcerated offenders, as some inmates present with coexisting psychiatric disorders, as well as substance abuse or dependence (U.S. Department of Health and Human Services, 1994). The BOP has established two residential drug-abuse units (one each for males and females) to address the needs of this special population. The programs integrate the existing residential drug-abuse program format with targeted interventions unique to inmates' mental illness. For example, relapse-prevention discussions might focus heavily on medication noncompliance as a significant relapse trigger and emphasize preventive strategies for avoiding mental health decompensations. Given the arguably greater risk for relapse, comprehensive aftercare and release planning is also a key component of the programs. Treatment staff consult extensively with half-way house providers, probation officers, BOP community-corrections staff, and others to educate themselves about inmates' dual diagnosis status and to recommend appropriate treatment, including psychiatric support.

FUTURE DIRECTIONS

Treatment Process Research

Preliminary indications of the success of BOP's residential drug-abuse treatment programs are encouraging and suggest that the current model is working. An important follow-up research question is: What specific program elements facilitate the most change among inmates participating in prison-based treatment? Disentangling the effects of different program elements is crucial to improving the efficiency and effectiveness of the agency's drug-treatment effort. Toward this end, a federally funded, joint research project, in collaboration with the Institute of Behavioral Research at Texas Christian University, commenced in 2001. Objectives of the project include: assessment of inmate-engagement indicators and change during treatment; monitoring of key inmate reactions to treatment that represent barriers to recovery; identification of program attributes and intervention strategies associated with treatment effectiveness; and dissemination of effective assessment systems and treatment models for correctional populations.

Community Reentry

After more than 10 years of working in the current treatment-model program, administrators are recognizing that inmates' treatment needs, both while incarcerated and upon release, are certainly not limited to drug abuse issues alone. An emerging realization is that, to adequately maintain treatment gains, more attention must be paid to associated problems, such as mental health and medical concerns, anger and violence problems, and learning disabilities. Program staff have begun to develop ancillary treatment strategies to address these problems within the institution. But such enhancements must also be considered when planning community reentry; released inmates may need access to a host of community resources during this reentry phase. In addition to substance-abuse aftercare, many will require reliable access to employment and financial services, medical and mental health services, educational and vocational services, housing assistance, religious services, and gang-intervention programs in order to ensure treatment success and enhanced community safety.

Neuropsychology

Neuroscience research continues to enlighten the field with new details of the intricate effects of drug use on biochemical and other brain functions.

As more is learned in this area, treatment regimens for addicted individuals will undoubtedly change. In recognition of this, the BOP has met with the NIDA and the National Institute of Justice to begin the process of determining how the BOP can best incorporate the latest science into practice. Initial reviews suggest that one area of future exploration should be the possible use of different or additional interview scales to determine what type of treatment or rehabilitation style best matches an inmate's particular drug-abuse profile. For example, a history of head trauma with evidence of resulting organic compromise would suggest that cognitive rehabilitation and/or pharmacological interventions may be in order to assist the inmate in comprehending and mastering the goals of treatment (cf., Amen, 1998).

SUMMARY

Providing drug abuse treatment in correctional settings poses significant challenges and opportunities. The BOP and other correctional agencies must respond to shifting public priorities, new legislative mandates, institution mission changes, staff turnover, and other factors as they face the formidable task of administering high quality and effective programs. Given this reality, correctional drug-abuse treatment programs must be carefully planned and implemented in accordance with the following principles:

- Strong support from top management communicates the importance of the program within the agency and encourages strict adherence to established parameters and rules of program development.
- A specific treatment orthodoxy (i.e., eligibility criteria, length of time in treatment, treatment philosophy) that is supported by scientific evidence must be established.
- Systematic treatment documentation must occur to foster replicability of functions (i.e., assessment, curricula, treatment for special populations, treatment plans, treatment summaries, and program policies) across institutions. Specific program documentation ensures program consistency throughout the system.
- A clearly defined system of incentives and sanctions must be in place to motivate inmates toward treatment, to reward positive behaviors, and to deter undesirable behaviors.
- A qualified, well-trained staff is essential. Clinical training for drug-abuse treatment staff should be conducted regularly, as should cross-training between treatment and correctional staff. This ensures all

staff understand their vital contribution to participants' treatment goals in the correctional environment.

- A community reentry component must continue the established treatment regimen in the offender's home community and treatment must be combined with appropriate supervision.
- A commitment to outcome and process evaluation is vital to maintaining treatment effectiveness. Administrators, funding sources, and staff require constant feedback on the successes and deficiencies of the program to allow program adjustments in response to measured results.

The BOP's most recent drug-abuse treatment initiative has been exhaustively reviewed and examined since its inception by Congress, Federal regulators, independent evaluators, and the Department of Justice leadership. Although it continues as a work in progress, it has been consistently judged as effective in positively changing inmate behavior, both in the institution and upon release to the community. BOP drug-abuse program documents are available on request through the National Institute of Corrections Information Center.

9

Treatment Accountability for Safer Communities: Linking the Criminal Justice and Treatment Systems

Foster Cook

Treatment Alternatives to Street Crime Programs (or, more recently, Treatment Accountability for Safer Communities), or TASC, is a case-management model developed in the United States in response to a growing understanding of the relationship between drugs and crime. Inciardi and McBride (1991) noted that TASC began in response to three fundamental assumptions:

1. That significant portions of the populations of major metropolitan areas had serious problems of drug abuse and addiction.
2. That drug addiction is often coupled with a cycle of crime, arrest, incarceration, release, and continued addiction.
3. That the frequency of contact between the addict and the criminal justice system provides viable opportunities to intervene.

The TASC model evolved to integrate substance-abuse treatment and to monitor drug-use behavior in criminal justice processing. The concept met the justice system's need for access to treatment, coupled with account-ability. It met the treatment system's need for predictable and supportive interaction with the justice system and provided the critical structures for coordinating supervision and treatment services across systems.

The Special Action Office of Drug Abuse Prevention first described the TASC concept in 1972. These strategies became organized administratively into "TASC" or TASC "model" programs, although the same concepts that are described in the TASC critical elements (Bureau of Justice Assistance, 1992) have found their way into other programs not called TASC. The original model, as well as the methodologies that have evolved from it now serve as the basis for many effective programs and practices for managing drug-dependent offenders. In other words, the success of a wide range of approaches for providing treatment services to persons involved in the justice system can be traced to the adoption of the client- and system-management strategies articulated in the TASC model (Peyton, in press).

TASC currently serves a variety of adult and juvenile populations. It is involved with pretrial, diverted offenders, and sentenced offenders. In some jurisdictions, TASC provides services for offenders throughout the justice process, from screening for drug use at arrest to managing the reentry of those returning to the community following prison or jail sentences. In some sites, TASC programs also work with justice clients who are mentally ill or dually diagnosed, or are involved in civil matters, including parental abuse and neglect cases. TASC is best characterized by its concept and functions rather than by its administrative structures and settings. Most programs are private nonprofits, but some are linked to statewide treatment or community-corrections programs. Some TASC programs serve juveniles and many others support drug courts. These programs incorporate the following basic functions: identifying appropriate candidates for treatment by screening offender populations using predetermined eligibility criteria; assessing the treatment and other needs of clients; assessing the treatment and other services; and providing client-centered case management to ensure that clients are admitted to treatment and/or receive other social services.

TASC also monitors clients by conducting regular drug testing and tracking client progress through the treatment and justice systems. It pro-vides regular and/or periodic reporting of program compliance to judges or other critical parties. TASC functions best with a comprehensive network of service delivery. Only within a continuum of care can the individualized needs of substance-involved justice populations be met. In many sites,

TASC has moved beyond its case management role to become the primary force in organizing, expanding, and transforming the continuum of treatment services available to offenders.

The need for TASC has been reinforced by numerous studies documenting the incidence of drug use by offenders. For example, DuPont (2000) reported that 44% of inmates in the Washington D.C. jail in 1969 were heroin users who tested positive for opiates by urinalysis. Toborg (1989) reported that the pretrial rearrest rates were 50% higher for released drug users than nonusers, with the rearrest rate directly related to the severity of drug abuse. For example, offenders who tested positive for one drug had a 22% rearrest rate. Those who used two drugs had a 28% rearrest rate, and those who used three or more had a 40% rearrest rate. State-prison inmates were also disproportionately found to be involved in serious drug use (Innes, 1988).

Early studies of the TASC model found its process to be effective in linking the justice and treatment systems (System Sciences, 1979), and TASC-monitoring involvement reduced rearrest rates (Lazar Institute, 1976), enhancing success rates with clients (System Sciences, 1979). TASC studies expanded from examining the process to interest in understanding *why* TASC worked with mandatory treatment to increase treatment retention and outcomes. It was noted that community treatment seemed to work best with structured case management (Collins & Allison, 1983). Case management improved access to substance-abuse treatment and retained clients in treatment. Length of time in treatment was shown to be the best predictor of treatment success (McLellan & McKay, 1998), which was supported when TASC and non-TASC clients were compared (Hubbard et al., 1989).

Inciardi and McBride (1991) reported that TASC programming demonstrated effectiveness in: (a) identifying populations of drug-involved offenders in great need of treatment; (b) assessing the nature and extent of their drug-use patterns and specific treatment needs; (c) effectively referring drug-involved offenders to treatment; (d) serving as a linkage between the criminal justice and treatment systems; (e) providing constructive client identification and monitoring services for the courts, probation, and other segments of the criminal justice system; and, perhaps most importantly, (f) retaining TASC clients in treatment longer than non-TASC clients, with better posttreatment success. Longshore, Turner, and Anglin (1998) reported that TASC clients received significantly more treatment and other services when compared with non-TASC controls, and showed reductions in drug use and drug crimes. Other studies reinforced the effectiveness of

TASC (Hepburn, 1996; Van Stelle, Mauser, & Moberg, 1994). There have also been several efforts to define TASC (Cook, 1992). In addition, the Center for Substance-Abuse Treatment (CSAT) is developing a TASC monograph (Peyton, in press) to emphasize TASC's continued success.

TASC is grounded in 13 elements: (a) a process to coordinate justice treatment and other systems; (b) procedures for providing information and cross training to justice, treatment, and other systems; (c) a broad base of support from the justice system with a formal system for effective communication; (d) a broad base of support by the treatment and other social services community; (e) organizational integrity; (f) policies and procedures for regular staff training; (g) a management-information system with a program-evaluation design; (h) clearly defined eligibility criteria; (i) performance of client-centered case management; (j) screening procedures for identification of TASC candidates within the justice system; (k) documented procedure for assessment and referral; (l) policies, procedures, and protocols for monitoring TASC clients' alcohol and drug use through chemical testing; and (m) competency with diverse populations.

ISSUES AND CHALLENGES

There are three major issues that challenge TASC programming: (a) the need for system-level approaches, including integrating treatment into the criminal justice system; (b) integrating TASC case management into drug courts; and (c) the need to better address the needs of mentally ill and dually diagnosed offenders in the justice system. These major issues are underscored by enforcement policies and mandatory/minimum sentences that are increasing the number of incarcerated inmates. It is also estimated that three fourths of these offenders are drug involved (Bureau of Justice Statistics, 1999). The overreliance on incarceration to address the drug problem has diverted state resources from public works, schools, and medical care. Community-based supervision and treatment networks must be strengthened if the costs of incarceration are to be brought under control.

The fragmentation of both the criminal justice and treatment systems, as well as the lack of centralized authority, to organize change present significant barriers to altering current practices. Budgetary authority, as well as the responsibility for the necessary components to change policy and provide more effective treatment are spread across state and local governments, and distributed among executive and judicial branches of government. In many states, managed care has compounded difficult system problems by restricting access to traditionally provided treatment, and services may not be available. Despite these problems, some states and local jurisdictions have managed to address offender drug use at a system level. The Breaking the Cycle projects (Harrell, Cook, & Carver, 1998), funded by the Office of National Drug Control Policy, and administered by the National Institute of Justice, are examples that have moved to create programs to drug test and treat *all* appropriate felony offenders in several jurisdictions. In two of the four jurisdictions, TASC provides the core infrastructure for drug testing of defendants, assessing and placing defendants in appropriate treatment, and monitoring compliance. Other system-wide initiatives include projects described as drug court "Systems" and the Criminal/Juvenile Justice Treatment Networks Projects. A challenge that some states have addressed is coordinating treatment services into and out of correctional institutions and aftercare services (see Inciardi, Surratt, Martin, & Hooper, this volume).

Drug courts are taking a more active role in programming that provides offenders with drug treatment (see Belenko, this volume). The structure of drug courts enhances the criminal justice leverage essential to successful TASC programming. In fact, Peyton and Gossweiler (in press) conclude that TASC and drug courts were "natural allies since about 11% of adult drug courts use TASC to provide screening, assessment and case management services." Drug courts can bring ongoing support to TASC and drug treatment by supporting offender compliance with treatment goals. TASC can provide drug courts with structures to ensure offenders get the services they need.

Offenders with serious mental illness and with co-occurring substance abuse and mental health disorders are overrepresented in the criminal justice system, with the prevalence of severe mental illnesses, including schizophrenia, bipolar disorder, and major depression, which range from 8% to 16% among inmates (Ditton, 1999). The mentally ill offender poses many challenges to the criminal justice and treatment systems because they are more likely to recidivate, be unemployed, and be homeless.

FUTURE DIRECTIONS

A majority of offenders use drugs and alcohol, which is coupled with a cycle of crime, arrest, incarceration, release, and continued addiction. The TASC model includes a program structure to coordinate treatment and case management supervision across criminal justice, treatment, and social service systems. The primary substance-abuse issue that confronts the criminal justice system is the need for system-level approaches. Current management structures cannot provide or coordinate individualized treatment for the large number of substance-involved offenders cycling through state institutions and local jails. TASC is uniquely positioned to manage care and treatment resources for the justice system. In fact, in some states, TASC is evolving as the central point for assessing levels of treatment need and contracting for these services. This new role requires TASC to move from being a client-management model to a client-*and*-system management model. This new role requires leadership and collaboration beyond traditional organizational boundaries.

10

Integrated Systems of Care for Substance-Abusing Offenders

Michael L. Prendergast
and William M. Burdon

Throughout the 1990s and continuing into the current decade, there has been an increased effort to introduce and sustain rehabilitative programs at all of the major points of the criminal justice system (CJS). At the arrest/pretrial stage, drug courts are being used to divert offenders with histories of substance-abuse into community-based, court-monitored substance-abuse treatment. Throughout the latter half of the 1990s, the number of drug courts has dramatically increased throughout the United States (Drug Courts Program Office [DCPO], 1998; General Accounting Office [GAO], 1997; Belenko, this volume). At the presentencing stage, diversion programs such as Treatment Accountability for Safer Communities (TASC) are being used to treat nonviolent, substance-abusing offenders as an alternative to incarceration (see Cook, this volume). As of 1996, there were more than 300 TASC programs operating in 30 states (Anglin et al., 1996).

At the incarceration stage, jail- and prison-based substance-abuse treatment programs are being increasingly used to treat substance-abusing offenders at both the state and federal levels. Taking the form of self-help groups (12-step), counseling, and intensive therapeutic community treatment, the number of inmates in drug-treatment programs in prisons, after increasing dramatically in the early 1990s and showing a decline in the mid-1990s, is once again increasing (Camp & Camp, 1998; Office of Applied Studies, 2000). At the parole stage, community-based treatment, especially for offenders who have received treatment during incarceration, is recognized as essential to reinforcing and consolidating the gains made in prison-based treatment, improving behavior while under parole supervision, and promoting long-term abstinence from drug use and criminal behavior (Inciardi, Martin, Butzin, Hooper, & Harrison, 1997; Knight, Simpson, Chatham, & Camacho, 1997; Prendergast, Wellisch, & Wong, 1996a, 1996b; Simpson, Wexler, & Inciardi, 1999; Wexler, De Leon, Thomas, Kressel, & Peters, 1999).

Central to the development and maintenance of these programs for treating substance-abusing offenders has been the continued recognition on the part of policymakers and criminal justice (CJ) professionals that treatment must exist as a viable alternative to the normal adjudication, incarceration, and supervision process, and that they must be willing to work with treatment providers within the CJS to treat substance-abusing offenders. The focus of this chapter will be on the organizational aspects of integrated systems of care. More specifically, the discussion will focus on the key elements of an integrated system of care for providing correctional-based treatment to substance-abusing offenders. Because correctional environments (i.e., jails and prisons) represent perhaps the most isolated and restricted aspects of the CJS in terms of its relationship and interaction with free society, it is believed that this part of the CJS presents the greatest obstacles and challenges to developing and sustaining an integrated system of care. As such, the principles applied to the development of an effective integrated system of care for correctional-based treatment are more likely to be applicable to the development of similar or extended systems of care at other points within the CJS (e.g., arrest, pretrial, presentencing) than vice versa. Finally, this chapter assumes that certain types of treatment for offenders, when properly implemented, can be effective, and, thus, does not review the literature on the effectiveness of treatment for offenders (see Cook; DeLeon, Sacks & Wexler; Inciardi, Surratt, Martin, & Hooper; and Peters & Matthews, this volume).

The discussion begins with a definition of *integrated system of care* and a discussion of the factors that have driven the trend toward a systems approach to treating substance-abusing offenders. This will be followed by a discussion of the key elements that make up an effective integrated system of care.

TOWARD A SYSTEMS APPROACH TO TREATING SUBSTANCE-ABUSING OFFENDERS

The term *integrated system of care* connotes the ability to unite the multiple components of a system into a fully functioning and unified whole. With respect to treating substance-abusing offenders, an integrated system of care must be able to mediate between the conflicting goals and operating procedures of stakeholders (Center for Substance-Abuse Treatment [CSAT], 1998; Rose, Zweben, & Stoffel, 1999; Silverman, 1985), and to take fragmented strategies and philosophies regarding substance abuse and treatment and combine them into a system that provides effective and comprehensive treatment in a "seamless continuum of care" for substance-abusing offenders (Wellisch, Prendergast, & Anglin, 1995; Taxman, 1998a). Such a system should be clearly defined, visible, and accessible (Glaser, 1990); should be organized around a common set of goals; should follow a set of common procedures; and should provide for a system of evaluation, information sharing, and feedback as a means of improving the overall quality of service delivery (Downes & Shaening, 1993).

Depending on where in the CJS treatment it is provided, the system responsible for delivering the treatment will be city-, county-, or state-based. Thus, multiple systems of substance-abuse treatment programs within the CJS may exist within a given state. In many jurisdictions, however, current arrangements for providing treatment to substance-abusing offenders fall short of what could be described as a true "system of care." The factors that prevent the formation of an effective system of treatment delivery are numerous. First and foremost among these factors is the fact that the delivery of treatment services is often poorly coordinated among the multiple agencies that are key stakeholders in the "would-be" system (corrections departments, parole departments, prison- and community-based treatment providers). Because of their different organizational and conceptual perspectives, there is a natural tendency for these stakeholder organizations to operate independently of each other, guarding their resources and organizational autonomy and continuing to pursue their own objectives and goals to the detriment of common system goals. As a result, screening, assessment, and referral procedures are poorly implemented and coordinated; comprehensive services are inadequate, if available at all; there is limited accountability for the outcomes of clients; and little attention is devoted to ensuring continuity of care across programs and systems.

Addressing these problems requires that the stakeholder organizations develop collaborations or linkages among themselves to be able to provide comprehensive, coordinated, and continuing care for substance-abusing offenders. But making such collaborations systems work effectively is not a trivial task. Numerous barriers need to be eliminated, or at least lowered, in order for the system as a whole to operate effectively and efficiently over the long term. The barriers will differ from one jurisdiction to another, but a number of the more important barriers that have been identified in the literature (CSAT, 1995b; Greenwood, 1995; Rose et al., 1999) include the following: (a) CJ and treatment organizations differ in their attitudes toward offenders and treatment and in their goals and expectations for treatment outcome; (b) CJ and treatment organizations tend to define the problem differently and have different standards and measures for success; (c) Staff from CJ and treatment organizations differ in their background and training and in the reward systems that motivate their activities; (d) In setting up new programs, CJ and treatment organizations have different time horizons for becoming operational and for observing effects of a program; (e) CJ and treatment organizations have different sources of funding that place restraints on what they can and cannot do and that call for different strategies for continuation of funding; and (f) Potential conflict arises from the organizational and financial demands of operating as either a government agency (CJ organization) or a private (either nonprofit or for profit) business (treatment organization).

In attempting to overcome these barriers, it is important that the committees or task forces established to address them include representatives from all affected stakeholder groups in order for multiple views to be represented, to encourage cooperation, and to avoid "bunker" mentalities. It is also crucially important that each of the participants in the organization clearly understand how the others operate in reality, not how they appear to operate on paper.

KEY ELEMENTS OF AN INTEGRATED SYSTEM

It follows from the definition set forth above that certain key elements are necessary in implementing and maintaining an effective integrated system of care. The following discussion of key elements of integrated systems for treating substance-abusing offenders is not intended to be exhaustive or to be overly prescriptive about how such systems should be set up. Rather, it is intended to raise issues that the stakeholders need to seriously consider in developing a system of care. In addition, these issues suggest topics that researchers and evaluators can examine to determine the effectiveness of particular systems in relation to others.

Stakeholders

Stakeholders can generally be divided into two broad categories: (a) those who have direct influence and control over the decision-making process, and (b) those who are affected by the decisions that are made (CSAT, 1995b). Often, when we think of stakeholders in an integrated system of care for correctional-based treatment, we tend to think of departments of corrections, parole departments or divisions, treatment providers (i.e., those agencies providing the correctional-based treatment), and community-based providers (where the system provides for continuity of care following corrections-based treatment). These organizations are the "primary" stakeholders in an integrated system of care. They have direct influence and control over the decision-making processes that define the structure and ongoing operations of the integrated system. In addition, primary stakeholders are directly affected by the decisions that they make. To varying degrees, each of the primary stakeholders may face political, financial, or operational consequences if the integrated system fails to provide effective treatment.

Stakeholders who do not participate in the decision-making process, but who are affected by the decisions that are made, are the "secondary" stakeholders in an integrated system of care. They do not participate in the decision-making process because they are not directly involved in the delivery of treatment services (the primary function of the integrated system). Indeed, their participation would likely complicate the decision-making process by unnecessarily and significantly expanding the breadth of viewpoints that must be considered. Nevertheless, to the extent that they are affected by the decisions that are made, their views, interests, and concerns should be considered, where appropriate, in the decision-making process. In this sense, they exert an indirect influence on decisions that are made. Three groups of secondary stakeholders, whose views, interests, and concerns may not receive adequate attention in the decision-making process, are legislators, correctional officer unions, and interested members of the general public.

Often, corrections-based treatment programs, especially those that are more intense and more costly (i.e., therapeutic community treatment), are initiated by legislation. Although the passage of legislation providing funding for these programs may lead one to conclude that they are supported by the legislature, it is important to remember that the legislature's interest does not stop there. Legislators have an ongoing and substantial stake in the outcome of such important initiatives. Therefore, the decision-making process should consider the legislature's need for some form of timely, accurate, and informative feedback regarding the effectiveness of the treatment delivered, regardless of how preliminary or general in scope it may be.

In many states, correctional officers who work in jails or prisons are unionized and have a direct impact on the ease with which treatment programs operate in the correctional environment. If the union is not supportive of correctional-based treatment, this may influence the support of individual correctional officers who might otherwise be supportive of prison-based treatment. This negative influence can be countered most effectively by taking into consideration union concerns regarding the impact of treatment programs on the operations of the institution and workload of correctional staff.

Finally, an important part of many correctional-based treatment programs is continued care in the community following release to parole. Decreased crime rates, especially drug-related crimes, and the feeling of living in a safer community are critical to the ongoing support of the communities where these programs operate. By contrast, poor relations between these treatment programs and the surrounding community will result in the programs continually reacting to community concerns and may have an adverse impact on the overall treatment initiative. Thus, obtaining and reinforcing the support of the communities where programs operate should be a key consideration of the primary stakeholders in the decision-making process.

Collaboration and Communication

Most discussions of systems development and maintenance have stressed the importance of collaboration and effective communication among the primary stakeholders as a prerequisite to the delivery of effective and efficient substance-abuse treatment (CSAT, 1994, 1995b; Greenley, 1992; Rose et al., 1999; Slayton, 2000; Taxman, 1998a, 1998b). Churchman (1968, 1979) emphasized that all systems exist within larger systems, which places constraints on what the smaller contained systems are able to accomplish (Wellisch et al., 1995). In the context of an integrated system for providing treatment services to substance-abusing offenders, this characteristic of systems presents an interesting paradox. Because treatment is being provided to substance-abusing offenders *within* the CJS, the CJS assumes the role of the superordinate system within which the treatment system must operate (i.e., as the subordinate system). Indeed, the relationship between the CJ and the treatment systems is likely to be contractually defined, with the CJ agency in the role of contractor. On the other hand, both parties exist as primary stakeholders in the integrated system of care. As such, effective collaboration among them is critical in order to provide effective treatment to substance-abusing offenders, and is largely dependent on the sharing of information in an atmosphere of "facilitative interdependence" (i.e., cooperation and trust), as opposed to "competitive interdependence" (i.e., mistrust and threat) (Litwak & Rothman, 1970), which often results in disputes that must be resolved through some form of adjudication or conflict-resolution process.

The types of information that are shared among organizations within an integrated system of care can be classified into three categories: system-, program-, and client-level information. System-level information is shared among participating organizations as a means of improving the overall effectiveness of the system. Examples of system-level information that is shared include procedures for improving screening, assessment, and referral to treatment; effective programming activities; coordination of treatment and institutional sanctions for noncompliant behavior; and procedures for transitioning clients from correctional- to community-based treatment following release from custody.

Owing to its nature, system-level information is best shared through regular meetings of the primary stakeholders. This may be accomplished through the development of a structure of committees, subcommittees, and ad hoc committees charged with sharing information, addressing issues of relevance, and proposing solutions. At the top of this structure should exist a superordinate committee through which the outcomes of the numerous subcommittees and ad hoc committees flow. System-level information can also be shared through the publication of periodic newsletters and a system Web site, which would allow for the dissemination of this information to secondary stakeholder organizations (e.g., legislators, correctional officers unions, interested members of the free community).

Program- and client-level information needs to be shared in order to ensure the delivery of effective treatment services to the client throughout his/her involvement with the continuum of care, thus improving the probability of successful outcomes. Program-level information includes primarily service and billing information (e.g., units of service delivered, program staffing changes, invoicing information). Client-level information includes the characteristics of individual clients, special needs they may have, the services they have received or been referred to, and their progress in treatment (or lack of it).

Program- and client-level information is most efficiently collected through a single, centralized, management-information system (MIS) (CSAT, 1994; Slayton, 2000). With such a system, organizations within the integrated system that contribute to and have a direct stake in the client's treatment outcome can submit and share information as a means of tracking the client's progress throughout his/her participation in the treatment continuum. However, treatment-provider organizations within the system are likely to have legitimate legal and ethical concerns related to disclosing (through information sharing) certain proprietary and client-level information.

As mentioned above, most integrated systems of care within the CJS are likely to be characterized by a contractual relationship between the CJ agency and the organizations providing treatment. As such, the CJ agency could assume the role of developing and administering the MIS. As the contractor, the CJ agency could require in the contract that all organizations participate in the centralized MIS. By doing so, the CJ agency can alleviate the ethical and legal concerns of the treatment providers by assuming final responsibility for determining the method and means by which information will be shared among participating organizations. Alternatively, a third party that is independent of the system could be recruited to develop and administer an MIS. In this case, the organizations that are part of the system would develop a memorandum of understanding with each other and enter into a contractual relationship with the third party as a means of establishing the policies and procedures about how and what types of information would be shared among the participating organizations, thus alleviating individual organizational concerns. Whatever the arrangement, a centralized MIS is a key element of an optimally functioning integrated system of care.

In summary, the goal of the integrated system with respect to collaboration and communication should be to create a "culture of disclosure" within the system, where participating organizations share system-, program-, and client-level information in an atmosphere of facilitative interdependence. Such an "interorganizational culture" will support "informal interaction," "reinforcement of attitudes and commitments," and "understanding and trust" among individuals and organizations from different parts of the system (Greenley, 1992), and will ultimately ensure that the client receives effective, appropriate, and sufficient treatment.

Common Goals

Next to collaboration and communication among the relevant stakeholders, perhaps the most important key element in implementing and maintaining an effective integrated system of care is the establishment of a common goal (or set of goals) by the primary stakeholders. The preexisting goals of the CJ and the treatment systems often differ substantially in terms of their focus and scope. The goals of the CJS are "society-focused." They are based on philosophies of punishment and incarceration (i.e., punishment, deterrence, protection of society) and are more concerned with "how well the system functions in its use of public funds and maintenance of the public trust" (CSAT, 1994, p. 10). Thus, the CJS is more focused on the crimes committed by the individual and the sanctions that must be imposed as a means of punishing the individual, deterring him/her from further criminal activity, and generally providing a safer community. On the other hand, the goals of the treatment system are more "person-focused." They are based on the view of addiction as a "progressive disease, with increasing severity of biological, psychological, and social problems over time," and are more concerned with providing "a system of services to assist individuals, their families, and communities in recovery from addiction" (CSAT, 1994, p. 15). Thus, treatment providers are more focused on treating the person for his/her substance abuse problem with the goal of preventing or reducing relapse to drug use and improving the mental and physical health of the individual.

These conflicting goals have their roots in the differing perspectives of the CJ and treatment systems with respect to the individual's substance abuse problem. The CJS views drug use as a crime that requires some form of punishment. Treatment is secondary to the primary goal of punishing the individual for committing the crime. This translates into a goal of abstinence by restricting (through incarceration) the offender's opportunity to engage in further drug use. The treatment provider, on the other hand, views occasional drug use by the individual being treated for substance abuse as a part of the recovery process, not as a crime that must or even should be punished (Rose et al., 1999).

It should not be assumed that the mere existence of a common set of goals will result in an automatic reconciliation of the conflicting means by which the CJ and the treatment systems attempt to achieve them. This reconciliation of conflicting means to common ends will require a collaborative effort on the part of the stakeholders toward achieving the common goals—an effort characterized by open communication and sharing of information in an atmosphere of trust and cooperation.

Although the goals of the CJ and treatment systems appear contradictory, it can be argued that both systems, in their efforts to achieve their respective goals, attempt to achieve a common outcome: the reduction or cessation of criminal activity on the part of the substance-abusing offender. The CJS attempts to achieve this through punishment aimed at incapacitating or deterring the offender, whereas the treatment system attempts to achieve this by helping the individual to remain drug free and lead a more productive life. As such, it has been suggested that the main (though not necessarily the only) common goal of an integrated system of care should be recidivism reduction (Taxman, 1998a, 1998b). In addition, given that the purpose of a corrections-based integrated system of care is to provide substance-abuse treatment to the client, another common goal of an integrated system should be the allocation of available resources to ensure that the effective and efficient delivery of treatment services to the client is optimized.

Resources

Without sufficient and properly allocated resources, no system of care is likely to function efficiently or effectively. Thus, most discussions of the elements of an integrated system of care address the issue of resources (Field, 1998; Greenley, 1992; Rose et al., 1999; Taxman, 1998a).

These resources are often financially based. Financial resources are the funds made available in operating budgets or through legislation authorizing the creation of the system of treatment programs. Often, these funds are administered by a designated CJ agency that is responsible for developing the system of treatment programs. The distribution of these funds usually occurs through a competitive bidding process, which awards contracts to treatment providers based on submitted proposals.

Other areas where the allocation of financial resources directly affect the ability of the system to deliver effective treatment services is in the funding made available for physical plant needs (i.e., construction or redesign of buildings to accommodate treatment staff and programming activities) and to the institutions where these treatment programs will be operating. Any new treatment program introduced into a correctional institution is certain to have an impact on institutional operations and resources (e.g., expenses relating to staffing, security, and inmate movement). Too often, however, correctional institutions expect that the new programs will operate within existing institutional parameters and that they do not have to change operating procedures and/or policies to accommodate the needs of the programs. This expectation is only reinforced when there is a lack of funding made available to the institution by the main funding agency as part of the agreement to host a treatment program.

Effective Screening, Assessment, and Referral

An essential component of an integrated system of correctional treatment is the procedures by which the CJ and treatment systems identify clients who need treatment, assess their treatment needs, and refer them to appropriate services. These tasks are difficult to carry out when attempting to coordinate the activities of separate organizations—corrections and treatment—that possess conflicting perspectives and goals with respect to substance abuse.

It is generally agreed that the most appropriate time to conduct the screening, assessment, and referral procedure is at the point where the individual enters the correctional system (Pacific Southwest Addiction Technology Transfer Center [PSATTC], 1999; Rose et al., 1999). Doing so has three distinct advantages. First, it informs the inmate at the front-end of the system (during the formal classification process) of his/her identification as an individual in need of, and designated to receive, substance-abuse treatment prior to release from prison. This will reduce the likelihood of inmate resistance and protest when the time comes to transfer the inmate into a treatment program. Second, it improves the efficiency of correctional management by identifying at the front-end of the system those individuals who need treatment and the modality and intensity of treatment that will be needed. Waiting until later may result in the expenditure of additional resources to locate and assess the inmate and transfer him/her to the appropriate facility for treatment. Third, it decreases the likelihood that inmates will have the opportunity to become "coached" in the screening and assessment process by other inmates, which would allow them to manipulate the process (PSATTC, 1999).

The goal of the screening, assessment, and referral process should be to maximize the match between individual need and treatment received. As such, the process should be able to distinguish between substance use, abuse, and dependence; assess motivation or readiness for treatment; include a broad needs' assessment that includes risk factors associated with substance abuse and criminal behavior (e.g., psychological, medical, occupational, educational, relationship); and measure variables that can be used to track clinical progress in treatment (i.e., changes in behavior, attitudes, and other dynamic factors) (PSATTC, 1999).

Once developed, the obstacles facing the implementation of an effective matching system may be more practical than theoretical. Not all substance-abusing offenders are alike in terms of their characteristics or needs. Addressing the unique and multiple needs of substance abusers requires a sophisticated matching system that is well developed and coordinated and contains a stable system of treatment options that have been found to be effective and that are acceptable to the system partners. The types and intensity of treatment services will be determined by a multitude of factors, such as client characteristics, type and severity of substance problem, criminal-risk classification, and psychological, social, and medical needs. In a comprehensive system of care, these treatment options within correctional settings may include self-help groups, substance-abuse education, cognitive skills programs, and short- and long-term therapeutic communities. In community settings, treatment options may include residential programs, outpatient programs, day treatment, sober living houses, and drop-in support groups.

Continuum of Care

At the beginning of the recent movement to develop treatment programs in prisons, Wexler and Williams (1986) noted that "the connection between rehabilitation efforts in prison and the process of integration into society after release is probably one of the most feeble links in the criminal justice system." Several recent studies of prison-based treatment programs have demonstrated the importance of aftercare as a means of reinforcing and consolidating the gains made in the prison-based program, improving clients' behavior while under parole supervision, and promoting long-term successful outcomes (Inciardi et al., this volume; Inciardi et al., 1997; Knight et al., 1997; Prendergast et al., 1996a, 1996b; Wexler et al., 1999).

Creating and maintaining the continuing care component of a statewide system of treatment for offenders can be a formidable challenge. Field (1998, pp. 96–97) has identified seven obstacles to establishing a system of continuity of care for substance-abusing offenders: "(1) segmentation of the criminal justice system, (2) lack of coordination between the criminal justice system and substance-abuse treatment programs, (3) lack of postrelease structure for offenders, (4) lack of incentives and sanctions at release,

(5) lack of services in the community, (6) lack of treatment-provider experience with offenders, and (7) community funding challenges." Overcoming these obstacles requires a high level of communication and coordination among all stakeholders who are responsible in some way for the individual during his/her involvement with the correctional system and treatment services. In short, despite the best intentions of all stakeholders, a well-functioning network of community providers may take several years to develop, and then only after hundreds of hours have been devoted to planning, problem solving, false starts, working through logistical problems, and overcoming practical, legal, and regulatory obstacles.

Three basic models have been identified as useful for ensuring continuity of care for individuals transitioning from prison-based to community-based treatment (CSAT, 1998; Field, 1998). In the *Institutional Outreach* model, the prison or prison-based treatment provider assumes the responsibility for contracting with community-based providers and coordinating the parolee's transition into aftercare. An example of this model is New York's Stay'n Out Program, a prison-based therapeutic community program that assumes primary responsibility for placing parolees into postrelease treatment (Wexler & Williams, 1986).

In the *Community Reach-In* model, community-based providers initiate contact with the prisons or prison-based treatment providers and inmates prior to their release to coordinate the individual's release and transition into aftercare. An example of this model is a demonstration project in the Oregon Department of Corrections, where community-based service providers offer treatment services to inmates prior to their release. Group treatment continues postrelease, usually with the same counselors and client cohort that received services in prerelease (Field, 1998).

The *Third-Party Coordination* model involves the use of a third party who acts as a broker of services and coordinates the parolee's release and transition into aftercare. The key components of this model include: (a) ongoing case management to ensure that parolees enter and remain in treatment following release; (b) provision of services under the direction and authorization of "supervision and treatment authorities," and (c) monitoring and reporting of offenders' progress to relevant officials and agencies. Two programs that exemplify this model are TASC and the Substance Abuse Services Coordinating Agency (SASCA) network recently established in California. TASC programs operate at the "front-end" of the CJS, identifying substance-abusing offenders early in their involvement in the system and diverting them into treatment as an alternative to adjudication and/ or incarceration. By contrast, the SASCA network operates at the "back-end" of the CJS by securing the placement of parolees in appropriate community-based treatment programs following their release from prison, and then monitoring their participation and progress in aftercare (Ossmann, 1999).

Evaluation: Monitoring, Effectiveness, Program Improvement

To ensure effectiveness, improve services, and maintain support from stakeholders, integrated systems need to establish evaluation procedures. According to Mark, Henry, and Julnes (1999), evaluations of programs or systems serve three purposes: oversight and compliance (monitoring), assessment of merit and worth (effectiveness), and program improvement. Monitoring is a function of the contracting or compliance agency and determines whether funds are being spent as authorized, whether contract or regulatory requirements are being complied with, whether staffing ratios are being maintained, whether the treatment beds are being fully utilized, and whether expected completion rates, referral rates, etc., are being met. While monitoring is an essential element of a system of care, it does not address the issue of whether the overall system or its various components are effective or whether the system or its components can be improved. These are addressed by the other two purposes of evaluation.

An evaluation of the merit or effectiveness of the system is needed to determine whether the goals and objectives of the system are being met and to assess posttreatment outcomes (either compared with a control group or with some agreed-upon standard of client behavior). This evaluation may also include an examination of the costs and benefits associated with the system of care. In this sense, the evaluation attempts to assess the value or worth of the system and its services to society. Initially, this evaluation should probably be conducted by an organization or consultant that has the technical expertise to conduct a well-designed outcome evaluation and can provide the credibility of an independent evaluator. Once an initial evaluation of effectiveness has been completed, the system partners (i.e., stakeholders) may decide to work with the evaluator to set up a routine data collection and analysis procedure that would allow for ongoing periodic assessments of effectiveness "in-house."

Evaluation activities concerned with program improvement are intended to feed information back to the system and its components in order to enhance their operations (CSAT, 1994; 1995b). Another term for this set of activities is "quality improvement" (CSAT, 1995a). Evaluation for improvement should occur at both the system and the program level, using standards and procedures that have been agreed to by all stakeholders. The types of information that can be used to identify opportunities for improvement can come from a variety of sources. An external evaluator can report qualitative and quantitative information about the characteristics and processes of the system and its components, which can be reviewed and, if necessary, acted upon by the system participants. The evaluator may assist the system participants in identifying effective organizational models and treatment techniques from the research literature. The treatment providers themselves, in collaboration with the participating CJ agencies, can conduct quality-improvement activities. Regardless of the source of information, a well-developed procedure for putting agreed-upon changes into practice, either throughout the system or within specific programs, needs to be in place to ensure that the intended changes actually occur.

CONCLUSIONS

Over the last decade, the CJS has experienced a substantial increase in the number of substance abusers who have become involved with and are continually being processed through the system. This form of revolving-door justice has spawned the need to provide operationally sound and cost-effective forms of treatment for substance abuse at all points of the CJS, as a means of decreasing recidivism among this population of offenders and the ineffective use of incarceration and punishment as a means of dealing with them.

The development and maintenance of integrated systems of care for treating substance-abusing offenders is beset with many obstacles, the most important of which are the differing philosophies regarding substance abuse and treatment and the resulting conflicting goals of those stakeholders representing the CJS (corrections departments, parole departments, courts, judges, prosecutors) and those representing the treatment system (prison- and community-based treatment providers). Overcoming these obstacles depends on the existence of a number of key elements, which were discussed in depth in this chapter: collaboration and communication in an atmosphere of mutual cooperation and trust; the establishment of a common set of system goals; sufficient and properly allocated resources; a procedure for effectively screening and assessing substance-abusing offenders and matching them with the appropriate modality and intensity of treatment; a means of ensuring offenders' continued involvement in treatment as they move through the CJS and eventually back into the community; and a system for assessing the overall effectiveness of the system and identifying opportunities to improve the quality of services delivered. These key elements stand as prerequisites upon which the success of any integrated treatment system ultimately depends.

Finally, despite the increased trend toward systems approaches to treating substance-abusing offenders, research on the interorganizational aspects of developing these integrated systems of care has been limited. Further research on integrated systems of care need to go beyond evaluation and assessment, which focus on single systems, to designs that compare and contrast different types of systems and, as a result, more clearly determine and assess predictors of and barriers to the effective delivery of treatment services in an integrated system of care.

ACKNOWLEDGMENTS

Supported by NIDA grants R01DA11483 and R01DA13114 and California Department of Corrections contracts C97.355 and 98.346. The views expressed in this chapter are those of the authors and do not necessarily represent the official positions of the funding agencies.

11

Therapeutic Community Treatment in Prisons

David A. Deitch, Susie Carleton, Igor B. Koutsenok, and Karin Marsolais

CURRENT STATUS

The prison population in the United States has grown, and more than 80% of the men and women in custody are seriously involved with drugs, alcohol, and associated crimes (Bureau of Justice Statistics, 1999). In addition to public health and public safety considerations, society is increasingly challenged to absorb the cost imposed by criminal activity and an expanding prison population, which is becoming one of the most hard-to-meet budgetary burdens. Facing the inability of traditional custody to improve the situation, the public's attitude has evolved from one demanding justice through incarceration to one open to the possibility of rehabilitation through effective treatment programs in custody settings. Research conducted during the past 50 years demonstrates that certain types of coerced treatment work, especially with the drug-addicted offender (Anglin & Maugh, 1992; Pearson & Lipton, 1999).

The most common types of addiction treatment in prison environments are self-help groups, individual and group counseling, cognitive restructuring, and the therapeutic community (TC) model. The types of treatment are usually determined by available budget, length of incarceration for inmates in treatment, assessment of treatment needs, experience and training of staff, available space, and treatment modalities used by community-based substance-abuse treatment providers. However, in selecting an appropriate treatment model, little attention focuses on scientific findings regarding treatment outcomes, and the most important reason for this seems to be a gap between research and practice (i.e., the findings do not get transferred into practical decision making).

One comprehensive meta-analysis of almost 30 years of research (Andrews, 1998; Pearson & Lipton, 1999) shows that general social work approaches are not effective and "behavioral" programs, such as Vision Quest, also have not demonstrated positive outcomes. A similar lack of positive impact was found in the evaluation of boot camps and periodic drug-related group counseling. Individual therapy and family interventions have very mixed outcomes. In general, behavioral training, cognitive behavioral treatment, and life-skill cognitive behavioral activities have been relatively successful and promising. But virtually all research findings support the positive impact of intensive TC model for the population of substance-abusing offenders. This is partially because the profile of this population is very similar to the profile of a typical client in community-based TCs—a long history of drug use, use of multiple substances, serious involvement in crime, lack of a social support system, an inadequate employment history, and limited social and survival skills. Another important factor of this model's effectiveness is that it is not drug-specific, as are others, such as methadone maintenance. The TC model views drug-taking behavior as a symptom of an overall systemic behavioral dysfunction. Therefore, the emphasis is not on the symptom, but on the need for learning (or relearning) totally new behaviors. The TC model is an intense rehabilitation process whose aim is to promote prosocial behavior, thereby overcoming drug taking. Since the 1970s, TCs have been able to work with all types of drug users, regardless of age, gender, ethnicity, or culture. Further, TCs have effectively treated those with the most pathology—little employment history, extensive multiple drug-taking histories, and high criminality— with remarkable success measured in terms of sharp drops in criminality and tax-consumptive behavior, and increases in employment, especially for those in treatment 6 months or longer (Knight, Simpson, & Miller, 1999).

Recent research on the effectiveness of this model in correctional settings continues to reveal gratifying data, particularly in terms of criminal and drug-taking recidivism. The long-term postrelease outcome studies consistently show a dramatic reduction in recidivism in treated groups. Wexler, Melnick, Lowe, and Peters (1999) reported 27% recidivism in offenders who completed both in-prison TC treatment and aftercare, versus 75% for those receiving no treatment. In addition, this reduced recidivism is accompanied by a marked improvement in community reintegration as measured by employment, family reunification, sustained relationships, and reduced psychological and psychiatric problems. Another study in Texas found that only 25% of those who completed both in-custody TC treatment as well as aftercare were reincarcerated at some point during the 3-year follow-up, whereas 42% of untreated offenders and 64% of aftercare dropouts had been reincarcerated (Knight et al., 1999). Inciardi, Surratt, Martin, and Hooper (this volume) also showed that completers of in-prison treatment with aftercare also had the lowest rate of recidivism 3 years' postrelease. This suggests not only a reduction in crime and an increase in public safety, but also a savings to taxpayers. A number of cost-benefit studies consistently reveal positive findings (Griffith, Hiller, Knight, & Simpson, 1999; Aos, Phipps, Barnoski, & Lieb, 1999).

Several recent findings suggest another aspect of the effectiveness of prison-based TC programs—the positive impact on prison management (Deitch, Koutsenok, McGrath, Ratelle, & Carleton, 1998; Deitch, Koutsenok, Burgener, Marsolais, & Cartier, 2000). Research findings strongly suggest a much safer, less problematic, and more satisfying work environment in the prison facilities where TC-substance-abuse treatment takes place. Custody personnel assigned to these facilities tend to have an overall better perception of their health, particularly their emotional conditions and stress levels as compared with staff members working in traditional custody environments. They also have significantly fewer illness-related absences and fewer on-the-job injuries (both assault- and nonassault-related). So these programs benefit not only offenders and society as a whole, but also reduce risks for custody staff.

HISTORY OF THERAPEUTIC COMMUNITIES IN THE UNITED STATES

Where and how the TC-treatment model emerged is both interesting and instructive relative to future growth. In the early 1960s, Senator Thomas Dodd visited Synanon and referred to this pioneering drug treatment effort as a "miracle on the beach." This miracle on the beach in Santa Monica, California, resulted in the development of a set of methodologies largely employed in what was to emerge as "residential TC drug treatment." At its onset, Synanon dealt primarily with heroin addicts, although over the years it has treated all types of drug use among all races with equal effectiveness.

Over the years, as more outcome evaluations demonstrated TC efficacy (De Leon, 2000; Sells, 1974) with many different types of drug users, there was an effort to understand the precise methods involved, and an opportunity to study how best to deploy these methods in terms of frequency and sequence. Several researchers have described a set of discrete important activities that take place in a hierarchy within these community settings (De Leon, 1997, 2000; Deitch & Solit, 1993). The primary change process is best described by De Leon's famous phrase, "Community as method." The TC purposively uses the peer community to facilitate social and psychological change in individuals. Deitch describes four categories that are at work within this community as method: (a) behavior management and behavior shaping; (b) emotional and psychological life; (c) intellectual, ethical, moral, and spiritual life; and (d) vocational and prosocial survival-skill development. Although these four distinct and quite extensive categories of TC activity can occasionally blend into and sometimes overlap with one another, each has quite a separate focus, method, and support theory. Surrounding these categories and community as method is the historical tradition of "agape," from the Greek meaning love, compassion, patience, understanding, care, and altruism (Knibb, 1987).

Critical to the TC model since its inception are: (a) an emphasis on the use of clients in recovery; (b) diminishment of the dichotomy of we/they (client/staff), normally found in most treatment models; and (c) an emphasis on participants all starting at the beginning as raw learners regardless of background, and then moving into positions of leadership and authority over time as a result of demonstrated behavior, while integrating these same behavior changes along the way.

Interestingly, the TC movement arose in the United States during a period in its history of recognizing racism and the struggle for dignity and human rights through nonviolent civil disobedience. The TC movement then grew during the struggle with Vietnam, and our nation's split created a group of people who were considered "outsiders." Synanon founder Charles E. Diederich certainly had a heady, often reckless, disregard for authority and the established system. Part of the early esprit de corps was in being outside the established system and providing a true alternative to the failures of institutional treatment of addiction. In the early 1960s, others were attempting similar models with different populations having a correctional-based profile. One of the earliest innovations in this approach to treating criminal opiate abusers occurred in 1963 in the second judicial district of the Supreme Court of New York in The Kings County Brooklyn probation department. It had secured funds from the National Institute of Mental Health, and started a program, Drug Addicts Treated on Probation (DATOP). These convicted felons were offered the opportunity of residential treatment taking place in the community under probation supervision, with the coerced threat of 5-year or longer sentences hanging over their heads if they failed to complete or left treatment against advice. During this time, DAYTOP referred to itself as Daytop and not as a TC but rather as a "humanizing community." Shortly after DAYTOP's inception in New York City, Efran Ramirez, a psychiatrist, was recruited by Mayor Lindsey to serve as the first "Czar" of drug abuse treatment for New York City. Dr. Efran Ramirez had been operating a drug-treatment community in a Puerto Rico mental health institution (Rio Piedras Hospital) using a protracted intake model. He began a close relationship with DAYTOP, and began to urge that DAYTOP adopt the language of TC because of its greater acceptance throughout the health and mental health communities. By 1967, a set of New York-based programs began operating TCs. A Chief Deputy to Ramirez, Dr. Mitchell Rosenthal (a child psychiatrist), began a group called Phoenix House. Another psychiatrist who had been influenced by Ramirez and DATOP, Dr. Judy Ann Denson Gerber, started the project called Odyssey. Simultaneously, small spring-ups began on Long Island with a group called Topic, and in the following 5 years, a number of programs emerged using similar methodologies and adopting the same nomenclature to describe themselves: TC (De Leon, 2000; Deitch, 1973).

HISTORY OF PRISON-BASED THERAPEUTIC COMMUNITIES

Both Synanon in the early 1960s and, later, DATOP because of its correctional association began projects in different prisons. In 1962, Synanon ran a project in the Nevada State Prison on a part-time basis. DATOP and, later, Phoenix House created a set of outpatient groups at Green Haven and other state prisons in New York.

By 1980, the emerging crisis of prison expansion, which was frequently developed at the expense of other tax revenue-dependent programs such as education, was having many prison administrations reconsider what they could do to stem the cost of this continuous prison building (Deitch et al., 2000). New York considered these issues and began to look at outcome data from many of the national studies that had occurred, principally the Drug Abuse Reporting Program (DARP), which had come out of Texas Christian University (Sells, 1974), and the Treatment Outcomes Prospective Study (TOPS) (Hubbard et al., 1989) from Research Triangle Institute. They began to look at the treatment-model studies to see if any dealt with clients resembling those which existed in the custody setting. They concluded that the TC model was dealing with a profile that had far more predatory crime than either methadone maintenance or outpatient drug-free models. Secondly, those people going into the TCs had a far worse work history, if any, than clients at either of the other two models. Thirdly, clients in community-based TCs had a series of drug problems, not just heroin, which was primarily the methadone model, or stimulants and hallucinogens, the outpatient drug-free model.

In summary, the TC showed promising outcomes with a highly predatory criminal who had little work history and a lot of other psychosocial problems, yet demonstrated success as much as 3 and 5 years later in terms of decreasing crime, increasing work productivity, and decreasing multiple types of drug taking.

FORCES AT WORK: IMPEDIMENTS TO IMPLEMENTATION OF THERAPEUTIC COMMUNITIES IN CUSTODY SETTINGS

Given the glowing outcomes and the apparent similarities of the TC and correctional mission—prosocial values emphasis, hierarchical structure, and demand for compliance—it would seem logical that these two systems would easily find common ground and act as willing partners. Yet reality has underscored the significant differences in the systems, not the similarities, and the blending process has been bumpy, convoluted, and painful. In this section, we will examine some of the impediments to implementation, both physical and philosophical.

When reviewing the mission statements of most correctional environments, one generally finds reference to the key concepts of safety, security, and return to the community. Although safety and security are readily reported goals of staff in these settings, rehabilitation has not fared so well and is, in some situations, so low on the list of priorities that it no longer represents a functional goal. The three primary issues are preventing escapes, reduction of violence (murders), and staying within budget. Rehabilitation, or habilitation for that matter, require some opportunity to test the individual ability to practice newly acquired skills. The introduction of treatment, and particularly a model that is so visible in the daily lives of inmates and staff, can pose a disruption to the routine and be experienced as a "security risk" by officer and inmate alike. The treatment providers, in turn, have their own beliefs and biases that can be counterproductive in the initial implementation of correctional treatment. Community-based TCs have relied on visible and active peer role models with historical and experiential credibility to engage inductees. Within the institution, the difficulty in hiring and retaining recovering or "ex-con" staff forces a reliance on academically trained staff who are less than TC fluent. Finally, the custody setting is a unique world with its own sets of standards, rules, and procedures for management of daily life. Leadership—wardens and senior staff—are bound by tradition, directives from legislatures, and the demands of courts. The ability of any institution to feed, clothe, and maintain 500 to 5,000 people, only a few of whom will be in the treatment environment, demands systems that leave room for little, if any flexibility. TCs, on the other hand, are fluid, dynamic environments that rely on a controlled chaos to facilitate the creative metamorphosis needed to effect lasting change. This oil and water mixture initially clashes and then transitions to a hybrid culture, often adopting the lowest common denominator (punitive response to resistance and noncompliance) as the reference point. David Farabee and his co-authors refer to overreliance on institutional versus therapeutic sanctions as one of six "common implementation issues for developing programs" (Farabee et al., 1999). The others are client identification and referral (assessment and access to inmates appropriate for treatment), recruitment and training of staff (work force depletion and non-TC skilled staff), reemployment of correctional staff (frequent shifting assignment as institutional policy), aftercare (availability and adequacy), and finally coercion (involuntary vs. voluntary program assignment).

Finally, cross training of correctional and treatment personnel focused on shared learning, demystification of each others' roles and experiences, and team building via concrete problem solving, will reap long-term benefits in increased communication, trust, and shared goals. Long-term outcomes of TCs in custody settings are difficult to feel or believe when struggling with daily management of inmates. Nonetheless, treatment and correctional staff can see the daily changes and emergence of a new person who could possibly have a fighting chance at a real human life.

CURRENT CONSIDERATIONS

Several specific issues need attention in the field in order for positive outcomes to continue to occur. What we now need is a work force trained in the appropriate methodologies to sustain this effort. With the current serious shortage of "soldiers" to carry out the mission, outcomes will begin to falter and rumors may fly that treatment does not work after all. The individuals need to deliver not only drug treatment, but treat criminogenic alcohol and drug users in a correctional setting—a relatively new and unique skill—and one absolutely critical to continued success. The issue has many facets: academically trained substance-abuse counselors who are simply not adequately prepared for the prison environment; ex-felons/ex-addicts who are eager to share their treatment experience and new lifestyles, but who have little academic or counseling background; and custody staff who have traditionally been trained to view the prison experience as a punitive rather than rehabilitative measure. Some attempts to mitigate this crisis are currently underway in California, Arizona, New Mexico, and other states. They include: core-curriculum substance abuse education for both custody- and treatment-provider staff; week-long cross trainings for custody and substance-abuse counseling staff to develop problem-solving and team-building skills; week-long work force development training in TC practice (again for both custody and provider staff); continuous quality improvement assessment and site visits for existing programs; several different types of technical assistance; and a certification program based on the Center for Substance-Abuse Treatment's *TAP 21: Addiction Counseling Competencies: The Knowledge, Skills, and Attitudes of Professional Practice*.

Special populations are another area for consideration. The community-based TC has a great deal of experience in addressing the special needs of unique populations: ethnic and cultural, women's issues, and acute and chronic physical disease. TCs were among the first to embrace the care and support of the HIV-infected addict, the special needs of disabled participants, and offer a safe place for sexual minorities to explore and begin recovery. The issue of women with children has been a special focus for TCs for the last 30 years, and this model has emerged as one of the leaders in women's treatment. These groups need a unique focus and the correctional environment has benefited by this work.

There are two groups that merit special attention in this discussion of correctional treatment: the sexual offender and the dually diagnosed offender. Recently, the University of California, San Diego, and the California Department of Corrections convened an expert panel to explore the issue of treatment for the drug-dependent sex offender within the context of the in-custody TC. The difficulty of disclosure of sexual crimes is of particular concern behind the prison walls, and can often condemn an inmate to brutal and humiliating treatment by other inmates. Avoiding disclosure results in a "secret" being kept by inmates and staff in direct conflict with the TC philosophy of disclosure and exposures of fears and failures, as well as hopes and dreams. Aftercare treatment is also a difficulty, due to legal and community restrictions on placement and residency of known sex offenders. These offenders would be best served in a treatment community dedicated to this special group (University of California, San Diego, 1999).

The second group that deserves comment in this chapter is the dually diagnosed inmate. Our modern social and judicial systems have altered the face of the prison inmate. The diagnostic and treatment capacity of most prison systems is mitigated by limited budgets, huge caseloads, and, again, the realities of prison life. Some TCs are finding that up to 30% of their clients have secondary psychiatric disorders. Although, for the most part, nonpsychotic disorders are well managed in the TC community, adequate treatment of both issues demands an intensive, team-treatment approach with the mental health and the TC community. Decisions about medication and intensity of therapy (both individual and group) must be made jointly and with the long-term focus of personal change needed for drug- and criminal-behavior recovery, as well as psychological and psychiatric stability.

POSSIBLE FUTURE CONCERNS

In conclusion, there is indeed a very brave and exciting history of treating the complicated multiple disorder of crime and drug taking by using a model that has demonstrated effectiveness in many cultures, with many types of predator criminals who use all types of drugs. The data we have presented is impressive. The question that remains is: Can we sustain this same degree of outcome, considering some of the emerging problems inherent in expanding TC and other drug treatment in custody and in community settings?

We feel obliged, in summary, to talk about a few of these problems. The first is the practice of awarding treatment contracts based on a higher number of points for the provider who offers to do the service for the least amount of cost. This "low-balling" is similar to that which occurs in managed care, where the expectation is for providers to do more for less in each ensuing year. Generally, this means that providers competing for large contracts take what they can out of the one place where flexibility occurs—in salaries.

Secondly, special competencies are required in how to address both criminal behavior and addiction in an environment that is decidedly criminogenic, and training in this area is severely lacking. Technical assistance as a follow-up to basic training is often necessary, especially since this work force experiences a high rate of turnover. Thirdly, to rely on treatment practitioners who often are less mature and stable in their own recovery is to risk what happened in the late 1800s in many of the asylum- and temperance-movement treatment approaches. The premature use of people who were in recovery might have influenced reported relapse. These issues have already created problems in many settings. Last, there is an emerging tension in many communities over the availability of treatment-bed space for people of the community who are on waiting lists seeking treatment; those returning from prison are an additional and unwanted burden.

As we do our work in this field in Texas, Arizona, New Mexico, and California, one recommendation heard repeatedly is to try to create a system of streamlined continuity of care. Our experience shows that a critical condition for effective treatment in prison and, later, in the community is the establishment of a close relationship and level of trust between both the parole officer and treatment providers. Our experience also suggests that one effective way to ensure establishment of this relationship is through a series of joint trainings. If all parties are familiar with the treatment model's operating methodology and philosophy, as well as the risk factors for relapse (both in addiction and crime) upon return to the community, this desired level of trust is far more likely to occur.

Separate from these specific issues, there is a general, "new innovation" pathway that is of grave concern to all who care about sustaining the outcomes toward which we are working. Often referred to as the "halo effect," the initial outcomes tend to look better than those that follow in future years. This is because the effort occurs on a small scale, in few locations, and is given much positive attention and intention by people who make sure that it works. Generally, such data are anecdotal, but in some instances, there are at least quasiexperimental outcomes. The model usually has top resources, and people become involved and excited about it. Usually the best personnel are assigned to it to ensure its success. At this stage of evolution, magical expectations begin to occur because of some of the early promising data. As the efforts grow larger, there is less positive attention, and more critical investigation and attention given to the projects. As the effort becomes more commonplace, the quality of the assigned work force decreases, and more research is funded.

In summary, we have a very promising approach that appears to work for many. This TC approach in prison may be receiving extraordinary comments, without being well-differentiated across different places and different inmate profiles (including the questionable claim that this works with the truly psychopathic inmate). Regardless, it appears that the TC model is capable of working with criminal and drug-taking lifestyles; it is definitely successful when people have volunteered, and, debatably, even when coerced. We will need to take care to provide enough time (or dosage) in treatment, and ensure that it is followed up with appropriate dosage in the community. In short, the TC model offers a promising history with considerations that we must carefully analyze, and if they are carefully analyzed and appropriately supported, these promising outcomes can be sustained.

12

Modified Prison Therapeutic Communities for the Dual- and Multiple-Diagnosed Offender

George De Leon, Stanley Sacks, and Harry K. Wexler

The last decade has witnessed an expansion of treatment approaches for special populations of substance abusers, including offenders in the correctional system and for mentally ill chemical abusers[1] (MICAs) in community-based and institutional settings. Notable has been the development of modified therapeutic community (TC) programs for treating substance abusers in correctional settings (Wexler, 1997). The feasibility and effectiveness of these prison-based programs is well documented (e.g., Simpson, Wexler, & Inciardi, 1999; Inciardi, Surratt, Martin, & Hooper, this volume), and recent evaluations have demonstrated the effectiveness of modified TCs for MICAs in community residences (e.g., De Leon, Sacks, Staines, & McKendrick, 2000). These developments

---

[1]This chapter uses the terms "MICA," "dual disorder," "co-occurring disorder," and "comorbidity" interchangeably.

have encouraged the application of modified TC models for treating MICAs in correctional settings.

This chapter summarizes the problem of comorbidity among offenders and current treatment approaches in both community-based and correctional settings. Focus is upon the modified TC approach for comorbid offenders. A brief history of TCs in relation to comorbidity is sketched, and a description from the Colorado prison system is presented. Some preliminary evaluation findings are also presented. The last sections outline treatment issues and policy recommendations as modified TC treatment for MICA offenders continues to expand.

COMORBIDITY AND OFFENDERS: CURRENT PROBLEM AND SOLUTIONS

For the past 20 years, research on co-occurring, substance-use disorders in patients with mental illness has yielded an extensive body of evidence documenting the prevalence of MICAs. For example, the National Institute of Mental Health's Epidemiological Catchment Area (ECA) study (Regier et al., 1990) and the National Comorbidity Survey (Kessler et al., 1994) are clear in showing that the lifetime prevalence of mental and substance-abuse disorders is high in the general population. The rates range from 19% to 30% for psychiatric and 15% to 18% for substance-use disorders. The ECA finding that is relevant here is that substance-use disorders co-occur with mental disorders more frequently than predicted by chance alone. Most studies suggest that 25% to 35% of persons with a mental illness also have a diagnosable substance-use disorder over the past 6 months (Mueser et al., 1995). Other studies of diagnostic patterns show that MICAs are more prevalent among treated samples than in untreated ones. Clinicians, practitioners, and researchers have documented client prevalence rates of 20% to 50% for co-occurring mental and substance-abuse disorders in *mental health settings* (Minkoff & Drake, 1991; Ross, Glaser, & Germanson, 1988; Rounsaville et al., 1991), as high as 90% in *substance abuse programs* (Sacks, De Leon, Bernhardt, & Sacks, 1997), and 30% to 40% in *homeless populations* (Michaels, Zoloth, Alcabes, Braslow, & Safyer, 1992). Thus, MICA clients are commonly encountered across many settings, with about half of all clients with severe mental illness experiencing diagnosable substance-related problems at some time in their life (Drake & Mueser, 2000).

PREVALENCE OF MENTALLY ILL CHEMICAL ABUSERS IN THE CRIMINAL JUSTICE SYSTEM

More recently in criminal justice settings, administrative and treatment professionals throughout the country have observed an increase in the number of offenders with co-occurring mental illness and substance-use disorders. Estimated prevalence rates for co-occurring disorders in the jail and prison populations have varied between 3% and 16% (Abramson, 1972; Pepper & Massaro, 1992; Peters & Hill, 1993; Steadman, Cocozza, & Melick, 1987; Tepin, 1990). Recently, the U.S. Department of Justice reported in the *Bureau of Justice Statistics: Special Report* (Ditton, 1999) that an estimated 283,800 mentally ill offenders were incarcerated in the nation's state prisons and jails, which represents 16% of that population. In addition, 547,800 probationers, or about 16% of probationers, responded that they had a mental condition or had stayed overnight in a mental hospital during their lifetime (Ditton, 1999). Of those incarcerated in state prisons, 34% exhibited a history of alcohol dependence based on the CAGE (a screening instrument for alcohol dependence or abuse whose acronym refers to its four drinking-related statements). As with state-prison inmates, 35% of probationers exhibited a history of alcohol use on the CAGE. Ditton (1999) also reported that mentally ill offenders were: (a) more likely than other offenders to be using alcohol or drugs when they committed their convicting offense (60% vs. 51%); (b) more likely to be incarcerated for a violent crime (53% vs. 46%); and (c) more likely to be homeless in the 12 months prior to their arrest (20% vs. 9%).

TREATMENT FOR MENTALLY ILL CHEMICAL ABUSERS IN THE CRIMINAL JUSTICE SYSTEM

Despite the rise in dual-disordered inmates entering prison facilities throughout the country, most states have not developed treatment programs to meet the needs of this large influx (Lurigio & Swartz, 1994). Various reasons have been cited for the slow implementation of corrections-based, dual-disorder programs. These involve the unique contextual issues of the prison setting, as well as system barriers (see Hills, 2000; Lurigio & Swartz, 1994; and Sacks, Wexler, Peters, & Sacks, 2000).

Notwithstanding these issues and barriers, treatment strategies and several treatment models and programs for dual-disordered offenders have been described in the literature (e.g., Edens, Peters, & Hills, 1997; Hills,

2000). These are mainly special unit programs within larger correctional facilities with specialized mental health services. Four of these are modified TCs (Turning Point, Oregon; Estelle Unit, Texas; Hackberry Unit, Texas; San Carlos and Arrowhead, Colorado). The other programs incorporate biopsychosocial concepts in eclectic models of treatment. These include the Dual Diagnosis Unit, Alabama; Crisis Care Unit, Delaware; and Dual Diagnosis Track, Kentucky.

The majority of the prison-based MICA programs evolved from previously established community-based substance abuse programs (Edens et al., 1997). However, all integrate components from mental health treatment (e.g., psychiatric consultation, medication education and compliance groups, individual counseling). Evaluation research on these initiatives is either preliminary or ongoing. Thus far, findings are encouraging in showing reasonable retention (von Sternberg, 1997) and reduced reincarceration rates (Field, 1995). The modified TC for comorbidity is the subject of the remainder of this chapter.

THERAPEUTIC COMMUNITIES AND COMORBIDITY

Psychiatric TCs have been implemented for offenders with substance abuse and other psychological problems for some 50 years. Indeed, the profile of admissions to the first hospital-based "psychiatric TC" established by Jones and others in Great Britain was marked by serious psychiatric and sociopathic characteristics, in addition to alcohol and drug abuse (e.g., Dolan, 1996; Jones, 1953; Rapaport, 1960). Notably, the utility of these TCs provided the rationale for implementing them in treating offenders in the commonwealth's correctional system.

A considerable research literature reports on both process and outcomes in the British prison TCs for offenders with personality and mental disorders (e.g., Dolan, 1994; Lees, Manning, Menzies, & Morant, in press; Rawlings & Yates, in press; Shine, 2000). Studies document the *management utility* of the TC in the prison setting. For example, longstanding TC programs, such as Grendon, report fewer inmate conflicts, less rule infractions, and better morale among the correctional staff (e.g., Shine, 2000).

Evaluations consistently affirm the efficacy of the Jones TC in improving the psychological status of offenders during their prison stay. Generally, however, the postprison follow-up studies in Great Britain show no significant differences in reconviction rates between former prison TC residents and control groups, although older residents show the better effects. The outcome studies indicate that the democratic (Jones) TC may not be effective in reducing criminal behavior among offenders with serious mental disorder, particularly those high in psychopathy.

The previous conclusion may reflect features of the offender samples, as well as the type of TC model used. The British TCs have focused mainly upon the criminal and psychiatric disorder of the offenders, rather than substance abuse. In their treatment samples, primary psychopathic personality has been the prominent characteristic, which, not surprisingly, is quite resistant to change. Moreover, unlike the Jones TC, the addiction TC model in North America appears more suitable for treating antisocial substance-abusers. Its hierarchical, autocratic structure and group techniques, such as confrontation, were developed by substance-abuser participants, themselves, to address their character-disorder features (see De Leon, 2000, chapter 2). More recently, the British TCs have been modified toward the addiction TC model to treat substance abuse in their offender populations.

Addiction Therapeutic Offenders and Dual Disorder

From their inception in the early 1960s, the community-based TCs in North America have served substance abusers with criminal histories, character disorder, and other psychiatric disturbance. Indeed, outcome research consistently documents improvements in psychopathological signs, along with reductions in substance abuse and criminal activity among long-term dropouts (beyond 6 months), and completers of standard or traditional TCs (De Leon, 1989). However, these studies indicate that only a certain group of comorbid clients are suitable for traditional TCs, even those programs with enhanced mental health services. Generally, these are the clients with less serious Axis I and those with Axis II personality disorders. Historically, substance abusers with serious Axis I diagnoses comprise only a small proportion of standard or traditional TC.

Within the last decade, however, standard TCs have modified to serve substance abusers with the more serious Axis I disorders. As described in the literature (e.g., De Leon, 1997), the evidence documenting the effectiveness of these community-based models provided the empirical basis for extending the modified TC for comorbid offenders within the correctional system. An instructive illustration of this adaptation of the TC is provided in the text that follows.

A MODIFIED THERAPEUTIC COMMUNITY FOR MENTALLY ILL CHEMICAL ABUSERS IN PRISON: CASE ILLUSTRATION

The Colorado Department of Corrections contracted with a private, not-for-profit agency to develop the Personal Reflections Therapeutic Community program at the San Carlos Correctional Facility in Pueblo, Colorado, in the mid-1990s, in response to the increasing number of inmates with co-occurring substance abuse and mental illness. The San Carlos program uses TC principles and methods as the foundation for recovery, and the structure within which a cognitive-behavioral curriculum focuses on the triple issues—substance abuse, mental illness, and criminal thinking and behavior—as a means of changing attitudes and lifestyles. The goal of the program is to use a positive peer culture to foster personal change and to reduce the incidence of return to a criminal lifestyle. The inmates progress through program stages, typically moving from orientation to primary treatment ("family" phase), then preparation for re-entry into the community at large. Upper level inmates in the TC program function as a positive, peer leadership group—or "structure"—to guide and support newer members as they begin to develop and apply new values, beliefs, and skills to their daily lives. Thus, the San Carlos TC, modified for the MICA population, functions as a healthy family for its members, reinforcing affiliation with the recovery community.

The San Carlos TC activities include psychoeducational classes that increase an inmate's understanding of the following: mental illness and the nature of dual diagnoses, addiction and drugs of use and abuse, the connection between thoughts and behavior, and emotional and behavioral coping skills. Therapeutic interventions in the TC include core groups to process personal issues, as well as modified encounter groups that address maladaptive behaviors, personal responsibility, and the use of the peer group for feedback and support.

In addition, the Colorado Department of Corrections has developed two other programs for MICA offenders. The program at Arrowhead provides a MICA track within a mainstream-prison TC. The program elements within this track include groups and activities designed to address mental illness, substance abuse, and criminal behavior. Inmates in this track also participate in all groups and activities of the mainstream TC. The program at Independence House is an aftercare program within the context of community corrections. MICA offenders are referred to Independence House from San Carlos and Arrowhead. The goals for the aftercare program are to continue personal growth, master community living, gain employment, and foster connection with the larger recovery community (Sacks et al., 2000).

Evaluation of the San Carlos modified TC is ongoing. Preliminary results indicate that the profiles of the MICA inmates show a substantial history of crime, mental illness, and substance abuse. In addition to their histories of criminal activity and incarceration, these offenders meet DSM-IV diagnostic criteria for mental illness and substance-abuse disorder as assessed by the Diagnostic Interview Schedule (DIS-IV). They show many similarities to a community-based MICA sample, and differ by the severity of their criminal behavior and greater frequency of antisocial personality diagnosis.

Treatment effectiveness is currently being assessed through comparative analysis of treatment outcomes between MICA inmates in the modified TC and similar inmates in an enhanced mental health (MH) model within the same correctional facility. Initial follow-up results at 6 months postprison indicate significantly lower criminal activity rates for the TC group.

MODIFIED THERAPEUTIC COMMUNITIES AS MENTAL HEALTH MODELS: SOME TREATMENT AND PLANNING ISSUES

The successful adaptation of the TC for special populations, such as MICA offenders in the special setting of the correctional facility, has surfaced important policy and training issues. Several of these, which have been identified in both clinical and research experience, are briefly discussed in this last section.

Emerging subtypes of MICAs. Comorbidity within the MICA population is heterogeneous. For example, TC research has identified five subtypes of substance abusers along a severity of mental-disorder dimension: (a) Axis I serious + Axis II ASP; (b) Axis II, ASP only; (c) Axis I, serious only; (d) Axis I, nonserious only; and (e) No nondrug diagnosis (De Leon, Sacks, Staines, & McKendrick, 1999).[2] Those subtypes that will benefit from modified TC models for comorbid offenders remain to be clarified.

Staff composition: Traditional and nontraditional. The multiple problems of the comorbid client and the unique features of the TC approach underscore the need for a special staffing composition of traditional mental

---

[2]Serious = the presence of a bipolar and/or schizophrenic diagnosis.

health and substance-abuse workers. Staffing issues in standard TCs and modified TCs are more fully discussed elsewhere (DeLeon, 2000, chapter 10). In the modified TC, the staff-to-client ratio is higher than in the standard TC, and lower than in the standard mental health facility. There is a greater proportion of staff with traditional, mental health training who work with nontraditional, TC-trained personnel.

Staff training and orientation. All staff is trained together in the TC perspective, mental illness, and substance use. Didactic instruction focuses upon TC theory and practice. Experiential training consists of brief exposures to the TC daily regime as residents themselves in cooperating standard or modified TCs. Ongoing training and technical assistance is provided by senior staff and mental health and TC consultants.

The main focus of training is to integrate staff to work effectively in the modified TC model, regardless of their varied educational background and professional orientation. The mental health staff must fully accept the TC self-help perspective and, especially, its impact on role relations with residents and the TC-trained staff. Rather than patients, residents are clients who are members of a community. Rather than treatment provider, staff members serve as guides and facilitators.

Conversely, nontraditional, professional staff with recovery or TC backgrounds must be oriented to mental health concepts, diagnoses, intervention strategies, and management of psychiatric crisis and pharmacotherapy. In particular, they must acquire more tolerance for individual differences in client rates of change and reset their expectations of client compliance, energy level, and responsivity. Perceptual and emotional issues of both staff should be routinely addressed (e.g., TC staff's fears of the mentally ill client and mental health staff's fears of the antisocial addict).

Continuity of care and the need for integrated services. Effectiveness notwithstanding, relapse is the rule in both drug abuse and mental illness. This highlights the central issue of continuity of care in the treatment of the dually disordered. Many of these clients will require continued involvement with human service agencies for an undetermined period. Some of the problems and issues in developing effective aftercare services for those leaving TCs are outlined elsewhere (De Leon, 1990–1991). These issues underscore the need to develop *integrated* systems of treatment delivery for the dually disordered.

In a fully elaborated and integrated system, different treatment settings articulate with each other under a *common TC-oriented recovery perspective* of dual disorder, and undergo a shared staff training and a coordinated case-management plan. Such a system may include the inpatient ward, day treatment and outpatient clinics, the homeless shelter, transitional community residence, and permanent housing. Each setting is designed to move the client to the next stage of recovery in another setting within the system. An example of a community-based system has been fully articulated in other writings of the authors (Sacks et al., 1997). A hospital-based integrated system is described elsewhere (Galanter, Egelko, De Leon, & Rohrs, 1993). An example of a developing integrated system within corrections is the Colorado illustration discussed earlier and described more fully elsewhere (Sacks et al., 2000).

Fidelity of the TC model. Surveys of various correctional programs for prison inmates, both TC and non-TC oriented, with co-occurring disorders, reveal common treatment components (see Edens, Peters, & Hills, 1997). However, the comparative effectiveness and cost-effectiveness of the modified TC will depend upon the fidelity in implementing the unique features of this model. Several recent developments address the issue of fidelity in TC programming. First, national standards have been disseminated to provide quality-assurance criteria for prison TC programs (Therapeutic Communities of America [TCA] Criminal Justice Committee, 1999). These recommend inclusion of services for the comorbid inmates, but delivered within the context of the TC approach.

Second, uniform training curricula are being developed or refined for generic, as well as modified TCs (Talboy, 1998). These will include modules addressing the needs of special populations in special settings, including inmates with co-occurring disorders.

In the last analysis, treatment fidelity refers to adhering to the key assumptions of the TC approach. These emphasize the relationship between the individual and community in the change process. Regardless of their level of function, comorbid individuals in the TC assume the primary responsibility for their recovery and change. They *use* community—the peers, staff, social relationships, and daily structure of activities—to foster the self-change. Thus, mental health, medical, and correctional elements must be integrated within the primary treatment component, which is community as method, to assure the fidelity of the TC approach.

POLICY RECOMMENDATIONS FOR TREATING
MENTALLY ILL CHEMICAL ABUSERS IN PRISON

The successful implementation and expansion of correctional TCs for the treatment of substance abuse in American prisons (Wexler, 1995; Wexler &

Lipton, 1993) offers important policy guidance for the treatment of MICAs and other mentally ill prisoners. Acceptance of the correctional TC is based on the positive outcomes of studies showing significantly lower recidivism rates for TC graduates (Lipton, 1995). Aftercare's contribution to reducing recidivism has been reported by recent studies in California (Wexler, De Leon, Thomas, Kressel, & Peters, 1999), Texas (Knight, Simpson, Chatham, & Camacho, 1997), Delaware (Inciardi, Martin, Butzin, Hooper, & Harrison, 1997), and by the Bureau of Prisons (Pelissier et al., 1998). Recent evaluation studies reported positive outcomes at 3 years' postrelease for inmates who completed both in-prison TC treatment and aftercare (Knight, Simpson, & Hiller, 1999; Wexler, Melnick, Lowe, & Peters, 1999).

The history of prison TC expansion is an unusual demonstration of a highly synergistic relationship between research, practice, and policy. The introduction of early, positive, prison TC outcomes (Wexler, Falkin, & Lipton, 1990), based on research in the 1980s, came at a time when the popular perception was "nothing works" in prison treatment, and "rehabilitation" was considered a politically incorrect term and the object of cynical disregard. However, the general public and policy makers were also very concerned with the public safety crisis of rising crime rates and the relationship between drug use and criminality (Lipton & Wexler, 1988), along with growing prison populations largely driven by crime that was drug related. A general need for a solution, or at least some hope, was shared by many and contributed to an atmosphere receptive to research showing "something works."

The self-help foundation of the modified TC focuses on empowerment of participants and the belief that a willingness to face one's problems and do the hard work of treatment can lead to successful postprison reentry. The self-help philosophy that guides treatment in modified TCs introduces a sense of hopefulness and long-term success that is not generally found in correctional, mental health programming. There are currently a paucity of good mental health treatment models in corrections and almost no continuous treatment that includes prison and aftercare. The Colorado work reported above is an important exception and provides a prototype for applying lessons learned from correctional substance-abuse treatment to MICAs.

With the spread of modified prison TCs for the treatment of substance abuse to all state prison systems and the federal prison system, important groundwork has been provided for the acceptance of a more *proactive* approach to correctional treatment for MICAs and other mentally ill inmates. Prison administrators have found that modified TCs are highly positive environments where inmates treat each other and all staff with respect. The programs are usually the cleanest and best-run housing units where custody staff prefers to work. A number of informal surveys have shown the cost benefits of TC units related to reduction in staff sick days, reduced rule infractions, and vandalism. The respectable return of the concept of rehabilitation (or habilitation), with the goals of recidivism reduction and healthy functioning in the community, becomes a realistic policy aim for the correctional mental health. It is a reasonable expectation that correctional policy makers and prison administrators will support modified TC treatment for MICAs and other mentally ill inmates based on the strong empirical support and successful implementation of modified, substance-abuse TCs into correctional systems.

The integration of substance abuse and mental health staff within modified TCs for MICAs has the potential to significantly advance the field rapidly and contribute to the expansion of the prison mission to better meet the needs of both public safety and public health. Evidence of the growing concern and resolve among policy makers to solve the problem of the mentally ill in corrections is seen in developments in the Department of Justice and other federal agencies. For example, a series of meetings are planned to focus on the mental illness crisis in corrections by the National Institute of Corrections, Correctional Programs Office, and the Office of National Drug Control Policy, to bring researchers, practitioners, administrators, and policymakers together in 2000 and 2001 (Wexler, 2000). As policy discussions transpire, the authors recommend that the problem be framed primarily as one of co-occurring disorders, and that the successes and lessons learned in correctional substance-abuse treatment (e.g., through modified TCs) be used as a guide to planning and implementing policy and new programming.

13

Drug Testing in Criminal Justice Settings

Adele Harrell and Mark Kleiman

Drug testing of offenders reflects the widespread recognition among criminal justice professionals that reductions in some forms of drug use among certain offenders result in reductions in crime. The relationship of crime and chronic hard-drug use has been well documented in the literature (Inciardi, Martin, Butzin, Hooper, & Harrison, 1997; Miller & Gold, 1994). Chronically hard-drug-involved offenders have high rates of criminal activity, with the frequency and severity of criminal behavior rising and falling with the level of drug use (Anglin, Longshore, & Turner, 1999). Drug addicts commit more crimes while they are addicted—some four to six times more than when they are not abusing narcotics, a pattern that is even more pronounced among habitual offenders (Vito, 1989).

Incarceration may temporarily halt offending by addicts, but many resume their drug use and crime upon release to the community. One study found that 60% of federal parolees who were opiate-dependent at the time of imprisonment were reincarcerated within 6 months of release, at a cost of more than $27,000 per person per year for incarceration. Intensive supervision failed to reduce their risk of recidivism; there was no significant difference between the rearrest and reincarceration rates of opiate-dependent parolees randomly assigned to "double parole," consisting of twice the amount of supervision by the parole office, and parolees on standard supervision (Cornish et al., 1996).

In addition to the impact of drug use on offender behavior, drug consumption by offenders has profound impact on illicit drug markets. By one estimate, 60% of the cocaine consumed in the United States in any given year is consumed by the subset of heavy users who are also arrested during that year (Kleiman, 1997). The financial contribution of offenders to those markets helps support the bloodshed, corruption, neighborhood disruption, and enticement of adolescents into criminal lifestyles that accompany illicit drug dealing, and reducing that contribution could be an important means of reducing those side effects. The failure of enforcement directed at drug distributors to raise prices or reduce availability (over the past 20 years, imprisonment for drug dealing has increased about tenfold, but the prices of cocaine and heroin are at about 25% of 1980 levels—at or near their all-time lows) gives added prominence to demand-reduction strategies (Reuter, 1997). Although demand reduction has tended to focus on preventive education and treatment, the capacity of the criminal justice system to reduce demand among the group where demand is highest should not be ignored.

Faced daily with the reality behind the statistics described previously, many judges, prosecutors, police, and corrections officers actively support efforts to reduce drug use among offenders, and are willing to use the authority of the justice system to encourage abstinence (or at least, reduced drug-use frequency) for offenders with cocaine or heroin problems and treatment for those who need it. Drug testing, alone or in combination with treatment, offers several advantages over other options for increasing offender accountability and managing offender behavior. Drug testing is a relatively inexpensive technique for monitoring and managing a behavior known to be linked to risk of offending. With proper concern for the chain of custody and the use of confirmation tests, results are reliable and can be introduced in court or at administrative hearings as evidence of continued drug use. Test results can also be used for assessment and treatment planning. Compared with alternative approaches for monitoring drug use, including self-reports, observation of symptoms, or informant reports, testing greatly increases the probability of detecting offenders'[1] drug use and

---

[1]For convenience, the term "offenders" will be used in this chapter for defendants (individuals who have been charged but not convicted), those who have been found guilty, and those who are participating in preprosecution diversion programs under court supervision. "Arrestees" refer to all individuals who are booked on an offense.

reduces the lag between the beginning of a relapse and its detection. Insofar as test results help break through the denial often characteristic of substance-abuse disorder, they can have a direct therapeutic benefit.

Varieties of Criminal Justice Drug Testing

Drug testing programs within the criminal justice system can be divided along three dimensions: purpose, stage of processing, and technology.

Purpose

Testing is used in three primary ways: (a) as a routine monitoring tool by first-line, community-corrections officers ("surveillance testing"), comparable to employer checks or face-to-face interviews, with the consequences of detected drug use determined on a case-by-case, discretionary basis; (b) to monitor compliance in connection with mandated treatment; and (c) as part of testing-and-sanctions programs (with or without treatment), in which each detected violation is designed to result in a prespecified sanction.

Surveillance testing, even if not tightly linked to sanctions, may serve as a deterrent to drug use and can help alert community-corrections officers to clients whose behavior needs special attention. Some community-corrections agencies regard the detection of technical violations and subsequent incarceration of the violators as an important part of their mission; for them, even infrequent testing serves as a highly cost-effective means of detecting such violations. The relatively narrow time-window of detection for most drugs using standard urine-testing technology limits the effectiveness of sporadic monitoring as a deterrent: an offender tested once per year—not an atypical frequency—faces a less than 1% risk of detection for any one incident of drug use, which for many falls below the threshold of efficacy as a threat.

Other agencies use surveillance tests linked to sanctions typically set in advance, and often graduated in severity, as a rehabilitation tool for changing offender behavior without resorting to long periods of incarceration. The basic logic is the same as that behind pure surveillance testing: that drug use can be deterred by threat of sanctions. However, this application uses contingency management strategies to change behavior through a closer linking of behavior to consequences. Tests can also be used to identify drug users for referral to treatment and then to work in partnership with treatment agencies to monitor treatment attendance and progress (testing linked to treatment). The goal of creating such testing-treatment links is to increase treatment entry and encourage treatment retention, compliance, and completion. Reductions in drug use achieved through treatment are expected to result in long-term reductions in offending.

Stage of Processing

Programs may test defendants (a) between arrest and case disposition, before or after formal charging, (b) between case disposition and sentencing (most often between a guilty plea and the imposition of a sentence), (c) as part of a postsentencing diversion program, or (d) as part of routine postsentencing probation or parole supervision. The stage of criminal justice processing has significant implications for how the results can be used. Results of pretrial testing before a defendant has been found or pled guilty (Stage 1) cannot be introduced as evidence against the person being tested or considered in case outcomes unless the offender has agreed to enter a preplea diversion program in which prosecution is deferred, pending successful completion of a drug treatment or intervention program. Stage 2 pretrial testing, used in most drug court and diversion programs, takes place after a guilty plea or finding, and requires that defendants[2] agree to drug testing and to waive certain rights in exchange for potential benefits. The benefits may be substantial—the dismissal of the charge or an offer of probation rather than incarceration upon successful completion of a treatment program or a specified period of drug abstinence. The waivers allow the courts to impose penalties or the original sentence if program goals are not attained.

Legal concerns about pretrial drug tests have been raised in many jurisdictions considering their adoption. The legal concerns stem from questions about the constitutionality of pretrial tests on the grounds of Fourth Amendment protections against unreasonable search and seizure, Fifth Amendment guarantees against self-incrimination, and Fourteenth Amendment pertaining to equal protections and due process. Although pretrial testing has withstood legal challenges in Washington, DC, most jurisdictions that have pretrial testing programs limit them to offenders who have agreed to participate in exchange for incentives.

---

[2]The term "defendants" is used as a general term to refer to those arrested and not yet charged, those charged with an offense and awaiting case disposition, and those who have pled guilty to charges with sentencing or final case disposition pending. The term "offenders" refer to those who have been sentenced.

Testing after an individual has been found guilty and sentenced (Stages 3 and 4) faces fewer legal restrictions in most states. Sentences that impose conditions related to drug involvement may require offenders to comply with all conditions imposed by supervising agencies (including drug treatment or testing) or may explicitly order offenders to undergo drug evaluation and treatment. Following sentencing, drug testing may be conducted by corrections agencies or by treatment or case-management agencies that provide services for offenders.

Technology

A variety of biochemical assays can be used to detect drug use, including the testing of urine, hair, saliva, and sweat for metabolites, and the testing of skin for residues. In addition, subjects can be examined physically and/ or behaviorally for signs of drug effects; these approaches can vary from the police officer's order to "walk the line" to measurements of gaze nystagmus (micromovements of the eyeballs) or various kinds of cognitive or eye-hand performance. Considerations of speed of results, accuracy, cost, operational feasibility, equipment and staffing, and detection window enter into the choice of technology (see Bureau of Justice Assistance, 1999, for a review of these issues).

Biochemical testing of urine is, by far, the dominant technology within criminal justice agencies. Compared with other approaches, it is highly accurate and inexpensive. Its greatest limitation is its relatively narrow "detection window": heroin, cocaine, and methamphetamine use remains detectable in urine for only 48 to 72 hours. Hair and sweat testing offer longer detection periods at higher costs and with much longer lags between test administration and results; the accuracy of hair testing remains in doubt.

Among urine tests, the most commonly used is Enzyme-Linked Immuno-Assay Testing (EMIT). Automated EMIT testing is often used by programs that conduct a large number of tests at a central location. Handheld tests are often used for spot checks or programs conducting fewer tests. Confirmation procedures usually involve gas chromatography or split-sample testing. At large volumes, a five-drug EMIT screen can be administered at a cost of as little as $5 per administration, with virtually instant results. Specimen cups with built-in reagents offer comparable immediacy, at somewhat higher cost, in low-volume settings. Given the behavioral characteristics of drug-abusing offenders, the importance of immediacy is hard to overstate.

Surveillance Drug Testing

Since the early 1980s, surveillance testing has been used by some pretrial, probation, and parole agencies for offenders on community release. One of the oldest, large-scale, pretrial surveillance-testing programs is operated by the Pretrial Services Agency (PSA) in Washington, DC. Since 1984, PSA has routinely tested all arrestees detained in jail within 72 hours of arrest. PSA recommends to the court that those who test positive for illegal drugs be required to submit to random, twice-weekly drug testing as a condition of release.

Because pretrial conditions of release prior to case disposition must be demonstrated to reduce the risk that a defendant will fail to appear for a hearing and/or reduce the risk to public safety, early research focused on the question of whether drug tests shortly following arrest predicted subsequent misconduct. Evaluations of the efficacy of tests in predicting pretrial misconduct in five of seven sites produced mixed results (Visher, 1992a, 1992b). In Washington, the tests predicted failure to appear at pretrial hearings *and* new arrests during pretrial release. In Phoenix, Miami, and New York, the tests predicted new pretrial arrest, but not failure to appear in court. In Milwaukee, the tests predicted failure to appear in court, but not pretrial arrest. In Tucson and Prince George's County, the tests predicted neither of these outcomes.

A detailed reanalysis of the data from these evaluations (Rhodes, Hyatt, & Scheiman, 1996) found that positive tests for opiates predicted new pretrial arrest consistently, and positive cocaine tests predicted failure to appear for hearings and, in some sites, pretrial arrest. Positive tests for other drugs did not predict either arrest or failure to appear. The researchers suggested the use of results from multiple tests and tests that detect drug use over a longer period of time to improve the prediction of offender misconduct. This approach is used in Washington, DC, where released defendants who fail or skip two or more tests are offered treatment linked to graduated sanctions that are designed to enforce attendance and compliance with treatment requirements.

Data from five of the seven sites were used to examine the question of whether pretrial drug testing reduced offender misconduct during pretrial release. In one site, drug testing was significantly related to lower rearrest rates, but not failure to appear rates. However, in another site, the reverse was found: drug testing was related to failure to appear rates, but not rearrest rates. More important to justice policymakers was the finding that no significant reductions in either form of pretrial misconduct were found in three of the five sites. In part, the lack of significant effects may be attributed to implementation problems. The evaluation review of the results notes that these programs encountered problems, such as failure to test the majority of arrestees at the time of arrest, failure to refer arrestees to drug-test monitoring, problems in getting drug-test results and related information to judges at arraignment and at later hearings, and lack of judicial support for sanctioning noncompliance, that made it difficult to assess what the impact might have been had the programs been fully implemented (Visher, 1992a, 1992b). Together, the implementation challenges and the lack of clear evidence of impact discouraged replication of the programs by other jurisdictions.

Surveillance testing following conviction and sentencing is more widely accepted and used by probation and parole agencies. However, testing practices vary widely by officer, agency, offender risk classification, and substance-abuse assessment results. Differences in the frequency and randomness of tests, use of the results, and reasons for testing may have a significant relationship to their utility as a behavior-control strategy. Testing may be conducted only occasionally, when drug use is suspected, or used as a routine element of supervision. Test failures may trigger a treatment referral, a request for a revocation hearing, a warning letter, or nothing. The time between test and response can vary from a few minutes to weeks or months. "Instant" tests and on-site laboratories allow some agencies to respond almost immediately, while others must wait to get test results from off-site laboratories. These variations make it impossible to generalize about the effectiveness of drug testing by probation and parole agencies.

One note of caution about surveillance testing is raised by the findings from a large experimental evaluation of Intensive Supervision Probation (ISP). The 14 participating ISP programs used small caseloads, very frequent offender-officer contacts, strict enforcement of probation/parole conditions, community service, curfew, work requirements, and unscheduled drug testing. In five programs, more than 96% of the participants were drug addicted. The frequency of testing and, thus, the risk of detection varied from site to site. In eight programs, unscheduled drug tests took place four to eight times per month, but random testing was less frequent or more variable in the other sites. Overall, ISP sanction severity was high (reincarceration), but the certainty of sanction was variable. The evaluation found that ISP participants had *higher* rates of technical violations (primarily for drug use), similar rates of arrest and street days to first rearrest, and *higher* rates of incarceration (as a result of the technical violations) than control subjects at 1-year follow-up (Petersilia & Turner, 1993). As the authors concluded, "Putting drug-dependent offenders in a program that forbids drug use, provides frequent testing, and provides no assured access to drug treatment virtually guarantees high violation rates" (p. 320). The ISP findings further suggested that outcomes for offenders in surveillance testing improve if combined with services that promote rehabilitation. In ISP, participation in employment services, counseling, community service, and payment of restitution was significantly related to recidivism; higher levels of participation were associated with a 10% to 20% reduction in recidivism, although it is possible that those most motivated to improve their lives took part in these services.

The ISP findings do not stand alone. A 5-year longitudinal experiment of testing for offenders who were 18 or 19 years old at the time of parole found that more frequent testing was associated with increased risk of a new arrest (Haapanen, 2000). This study also indicated that positive drug tests in the first few months of parole predicted increased likelihood of a subsequent arrest and could be used as a risk-assessment procedure.

There is evidence, however, that pretrial surveillance testing, if linked to graduated sanctions, can deter drug use and crime. An experiment conducted in Washington, DC, compared voluntary, surveillance drug testing linked to graduated sanctions, but not enhanced access to treatment, with surveillance testing without sanctions or treatment referrals. Drug-felony defendants randomly assigned to the two different court dockets were tested twice weekly, and results were provided to judges via computer screens located at the bench. Those on one docket who were offered the chance to join a graduated sanctions program in exchange for an increased chance of receiving probation in lieu of incarceration were compared with a similar group of defendants assigned to the other docket. The sanctions for skipping a test or testing positive included 3 days in the jury box for the first test failure, 3 days in jail for the second, mandatory detoxification for the third, and a week in jail for the fourth.

These sanctions were implemented surely and swiftly: 97% of the test failures resulted in the scheduling of a review hearing; the large majority of the hearings occurred within a week of the test failure; and the sanctions were applied with great consistency. The evaluation found that testing linked to sanctions reduced both crime and drug use. Those subject to graduated sanctions were significantly less likely to fail or miss a drug test in the month before sentencing, less likely to be rearrested in the year after sentencing, and averaged more days on the street prior to a rearrest than defendants tested twice a week without sanctions (Harrell, Cavanagh, & Roman, 1999). Those in the sanctioning program who voluntarily participated in NA/AA groups showed the greatest reductions in drug use, again possibly because their motivation to change was higher than those who did not participate. Focus-group interviews found that participants were motivated to comply with testing requirements because they believed that the tests were accurate, had agreed to the rules in advance, and thought the judges were fair in applying the sanctions. In contrast, testing drug offenders during pretrial release and probation without systematic sanctions or treatment referrals had no significant impact on recidivism (Cavanagh & Harrell, 1995).

Testing Linked to Treatment

Drug testing has long been used by court-affiliated treatment providers. For more than 25 years, courts and corrections agencies have referred offenders to TASC (Treatment Alternatives to Street Crime), a network of specialists who find treatment placements for court-referred clients and then monitor their progress. Referrals to TASC included pretrial defendants (before and after plea), those accepted into specific diversion programs, and those sentenced to probation. TASC providers and their affiliated treatment agencies use drug testing to assist clients to confront their drug problems and to provide information on continued drug use for treatment guidance.

Evaluation of six TASC programs found reductions in self-reported drug use, but no evidence of reductions in subsequent arrests or violations of probation, when TASC participants were compared with comparable offenders (Anglin et al., 1999). In fact, arrest rates and technical violation rates were higher among TASC participants at the two sites with the most rigorous surveillance. However, many offenders referred to TASC programs do not ever report and others drop out, largely because justice agencies often fail to monitor compliance with treatment referrals or the results of drug tests. The failure of TASC to impose consequences for noncompliance is likely to have a negative effect on treatment entry and retention treatment. One evaluation of community-based treatment for offenders found that treatment combined with urinalysis and court monitoring with sanctions had higher rates of success than treatment alone (Falkin, 1993).

Drug diversion and drug courts represent efforts by the judiciary to reduce drug taking by offenders by monitoring treatment participation and making decisions contingent upon specified aspects of offender behavior.

Drug diversion involves offering defendants the option of a deferred, suspended, or probationary sentence in lieu of possible incarceration on the condition that they undergo substance-abuse treatment. Diversion programs vary enormously. Some are formal treatment plans administered under the rubric of TASC. Others are as simple as a judge's demand for "thirty in thirty" (attendance at thirty 12-Step meetings in the next 30 days) from someone accused of public intoxication or drunken driving. Many of these programs rely heavily on drug tests to provide an independent measure of progress toward abstinence.

In drug courts, the judge acts as the case manager, rather than delegating that responsibility to TASC. Defendants come in frequently to review their treatment compliance and drug-test results, and are praised or rebuked for good or bad conduct by the judge in open court, and sometimes given additional sanctions. After a period of months, the defendant is sentenced on the original offense, with the promise that the sentence will reflect his presentencing behavior.

Because diversion programs and drug courts are built around the idea of treatment, they tend to put as much stress on showing up for treatment sessions as on actual desistance from drug use. The programs also vary in operation. Some are set up to handle only first-time offenders or those charged with minor offenses. In others, a broader range of offenders is eligible to participate. Some drug courts accept offenders before a plea is entered, whereas others take offenders only postplea. Some are quick to apply punitive sanctions, ranging up to discharge from drug court and imposition of sentence, when participants continue to use drugs. Other courts view occasional lapses as a part of recovery and will retain drug-positive participants so long as they attend treatment and commit no new crimes. Many drug-court judges believe that praise and reprimand from the bench, backed with the judge's reserve powers of incarceration, will serve as sufficiently potent and immediate rewards and punishments without resorting to more material sanctions; others sanction routinely and by formula. (One drug-court judge who believes in formulaic sanctions likes to tell new defendants: "From this moment on, I have no control over what happens to you. The prosecutor, the probation officer, your attorney, the court clerk: none of them has any control over what happens to you. You control what happens to you.")

What drug diversion and drug courts have in common with other pretrial programs is that participation is voluntary (defendants can, and some do, choose routine sentencing instead) and restricted to defendants who the court and the prosecution are prepared *not* to incarcerate if the defendants will comply with program rules and stop using drugs. By definition, this excludes offenders whose crimes have been especially severe or violent. The federal law providing funding for drug courts specifies that defendants admitted to drug-court treatment must have no prior violent offenses. Thus, many of the most troublesome offenders, whose drug consumption it would be most valuable to influence, are not eligible for these programs.

As Table 13.1 indicates, eight evaluations using experimental or strong quasi-experimental designs report that drug-court participants are less likely to be rearrested following the end of the program than otherwise comparable offenders not enrolled in drug court. A smaller number of studies report no significant differences in recidivism between drug-court participants and others, including offenders randomly assigned to probation with or without drug testing, and comparison groups of similar offenders. Related findings include no difference in technical violation rates between: (a) drug-court participants and offenders randomly assigned to probation with or without drug testing, or (b) offenders in matched comparison groups, and a longer time to first rearrest than a comparison group. However, none of these studies has examined the effects of variation in frequency of testing or use of results as a determinant of drug-court outcomes. Drug courts and other programs that link offenders to treatment are currently trying alternative incentives and sanctions as a means of increasing offender compliance with treatment and testing requirements.

Lessons From the Offender Drug-Testing Experience

The preceding overview of drug-testing programs in the criminal justice system illustrates their diversity. Several key principles of effective use of drug testing emerge from evaluations of these programs.

- A combination of testing and treatment is likely to be better than surveillance testing or treatment alone. ISP programs in California that combined treatment with strict surveillance reduced recidivism by as much as 15% over high levels of surveillance alone, leading to recommendations that treatment be included as a part of efforts to reduce criminal activity among drug-felony offenders (Petersilia & Turner, 1993; Petersilia, Turner, & Deschenes, 1992). Treatment combined with urinalysis and court monitoring with sanctions is more likely to be successful than treatment alone (Falkin, 1993).

TABLE 13.1 Synopsis of Drug Court Impact Evaluations

Name of program	Design	Findings	Issues/concerns
Baltimore City Drug Treatment Court (Gottfredson & Exum, 2000). Program targets nonviolent, substance-abusing offenders. Treatment is comprised of 4 modalities: intensive outpatient, methadone maintenance, inpatient, and transitional housing.	Randomized experiment • Preliminary report compared 139 offenders randomly assigned to drug court with 96 offenders randomly assigned to traditional parole and probation services.	*Rearrest:* 44% of the participants were rearrested 12 months after disposition compared with 56% of the comparison group ($p = .06$).	Selection bias: Although authors used random assignment, this occurred after participants volunteered for the program. Therefore, self-selection into treatment may not be fully controlled. Short follow-up period (for some participants)
Maricopa County First Time Drug Offender Program (Deschenes et al., 1995). Program targets first-time convicted, felony-drug offenders. The 3-phase, 6- to 12-month program consists of drug education, social-skills training, relapse prevention, and attendance at 12-step programs.	Randomized experiment • 639 offenders were randomly assigned to: 1. Drug-court program, standard probation, no drug testing. 2. Standard probation with random, monthly drug testing. 3. Standard probation with testing scheduled bi-weekly.	*Rearrest:* 33% of probationers versus 31% of drug-court participants were rearrested during the 12-month follow-up. (Differences not significant.) *Technical violation:* 46% of probationers versus 40% of participants received technical violations at the 12-month follow-up. (Differences not significant.)	The GAO, in their review of this program, noted, "The results, especially those involving recidivism, fail to establish strong effects of testing and treatment. Part of the reason for this may be due to the fact that various programs were not always implemented as designed" (GAO, 1997, 102).

TABLE 13.1 *(continued)*

Name of program	Design	Findings	Issues/concerns
Dade County Drug Court (Smith, Davis, & Goretsky, 1991) (As described in GAO, 1997). Three-phase, 12-month program targeting offenders charged with third-degree felony-drug possession with no prior convictions. Treatment consists of detoxification, counseling, acupuncture and educational/vocational assessment.	Three-group, quasi-experimental design • Compared rearrest rates for: 1. Persons assigned to the drug court (*n* = 318). 2. A subgroup of persons assigned to the drug court who actually participated in it (*n* = 148). 3. A sample of pre-drug-court narcotics cases from early 1988 (*n* = 99).	*Rearrest rates:* Participants had the lowest rearrest rate (15%), followed by persons assigned to the drug court (32%) and pre-drug-court narcotic cases (33%). The length of the follow-up period and statistical significance was not reported.	Selection bias • Eligibility requirements changed over time. • Participation voluntary and, therefore, motivation may be driving the results.

(continued)

TABLE 13.1 *(continued)*

Name of program	Design	Findings	Issues/concerns
Dade County Drug Court (Goldkamp & Weiland, 1993). Three-phase, 12-month program targeting offenders charged with third-degree felony-drug possession with no prior convictions. Treatment consists of detoxification, counseling, acupuncture (if interested), and educational/vocational assessment.	Six-group, quasi-experimental design study compared: 1. Offenders admitted to the drug-court program ($n = 326$). 2. Felony-drug defendants not eligible due to more serious offenses ($n = 199$). 3. Non-drug-felony defendants in the same period ($n = 185$). 4. Non-drug-felony drug defendants in earlier years ($n = 302$). 5. Felony nondrug defendants from earlier years ($n = 536$). 6. Offenders assigned to the drug court but did not participate.	*Rearrest rates* showed 33% of drug-court participants were rearrested compared with between 48% and 55% of the comparison group during the 18-month follow-up period. (Statistical significance not reported.)	Selection bias • Participation was voluntary. Therefore, motivation may be driving the results. • Report states there was flexibility in the eligibility requirements. • Authors estimate that between 17% to 31% of defendants identified as eligible were not admitted to the program for numerous reasons.

TABLE 13.1 *(continued)*

Name of program	Design	Findings	Issues/concerns
Denver Drug Court (Granfield & Eby, 1997). Three-phase, tailored-treatment program. The levels range on a continuum of no treatment but judicial supervision (level 1) to therapeutic community placement (level 6). Level 7 consists of intensified surveillance but no treatment.	Three-group, quasi-experimental design • Study compared: 1. A random sample of 100 drug-court participants. 2. A random sample of 100 subjects from pre-drug-court years 1992/1993. 3. A random sample of 100 subjects from pre-drug-court years 1993/1994.	*Rearrest rates:* 58% of the drug-court participants, 53% of the 1993–1994 cohort, and 53% of the 1992–1993 cohort rearrested at 12 months. (Differences not significant.) *Revocations for violations of probation:* 22% of the participants versus 15% of the 1993–1994 cohort and 14% of the 1992–1993 revoked within 6 months. (Differences not significant.)	Sample size • Short follow-up period for revocations (6 months) and arrests (12 months, which includes the time in treatment). Selection bias • Random assignment was not used.
Oakland (FIRST) Drug Court (Bedrick & Skolnick, 1999). The program targets first-time possession-for-use cases eligible for diversion. Treatment consists of AIDS and drug-education classes, counseling, and group probation sessions.	Two-group, quasi-experimental design • Compared 110 drug court participants with 110 defendants assigned to diversion prior to inception of the FIRST program.	*Felony rearrests:* 18% of participants rearrested at 12 months compared with 35% of comparison group. At year three, 41% of participants, compared with 55% of comparison group rearrested. At year four, 47% of participants versus 55% of the comparison group rearrested. (Significance at 3 years $p = .05$.)	Selection bias • Author notes that eligibility requirements were waived for some defendants. • One third or more of diversion-eligible defendants failed to show for placement into the FIRST program.

(continued)

163

TABLE 13.1 (continued)

Name of program	Design	Findings	Issues/concerns
Florida's First Judicial Circuit Drug Court (Peters & Murrin, 1998). Three-phased treatment program lasting approximately 12 months. Treatment consists of counseling, group therapy, peer support, community-support systems, aftercare groups, and vocational training.	Three-group, quasi-experimental, matched design • Study compared completers, noncompleters, and a matched sample of court probationers from Okaloosa (n = 58) and from Escambia (n = 168).	*Rearrest rates*: 48% of completers compared with 63% of matched and 86% of noncompleters were rearrested over 30 months (p < .001) in Escambia. In Okaloosa, 26% of completers compared with 55% of matched and 63% of noncompleters rearrested (p < .01).	Selection bias • Participation voluntary and, therefore, motivation may be driving the results. • Completers differed significantly from noncompleters on education, race, employment, and arrest history. Small sample size in Okaloosa
Jackson County Drug Court Diversion Program (Jameson & Peterson, 1995). Three-phase, 12-month program consisting of drug testing, acupuncture, AA/NA meetings, and individual, group, and family counseling.	Two-group, quasi-experimental design • Compared rearrest rates for 450 program participants with a group of 4,755 comparable offenders admitted to the Jackson County Department of Corrections between 1991 and 1994.	*Rearrest* data found that 4% of participants were rearrested within the first year compared with 13% of the comparison group. (Statistical significance of the difference was not reported.)	Selection bias • Participation voluntary and, therefore, motivation may be driving the results. • Short follow-up period.

TABLE 13.1 (*continued*)

Name of program	Design	Findings	Issues/concerns
Multnomah County STOP Drug Diversion Program (Finigan, 1998). Three-phase, 12-month diversion program targeting defendants charged with felony possession with no evidence of drug dealing and no violent crime charges pending at the time of arrest. Treatment consists of group and individual counseling, acupuncture, and life skills.	Three-group, quasi-experimental, matched design • Study compared: 1. Random sample of 150 completers. 2. 150 noncompleters. 3. A matched sample of arrestees who were eligible for the program, but did not receive it.	*Rearrest rates:* .59 arrests (.23 for serious felony arrests) per drug-court participant compared with 1.53 (1.17 serious felony arrests) per comparable defendants who did not enter drug court at 2-year follow-up ($p < .001$). Completers had .36 arrests per drug-court graduate compared with .71 per noncompleter ($p < .001$) and 1.53 for the comparison group ($p < .001$).	Selection bias • Participation voluntary, and therefore, motivation may be driving the results.

(*continued*)

TABLE 13.1 *(continued)*

Name of program	Design	Findings	Issues/concerns
Santa Clara County Drug Treatment Court (Office of Justice Programs, 1998). The program targets repeat narcotics offenders with nonviolent criminal histories. Defendants with prior sales and trafficking convictions are not eligible. Description of the treatment program was not provided in the report.	Five-group, quasi-experimental design • Study compared: 1. Completers and still active (n = 269). 2. Participants (n = 388). 3. Eligible but did not participate (n = 325). 4. Defendants granted deferred entry of judgment (n = 2713). 5. Defendants on probation, but not participating in the drug-treatment court (sample size not indicated).	*Rearrest:* 1) 8% of completers and still active; 2) 13% participants; 3) 47% eligible but did not participate; and 4) 27% deferred entry of judgment rearrested in 2 years. 4.8% of the completers, 10.5% of the participants, 29.5% of the eligible but did not participate group, and 14.2% of the deferred entry of judgment group rearrested for drugs during the 14-month follow-up period. (Significance not reported).	Selection bias • Participation voluntary and, therefore, motivation may be driving the results. • Comparisons included persons still participating in the drug program. Therefore, the treatment group had a much lower risk for rearrest and relapse than the comparison groups.

- Surveillance testing linked to consistent and timely sanctions can reduce drug use and crime. In Dade County, felony defendants in the drug court were less likely to recidivate and had longer periods to rearrest than other felony-drug defendants (Goldkamp, 1993). In Washington, DC, defendants offered graduated sanctions, judicial monitoring, and referrals to treatment for drug-testing. Violations were more likely to test drug negative during the month before sentencing than a randomly assigned group of defendants on a docket that offered only judicial monitoring of test results (Harrell et al., 1999). Sanctions that are treatment oriented (e.g., remand to detoxification or more intense treatment) have been shown to hold great promise (Lipton, 1994).
- Surveillance testing may have unintended negative consequences. Increased surveillance and threats of penalties may also increase the detection of violations and failure-to-appear rates, thus increasing the overall level of incarceration unless the deterrent effect of testing outweighs the effect of increased levels of detection (Petersilia et al., 1992; Goldkamp & Weiland, 1993).
- Offenders should face negative consequences for drug-test failures. Drug-testing programs that do not provide sanctions for test failures generally are ineffective in reducing subsequent offending. Drug-court participants in Maricopa County did not differ from traditional probationers in positive urinalysis or recidivism rates following the court intervention (Deschenes, Turner, & Greenwood, 1995). However, these drug-court participants had fewer contacts with justice personnel and fewer alcohol and drug tests administered than the control group. System-wide drug testing that was not linked to systematic monitoring, sanctions, or treatment was found to have no impact on recidivism (Harrell & Cavanagh, 1995).
- Offenders need to understand the sanctions they face. At the heart of increased accountability is the forging of an understanding between the court and the offender on behavioral requirements and consequences. When drug-court defendants enter into an agreement with a judge, they accept a "contingency contract" that makes them accountable for participating in treatment and complying with a known set of rules, which offer sanctions and incentives that they can control through their behavior (see Inciardi, McBride, & Rivers, 1996). In focus groups, participants in the D.C. Drug Intervention Program emphasized the importance of knowing rules in advance (Harrell & Smith, 1996). This is likely to apply to offenders on probation and parole, as well as those in drug courts.

Major Issues

Drug testing raises a number of issues for justice agencies. There is an inherent tension in justice policies between the goals of offender rehabilitation, which often call for community placement, and the immediate need to protect the public from reoffending, which may call for incarceration. Moreover, those with the most serious drug problems may not be those with the most serious histories of nondrug offending. Different agencies and individuals place different values on these objectives. Although most would agree that criminal justice policy needs to balance these goals, there is no agreement on the optimal balance.

There is also insufficient empirical evidence on questions related to the tradeoffs that must be made. Too little information is available on how to use drug testing to manage the behavior of offenders released to the community. How often must tests be administered? What kinds of responses affect decisions to abstain from drugs, enter treatment, and remain in treatment? What kinds of treatment options are needed and how should those in need of treatment be identified? Should treatment be mandated or merely offered? (These last two questions grow in importance where treatment capacity is inadequate to handle even the voluntary caseload, and where criminal justice referrals compete with nonoffender clients for scarce treatment slots; it would be ironic if one had to commit a crime to get drug treatment.) Should responses to positive tests be different for addicted offenders waiting for an available treatment slot than for the responses to positive tests from those assessed to have less severe substance-abuse problems? Do the former deserve a grace period to allow them to get into treatment? Are incentives needed and how should they be used? While surveillance drug testing should theoretically increase the certainty of facing a penalty and thus deter drug use, refusal rates and other evidence in the ISP evaluation indicated that some offenders perceived the intense supervision as more punitive that the alternative incarceration, particularly since the supervision period often lasted much longer than the period of incarceration.

Effective use of drug tests by the criminal justice system is also plagued by the fact that this collection of agencies is not, in fact, a system. Agencies with different mandates, funding sources, and management that discourage collaborative resolution of common problems cannot be expected to work together unless prompted by some outside force. Jails and prisons are worried about space. Courts are worried about caseloads. Community corrections' officers face daunting caseloads that make individualized monitoring difficult. Their information systems are frequently inadequate—many lack even desk-top computers—and are rarely linked to other systems with information about their clients. They lack procedures for reporting the status of offenders to each other on a timely basis. Overloaded court dockets and crowded jails in many areas create delays in responding to reported violations. Procedures for obtaining and using reports from community-based treatment providers are even weaker. The incentive to look beyond immediate problems to systemic reform is weak. Despite these challenges, interest in and use of drug testing by criminal justice agencies continues to grow. As the following section indicates, newer programs are being designed to address these challenges.

Combining Surveillance Testing with Graduated Sanctions and Treatment

The popularity of drug courts, the generally positive evaluation findings on their impact, and indications that combining treatment and graduated sanctions with surveillance testing has given rise to new programs, now in the demonstration phase, that combine aggressive monitoring of offender drug use through testing with behavior-change strategies, including graduated sanctions and treatment. In these programs, the authority of the criminal justice agency to impose conditions on offenders is used to influence offenders' drug use and treatment participation. These programs generally offer incentives for entering and complying with treatment, sanctions for treatment noncompliance and testing failures, and judicial monitoring of results. They generally use drug testing to increase offender accountability by using relatively mild sanctions for a positive drug test rather than traditional revocation of bond or probation (accompanied by long periods of incarceration), on the grounds that relapses are expected, and that such sanctions can play a therapeutic role in encouraging offenders to persist in their recovery efforts.

Application of sanctions that are certain, swift, and appropriate to the offense has long been identified as theoretically important in the deterrence model of justice. Graduated sanctions, compliance hearings, and more frequent drug testing have been used by drug courts to respond to violations of the contingency contract. Similarly, incentives such as ceremonies, token gifts, and reduced intensity of drug testing, monitoring, and treatment have been used to reward treatment progress and compliance with requirements of drug testing.

Two large federal initiatives are currently examining the use of drug testing for early case identification and service referral.

*   Breaking the Cycle (BTC), a multisite demonstration program funded by the Office of National Drug Control Policy and the National Institute of Justice, is testing a model of intervention that uses drug tests immediately following pretrial release, with screening interviews to assign drug-using defendants to drug-testing surveillance and treatment as needed. Compliance with the testing and treatment is monitored and failures addressed using graduated sanctions. Findings from the Birmingham site indicate that BTC resulted in improvements across a 9- to 15-month period on two key scales of the Addiction Severity Index: the drug-severity composite score and the family-functioning composite score (Harrell, in progress).
*   Operation Drug TEST (ODT) began operation in 24 of the 94 federal judicial districts in the United States in Fiscal Year 1997. The TEST model calls for universal Testing prior to the initial hearing to identify drug-involved defendants; Effective Sanctions when defendants on release are found to be using drugs; and referral of drug-using defendants to Treatment as needed.

Other programs are focusing on offenders sentenced to prison or probation.

*   Connecticut has passed legislation to provide drug testing to monitor drug abstinence among convicted offenders offered community-based treatment in lieu of prison.
*   Maryland has mandated drug testing and graduated sanctions for drug-involved probationers.
*   Some judges are now monitoring probationers with regular postsentence hearings during which reports on compliance, including drug-test results, are reviewed.

Research on these initiatives is underway. Hopefully, results will provide guidance on a number of key issues, including: (a) what sanctioning procedures are most effective, (b) how the impact of sanctions for drug-test failures is affected by the balance between the certainty, swiftness, and severity of sanctions, (c) the difference in effectiveness of sanctions administered by judges, corrections officers, or administrative review panels, and (d) the role of incentives in gaining cooperation and compliance with treatment and testing requirements. Far more research on the effects of interventions on drug use is needed. Few studies have examined the likelihood or magnitude of reductions in drug use following intervention, which, even if temporary or short of abstinence, may result in benefits to the individual and community. Research also needs to examine the power of drug tests, combined with other simple screening procedures, to predict the risk of criminal activity while on community release and how this information should be combined with existing procedures for classifying offender risk. Perhaps the most important gap in the existing research is the failure of most studies of criminal justice testing programs to offer and test theories of offender behavior management that could be generalized to the wide variety of criminal justice settings in which drug testing has a potentially useful role.

14

HIV and AIDS Prevention Strategies

David Farabee and Carl G. Leukefeld

IV seroprevalence, the condition leading to AIDS, is substantially higher among U.S. prison and jail populations than among the general population. As of 1996, 2.3% of all prison inmates (both state and federal systems) were known to have HIV; of these, 23.6% had confirmed AIDS. Not controlling for demographic differences associated with risk of acquiring HIV/AIDS, U.S. prison inmates are approximately six times more likely than the general population to be infected with AIDS, with the rates of confirmed AIDS occurring in about 54 per 10,000 inmates versus 9 per 10,000 persons in the general population.

In order to appreciate the full magnitude of these prevalence figures, it is necessary to take into account the dramatic increases in the U.S. prison population over the past several years. HIV seroprevalence among male prison inmates has remained relatively stable from 1991 to 1996, ranging from 2.2% to 2.6% (see Figure 14.1). However, when these percentages are attached to population figures for each year, we see that the actual number of HIV-positive male inmates has steadily increased from 16,150 in 1991 to 21,799 in 1996—an increase of 34.9% over a 6-year period. Among female prison inmates, HIV seroprevalence has remained consistently higher than that found among male inmates, ranging from 3.0%

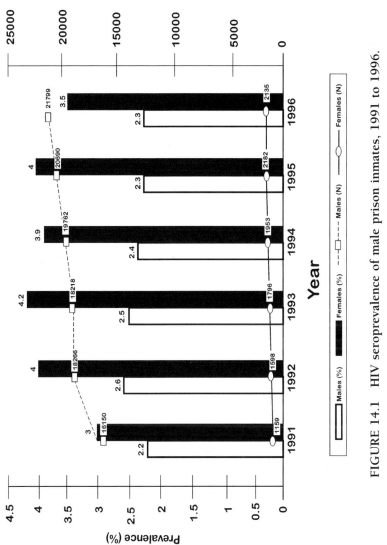

FIGURE 14.1 HIV seroprevalence of male prison inmates, 1991 to 1996.

Sources: BJS, National Prisoner Statistics; Hammett, Harmon, and Maruschak, 1999.

to 4.2%. Although females account for approximately 6% of the prison population (Bureau of Justice Statistics, 1999), their higher prevalence of HIV, combined with the growth of the female inmate population, has resulted in even greater relative increases in the number of known HIV cases. The number of female inmates infected with HIV grew from 1,159 in 1991 to 2,135 by year end 1996—an increase of 84.2%.

One of the most powerful predictors of HIV serostatus is prior drug use. According to Hammett, Harmon, and Maruschak (1999), the likelihood of testing positive for HIV increases linearly as a function of self-reported drug use, with a prevalence of 2.3% among inmates who had ever used drugs, 2.7% of those who had used drugs in the month prior to their commitment offense, 4.6% of those who had ever injected drugs, and 7.7% of those who reported ever sharing a syringe.

The strong association between drug use, particularly injection drug use, and HIV infection has drawn increasing attention from public health officials. This association is of particular concern for the inmate population, given their high prevalence of injection drug use. According to a nationally representative sample of U.S. prison inmates, 25% reported injecting drugs (most commonly heroin or cocaine) for nonmedical purposes at least once in their lifetimes. Twelve percent of the inmates reported at least one incidence of needle sharing (Bureau of Justice Statistics, 1991). Consequently, the higher levels of injection drug use found among the criminal justice population place them at increased risk of acquiring HIV. In fact, a recent comparison of all persons with AIDS, reported from January 1994 through December 1996, found that, while injection drug use accounted for 27% of AIDS cases diagnosed in the general population, it accounted for 61% of the cases diagnosed in a correctional facility. Conversely, while male-to-male sex was associated with 43% of reported AIDS cases among the general population, it accounted for only 12% of cases diagnosed in correctional facilities. Heterosexual contact accounted for 6% and 12% of the inmate and general population cases, respectively (Dean-Gaitor & Fleming, 1999).

The link between drug use and HIV, however, cannot be attributed exclusively to injectors. Edlin and colleagues (1992) found that female crack smokers were six times more likely than nonusers to have had more than 20 sexual partners, 15 times more likely to have engaged in prostitution, and four times more likely to have ever had a sexually transmitted disease. Although the advent of AIDS initiated an apparent trend toward safer sexual practices, particularly among urban men who have sex with men (Jones et al., 1987), HIV risk associated with drug use has proven to be less tractable. In fact, the proportion of new AIDS cases attributed to injecting drug use has steadily increased over the last several years, in contrast with the declining incidence of infection acquired through male-to-male sexual contact.

CONCEPTUAL ISSUES

Although a substantial literature already exists concerning HIV-prevention interventions in the community, implementing programs in correctional settings requires an understanding of some of the unique issues surrounding correctional systems and the inmate population. In this section, we focus on three areas: (a) the criminal justice setting as an opportunity for prevention, (b) vectors of transmission among the inmate population, and (c) strategies for prevention.

The Criminal Justice Setting As an Opportunity for Intervention

The high levels of injection drug use—and of illicit drug use in general—among inmates makes the criminal justice system an ideal point of contact for primary and secondary HIV-prevention efforts (Wish, O'Neil, & Baldau, 1990). Moreover, given the limited resources for widespread HIV prevention, there is a clear and urgent need to ensure that these services are provided to those who are at highest risk for acquiring HIV, such as substance abusers and criminal offenders.

Although the overall availability of corrections-based prevention services has increased somewhat over the past decade, many offenders still move through the criminal justice system without ever being exposed to any form of HIV prevention. In a study of prevention exposure among out-of-treatment injection drug users and crack users, Farabee and Leukefeld (1999) examined the likelihood of receiving HIV/AIDS-prevention information or supplies (e.g., condoms and bleach) as a function of having prior criminal justice involvement. Despite evidence of high HIV risk among criminal justice-involved subjects (particularly with regard to crack use and prostitution), prior incarceration was only minimally associated with prior HIV-prevention exposure or HIV testing.

The importance of reducing HIV risk among inmates is critical, not only because inmates represent a clearly defined high-risk group, but also because their separation from the general population is almost always temporary. According to a recent analysis by the Bureau of Justice Statistics (2000), the average jail sentence for felons in the United States is approximately 6 months. Felons remanded to a state prison in 1996 had an average sentence of approximately 5 years. However, based on current projections of actual time served, an inmate sentenced to 5 years in prison can be expected to be released in 2 years and 4 months. Overall, only 1.2% of felons are sentenced to life in prison. Hence, for all but a small proportion of state prison inmates—and for virtually all jail inmates—the impact of corrections-based HIV testing and prevention reaches far beyond the correctional setting.

Vectors of Transmission

Among inmates, the primary routes of HIV transmission, as in the general population, are through sexual contact and the sharing of infected drug-injection paraphernalia. Although most cases of HIV infection among inmates occur prior to incarceration (Withurn, 1993), mounting anecdotal and empirical evidence suggests that there is a continuing risk of transmission while in prison.

Sexual Contact

The most common route of HIV transmission (57%) among males in the United States is male-to-male sexual contact; among females, the primary risk categories are evenly split between injection drug use (42%) and heterosexual contact (40%) (Centers for Disease Control and Prevention, 1999). Consequently, there is a need to assess the rates of sexual contact among inmates. Estimating the prevalence of sex in prison has been problematic due to the reluctance of administrators to acknowledge the existence of banned activities in prisons, coupled with the problems of gaining accurate self-reports for such highly stigmatized behaviors. In-prison sexual activity, then, must be gauged generally from more than a single study. In these broad terms, estimates of male-to-male sexual activity (almost always unprotected) among prisoners range between 8% to 30% of the prison population (Nacci & Kane, 1983). Nonconsensual sex, or prison rape, among male inmates has also been cited as a risk factor. One study estimated that as many as 131,000 male inmates are forced to engage in sex every year (Donaldson, 1994). Among female inmates, occurrences of sexual contact are even less likely to be reported. Of special concern are the anecdotal reports of sexual contact between male correctional officers and female inmates (Solursh, Solursh, & Meyer, 1993).

Injection-Related Practices

HIV can be spread among injectors through direct or indirect needle sharing. Direct needle sharing, considered the riskier behavior, involves the use of inadequately cleaned needles or syringes by two or more people. Indirect needle sharing refers to the common use of potentially infected injection paraphernalia, such as cookers, rinse water, and cotton filters.

Self-reported in-prison drug use, like sexual contact, is likely to be underreported. Attempts to circumvent this problem by collecting inmate urine samples have also been difficult, due to inmates' being "tipped off" by corrections officers who provide illicit drugs at exorbitant cost (Inciardi, Lockwood, & Quinlan, 1993). However, one study of 4,800 randomly selected inmates in the state of Wisconsin found 27% of the inmates tested positive for illicit drugs. Although marijuana was the most common drug found, injectable drugs such as cocaine, opiates, and amphetamines were found as well (Vigdal & Stadler, 1989). But regardless of the types of drugs used, the fact that illicit drug use does occur in prison has empirical support. Exacerbating this problem is the increased risk associated with sharing injection works in prison. Because of the scarcity of needles and other paraphernalia, as well as cleaning agents such as bleach, inmates tend to share their inadequately cleaned works with large networks of injectors (Horsburgh et al., 1990). In fact, one study in Scotland found that the number of inmates sharing single syringes while in prison ranged from 5 to 100 (Kennedy, Nair, Elliot, & Ditton, 1991).

While the vast majority of HIV/AIDS cases are "imported" into the correctional system, several studies have documented seroconversion within the prison system. These studies found seroconversion rates of approximately 1% per year. However, statistical models including injection drug use as a factor estimate annual seroconversion rates ranging from 1.7% to 3.3% (Horsurgh et al., 1990).

Prevention Strategies

This section provides an overview of the four primary classes of HIV risk-reduction approaches used in U.S. correctional systems: HIV testing, education, psychoeducational programs, and substance-abuse treatment. Prison-based needle exchange and condom-distribution programs are also discussed, although such programs are rare in the United States.

Testing

Although HIV-antibody testing does not really qualify as primary prevention, it can be an effective component of secondary prevention. A number of recent pharmaceutical advances (e.g., protease inhibitors and combination antiretroviral therapy) have been shown to significantly delay the transition from HIV to AIDS, but the effectiveness of these medications is predicated on early detection of the virus. In addition, persons testing positive for HIV will typically show substantial reductions in risky drug use and/or sexual behaviors, thus reducing the rate of further infection.

Virtually all correctional systems in the United States provide HIV-antibody testing (Bureau of Justice Statistics, 1996). However, the policies that determine when and why an inmate is tested vary considerably. For example, the Federal Bureau of Prisons (BOP) provides HIV testing under three conditions: upon inmate release, upon inmate request, and to verify cases where there is clinical indication. BOP also conducts random HIV tests in order to estimate prevalence. Among state correctional systems (including the District of Columbia), inmates are most commonly tested at their request (78%) or to confirm clinical indications (74%). Only 32% of the state correctional systems test inmates as they enter the system. Perhaps the most disconcerting figure, however, is the lack of testing prior to institutional release, which was reported by only three (6%) states.

Education

The most common form of corrections-based HIV/AIDS prevention involves education. In 1997, instructor-led HIV education was reported by 94% of state and federal prisons, and 73% of city/county jails—a substantial increase over 1994, in which HIV education was offered in 75% of prisons and 62% of city/county jails (Hammett et al., 1999). The majority of instructor-led education programs tend to focus on basic information regarding the modes of exposure to HIV/AIDS and the interpretation of test results, rather than specific behaviors that can reduce HIV risk, such as practical suggestions for safer sex and injection practices.

Even if these educational programs were expanded to include these specific risk-reduction behaviors, however, it is unclear that education alone would result in meaningful changes in behavior. A recent study of incarcerated adolescents found significant increases in knowledge regarding HIV between 1988 and 1996. However, in spite of this increase in knowledge, this same study revealed that sex-related HIV risk had actually increased for the later cohort (Lanier, Pack, & DiClemente, 1999).

Psychoeducational Programs

There is evidence to suggest that the failure of didactically oriented education programs to bring about lasting behavior change can be attributed to the limited amount of cognitive processing this approach requires (Dees, Dansereau, Peel, Boatler, & Knight, 1991; Farabee, Simpson, Dansereau, & Knight, 1995). These studies indicate that, in order to be effective, a method of presenting prevention information must encourage the client to actively integrate personal and expert-generated knowledge. To this end, a number of promising "psychoeducational" strategies have emerged to address social and cognitive factors that lead to and maintain engagement in high-risk behaviors.

Among psychoeducational programs, there are considerable variations in philosophies and presentation formats. Grinstead, Zack, Faigeles, Grossman, and Blea (1999) argue that peer education is the most appropriate method of HIV intervention for inmates. According to these researchers, inmate peer educators possess the most knowledge regarding actual HIV risks for this population, particularly those risks that are heightened during incarceration. Moreover, because male-to-male sex accounts for a minority of HIV infections among inmates, it was argued that a prison-based program should primarily target the needs and motivations of heterosexual men. Using a randomized design, Grinstead et al. (1999) evaluated the effectiveness of a peer-led prerelease intervention intended to reduce HIV risk behaviors of inmates returning to the community. Although this study only had a 2-week follow-up response rate of 43%, results suggested that men who had received the peer-led intervention were significantly more likely to use a condom the first time they had sex after paroling. Intervention participants were also less likely to report using drugs, injecting drugs, or sharing injection equipment during the first 2 weeks following institutional release.

Employing a combination of social learning, self-help, and therapeutic community principles, Wexler, Magura, Beardsley, and Josepher (1994) developed and evaluated an HIV-prevention program for drug-injecting parolees entitled, "ARRIVE" (AIDS Risk Reduction for IV Drug Users on

Parole). This 8-week, 24-session program was led by recovering substance abusers, and consisted of eight content areas: creating a support group; epidemiology of AIDS; AIDS risk-reduction methods; AIDS among minorities; student presentations; links between depression and addiction; needs of persons with AIDS; and review of AIDS transmission, prevention, and treatment. One year later, parolees who had graduated from the program (68% of those who attended initially) were less likely than noncompleters to inject drugs and less likely to use illicit drugs in general. With respect to sexual risk, ARRIVE completers were less likely to have had sexual relations with high-risk persons and more likely to use condoms than were noncompleters.

Although HIV seroprevalence is higher among female than male inmates, relatively few studies appear in the research literature that evaluated female-specific prevention interventions. One such study compared a program based on social-cognitive theory with another based on gender and power theory (St. Lawrence et al., 1997). The program, based on Bandura's (1994) social-cognitive theory, addressed four key components: (a) information provision, (b) mastery of self-protective skills and self-efficacy for implementing these skills, (c) social competency, and (d) social support for precautionary changes. The other program, based on the theory of gender and power, emphasized gender-related power inequities, particularly in heterosexual relationships, that foster male dominance and coercion over females. Six-month follow-up interviews revealed somewhat positive effects for both strategies, with participants in the social-cognitive theory-based program demonstrating greater improvement in condom-application skills and participants in the gender and power program showing greater commitment to changing high-risk behaviors. However, whereas the between-group comparisons revealed minimal differences, there was a positive main effect over time for both groups on measures of self-efficacy, HIV knowledge, communication, condom use, and motivation for change.

Substance-Abuse Treatment

As mentioned earlier, injection drug use is associated with 61% of the cases diagnosed in a correctional facility, compared with only 27% of AIDS cases diagnosed in the general population (Dean-Gaitor & Fleming, 1999). Likewise, illicit drug users with prior or current criminal justice involvement are more likely to have traded sex for money or drugs than illicit drug users with no criminal justice involvement (Farabee & Leukefeld, 1999). It should also be noted that the level of substance problems among prison inmates is often quite severe. In fact, a recent study of the prevalence of DSM-IV-defined substance disorders among male inmates entering Texas prisons found that 56.4% of those interviewed met the diagnostic criteria for drug or alcohol abuse or dependence during the 30 days prior to incarceration (Peters, Greenbaum, Edens, Carter, & Ortiz, 1998). In contrast, it is estimated that substance-abuse treatment is available for about 12% to 20% of all state prison inmates (Bureau of Justice Statistics, 1995).

While the correctional treatment literature evaluating the effectiveness of substance-abuse treatment on reducing HIV risk is limited, the community-based treatment literature offers compelling support. A recent study of opiate addicts admitted to a 90-day methadone detoxification program demonstrated significant reductions in opiate use during treatment. Furthermore, these reductions were accompanied by substantial reductions in needle sharing, particularly with strangers (Iguchi, 1998).

Although studies of the effects of prison-based substance-abuse treatment on postrelease HIV risk are rare, at least one study suggests that such treatment can be effective, but only if provided in a continuous, staged approach that includes aftercare. The evaluation of Delaware's Key-Crest prison-based therapeutic community demonstrated significant reductions in 6- and 18-month postrelease drug use for treatment participants relative to comparison subjects (Inciardi, Martin, Butzin, Hooper, & Harrison, 1997). More importantly for the present discussion, inmates participating in the Crest (aftercare) program were less likely than those who did not participate to report any injection drug use during the posttreatment period (Inciardi, 1996). Furthermore, this same study revealed that the length of time spent in the in-prison (Key) phase of treatment was associated with increased rates of condom use following treatment.

Although HIV risk reduction was not specifically examined, a number of prison-based therapeutic community evaluations have demonstrated reductions in drug use among parolees who successfully complete treatment (Inciardi et al., 1997; Inciardi, this volume; 1996). It should be noted, however, that the impact of these programs is largely contingent on whether inmates participate in aftercare following parole. In fact, one recent evaluation revealed that inmates participating in prison treatment without aftercare tend to have similar long-term posttreatment outcomes as those receiving no treatment at all (Lowe, Wexler, & Peters, 1998). Thus, while it would be advantageous to include HIV interventions in substance-abuse treatment programs, the strong association between drug use and HIV infection among correctional populations ensures that even substance-abuse treatment alone can be a powerful strategy for reducing HIV risk.

We conclude this section on prevention with a brief discussion of two harm-reduction approaches: needle exchange and condom distribution. While neither of these strategies has gained much support in state or federal criminal justice systems, their popularity outside of correctional settings and in other countries merits some attention.

Bleach Availability and Needle Exchange

Currently, the possession of injection equipment is illegal in all federal, state, and local correctional facilities in the United States. Bleach for any purpose, although not specifically for disinfecting syringes, is available to inmates in 10 state and federal prison systems and 8 city or county systems (Hammett et al., 1999). While bleach availability is limited, a primary argument against needle-exchange programs, especially in a prison setting, is that the increased availability of needles, combined with tacit administrative approval of drug use in prison, will result in increased injection drug use by inmates. However, a report on a needle-exchange program for female inmates in Switzerland found that providing clean syringes did not increase drug use; however, it did result in significant reductions in needle sharing (Nelles & Fuhrer, 1995). Likewise, a recent study of a community-based syringe-exchange program in New York City revealed substantial reductions over time in the proportion of program participants who engaged in risky injection practices—from 26% to 3% over a 90-day period (Paone, Des Jarlais, & Shi, 1998).

Condom Distribution

Unprotected homosexual contact among males is not uncommon in prison, although specific estimates are difficult to obtain (Solursh et al., 1993). Outside of the United States, the high prevalence of risky sexual practices among inmates has led to administrative efforts to reduce the risk of HIV spread through sexual contact. In fact, a recent review of correctional public health efforts indicates that condoms and dental dams are currently distributed to inmates in 18 countries (Dolan, Wodak, & Penny, 1995). In addition, the World Health Organization (1993) recommended that all inmates have access to both condoms and cleaning supplies for syringes. In the United States, however, condoms are available to inmates in only two state or federal prison systems and four city or county jail systems (Hammett et al., 1999). A study of former New York prison inmates found that many male prisoners use makeshift materials, such as the fingers of plastic gloves, to protect themselves from acquiring HIV (Mahon, 1996). These same inmates, however, said that sexual activity within the prison is so highly stigmatized that the method of condom distribution would have to be extremely discreet in order to be effective.

Not unlike debates surrounding similar harm-reduction programs outside correctional settings, the critical arguments regarding condom-, syringe-, and bleach-distribution programs in prison appear to be largely philosophical. As briefly summarized above, there is substantial empirical evidence supporting the effectiveness of harm-reduction programs in reducing the institutional spread of HIV. However, correctional administrators are understandably reluctant to provide materials that directly facilitate—if not encourage—behaviors that are prohibited in prison. There is, in spite of research literature supporting the efficacy of these programs, a defensible perspective that sexual activity and drug use are behaviors under the control of the inmate and, therefore, a matter of individual responsibility.

CONCLUSIONS

The epidemiology of HIV/AIDS in U.S. correctional systems provides both reasons for optimism and concern. While the seroprevalence of confirmed HIV has remained relatively stable throughout the past decade, the growing correctional population has resulted in a 34.9% increase in the number of HIV-infected males, and an 84.2% increase in the number of HIV-infected females (Bureau of Justice Statistics, 1999). The rates of infection remain significantly higher among inmates than among the general population, with inmates being six times more likely to be HIV positive.

A number of HIV interventions are currently in place in federal, state, and local correctional systems. HIV education and testing are the most common interventions, with virtually all inmates being exposed to either or both while in prison. Unfortunately, testing policies are inconsistent between, and even within, correctional systems, and the HIV education offered in many institutions is cursory. In fact, Hammett et al. (1999) report that only 10% of state and federal correctional systems offered instructor-led education, peer-led programs, pre- and posttest counseling, and multisession prevention counseling. This is unfortunate, because several multisession psychoeducational programs show quite promising results.

Substance-abuse treatment is also considered to be a method of HIV prevention. As indicated above, HIV cases diagnosed in jail or prison are more than twice as likely to be associated with injection drug use than those cases diagnosed in the general U.S. population (Dean-Gaitor & Fleming, 1999). Thus, drug abuse treatment is particularly germane to preventing HIV risk among offenders.

Despite significant research support for harm-reduction measures such as condom-, syringe-, and bleach-distribution programs, and the increased use of these approaches internationally, correctional systems in the United States remain hesitant to implement these programs. Instead, many correctional administrators argue that the responsibility of sex- and drug-related HIV risk reduction is on the inmate—and that abstinence from these behaviors is a viable alternative.

FUTURE DIRECTIONS

This review of the epidemiology of HIV in corrections and the most common prevention strategies reveals a number of opportunities for future research, clinical, and policy development. Specifically, two areas are presented for consideration: (a) targeting personality and cognitions to reduce drug use, crime, and high HIV-risk behaviors, and (b) documenting prison seroconversions.

Targeting Personality and Cognitions

A body of literature suggests that a common set of psychological traits are associated with HIV risk, drug use, and criminal activity. For instance, Gottfredson and Hirschi's (1990) general theory of crime is based on the concept that individuals vary from one another in their levels of self-control and thus, in their ability to refrain from engaging in crime. According to these researchers, self-control is a continuous dimension, relatively stable throughout one's life course, and can account for a broad range of deviant activities, including drinking to excess, illicit drug use, and promiscuity. Indeed, impulsivity, a component of self-control, has been shown to be positively related to both HIV risk (Seal & Agostinelli, 1994) and the frequency of criminal activity (Luengo, Carrillo-de-la-Pena, Otero, & Romero, 1994; White et al., 1994). Likewise, decision making, which can be defined as an ability to consider various behavioral response options to a given situation, has also been identified as a predictor of risky sexual practices (Pinkerton & Abramson, 1995) and violence (Indermaur, 1999).

Hence, just as few criminals specialize in a narrow category of crime (Simon, 1997), high-risk sexual and injection behaviors are rarely isolated events.

Documenting Prison Seroconversions

As we indicated earlier in this chapter, empirical studies of seroconversions within the prison system are rare (Horsurgh et al., 1990). Given the growing number of incarcerated persons living with HIV, the rate of seroconversions is likely to increase. Since only three state correctional systems have a policy of testing inmates for HIV prior to release (Hammett et al., 1999), it seems that HIV testing should become part of medical examinations at prison entry, as well as upon release. This would provide for a valid estimate of seroconversions in prison, as well as reduce the likelihood of collateral infection once the inmate is released to the community.

The stable prevalence of HIV and AIDS in U.S. correctional systems offers a basis for cautious optimism. But the rapidly growing number of inmates these percentages represent underscores the need for continued pursuit of effective prevention strategies for this high-risk population. Inconsistent HIV-testing policies and education programs are, in and of themselves, clearly not adequate for decreasing the spread of HIV. Given that HIV is generally a behaviorally spread disease, effective interventions must target HIV risk behaviors directly, as well as the cognitive and personality styles that promote them.

15

Jail Treatment for Drug Offenders

Roger H. Peters and Charles O. Matthews

SUBSTANCE-ABUSE PROBLEMS AMONG JAIL INMATES

Correctional populations in the United States have expanded tremendously in the last 15 years, with more than 600,000 inmates occupying local jails (Gilliard, 1999). Jails now house up to 25% of state prisoners due to overcrowding in prisons (Beck, 1999), and increasingly have been used to detain individuals who are arrested for drug-related offenses and who have serious drug problems. For example, approximately two thirds of recent adult arrestees in metropolitan jails tested positive for drugs (Bureau of Justice Statistics, 2000), and 77% of local jail inmates have substance-abuse problems (Belenko, Peugh, Califano, Usdansky, & Foster, 1998), including a significant number who are polydrug users.

Although legislative, law enforcement, and correctional initiatives developed in response to emerging substance-abuse problems have focused heavily on reducing the supply of drugs and incapacitating drug offenders, there is growing sentiment that building new jails and prisons does not provide a satisfactory long-term solution to deal with this problem. The costs of building new jails and prisons are staggering, with construction costs for these institutions rising from $7 billion in 1980 to $38 billion in 1996 (Belenko & Peugh, 1998). Many jurisdictions have begun to reexamine the need to develop substance-abuse treatment programs in jails and prisons, and a number of such programs have been developed (Peters & Steinberg, 2000). These programs provide a range of promising alternative strategies to reduce criminal recidivism and to restore substance-abusing offenders to productive lives in the community.

THE ROLE OF JAILS IN PROMOTING REHABILITATION

In the past, jails have served primarily to detain pretrial inmates or inmates serving a sentence of less than 1 year. In this capacity, jails serve as a receiving facility for individuals who are waiting for arraignment hearings, trial, or sentencing. Jails also serve to hold violators of probation, parole, or bail bond, and those absconding from court-ordered programs or other community placements. Many juveniles are held in jail pending transfer to juvenile justice authorities, and a number of jails also hold federal or state prisoners. In some jurisdictions, the mentally ill are housed in jails until they can be civilly committed to community or state hospital facilities.

The role of jails has changed significantly in the last several decades, as funding for community mental health and substance-abuse services has diminished, and as local detention facilities have begun to adopt a broader mission to serve the community as "gatekeepers" in identifying and addressing a range of psychosocial problems, such as HIV/AIDS, domestic violence, educational deficits, homelessness, and mental health and substance-abuse disorders (National GAINS Center, 1997; Peters, 1993; Peters, Strozier, Murrin, & Kearns, 1997). This changing mission has been influenced by the recognition that jails serve as the repository for growing numbers of disadvantaged individuals who have been displaced from traditional societal "safety nets" such as state hospitals, and by the fact that without meaningful interventions, these individuals often cycle repeatedly through the courts, jails, and prisons.

Jails provide an important opportunity to identify substance-abuse and other psychosocial problems, to provide stabilization of acute needs (e.g., detoxification from alcohol or opiates, medication for psychotic or depressive symptoms), and to refer inmates to appropriate services within the institution or in the community. Jails often serve as the first point of contact for offenders who have substance-abuse problems. At the point of arrest and incarceration in jail, inmates may also be more aware of the negative consequences related to their substance abuse and more willing to enter a treatment program. Most of these individuals have not previously initiated contact with treatment agencies, and their first involvement in treatment services is frequently after involvement with the criminal justice system (Mumola, 1998).

OUTCOMES OF JAIL SUBSTANCE-ABUSE TREATMENT

In comparison to the research literature examining prison-treatment outcomes (Pearson & Lipton, 1999), there are relatively few studies describing outcomes from jail substance-abuse treatment. Several methodological limitations of jail-treatment research include a lack of high-quality, randomized, experimental designs, a restricted range of outcome measures, and an absence of lengthy follow-up periods. Despite these limitations, an increasing body of research has developed during the past 10 years, which provides reasonably consistent and encouraging results.

A number of studies document reduced rates of criminal recidivism associated with participation in jail-treatment programs. Several of these studies demonstrate reduced rearrest or reconviction rates among jail inmates who complete treatment relative to untreated matched comparisons (Peters, Kearns, Murrin, Dolente, & May, 1993; Santiago, Beauford, Campt, & Kim, 1996; Taxman & Spinner, 1996; Tucker, 1998; Tunis, Austin, Morris, Hardyman, & Bolyard, 1996), and program dropouts (Hughey & Klemke, 1996; Tunis et al., 1996). Reductions in arrest rates range from 5% to 25% in comparison to untreated inmates, over follow-up periods of 6 months to 5 years. Treated jail inmates have also been found to have a longer duration to rearrest following release from incarceration relative to untreated comparisons (Hughey & Klemke, 1996; Peters et al., 1993; Santiago et al., 1996; Taxman & Spinner, 1996; Tunis et al., 1996), and to have fewer average arrests during follow-up (Hughey & Klemke, 1996; Peters et al., 1993).

Other positive outcomes associated with in-jail treatment include reduced rates of relapse among treatment participants (Tucker, 1998), lower levels of depression (Santiago et al., 1996), and fewer disciplinary infractions (Tunis et al., 1996). Cost savings associated with jail-treatment programs have been reported from $156,000 to $1.4 million per year (Center for Substance Abuse Research, 1992; Hughey & Klemke, 1996). The only study reported in the literature that did not find improved outcomes among treated jail inmates examined a minimally intensive program (72 hours of treatment services) that employed a "Reality Therapy" approach (Dugan & Everett, 1998). The authors report that the short duration of treatment, the limited scope and intensity of program services, the absence of transition services, and lack of separation between treatment participants and the general jail population may have contributed to the absence of treatment effects.

Several studies have investigated the effects of duration of jail substance-abuse treatment on outcomes. Recidivism rates for offenders treated in a large, long-term, modified therapeutic community (TC) program were inversely related to the length of jail treatment, up to an optimal duration of 91 to 150 days of treatment (Swartz, Lurigio, & Slomka, 1996; Swartz & Lurigio, 1999). Greater length of treatment was also associated with fewer new offenses, fewer new arrests, and a longer duration until rearrest. A study of minimally intensive, jail substance-abuse education/treatment programs (Tunis et al., 1996) found that those involved in less than 1 month of jail programming had slightly higher rates of reconviction, in comparison to participants with longer program participation. Santiago et al. (1996) also report a positive correlation between the length of jail treatment and duration until rearrest, with an optimal length of treatment of 46 to 60 days.

Several studies highlight the importance of aftercare substance-abuse treatment services for inmates released from jail. Swartz et al. (1996) found that individuals receiving community aftercare services were half as likely to be rearrested, in comparison to those who did not receive these services, and had fewer new arrests. Similarly, Santiago et al. (1996) found that linkage with either residential or outpatient treatment services was associated with lower rates of rearrest during a 1-year follow-up period. Finally, Taxman and Spinner (1996) reported that nearly 50% of individuals receiving in-jail treatment received postrelease treatment in the community, in comparison to only 6% of untreated inmates.

THE SCOPE OF JAIL SUBSTANCE-ABUSE TREATMENT SERVICES

Findings From Previous Surveys

A number of efforts have examined the scope of substance-abuse treatment programs in U.S. jails. The American Jail Association (AJA) conducted a nationwide survey (Peters, May, & Kearns, 1992) examining the scope of substance-abuse services in jails. Although 28% of jails reported substance-abuse treatment services, only 18% involved nonvolunteer staff, and only 7% had a comprehensive level of services. More than 6,000 inmates in 3,328 jails across the country were interviewed in 1996 for the Bureau of Justice Statistics Survey of Inmates in Local Jails (Bureau of Justice Statistics, 2000). Although 25% of inmates with a substance-abuse history had previously received treatment services in jail or prison, only 4% of jail inmates received any type of treatment services during their current incarceration, and only 1.4% received counseling services. The Uniform Facility Data Set (UFDS) Survey of Correctional Facilities (Office of Applied Studies, 2000) surveyed 97% of U.S. jails ($N = 3,067$) in 1997, with 34% of jails reporting substance-abuse treatment programs (ranging from 0% of jails in Alaska to 91% of jails in New Hampshire), in comparison to 56% of state prisons and 94% of federal prisons. The Bureau of Justice Statistics (2000) conducted a survey in 1998 of more than 800 jurisdictions, finding that 43% of jails reported substance-abuse treatment programs, with rather wide disparities in the proportion of services reported among larger jails (74%) and smaller jails (34%).

Findings From a Survey of Metropolitan Jail-Treatment Programs

In order to highlight recent trends in U.S. jail substance-abuse treatment programs, a survey was conducted of 17 programs from 16 geographic areas. Jail-treatment programs were selected based on the following criteria: (a) programs that were developed in major metropolitan areas, (b) programs representing geographic diversity from each of the major regions in the country, and (c) programs that had been identified in the literature or by staff from the AJA, or that were known by the authors. Metropolitan jails were selected because they represent the largest inmate populations in the country, and because the literature indicates that these jails are more likely to provide comprehensive treatment programs (Peters et al., 1992).

Jail substance-abuse treatment programs were sampled from the following metropolitan areas: Albuquerque, Boston, Chicago, Dallas, Detroit, Houston, Fort Lauderdale, Los Angeles, Philadelphia, Portland (Oregon), San Diego, San Francisco, Seattle, St. Louis (Missouri), Tampa, and New York. A 65-item survey instrument was developed to describe qualitative and quantitative characteristics of existing jail substance-abuse treatment programs. Substance-abuse treatment program administrators within each jail were contacted, and all agreed to participate in phone interviews that averaged 45 minutes in duration. Estimates were obtained in cases in which exact data were not available. Meta-analytic weighting techniques were used to convert percentages and means reported at individual jail sites into valid estimates, based on the size of the relevant population (e.g., jail census, jail-treatment program enrollment).[1]

Characteristics of Jails Surveyed

The size of jails sampled in the survey varied from an average daily census of 281 to 19,500, with an average census of 5,687 (see Table 15.1). Most jails were operating near their rated capacity. Respondents reported that 80% of their jail populations had substance-abuse problems. Only 3% of the inmates described as having substance-abuse problems were actually receiving treatment in the jails, with a range from 1% to 18% in each jail surveyed.

Size and Duration of Treatment Programs

As indicated in Table 15.1, the number of substance-abuse treatment slots within a given program varied from 56 to 625, with an average of 160 slots. Jail-treatment programs averaged 13 weeks in length, although 19% of programs included 6 or fewer weeks of treatment. Programs averaged 26 hours of treatment per week, although this varied widely by program, as did the inmate-to-staff ratio.

Treatment Costs and Funding Sources

Annual costs of jail substance-abuse treatment programs varied from $105,000 to $1.5 million, with a mean of $671,367. The daily cost per

---

[1]For example, jail program administrators were asked to estimate the proportion (%) of their jail population that had substance-abuse problems. Each percentage total was multiplied by the corresponding jail census to produce an estimate of the number of inmates in each jail with substance-abuse problems. Totals from each jail were pooled to provide an estimate of the number of inmates in all of the sampled jails with substance-abuse problems. This total was divided by the total (combined) census of all jails sampled to produce a valid estimate of the overall proportion of inmates with substance-abuse problems.

TABLE 15.1   Characteristics of Jail Substance-Abuse Treatment Programs
and Participants

Characteristics	M	SD	Range
Jail			
Daily census	5,687	5,394	281–19,500
Percentage with substance problems	80%	—	60%–93%
Percentage receiving treatment[a]	3%	—	1%–18%
Program			
Annual budget	$671,367	452,570	$105,000–1,500,000
Inmate cost per day	$12.90	8.12	$4–33
Years of program operation	8.4	7	2–27
Admission waiting time (days)	23	—	0–60
Treatment slots	160	144.46	56–625
Treatment length (weeks)	13	7.75	3–52
Treatment hours/week	26	16.77	2–56
No. of paid treatment staff	10	6.75	3–27
Inmate/staff ratio	14.77	5.02	7–23
No. of volunteer staff	6.9	8.30	0–32
Participants			
Age	31	—	18–43
Gender			
Male	76%	—	0%–100%
Female	24%	—	0%–100%
Ethnicity			
African American	42%	—	4%–73%
Caucasian	39%	—	8%–80%
Hispanic	16%	—	1%–58%
Other	3%	—	0%–15%
Legal			
Prior felonies	4	—	0%–10%
Sentenced	59%	—	20%–100%
Unsentenced	50%	—	0%–100%
Court ordered to program	58%	—	0%–100%
Percentage with major mental disorders	26%	—	0%–60%

Note. Survey responses in the form of means and percentages were summarized as total means
and percentages using meta-analytic weighting techniques for accuracy; standard deviations could
not be calculated for these statistics. Due to missing data, percentages do not always sum to 100%.
Ranges are for unweighted data.
[a]Of those with substance problems.

jail-treatment participant ranged from $4 to $33. Programs with higher daily treatment costs offered more hours of weekly treatment services and had smaller inmate-to-staff ratios. There did not appear to be a direct relationship between the number of treatment slots and daily treatment costs per inmate. The cost per jail-treatment episode ranged from $329 to $2,008, with an average of $979 per episode. Programs with higher costs per jail-treatment episode featured a longer duration of treatment.

The most frequent funding source among jail-treatment programs surveyed was through the County Sheriff's Office budget, although supplemental funding was often received from federal, state, and local grants. Several state agencies provided funding for the jail-treatment programs surveyed, including departments of corrections, community corrections, and health/public health. The Governor's Office provided funding for treatment in one jurisdiction. Several program administrators expressed frustration that most grants support treatment programs of at least 6 months' duration, and that these grants are typically received by state corrections departments. Several innovative sources of funding for jail-treatment programs included state liquor excise taxes, inmate "canteen" and telephone funds, and inmate employment contracts.

Participant Characteristics

The characteristics of jail-treatment participants varied widely across programs, as indicated in Table 15.1. Jail-treatment programs serve a population that is young (M = 31 years), largely male (76%), and fairly evenly distributed among African Americans (42%) and Caucasians (39%). The majority (58%) of participants are court ordered to treatment programs as a condition of their sentence, and most have prior felony convictions. Twenty-six percent of participants were identified as having a major mental health disorder, and several programs reported that this proportion was significantly higher (42% to 46%) among female participants.

Staffing

Jail-treatment programs averaged 10 paid treatment staff, although the staff size varied considerably (see Table 15.1). An average of 83% of paid staff were licensed or certified, and 50% were in recovery from substance-abuse. Treatment services were provided by jail employees in 59% of programs surveyed, by contract staff in 18% of programs, and by both jail and contract staff in 24% of programs. One survey respondent noted that use of jail employees rather than contract staff allowed a greater level of "relationship-building" and cooperation between treatment and security staff. A number of respondents noted that high staff turnover was a problem in the early stages of program development.

Volunteers provided services in 88% of programs surveyed, and were most frequently engaged in providing 12-step groups. Volunteers also provided religious services, AIDS awareness/education, individual counseling, alumni services, health education, adult literacy, and parenting and anger-management workshops. An average of seven volunteers participated in jail-treatment programs, and volunteers provided an average of 4 hours of services per week.

Eligibility Criteria and Screening

All treatment programs surveyed require participants to have a history of substance-abuse problems or substance-related offenses as a prerequisite for program admission. Other important factors considered for program admission include a willingness to participate in treatment, security classification, sentence status, probation status, and whether treatment is ordered by the court. In some cases, priority placement is provided for sentenced inmates. Individuals who have severe mental health or medical problems or who have been receiving methadone maintenance are typically excluded from jail-treatment programs due to an absence of adequate ancillary treatment resources. Inmates with histories of violence or who are convicted of sex crimes, homicide, arson, child abuse, domestic violence, weapons offenses in jail, jail escapes, and drug dealing are also excluded from many metropolitan jail-treatment programs. Drug testing was performed by 41% of jail-treatment programs, and was conducted randomly in 35% of jails, at intake (17%), and upon suspicion of drug use (17%).

Referral Sources

Jail-treatment programs receive referrals from judges, attorneys, probation officers, inmates (self-referrals), and other jail staff (e.g., treatment staff, security, medical and psychiatric staff, and chaplains). Some treatment programs apparently screen all general-population jail inmates to identify those eligible for treatment, particularly those programs with restrictive admission criteria. One treatment program actively recruits new inmates during orientation meetings and in the jail "admission dorms" that house new detainees.

Assessment

Over two thirds of treatment programs surveyed administer a psychosocial interview, and 58% report use of standardized instruments during assessment. Assessment is typically provided at intake to the program, and the most common instruments used were the ASI (41%) and the SASSI (24%). In some cases, jails used only brief screening instruments (e.g., the SMAST, DAST) to select program participants, and in other cases, participants were selected largely by classification staff.

Programmatic Approach and Treatment Services

Most jail-treatment programs (76%) endorsed more than one therapeutic orientation or treatment philosophy, and several respondents described their programs as "eclectic," "integrated," or "holistic." Programs described the following type of treatment orientations: 12-step approach (76%), cognitive-behavioral (65%), relapse prevention (52%), and educational (47%). One program reported use of a boot camp approach. Almost 50% of the treatment programs reported use of TC models. Many programs reported that they had modified the TC model to provide a less intensive treatment approach of shorter duration, and with less emphasis on discipline, confrontation, and peer hierarchy, and more emphasis on enhancing treatment motivation and using group "process" interventions.

All but one of the programs surveyed (94%) reported that their substance-abuse treatment unit was isolated from other general-population jail inmates. The majority of programs (88%) reported that male and female inmates are treated in separate units, and only two programs (12%) provided co-ed programming. Several programs have discontinued co-ed programming because it proved too distracting for treatment participants.

Table 15.2 describes the range of treatment services offered in jail substance-abuse treatment programs. Each of the programs reported offering relapse-prevention groups and HIV education/prevention, and the vast majority also provided 12-step groups (e.g., Alcoholics Anonymous [AA]/

TABLE 15.2   Type of Jail Treatment Services Provided

Type of Service	Programs providing	Mean hours/ week	SD	Range
HIV education/prevention	17 (100%)	1.33	1.18	.1–4
Individual counseling	17 (100%)	1.00	.28	.5–1.5
Relapse-prevention services	17 (100%)	6.70	8.92	2–30
Education/GED	16 (94%)	11.73	8.65	1–30
Parenting skills	16 (94%)	1.94	1.61	.3–6
12-step groups	16 (94%)	6.27	3.70	1–12
Modifying criminal thinking	14 (82%)	7.69	10.14	1–30
Domestic violence treatment	13 (77%)	6.19	10.42	.5–30
Vocational/job training	11 (65%)	9.63	14.38	1–40
Dual-diagnosis treatment (mental health/SA)	8 (47%)	10.25	13.52	1–30
Acupuncture	3 (18%)	NR	—	—
Anger management	3 (18%)	2.00	0	2
Medically supervised detoxification	3 (18%)	NR	—	—
Family therapy	2 (12%)	NR	—	—
Sexual trauma treatment	2 (12%)	NR	—	—

Note. Means, standard deviations, and ranges were calculated of those programs that offered a particular service and were able to quantify the weekly hours of that service. NR, not reported by programs.

Narcotics Anonymous [NA]). Although all programs provided individual counseling, this was typically limited to managing crisis situations. Most jail-treatment programs provided parenting skills' classes, interventions to address criminal thinking, and services to address domestic violence, although these services ranged from marginally intensive to use of lengthy, structured curriculum. All but one program surveyed provided education or GED services, although only 65% reported providing vocational training. HIV education and medically supervised detoxification were frequently provided by other departments within the jail (e.g., health or medical services). A few programs also reported providing acupuncture, sexual-trauma treatment, and family therapy.

Specialized Mental Health Services

Most metropolitan jail-treatment programs (71%) refer inmates who have co-occurring mental health disorders to psychiatric or mental health departments for consultation, evaluation for medication, and/or stabilization. Several jails also provide psychological evaluation, individual and group counseling, and case-management services. Two programs had developed specialized dual-diagnosis units, with one unit located in a jail mental-health department, and the other located in a modified TC for mentally ill chemical abusers (MICAs). Three programs (18%) provided no specialized services for participants with co-occurring disorders, and in several cases, these individuals were deliberately screened out of programs.

Program Phases

More than half (59%) of survey respondents reported that they provided different "phases" of in-jail treatment, typically involving three levels of varying treatment intensity. Initial phases of jail treatment include assessment, intake, orientation, motivational enhancement, and medical detoxification. Intermediate phases of treatment are more intensive and provide a focus on skill building, psychoeducational activities, and 12-step groups. Final phases of treatment tend to emphasize relapse prevention, transition planning, and community linkage.

Transition and Reentry Services

Each of the jail-treatment programs provided transition and reentry services. The most common types of transition services provided were assessment of aftercare needs, discharge planning, placement planning, and linkage with community-treatment agencies. Transition and reentry services are typically provided by jail aftercare coordinators, community resource coordinators, jail-treatment counselors, aftercare counselors, and case managers. Specialized reintegration programs are provided in several jail programs, including reentry classes and groups in which inmates are actively involved in postrelease planning. Several jail-treatment programs prepare individualized postrelease plans related to housing, aftercare, relapse prevention, and employment. One program reported sharing participants' postrelease plans and other information with community-treatment and criminal justice agencies, and also provided transportation to community-treatment providers upon release and arranged for participants' medications needs. These interventions have apparently reduced recidivism among the program's graduates, particularly those "revolving-door" inmates who have co-occurring mental health and substance use disorders.

Several jail-treatment programs fund aftercare services through contracts with community-treatment providers. Other programs provide graduated release through community corrections work-release programs that include use of electronic monitoring and involvement in court-monitored treatment. In-reach services are provided by community agencies prior to inmates' release in several jail programs, including treatment-placement interviews, family liaison, counseling services, transportation to community-treatment programs, and tracking to monitor postrelease involvement in community-treatment services. Barriers to effective aftercare and transition services include homelessness and lack of stable housing among program participants, and limited availability of community-treatment services. Coordinating and timing inmates' release from jail treatment is also difficult due to the limited availability of community-treatment slots and to the uncertain dates of hearings and release from jail for pretrial inmates.

Linkage with Drug Courts and Other Diversion Programs

All respondents reported the availability of programs designed to divert substance-abusing offenders from jail or prison to community treatment, including drug courts and community supervision coupled with treatment and regular drug testing. Sixty-five percent of jail-treatment programs admitted drug-court participants who had received jail time as a sanction. Among these programs, the mean duration of treatment for drug-court participants was 51 days (range = 3.5 to 150 days). Benefits associated with drug-court involvement included a greater likelihood that participants will complete treatment and the inclusion of jail programs in a continuum of community-treatment services. Problems related to drug-court involvement have resulted from the absence of available treatment slots, which has led to lengthy periods of confinement prior to placement in some jail-treatment programs. Conversely, some drug courts do not provide sanctions that allow adequate time for participants to complete the jail-treatment program. Other diversion arrangements include an in-jail day-treatment program for women who are allowed to reside in the community, boot camps providing drug education for youthful offenders, and court-ordered treatment in secure community-based facilities.

Program Completion and Disposition Status

Survey respondents indicated high rates of completion from jail-treatment programs (67%). Most program graduates were released to the community

(76%) and were typically placed on community supervision (62%). However, less than 50% of graduates were court ordered to receive substance-abuse treatment in the community following release from jail. About 25% of program graduates were transferred to other jail units to complete their sentence.

Program Modification and Development

Many jail programs reported significant changes that had occurred over time, most frequently involving improved linkages to community services, including drug courts, community providers, and Treatment Alternatives for Safer Communities (TASC) services. Several programs also indicated improved coordination with corrections staff, enhanced funding, and development of new treatment curricula (e.g., the addition of domestic violence and parenting skills' curricula). A number of treatment programs were relocated, and others reported changes in the eligibility criteria, treatment approach, and program size. In one program, aftercare services have been augmented during the month following release in response to research showing significant rates of relapse and recidivism during that period of time. Many jail programs reported an increasing demand for treatment slots from the criminal courts, although this has not typically been accompanied by additional funding to expand treatment services. Additionally, in a number of programs, funding had been discontinued or reduced, in some cases due to expiration of federal grants.

Several innovative approaches described by respondents included development of specialized "tracks" for juveniles charged as adults, blending domestic violence and substance-abuse treatment services, integrated dual-diagnosis treatment services for inmates with co-occurring disorders, DUI-focused treatment, and gender- and culture-appropriate programming. A number of programs reported use of alumni groups, peer-based programs, and peer-support/monitoring groups. Other programs feature criminal-thinking classes, parenting skills, and acupuncture. One program reported a unique track combining relapse-prevention approaches with achievement and entrepreneurship training.

Seventy-one percent of respondents reported plans to develop new program components, including three jails (18%) planning services for juveniles charged as adults, two jails (12%) developing dual-diagnosis tracks (including a specialty track focused on ADHD and substance-abuse), and one jail planning to develop a separate track of shorter duration (e.g., less than 6 months). One jail will soon begin to offer follow-up services to program graduates who have been transferred to the general jail population. Another jail is planning to develop culturally appropriate programs and bilingual staff to serve the needs of Hispanic inmates.

Barriers to Program Implementation

The most common barrier to program implementation cited by survey respondents was a lack of adequate funding (68%), followed by difficulties in communication and coordination between corrections and treatment staff (38%), and lack of support and commitment from correctional administrators (31%), which was often related to changes in correctional administration. Two programs (13%) described shortages of space for treatment activities, and other programs indicated difficulties finding adequate participant time for treatment due to facility constraints on inmates' schedules and competing institutional activities.

POLICY IMPLICATIONS AND DIRECTIONS FOR FUTURE RESEARCH

The contours of U.S. jail populations have clearly been shaped by the massive influx of drug offenders in the last 15 years. This trend has been influenced by new drug enforcement and sentencing policies and by the absence of a comprehensive strategy to enhance demand reduction through treatment programs for offenders diverted from incarceration. In the absence of legal mandates to provide treatment services for the 70% to 85% of jail inmates who have substance-abuse problems (Belenko et al., 1998; National Center on Addiction and Substance-abuse, 1998; National Institute of Justice, 1998), it is encouraging that the proportion of jails providing substance-abuse treatment services has apparently expanded from 28% to 43% between 1990 and 1998 (Bureau of Justice Statistics, 2000; Peters et al., 1992). Despite this expansion, there has been simultaneous growth in the number of substance-involved inmates housed in jails. Additionally, in-jail treatment programs typically have relatively few slots in comparison to the overall jail population. As a result of these factors, only 4% of jail inmates needing substance-abuse treatment currently receive treatment services (Bureau of Justice Statistics, 2000).

The "gap" between the need for treatment and available treatment-services delivered appears to be significantly greater in jails than in federal and state prisons, where 10% and 13% of respective inmate populations are involved in treatment (National Center on Addiction and Substance-abuse, 1998). The largest gap in treatment services appears to be in small jails (Bureau of Justice Statistics, 2000), which are the least likely to provide treatment. The gap between the need for treatment services and available services reflects an oversight in public policy designed to reduce crime in the United States, and a "missed opportunity" (National Center on Addiction and Substance-abuse, 1998) to intervene with a large group of offenders who are unlikely to voluntarily enter community-treatment programs and who are at high risk for reincarceration. Potential cost savings associated with jail treatment appear to far outweigh the modest costs of treatment. Societal cost savings related to correctional treatment are estimated at approximately $69,000 for each successful treatment participant (National Center on Addiction and Substance-abuse, 1998), while the cost per jail-treatment episode[2] averages less than $1,000.

The research literature provides consistent support for the effectiveness of jail substance-abuse treatment in reducing recidivism and extending the length of time that participants are arrest free in the community. Although reductions in recidivism related to participation in jail treatment are less impressive than those resulting from prison-treatment programs, the costs of jail-treatment programs are significantly lower, due to the shorter duration of treatment in jails. While duration of up to 90 days of jail treatment appears directly related to criminal justice outcomes (Santiago et al., 1996; Swartz et al., 1996; Tunis et al., 1996), positive outcomes have also been detected among programs of significantly shorter duration (e.g., 6 weeks; Peters et al., 1993). Another benefit of jail-treatment programs is their ability to provide an effective transition to community-treatment services, due to their close proximity to the inmates' home environment. Research confirms that transition/aftercare services are an important predictor of positive treatment outcomes (Santiago et al., 1996; Swartz et al., 1996).

Findings from jail-outcome research indicate a clear need to expand the scope of substance-abuse treatment services available in U.S. jails. The range of diversionary programs (e.g., drug courts) should also be expanded throughout the country, to provide treatment opportunities for offenders who do not require treatment services in a secure setting. Unfortunately, the majority of federal grant programs currently restrict funds for correctional

---

[2]Excluding normal costs of incarceration.

treatment to programs of at least 6 months' duration, which is too long a duration to be implemented in most jail settings due to the relatively short periods of confinement. Moreover, the decentralized location of jail operations and funding through county governments inhibit advocacy efforts at the state and federal levels to expand inmate services, and generally discourage a "systems" approach to developing jail services at more than just the local level. An important first step toward addressing the treatment gap in jails would be to expand eligibility for federal grant programs, such as the Residential Substance-abuse Treatment (RSAT) program, to support development of jail-treatment programs of moderate duration (e.g., at least 2 months). A review of the RSAT grant eligibility requirements is currently underway to address this issue. State jail authorities are also needed to develop guidelines for inmate services and other aspects of jail operations, to monitor implementation of key services, and to work with legislatures and local government to obtain appropriate funding for these services.

According to the current survey results, metropolitan jail programs are characterized by high intensity, moderate duration, and a comprehensive scope of substance-abuse treatment services. Over two thirds of participants complete jail-treatment programs, which is a significantly higher rate than in community-treatment programs (Onken, Blaine, & Boren, 1997). However, these programs provide services to only a small fraction of jail inmates who need substance-abuse treatment services. The current survey indicates that scarce jail-treatment slots have increasingly been allocated to inmates sentenced by the criminal courts. As a result, there are fewer slots available for unsentenced, pretrial inmates. Despite more frequent court referrals to metropolitan jail-treatment programs, less than 50% of treatment graduates are required to participate in postrelease treatment services. Research indicates that a lack of postrelease services undermines the effects of in-jail treatment. Another problem identified by the survey is that 25% of metropolitan jail-treatment graduates are transferred to general-population units, where they are exposed to the potentially corrosive effects of untreated jail inmates. Greater coordination is needed by these programs to ensure that treatment graduates are released directly to community-treatment programs or to "alumni" or "transition" dorms within the jail that provide ongoing services (e.g., 12-step groups, transition services) in an environment that supports ongoing recovery.

The current survey also identified increasing needs within jails to develop treatment services for special populations, including females, juveniles, and inmates with co-occurring mental health disorders. Innovative approaches developed within several metropolitan jails to address these growing populations include specialized, dual-diagnosis units for inmates with co-occurring mental health disorders, as well as specialized treatment programs for females, juveniles, and domestic violence offenders and DUI offenders. There is also an urgent need to expand transition and community-linkage services within jail substance-abuse treatment programs, as reflected by the significant number of program graduates who are released to the community without court orders to participate in continuing treatment. Transition services are often the last to be funded and implemented within jail-treatment programs, although they are perhaps the most important in preventing substance-abuse relapse and recidivism. Many of the metropolitan jail-treatment programs surveyed are attempting to develop better linkages with community-treatment agencies and drug courts through "in-reach" and "out-reach" services, and through contracts developed with community-treatment providers to ensure continuity of postrelease services. However, a lack of funding to support aftercare services, and a shortage of available community-treatment slots remain major barriers to improving transition services. Consistent with other studies (Bureau of Justice Statistics, 2000; Office of Applied Studies, 2000), the current survey identified a critical shortage of detoxification services in jails. The current survey also detected the need for additional cross-training of substance-abuse treatment and correctional staff, including jail administrators.

Additional jail-treatment research is needed to identify inmate characteristics that predict retention and other positive outcomes of treatment, as well as to identify treatment-matching strategies for placement in jail and postrelease services. Optimal lengths and types of jail-treatment also need to be explored more carefully. Research should also examine the effectiveness of innovative jail-treatment approaches that have emerged in the last several years, including specialized tracks, supplementary groups, and special units designed for high-risk populations, and partnerships between jail-treatment programs and drug courts. Successful models of collaboration between jail treatment and corrections staff also need to be identified.

Jail-treatment outcome studies would benefit from use of randomized, experimental designs, extended follow-up periods (e.g., several years), and multiple outcome measures (e.g., rearrest, substance-abuse, utilization of public services, and employment). Continuing research is clearly needed to examine the cost effectiveness of jail substance-abuse treatment, for example, through assessment of the economic impact of treatment on crime and utilization of health care and other services. Without further evidence of cost effectiveness, it is unlikely that significant policy change will occur to enhance the scope of jail substance-abuse treatment services.

16

The Importance of Aftercare in a Corrections-Based Treatment Continuum

James A. Inciardi, Hilary L. Surratt, Steven S. Martin, and Robert M. Hooper

Relapse is a constant among individuals undergoing treatment for substance-abuse disorders. High relapse rates are common across addictions, and most typically occur during the first 3 months following treatment initiation (Hitchcock, Stainbeck, & Roque, 1995). Relapse is also a significant problem for patients who have completed treatment. And importantly, high relapse rates following treatment tend to push up the costs of effective care due to the necessity of multiple treatment episodes. In the face of this evidence, researchers and clinicians have suggested that one effective way to maintain initial treatment gains and to bolster the recovery process is through participation in aftercare beyond that of primary treatment (De Leon, 1990–1991).

NATURE OF AFTERCARE

Aftercare treatment is defined as a set of supportive and therapeutic activities designed to prevent relapse and maintain behavioral changes achieved in previous treatment stages (Fortney, Booth, Zhang, Humphrey, & Wiseman, 1998). Aftercare provides social support, linkages to resources, and the coping strategies needed to buffer the stress and anxiety associated with the transition to community-based life. Aftercare also facilitates the detection of minor relapse episodes, thereby helping to prevent complete reversion to problem drinking and/or drug use. Often there are behavioral, attitudinal, emotional, or cognitive signs of relapse that precede actual reuse of a drug (De Leon, 1990–1991). Aftercare programs that have the capability of detecting these early warning signals can take the necessary steps to prevent a full relapse.

Another essential component of the successful aftercare program is the location and development of a community-resource network that can actively support the client's changing lifestyle. It is likely that many recovering addicts will have had limited experience in dealing with day-to-day problems in an effective and functional manner (Brown & Ashery, 1979). Moreover, members of an individual's social circle and community are likely to persist in their perception of the client as a drug user. As such, there is little reason to believe that the client can assume and maintain the unfamiliar roles of stable employee or responsible family member without consistent support (Brown & Ashery, 1979; De Leon, 1990–1991). Aftercare programs may assist in this process by linking individuals with a variety of essential services, including housing, legal aid, educational assistance, and employment assistance.

Although the effectiveness of aftercare has been understudied, there is evidence that greater participation is associated with better alcohol- and drug-use outcomes (McKay et al., 1998). Several studies have reported that longer treatment duration predicts improved outcome, including abstinence or less frequent drug use at follow-up (Higgins & Budney, 1997; Lash, 1998). Thus, providing aftercare as a follow-up to inpatient treatment may improve overall treatment effectiveness. Relapse rates for alcoholics who participate in aftercare, for example, are substantially lower than rates for those who do not participate in aftercare (Lash, 1998). Aftercare participation following inpatient treatment has also been associated with greater social stability, as well as better cognitive and psychological functioning. Even when the primary treatment phase is relatively brief, the duration of aftercare can significantly postpone time to relapse (Rychtarik, Prue, Rapp, & King, 1992). The gains accrued in the primary phase of treatment, however, are nevertheless critical to overall success. Cocaine and alcohol abusers, for example, who fail to sharply reduce or eliminate drug abuse during primary treatment tend to have significantly worse attendance in aftercare (McKay et al., 1998).

Although these studies point to the importance of aftercare services, they also raise questions about the causal role of aftercare in promoting better drug-use outcomes. Most studies suggesting a positive relationship between aftercare and successful outcome are correlational, and, therefore, do not exclude the possibility that those most motivated to succeed are the individuals who consistently attend aftercare sessions, or that doing well leads to greater use of aftercare services. Despite these contentions, researchers using cross-lagged designs have argued that the pattern of correlations between substance use and aftercare attendance over time was consistent with aftercare promoting sobriety, rather than sobriety promoting aftercare attendance (Vanicelli, 1978).

The need for aftercare in corrections-based treatment programs was first noticed more than 50 years ago. Toward the close of the 1920s, as growing numbers of heroin addicts were being sentenced to federal penitentiaries, several members of Congress advocated the establishment of federal "narcotics farms" for the treatment of drug-addicted prisoners. The result was the Porter Narcotic Farm Act in 1929, which led to the establishment of narcotics farms (later called Public Health Service hospitals) in Lexington, Kentucky, in 1935, and in Fort Worth, Texas, in 1938 (Eddy, 1973, p. 25). Under the Porter Act, drug offenders convicted in federal courts could be sent to the farms by the sentencing judge in lieu of conventional imprisonment. This became the principal function of the Lexington and Fort Worth facilities, which were, in fact, run like medium-security prisons (King, 1972, p. 157). The 6-month treatment regimen included detoxification, psychotherapy, and vocational counseling, but follow-up studies found the programs to be quite ineffective, primarily because of the lack of community-based aftercare (O'Donnell & Ball, 1966, pp. 175–176).

Although corrections-based treatment for substance abusers has been a growing trend since the late 1980s (Inciardi, 1993), only recently have prison-based programs included aftercare components. Preliminary outcome data, furthermore, highlight the importance of aftercare in such a setting (Wexler, in press). In recent follow-up studies of drug-involved offenders receiving treatment in a prison therapeutic community (TC) in the California correctional system, for example, there were more positive outcomes for those who received treatment with aftercare than those who did not receive aftercare programming (Wexler, Melnick, Lowe, & Peters, 1999). More specifically, comparisons across the 12-, 24-, and 36-month follow-up periods demonstrated consistent positive outcomes with the completion of aftercare. Although recidivism rates increased for all study groups (control, TC dropouts, TC graduates, aftercare completers) as time at risk increased from 12 to 36 months, those who completed both the in-prison and aftercare phases of treatment had the lowest rates of recidivism. Studies in Texas not only document the effectiveness of intensive prison-based treatment when it is integrated with aftercare (Knight, Simpson, & Hiller, 1999), but also demonstrate that treatment is more cost effective when aftercare is included (Griffith, Hiller, Knight, & Simpson, 1999). The design of the Delaware corrections-based treatment continuum provides an additional opportunity to examine the impact of aftercare on long-term treatment outcome.

THE CORRECTIONS-BASED TREATMENT CONTINUUM

Based on experiences with correctional systems and populations, with corrections-based drug treatment, and with the evaluation of a whole variety of correctional programs, it would appear that the most appropriate strategy for effective treatment intervention with inmates would involve long-term TC treatment in a three-stage process (Inciardi, Lockwood, & Martin, 1991). Each stage in this regimen of treatment would correspond to the inmate's changing correctional status—incarceration, work release, and parole (or whatever other form of community-based correction operates in a given jurisdiction).

The *primary stage* should consist of a prison-based TC designed to facilitate personal growth through the modification of deviant lifestyles and behavior patterns. Segregated from the rest of the penitentiary, recovery from drug abuse and the development of prosocial values in the prison TC would involve essentially the same mechanisms seen in community-based TCs. Therapy in this primary stage should be an on-going and evolving process. Ideally, it should endure for 9 to 12 months, with the potential for the resident to remain longer, if necessary. As such, recruits for the TC should be within 18 months of their work-release date at the time of treatment entry.

It is important that TC treatment for inmates begin *while they are still in the institution* for a number of reasons. In a prison situation, time is one of the few resources of which most inmates have an abundance. The competing demands of family, work, and the neighborhood peer group are absent. Thus, there is the *time* and opportunity for comprehensive treatment, perhaps for the first time in a drug offender's career. In addition, there are other, new opportunities presented—to interact with "recovering addict" role models, to acquire prosocial values and a positive work ethic, and to initiate a process of education, training, and understanding of the addiction cycle.

Since the 1970s, work release has become a widespread correctional practice for felony offenders. It is a form of partial incarceration whereby inmates are permitted to work for pay in the free community, but must spend their nonworking hours either in the institution, or more commonly, in a community-based, work-release facility or "halfway house." Inmates qualified for work release are those approaching their parole eligibility or conditional-release dates. Although graduated release of this sort carries the potential for *easing* an inmate's process of community reintegration, there is a negative side, especially for those whose drug involvement served as the key to the penitentiary gate in the first place.

This initial freedom exposes many inmates to groups and behaviors that can easily lead them back to substance abuse, criminal activities, and reincarceration. Even those receiving intensive TC treatment while in the institution face the prospect of their recovery breaking down. Work-release environments in most jurisdictions do little to stem the process of relapse. Since work-release populations mirror the institutional populations from which they came, there are still the negative values of the prison culture. In addition, street drugs and street norms tend to abound.

Graduates of prison-based TCs are at a special disadvantage in a traditional work-release center since they must live and interact in what is typically an antisocial, nonproductive setting. Without clinical management and proper supervision, their recovery can be severely threatened. Thus, secondary TC treatment is warranted. This *secondary stage* is a "transitional TC"—the TC work-release center.

The program composition of the work-release TC should be similar to that of the traditional TC. There should be the "family setting" removed from as many of the external negative influences of the street and inmate cultures as is possible. Additionally, there should be the hierarchical system of ranks and job functions, the rules and regulations of the environment, and the complex of therapeutic techniques designed to continue the process of resocialization. However, the clinical regimen in the work-release TC must be modified to address the correctional mandate of "work release."

In the *tertiary* or *"aftercare" stage,* clients will have completed work release and will be living in the free community under the supervision of parole or some other surveillance program. Treatment intervention in this stage should involve out-patient counseling and group therapy. Clients should be encouraged to return to the work-release TC for refresher/reinforcement sessions, to attend weekly groups, to call on their counselors on a regular basis, and to participate in monthly one-to-one and/or family sessions. They should also be required to spend 1 day each month at the program, as well as a weekend retreat every 3 months.

This three-stage model has been made operational within the Delaware correctional system, and is built around a series of four prison-based TCs, three work-release TCs, and an intensive aftercare component. The prison-based and work-release programs were implemented during the period 1988 through 1992, and as such, their clinical content has been described at length in the literature (Hooper, Lockwood, & Inciardi, 1993; Inciardi, Martin, Butzin, Hooper, & Harrison, 1997). Because the aftercare programs were not implemented until 1996, the opportunity exists to examine program effects with and without aftercare.

AFTERCARE DEVELOPMENT

Prior to 1996, only a rudimentary aftercare program was in operation. Linked with the work-release TC, one staff member provided minimal supervision to 35 clients who had completed the residential phase of treatment. As the number of program graduates increased, a specific aftercare regimen was developed in which clients would participate for 6 months.

In order to be accepted into aftercare, the client must be referred by a feeder program—the prison-based and/or work-release TC. In order to make the transition into aftercare, the client is required to find stable employment, as well as an approved living situation. During the first week of aftercare participation, an intake interview is completed with the client. In addition, the Addiction Severity Index is administered and a Master Treatment Plan is developed within 30 days of admission. The client and counselor jointly construct the Master Treatment Plan, which includes a statement of problems, long- and short-range goals, and specific action steps and target dates for meeting these goals.

The list of problems, goals, and action steps are typically updated on a monthly basis, but this can occur more frequently if the situation requires. During the first 30 days of aftercare, the client is expected to participate in two therapy groups per week, two outside Alcoholics Anonymous (AA)/Narcotics Anonymous (NA) meetings per week, and one individual counseling session. The therapy groups are designed to deal with issues related to relapse prevention, relationship and employment difficulties, and economic challenges.

After the first 30 days of aftercare, clients who are adjusting well to life in the community are permitted to discontinue one of the weekly group sessions, but are expected to continue attending the community-based AA/NA meetings, as well as the monthly individual session. Additionally, aftercare clients are expected to serve as peer role models for clients in the work-release TC by conducting seminars on issues surrounding community re-entry, as well as assisting newer clients with employment searches and job-interviewing skills.

The early detection of breakdowns in the recovery process is facilitated by random urine testing conducted among aftercare participants. When clients have a positive urine test or self-report having used a drug, their aftercare program is adjusted, provided they have not become reinvolved in criminal activity. Typically, a person obtaining a positive screen for alcohol is expected to increase their therapy group attendance to twice a week, and must attend an additional AA meeting each month. In addition, the client must spend at least 1 weekend day at the work-release TC facility participating in a relapse-prevention group. Any client testing positive for illegal drugs must remain at the work-release TC facility as a weekend resident, and attend an increased number of treatment groups during the week. There is flexibility in accommodating aftercare clients in the work-release TC housing unit on weekends because there are always a number of residential clients on weekend furloughs. Those testing positive for heroin are brought back to the work-release TC immediately, given a medical examination, and detained. A staff assessment is conducted within 24 hours to determine the appropriate next steps. These additional measures are designed to assist individuals who are in danger of complete relapse, but who indicate a need and willingness to obtain help.

The aftercare program has been integrated with the probation and parole system. Specific probation and parole officers have been selected and cross-trained with the TC treatment staff. Because these officers understand and support the TC method of treatment, they are assigned to supervise a caseload of aftercare clients. This, in turn, results in a higher level of accountability among the aftercare clients. When there are indications that a client is having difficulty, a case-management session is held that includes the client, the probation/parole officer, and treatment staff. In such cases, the client must agree to close supervision in order to remain in the aftercare program. This type of early intervention strategy helps to reduce the number of clients who might succumb to a full relapse and/or become reinvolved in criminal activity. A concerted effort is made by all staff to maintain clients in the community if they demonstrate a willingness to address their existing problems. By having a united probation/parole and treatment staff intervention, a clear signal is given to the client that there is concern for his or her ongoing recovery—provided the client continues to work on his or her issues.

PROGRAM EFFECTIVENESS

The Center for Drug and Alcohol Studies at the University of Delaware has been funded for more than 10 years by the National Institute on Drug Abuse (NIDA) to evaluate the relative effectiveness of the prison and work-release treatment programs described above. In recent years, evaluation funding has also come from the National Institute of Justice and the Center for Substance-Abuse Treatment. Client selection for the present study has involved both random assignment and purposive sampling, and four groups have been followed—a no-treatment comparison group, treatment drop-outs, treatment graduates, and treatment graduates *with* aftercare.

Participation in the project is voluntary, and clients are protected by a Certificate of Confidentiality issued by NIDA. About 95% of all eligible clients have agreed to participate in the study at baseline, and more than 80% of those interviewed also provided a urine specimen. Follow-up rates for all study participants have been about 80%. The data presented here pertain to those clients who have completed the 42-month follow-up interview, resulting in a sample size of 518.

The baseline interview was administered in prison, just prior to the client's transfer to work release. The baseline assessment collected self-report data on basic demographics, prior living situation, criminal history, drug-use history, treatment history, sexual-behavior history, sexual attitudes, HIV risks, and physical and mental health. Previous use of a series of illegal drugs was measured on an ordinal scale, ranging from 0 (no use) to 6 (use more than once a day) in the 6 months prior to incarceration.

The first follow-up assessment occurred 6 months after release from prison, corresponding with graduation from work release. Subsequent interviews were conducted 18 months and 42 months after release. Treatment dropouts were also followed up at these time points. Follow-up surveys elicited detailed information about drug use and criminal activity during the intervening time periods. In addition, the follow-up interviews collected information on the amount of time spent in any drug treatment program since release from prison. This is important because the comparison group was not truly a *no-treatment* group. Many of these offenders sought treatment on their own during work release, and this treatment status should be controlled for outcome analyses.

The dependent variables for the analyses presented here are dichotomous measures of relapse to illegal drug use and rearrest at the 42-month follow-up. Each outcome measure was constructed from repeated self-report data and objective criteria. To be considered "drug free," the respondent must have reported *no* illegal drug use *and* have tested negative for drugs on the urine screen at each follow-up point. As such, this is an extremely conservative criterion since drug use on even one occasion during the follow-up period would negate the "drug free" status. Similarly, the criteria for "arrest free" included no self-reports of arrest and no official arrest records for new offenses since release from prison.

The data were analyzed using a multivariate, logistic, regression technique, with treatment status (treatment graduates with aftercare, treatment graduates with no aftercare, treatment dropouts, and no treatment), and a number of other putative predictors of relapse and recidivism included as possible explanatory variables in the model. These additional predictors included age, gender, race/ethnicity, age at first arrest, number of previous arrests, number of times in prison, frequency of prior drug use, and prior drug treatment. These control variables are not only potential predictors of treatment outcome, but more importantly, they are factors that may differ across groups since group membership was not randomly assigned.

Figures 16.1 and 16.2 present the results of the logistic regressions predicting rearrest and relapse to drug use at 42 months by treatment status, holding the control variables constant. An examination of the arrest-free panel (Figure 16.1) reveals that all three treatment groups are far less likely than the comparison group to be arrested on a new charge. In addition, those that complete treatment fare significantly better, and those who complete treatment with aftercare are the most likely to be arrest free. More specifically, less than 50% of the clients completing treatment with aftercare have been rearrested, while three fourths of the comparison group have been rearrested by the 42-month follow-up.

The beneficial effects of both treatment and aftercare are equally apparent when drug-free status is examined in Figure 16.2. When contrasted with the comparison group in which only 4% remained drug free 42 months after release from prison, treatment dropouts and graduates are four to five times more likely to be drug free, and treatment graduates with aftercare are nine times more likely to be drug free.

As noted, "drug free since release" is an extremely conservative measure of treatment outcome. Anyone who has ever gone on a diet, attempted to

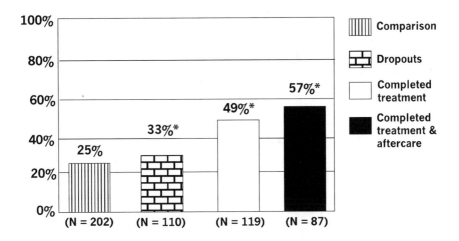

FIGURE 16.1   Delaware corrections-based therapeutic community treatment continuum, percentage arrest free since release at 42-month follow-up.

Significantly different from comparison group at $p < .05$ controlling for age, race, gender, criminal history, prior treatment, and drug-use history.

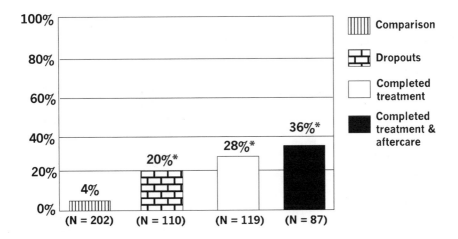

FIGURE 16.2   Delaware corrections-based therapeutic community treatment continuum, percentage drug free since release at 42-month follow-up.

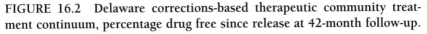

Significantly different from comparison group at $p < .05$ controlling for age, race, gender, criminal history, prior treatment, and drug-use history.

stop smoking, or made a New Year's resolution understands the nature of relapse. As such, a more realistic measure of treatment impact appears in Figure 16.3. Being drug free in the last 30 days suggests that an enduring relapse has not occurred, and that the client continues to be functional. Clearly, clients receiving treatment and aftercare did better than any other group.

DISCUSSION

The typically long-standing drug and criminal careers of offenders coming to the attention of the criminal justice system are not specific to Delaware, and any endeavor to curtail these behaviors requires substance-abuse treatment that is both intensive and extensive. Delaware has responded to this need by instituting its continuum of *primary* (in prison), *secondary* (work release), and *tertiary* (aftercare) TC treatment corresponding to sentence mandates. Earlier analyses of the Delaware continuum (Inciardi et al., 1997), as well as the outcome data presented here, indicated that clients who completed *secondary* treatment (some of whom also completed *primary*

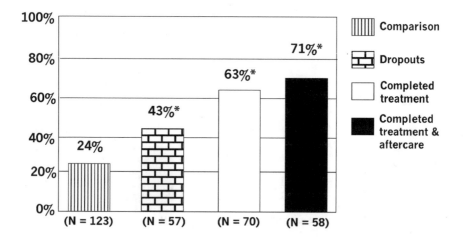

FIGURE 16.3   Delaware corrections-based therapeutic community treatment continuum, percentage drug free in last 30 days at 42-month follow-up.
Significantly different from comparison group at $p < .05$ controlling for age, race, gender, criminal history, prior treatment, and drug-use history.

treatment) were significantly more likely than those with no treatment or those who dropped out of treatment to remain drug free and arrest free at 42 months after release from prison. In addition, the first analyses of data now available on Delaware clients who received *tertiary* treatment (a TC aftercare program implemented in 1996) suggest that treatment graduates who participate in aftercare programs surpass treatment graduates who do not receive continuing care in remaining drug and arrest free at 42 months. These results provide continuing support for the beneficial effects of participation in institutional, transitional, and community TC treatment for drug-involved offenders.

It should be noted that the 42-month outcome data presented here are still preliminary, and are based on modest sample sizes that are insufficient for analyses of all possible combinations of treatment participation. As long-term follow-up data on more clients become available, several more comprehensive analyses will be conducted. In particular, the effects of length of time in each phase of treatment, as well as completion of each phase, will be examined more fully. The analyses presented here did not examine the unique effects of participating in the in-prison TC program, although there is some indication that graduates of the institutional TC are more likely to remain in treatment through work release and aftercare. As more follow-up data are collected, it will be possible to examine the differential effects of all treatment-continuum stages simultaneously.

Treatment participation and completion are the focus of these analyses, but it is obvious that treatment participation comprises only part of the explanation for the phenomena of relapse and recidivism. The current analyses attempted to address some other possible explanations by modeling the effects of demographic characteristics, prior criminal activities, and drug-use history on relapse and rearrest. Nonetheless, important control or confounding variables are undoubtedly lacking. In this regard, there are two areas of major theoretical and practical interest that should be examined. First, there is the appropriateness of the TC-treatment modality for the client. There is a growing literature that suggests that assignment to the appropriate treatment milieu can have important implications for treatment success (De Leon, Melnick, Kressel, & Jainchill, 1994). To some extent, this has been addressed in our study by conducting detailed assessments of each client's substance abuse-treatment history, but more comparative outcome analyses of these data are needed. A second area that will be considered in future analyses is the compulsory or voluntary nature of the treatment entry (Leukefeld & Tims, 1988; De Leon, Inciardi, & Martin, 1995). The Delaware TC programs contain both treatment volunteers and those with parole or judicial mandates for treatment. Examining the appropriateness of TC treatment for a particular client and the differential effects of self-selection versus involuntary selection will be important methods with which to further our understanding of the impact of treatment on relapse and recidivism.

Despite these limitations, the present data speak to the value of treatment in work-release and parole settings and the importance of retention in treatment in increasing long-term abstinence from drug use and criminal activity. More importantly, the data also support some long-held beliefs about the beneficial effects of aftercare (e.g., De Leon, 1990–1991; Knight, Simpson, & Hiller, 1996; Wexler et al., 1999). Aftercare programs appear to provide a critical bridge between institutional confinement and community reentry by providing assistance for the psychological, social, and legal obstacles that can place drug-involved offenders at risk for relapse and recidivism during work release and parole.

17

Clinical Issues in Treating Substance-Abusing Women

Michele Staton, Carl G. Leukefeld, and T. K. Logan

Women continue to use drugs and alcohol at high rates in the United States. A 1996 Center on Addiction and Substance Abuse (CASA) report estimated prevalence in the United States at about 4.5 million women 18 years and older who are alcoholics or alcohol abusers, 3.5 million who misuse prescription drugs, and 3.1 million who regularly use illicit drugs. Current research has begun to clarify differences in the substance abuse between men and women, with implications that there are differences in the ways women use drugs, the reasons women initiate drug use, the barriers to treatment, and the health/mental health consequences resulting from use. There is growing evidence that women may become addicted to drugs and/or alcohol more easily than men because of biological/metabolic differences (Blume, 1998). There are also related sociological issues in that women initiate drug use in a manner that is closely linked to their relationships with significant others, particularly males (Blume, 1998; Hutchins, 1995). In addition, women face increased treatment barriers for substance-abuse problems, including lack of child care, fear of losing their children, shame or guilt of being an alcoholic or drug addict, denial of their addiction, and transportation issues (Hall, 1998).

Although women's substance-abuse issues may be different than men, a commonality is that drug and alcohol use are often linked to criminal justice system involvement (Leukefeld & Tims, 1992). In fact, an estimated 80% of incarcerated individuals have substance-abuse issues (Blanchard, 1999). Nearly one of every 144 American adults is currently incarcerated for a charge related to drug and/or alcohol involvement, and nearly 75% of those incarcerated report using drugs regularly during the month prior to their arrest (CASA, 1998). Almost 84,000 women were incarcerated in prisons in 1998, at a rate of nearly one in every 109 U.S. women who is involved in some way with the criminal justice system (Bureau of Justice Statistics [BJS], 1999). Women represent the fastest growing population in prison settings, which is related to their drug use and drug-related offenses (Henderson, 1998). A large number of female offenders, reported as high as 98%, have a history of substance abuse, and many indicate that they were under the influence of alcohol or drugs at the time of their offense (Brewer, Marquart, Mullings, & Crouch, 1998; Cotton-Oldenburg, Jordan, Martin, & Kupper, 1999). With that background, the purpose of this chapter is to overview the literature related to treating incarcerated women, to discuss special issues among women, and to provide recommendations for establishing effective treatment programs within prison and jails.

TREATMENT FOR WOMEN

Overall, there are a limited number of prison- and jail-based treatment programs in the United States. Although approximately 80% of offenders are substance abusers, only about one third of former state and federal prisoners report they had participated in drug or alcohol treatment while incarcerated (Blanchard, 1999). In fact, the number of inmates in need of substance-abuse treatment increased by 22% between 1993 and 1996 (Camp & Camp, 1996).

Research on treatment effectiveness for women is very limited. In general, most of the treatment research has focused on programs that are male oriented. Residential treatment in the form of therapeutic communities (TC) is one of the most effective approaches for prisoners, particularly males (Inciardi, this volume; Martin, Butzin, Saum, & Inciardi, 1999). Therapeutic community treatment focuses on drug use that is perpetuated environmentally, and behavior is addressed using confrontational groups, strict enforcement of specific rules, job functions, and other restrictions (Harrison, Butzin, Inciardi, & Martin, 1998; Hartmann, Wolk, Johnston, & Colyer, 1999). Therapeutic community models tend to be effective with both male and female offenders (Lockwood, McCorkel, & Inciardi, 1998). A specific goal of TC treatment is drugs and/or alcohol abstinence, as well as a lifestyle free from antisocial behaviors and attitudes (CASA, 1998). While TC programs have shown effectiveness in reducing recidivism (Gerstein, 1999; Wexler, Melnick, Lowe, & Peters, 1999), there is a high dropout rate, which is commonly related to treatment intensity.

Prison and jail treatment programs often incorporate case management to link offenders with drug treatment and other community services (Martin & Inciardi, 1997; Siegal, Rapp, Li, Saha, & Kirk, 1997). Intensive outpatient settings, therapy-based programs, psychoeducational approaches, and 12-step programs are commonly used community-treatment approaches (Office of National Drug Control Policy, 1996). Due to the limited treatment availability in prisons and jails for females, female offenders are frequently referred to community aftercare programs following release from prison (Wellisch et al., 1993). Aftercare programs generally strive to empower women to implement changes in their drug use, criminal activity, criminal thinking, risky sex behavior, intimate relationships, and family lives.

Successful aftercare programs, following prison- or jail-based treatment, assist clients in establishing strong community networks and service-utilization resources. One specialized program in Rhode Island was designed to link incarcerated HIV-positive women with care coordinators to plan for their release and then to doctors, social workers, and peer counselors following release (Vigilante et al., 1999). Prerelease counseling is also used to focus on medical care, housing, substance-abuse treatment, and family support. A specific goal is to provide linkages to community resources in order to maintain long-term therapeutic relationships as a means of support for problems, such as HIV. One outcome study found that compared with a randomly selected sample of seropositive women, those who completed the prerelease program had lower percentages of recidivism at 6-month follow-ups (12% vs. 22%) and at 12 months (17% vs. 39%), indicating that coordinated aftercare efforts may have particular relevance for offenders.

Although some treatment approaches are more effective for incarcerated women, a consistent finding is that increased time in treatment, followed by structured aftercare, is associated with treatment success (Lipton, 1995). In addition, programs that were more likely to reduce recidivism should be at least several months in duration, target criminal thinking, and incorporate social skills (Gendreau, 1996). For women, specific treatment approaches that are most beneficial are those that utilize the relational/connectedness model. For example, several studies point to the importance of relationships and connectedness for women (e.g., Covington, 1998). For drug users, it has been reported that women's episodes of use, abstinence, and relapse are closely related to their significant opposite-sex relationships (Henderson, 1998). Thus, strengthening positive social-support networks and relationships in treatment and aftercare is extremely important for achieving sobriety and maintaining recovery (Finkelstein, Kennedy, Thomas, & Kearns, 1997).

In summary, while treatment programs in prisons and jails are needed, gender-specific programs that target the needs of women are extremely limited. The male-focused approaches used in existing treatment programs do not embrace women's issues and do not address special needs of women in the areas of substance abuse, health, mental health, victimization, and parenting. Without adequate programming while incarcerated, women with limited skills and education return to the community with limited opportunities, compounded by the stigma of having been incarcerated (Winifred, 1996).

TREATMENT NEEDS

In the past 20 years, the number of specialized programs for addicted women has steadily increased. For instance, Grella, Polinsky, Hser, and Perry (1999) conducted a secondary data analysis using a regional database of U.S. drug treatment programs, and found that approximately 19% could be classified as women-only programs. Differences between programs that were female focused and those for both men and women were related to specialized services offered. For example, women's programs were more likely to provide parenting classes, pregnancy care, housing assistance, and vocational services. Within the criminal justice system, 49 state Departments of Corrections indicated that they had programs specifically for women—primarily in the areas of parenting, substance abuse, victimization, and life skills (National Institute of Corrections, 1998). However, the services provided and the effectiveness of these treatment approaches were not discussed. As indicated in the research literature, women have specific treatment needs in each of the following areas:

Victimization

It has been shown consistently that high percentages of incarcerated, drug-abusing women have detailed histories of physical, mental, and sexual abuse (e.g., Bond & Semaan, 1996; Sheridan, 1996). In fact, it has been estimated that almost 50%—four in 10 female inmates—reported they had been abused at least once before their current incarceration, with about one third reporting physical and sexual abuse (BJS, 1994). Lake (1993) reported that more than 85% of female inmates had at least one type of victimization experience in her life, with reported sources of abuse ranging from intimate partners to family members. In addition, Bond and Semaan (1996) found that 72% of an incarcerated sample reported being beaten by a boyfriend or a spouse and 44% had been abused by one or both parents. Consequently, victimization services need to be incorporated into female-offender treatment.

Mental Health

Women prisoners experience a variety of mental health issues (Singer, Bussey, Song, & Lunghofer, 1995). For example, 64% of incarcerated women reported lifetime psychiatric disorders, including drug abuse or dependence, alcohol abuse or dependence, personality disorders, major depressive episodes, and dysthymia (Jordan, Schlenger, Fairbank, & Caddell, 1996). Depression and anxiety are the most common mental health issues, and in some cases, the symptoms are severe. A high percentage of women prisoners also present characteristics associated with suicide risk (defined as a history of psychiatric treatment, previous suicide attempts, alcohol or drug abuse, social and economic disadvantages, a history of physical and/or sexual abuse). Consequently, there is need for mental health services for women offenders. Correctional services range from psychiatric evaluations to medication to outside hospital referrals. However, despite the fact that mental health services are often available for incarcerated individuals, there may be a disparity in those who receive needed services. For example, Teplin, Abram, and McClelland (1997) found that only 24% of those who were determined to need mental health services received them during their jail stay.

Health

In addition to mental health issues, many women prisoners have multiple health problems that are compounded by risky lifestyles and limited health care before incarceration (Ingram-Fogel, 1991). While correctional facilities are likely to provide health care, the quality and opportunity for adequate health care may be limited. The most frequently cited health concerns among incarcerated women are drug and alcohol abuse or dependence, HIV, pregnancy-related problems, hepatitis, back and neck pain, severe headaches, obesity, dental problems, and chronic health problems such as hypertension, emphysema, and asthma (Ingram-Fogel, 1991; Ross & Lawrence, 1998). Kidney and bladder infections are also common with untreated urinary tract infections and bladder infections (Marquart, Brewer, & Mullings, 1999). Poor health care before prison may predict increased illness and poor health during incarceration. Prison officials often fail to ensure that women can receive quality health care, despite the fact that, for many women, incarceration is the first opportunity to address their health needs when they are not abusing drugs/alcohol (Smith & Dillard, 1994).

STDs, HIV, and AIDS

Sexually transmitted diseases (STDs) are more commonly reported among offenders than the general population (Hammett & Harmon, 1999). A history of STDs, including chlamydia, human papillomavirus, herpes simplex, cystic and mymatic conditions, dysmenorrhea, and chronic pelvic inflammation, are commonly reported by female offenders (Ross & Lawrence, 1998). One of the most prevalent STD health concerns for incarcerated women is HIV. In general, the rate of HIV infection is about six times higher among male and female prisoners than in the general U.S. population (Maruschak, 1999).

Exchanging sex for money or drugs is a high risk factor for HIV among female offenders (Cotton-Oldenburg, Martin, Jordan, Sadowski, & Kupper, 1997). Other consistently reported HIV-risk behaviors that increase a female offender's risk for HIV include sharing drug-injection equipment, engaging in unprotected sex with drug-injecting partners, having sex with multiple partners, exchanging sex for money or drugs, reporting a history of a diagnosed STD, inconsistently using condom with multiple sex partners, and using alcohol and other noninjection drugs (Cotton-Oldenburg et al., 1999). Thus, HIV infection among female inmates is a serious health concern.

Children and Parenting

Since the majority of women who abused drugs before prison have children (Coll, Surrey, Buccio-Notaro, & Molla, 1998), the mother/inmate relationship with her children is a difficult issue. Society seems to view these women as inadequate, incompetent, and unable to provide for the needs of their children. In addition, being a prisoner separates mothers from their children, and this loss of relationship increases a woman's sense of inadequacy, despondency, and fear of permanently losing her children, and most mothers feel intense guilt and shame, and experience fear of being rejected by their children (Coll et al., 1998). Dealing with involuntary separation from their children has increased consequences for incarcerated drug-abusing women at release since mothers can face a variety of reunification issues with their children. This increasingly stressful situation can increase a woman's risk for relapse. Relapse often results in reincarceration, and another cycle of separation from their children usually occurs within the first 6 months of release (Harm, Thompson, & Chambers, 1998).

CLINICAL APPROACHES

Existing prison and jail substance-abuse treatment programs for women have been described as: (a) no specialized services; (b) drug education and/or drug abuse counseling; (c) residential units with drug treatment; (d) client-initiated and/or client-maintained services such as Alcoholics Anonymous (AA) and/or Narcotics Anonymous (NA); and (e) specialized services that do not directly focus on substance abuse (Peters, 1993). However, only a few studies have addressed specific program components for female-offenders. The following areas have been identified as critical for female offender substance-abuse treatment (Morash, Haarr, & Rucker, 1994; Peters, 1993; Singer et al., 1995), which include: (a) multimodality treatment; (b) isolated treatment units; (c) competent and professional staff; (d) cross-training sessions for program and prison staff; (e) developing strong peer networks; (f) separate prison sanctions and treatment-program sanctions; (g) consistent and sustained treatment participation; (h) vocational training; (i) specialized health care; (j) parenting education; (k) HIV and STD education; (l) victimization counseling; and (m) prerelease planning.

Since the number of women in the criminal justice system is continuing to increase, incarcerated women have specific needs that require specialized attention in treatment programming. Prison and jails are opportune places to provide services to these women, yet in-custody treatment is limited. Women need services, and they specifically need gender-specific services that are designed with knowledge and expertise to address special issues. In addition, initial in-custody services should be developed with the goal of establishing a continuum of care and aftercare that follows the client into the community.

FUTURE DIRECTIONS

One approach is to more effectively target women before they are incarcerated. A large percentage of female offenders are minority women with few job skills, no health insurance, inadequate housing, dependent children, and with limited access to community-based health and treatment systems (Ross & Lawrence, 1998), which is associated with drug and alcohol use (Staton, Leukefeld, & Logan, in press) as a major barrier. In fact, the fear of legal consequences from drug use, as well as general neglect of their bodies are often major reasons for not seeking care. Targeted assessments and outreach to at-risk women as they enter treatment systems, including health departments and emergency rooms, could enhance services for female drug users.

Individualized programming for women prisoners, particularly substance abusers, could be successful. In addition, the severity and reoccurring nature of substance abuse create a need for continued intervention after incarceration. In order to facilitate aftercare treatment, case managers and recovering women who work with treatment staff and correctional officers can facilitate treatment planning during custody and community transition (Wexler & Lipton, 1993). Aftercare can include residential community-treatment programs, halfway houses, intensive supervision with sanctions, and random urine testing (Henderson, 1998).

Treatment programs for female inmates should also intensify efforts to address sexual abuse and domestic violence in order to develop greater assertiveness and autonomy in relationships (Peters, Strozier, Murrin, & Kearns, 1997). Prison-based programs should closely communicate with and coordinate services with community-based agencies to continue interventions with female inmates. Increased community linkages with victimization services after prison also need to be a priority, since many women will return to high-risk situations. These programs should assist women in overcoming barriers to seeking victimization services, including substance abuse, cost, guilt, fear, and denial (Brewer et al., 1998; Staton et al., in press). An additional focus of prison-based programs for women must be HIV prevention. Intervention programs should target decreasing risk-taking behaviors, including sex exchange, sex with multiple partners, inconsistent condom use, and unprotected oral sex (Cotton-Oldenburg et al., 1999).

In conclusion, although the needs of substance-abusing women are varied, continued research into understanding the female substance abuser is critical. Specific research questions should focus on health, mental health, substance abuse, HIV risk, victimization, and parenting. For example, (a) Do women use services differently than men? (b) If so, how can women be targeted more effectively? (c) What are the essential features of gender-specific treatment? (d) What factors could we more effectively address in prerelease planning to lengthen aftercare supervision? and (e) How should resources be allocated—treatment, policy, and/or research?

ACKNOWLEDGMENTS

This project is supported by Grant No. DA08154 awarded by the National Institute on Drug Abuse. Opinions and points of view expressed are those of the authors and do not represent the official position or policies of the National Institute on Drug Abuse.

18

Treatment for Drug-Involved Youth in the Juvenile Justice System

Richard Dembo, Stephen Livingston, and James Schmeidler

Treatment of adolescents for alcohol/other drug abuse and related problems in the juvenile justice system remains an issue of critical importance for several reasons. First, there has been an increase in youth crime and its effects, as well as a growing awareness of the magnitude of these and related problems among various high-risk groups (Butts & Harrell, 1998). This increase, together with a higher rate of law-violation referrals to juvenile court (a 57% increase between 1980 and 1995), has resulted in an increasingly clogged and backlogged juvenile court system and less involvement in case deliberation (Snyder & Sickmund, 1995). Younger offenders are entering the juvenile system in increasing numbers, and bringing with them a number of serious, interrelated problems, including drug use, educational deficits, and emotional/psychological issues (including abuse and neglect) (Dembo, Schmeidler, Nini-Gough, & Manning, 1998a). Demographic projections indicate a substantial increase in the U.S.

youth population in the next 10 to 20 years, which threatens to create an increasingly overburdened juvenile justice system. Second, drug-testing results from national studies (National Institute of Justice, 1999) of juvenile arrestees indicate continuing high levels of drug use. Third, evidence indicates an increased co-occurrence of mental health and drug abuse problems among juvenile offenders (Winters, 1998).

A knowledge base deriving from experience in treating youths has begun to be established. However, rigorous, comprehensive impact and cost studies of treatment interventions in the juvenile justice system remain relatively infrequent. Rates of failure of adolescents to enter and remain in treatment present continuing challenges to service delivery. Posttreatment relapse rates among adolescents with drug abuse problems (Catalano, Hawkins, Wells, Miller, & Brewer, 1990–1991), particularly those involved in the justice system, remain high (Armstrong & Altschuler, 1998), reflecting the often chronic nature of these problems.

Many youths entering the juvenile justice system have multiple personal, educational, and family problems. These problems include physical abuse, sexual victimization, emotional/psychological functioning difficulties, educational problems, and alcohol and other drug use (Dembo, Williams, & Schmeidler, 1998). These difficulties can often be traced to family alcohol/ other drug use, mental health, or crime problems that began at an early age (Dembo, Williams, Wothke, Schmeidler, & Brown, 1992). One in four U.S. children, or 19 million, is exposed to alcohol abuse or dependence at home before reaching the age of 18 (Grant, 2000). Juvenile offenders, particularly minority and inner city youth, are also at high risk of being infected by or transmitting HIV via injecting drugs or crack cocaine-driven sexual activity involving multiple partners (Inciardi & Pottieger, 1991), so they are an important HIV/AIDS risk-reduction target group.

There is increased recognition that integrated systems of care need to be developed to identify and complete quality assessments of troubled youths, link them with appropriate intervention programs, and provide them with supportive posttreatment or aftercare services. Identifying and responding effectively to these drug abuse and related problems as early as possible by involving the youth in effective intervention services (Klitzner, Fisher, Stewart, & Gilbert, 1991), would reduce: (a) the risk of escalation of their types and patterns of drug use and related problems, especially crime (Dembo et al., 2000); (b) their moving into the adult criminal justice system; and (c) the enormous societal costs associated with crime, drug abuse, and mental illness (Office of National Drug Control Policy, 1997).

PAST AND RECENT WORK

A 1990 Institute of Medicine report on drug treatment (Gerstein & Harwood, 1990) indicated the goals of treatment were multiple, and include the following: reduce individuals' drug use and the overall demand for illicit drugs; reduce street crime; change users' personal values; develop educational or vocational capabilities; restore or increase employment or productivity; and improve the users' overall health, psychological functioning, and family life. However, this report, which reflected knowledge derived from adults, had limited usage for juveniles. Dembo, Williams, and Schmeidler (1993) suggested that alcohol/other drug abuse in juveniles differed from adults in several ways: (a) there was no widely accepted definition of "abuse" in juveniles; (b) the course of youth alcohol/other drug abuse was often different from that of adults; (c) the severity of youth alcohol/other drug use problems needed to take the factor of age into account; (d) troubled youths tended to have multiple problems—their alcohol/other drug use may not be primary; (e) youths tended to be more fascinated with the drug-related lifestyle and less fatigued with failure and the negative social consequences of their drug use (DeLeon & Deitch, 1987); and (f) youths require a greater emphasis on addressing educational needs and parental/family support in the treatment process.

Klitzner et al. (1991) urged that early intervention services be directed to individuals/groups: (a) whose use of alcohol/other drugs put them at high risk of negative consequences, (b) whose use of alcohol/other drugs resulted in clinically significant dysfunction or consequences, and (c) who exhibited particular problem behaviors that were precursors to alcohol/other drug problems (e.g., youths failing at school). Dembo et al. (1993) noted that the juvenile justice system generally does not become concerned over the behavior of a youth until he or she has appeared in court several times. At this point, the youngster has probably failed in a number of informal and loosely structured programs, and developed serious problems in school and delinquent behavior, including the use of various drugs. Many have developed a delinquent lifestyle, and it is often very difficult to turn them around.

Treatment entry and retention present considerable challenges in treating drug-abusing adolescents (Battjes, Onken, & Delany, 1999). Many drug-involved youth do not enter treatment or leave prematurely, with associated high rates of return to drug use, involvement in crime, and increased risk of HIV/AIDS, and other health and social problems. Treatment programs may have stringent rules, regulations and goals (e.g., clients must be drug or medication free), resulting in clients believing that programs are insensitive to their needs. Individual issues, including readiness to change, also need to be addressed for successful treatment entry and engagement to occur (DiClemente & Prochaska, 1998). In particular, as Battjes et al. (1999) note, there is a need to focus on what clients are ready for and want in seeking to involve them in programs and build on their strengths.

Regarding treatment impact, Catalano et al. (1990–1991) identified a number of background, or pretreatment, during-treatment, and posttreatment factors associated with relapse or failure to complete treatment: *Background or pretreatment factors*: (a) drug use: the younger the age of onset, the more serious the primary drug of abuse, and the abuse of multiple drugs was related to not completing treatment; (b) criminality: the amount of lifetime criminal involvement was related negatively to posttreatment outcome; and (c) educational level was related positively to completion of treatment and posttreatment outcome; *During-treatment factors*: (a) length of time in treatment was related positively to treatment outcome; (b) voluntary versus mandated treatment entry: mandated (often legal sanction) clients fared better than one might expect in completing treatment and in posttreatment outcome—the key was length of treatment (perceived choice regarding treatment was also predictive of positive during- and posttreatment outcomes); (c) staff characteristics: quality staff, who establish positive role relationships with clients, can improve treatment outcome; and (d) involvement of family/parents in treatment was positively related to program completion; *Posttreatment factors*: (a) thoughts and feelings about drugs and drug cravings were related negatively to posttreatment outcome; (b) involvement in productive activities, such as school or work, was related positively to posttreatment outcome; and (c) few and less satisfactory active leisure activities were related positively to relapse.

These factors (Catalano et al., 1990–1991) associated with relapse or failure to complete treatment have important implications for the development of more effective programs: Pretreatment factors tend to be fixed entities and there is little a treatment program can do to manipulate these factors with a view to reducing posttreatment relapse (Catalano, Wells, Jenson, & Hawkins, 1989). Drawing on treatment-outcome studies involving adults, and the few such inquiries involving youth, pretreatment and during-treatment factors combined account for a smaller amount of the variance in posttreatment relapse than posttreatment experiences (Catalano et al., 1989). The posttreatment success factors indicate the importance of involving youth in productive roles, providing an environment supporting positive change initiated in treatment, and reducing their alcohol/other drug use. Identification of risk factors associated with posttreatment relapse among treated clients can suggest program components to reduce factors associated with higher relapse rates and increase factors associated with lower relapse rates (Hawkins, Catalano, & Miller, 1992).

Recent meta-analyses completed by Weisz, Weiss, Han, Granger, and Norton (1995) and Lipsey and Wilson (1998) have found a number of positive effects of treatment (e.g., reduced drug use and delinquency). Treatment for drug dependence and related psychosocial difficulties can be effective in reducing criminality (Anglin & Speckart, 1988). Programs based on social-learning theories are particularly effective among drug-involved persons who have developed their drug-use lifestyle over a period of years (Wexler & Williams, 1986). Treatment-evaluation studies show clear evidence regarding the efficacy and cost effectiveness of treatment (Pickens, Leukefeld, & Schuster, 1991; Simpson, Wexler, & Inciardi, 1999).

Aftercare services are a vital link in the service continuum. Although seriously needed, these services remain infrequent, underdeveloped, and tend to be narrowly focused on single problem areas, such as school placement or peer networks (Armstrong, 1991). They also tend to be heavily surveillance oriented. Aftercare services remain the weakest link in the program service chain. It is counterproductive to treat youth in residential settings, only to return them unassisted to environments that supported their problem behavioral in the past (Altschuler & Armstrong, 1991; Catalano et al., 1989; Armstrong & Altschuler, 1998). If behavioral change influenced by treatment programs is to last, it needs to be supported after the youth reenter the community. Youth often return to stressful environmental circumstances, including austere economic conditions, social or family disorganization, deviant peers, and other social pressures. These stressors, together with the lack of educational or vocational skills, as well as additional problems, present formidable challenges to their involvement in conventional activities. Aftercare programs need to include elements that deal quickly with relapse to substance use, responding to these relapses in a manner that discourages continued drug use and supports a return to abstinence (Catalano et al., 1989). It is also important that aftercare programs maintain contact with youth during their transition from institutional to aftercare services—perhaps involving continuity of staff across institutional-community program placement (Altschuler & Armstrong, 1991).

Several factors have led to a continued, high level of interest in juvenile aftercare programs. In spite of the fact that residential-commitment programs for troubled youth have been found ineffective in reducing recidivism, a strong tendency continues to place youth displaying troubled behavior in the community in large and frequently crowded residential facilities (Altschuler & Armstrong, 1991; Greenwood & Zimring, 1985). These facilities are often intimidating and otherwise stressful environments, at considerable distances from the youths' families, where their educational and other rehabilitative needs are often ignored or insufficiently addressed. These expensive programs serve primarily to isolate youths from the general society.

In 1991, Altschuler and Armstrong completed an important review of intensive community-based aftercare programs, which resulted in some striking findings: (a) A relatively small proportion of the literature on aftercare programs focused on programs for juveniles; most of the literature tended to be descriptive, anecdotal, and impressionistic, rather than evaluative and empirical; most evaluation studies involved such nonexperimental designs as case studies. This literature did not provide a firm basis for developing particular approaches and practices for use in different settings; (b) The basic concept and rationale for the design of many programs and their operation were not clearly articulated, consistently and logically explained, and implemented in program activities; (c) Aftercare programs needed to include a comprehensive system of services, use graduated sanctions, and place emphasis on incentives and positive reinforcements; and (d) Site visits to programs collected descriptive information in a number of important areas (e.g., history, background, and overall context of the aftercare program, organization/structure, number of clients, program philosophy and content). However, few of the programs had ever been evaluated.

Altschuler and Armstrong (1991) proposed a Intensive Aftercare Supervision model, including elements of social control, strain, and social-learning theories, to serve as a conceptual foundation to design and implement effective aftercare programs. A number of intensive aftercare programs being implemented in various states (e.g., Colorado, Nevada, New Jersey, and Virginia) reflect a sensitivity to providing support and treatment services to youth released from commitment programs. However, many more of these types of programs are needed, particularly those that, in addition to addressing traditional surveillance concerns, are treatment and service oriented (Armstrong & Altschuler, 1998).

Finally, long-term care may be needed by drug-involved youth in the juvenile justice system—beyond the time their court-imposed sanctions end (Dembo et al., 1993). Juvenile justice agencies tend to have an episodic interest in troubled youth. Interest centers around the behavioral reason for the youth's contact with the system and the judicially imposed consequences of that behavior. Once the period of program involvement ends, agency interest in the youth's case ceases—unless he or she comes to the attention of a juvenile justice agency again. This manner of responding to troubled youth fails to incorporate the experience that many of their problemed lives can be traced to their early years, and that their problems became more serious as they proceed through adolescence. The delinquent behavior of these youth frequently reflects a chronic involvement in personally and socially damaging activities (Farrington & West, 1990; Moffitt, 1993). Repeated interventions over a protracted period, which are reinforced by improvements in the social, vocational, and educational skill levels of the youth in treatment, are most likely to be successful (Pickens et al., 1991). Service-delivery systems and associated support services should accommodate themselves for repeated intervention. Seriously troubled youth (many of whom will pursue law-violating activities into adulthood), and, where indicated, their families, need to be involved in long-term, intensive service and supervision programs to remedy their difficulties that find expression in delinquency/crime.

Some Promising Developments

Centralized Preliminary Screening, In-Depth Assessment, and Service Referral

In the late 1980s and early 1990s, a number of program models and efforts were pursued to complete preliminary screening and in-depth assessments of drug-involved youth, and to refer them to needed services (Dembo et al., 1987; Rahdert, 1991; McClellan & Dembo, 1993). Elements of these approaches were incorporated into a Juvenile Assessment Center (JAC), a centralized intake facility established in Tampa, Florida (Dembo & Brown, 1994). JACs have spread to 20 other locations in Florida, Kansas, and other states. JACs involve a variety of community agencies, including law enforcement, juvenile justice, and human service agencies, which are also located at the facility. They can systematically collect sociodemographic, delinquency, abuse and neglect history, educational history and needs, and psychosocial functioning (e.g., mental health problems and substance use, including urine testing) information on arrested youth. JACs can also refer youths to substance abuse and mental health programs. At the community level, JACs can increase interagency coordination in meeting the needs of troubled youth and their families, reduce duplication of effort, smooth the transition of youth from one program/agency to another, and improve the quality and appropriateness of referrals to help overcome major workload and juvenile justice "systemic" problems. JACs also serve as a focal point for multiagency, early intervention efforts for arrested youth.

Intervention

Two critical service-delivery issues involving at-risk youth are: (a) low rates of treatment entry and retention (Battjes et al., 1999), and (b) lack of rigorous, comprehensive impact and cost studies of innovative interventions for substance-abusing youth in the juvenile justice system. Innovative services are especially needed by minority and inner city youth and their families, who have historically been underserved (Dembo & Seeberger, 1999). The Youth Support Project, which operated out of the Tampa JAC, implemented a systems-oriented, home-based Family Empowerment Intervention (FEI). Families were served by field consultants, who were not trained therapists, but were trained by and worked under the direction of licensed clinicians. Twelve-month follow-up recidivism analyses indicated that youth who completed the FEI experienced significantly lower rates of new charges and significantly fewer new arrests than youth not completing the FEI (Dembo et al., 2000). In addition, 12-month psychosocial outcome analyses indicated that, compared with ESI youth, youth receiving FEI services reported: (a) fewer drug sales during the follow-up period, (b) getting very high or drunk on alcohol less often, (c) less marijuana use, and (d) had a lower hair-test positive rate for marijuana use at follow-up interview. Further, analyses found youth completing the FEI had much better psychosocial outcomes than youth not completing the FEI (Dembo et al., in press).

Several other community-based family interventions, informed by an ecological systems view have demonstrated effectiveness (e.g., Rahdert & Czechowicz, 1995; Kumpfer & Alvarado, 1998). In multisystemic therapy (MST) (Henggeler et al., 1994; Henggeler, Pickrel, Brondino, & Crouch, 1996; Henggeler, 1997), trained therapists at community mental-health centers have provided services to four to six "at-risk youth" and their families for as long as 4 to 5 months. From a structural family-therapy perspective, the first step is to develop parental competencies to restructure the family and establish parental control. A second goal is to teach parents how to use agencies and services, including schools, more effectively. In functional family therapy (Alexander & Parsons, 1982), a wide variety of trained interventionists, working in one- or two-person teams, provide between 8 and 26 hours of in-home services, involving five phases (engagement, motivation, assessment, behavior change, and generalization) to referred youth and their families.

For youth needing residential-treatment services, TCs for adolescents are currently being evaluated and are showing promising results. For example, Jainchill, Hawke, DeLeon, and Yagelka (2000) studied the 1-year posttreatment outcomes of 485 youths admitted to six drug-free residential TCs across nine sites. Thirty-one percent of the youth completed residential treatment, 52% dropped out of treatment, and the remainder were terminated for different reasons (e.g., referred elsewhere). Based on self-report data, significant reductions in drug use and criminal activity were found, with reductions in both being greater for those who completed treatment. The most consistent predictors of positive outcomes were completion of treatment and not associating with deviant peers upon return to the community.

Hawkins, Jenson, Catalano, and Wells (1991) assessed the effectiveness of a cognitive-behavioral skills training program among institutionalized juveniles in reducing recidivism and substance abuse. The program was conducted in two phases: (a) a 10-week first phase involving group sessions to develop skills in consequential thinking, self-control, avoiding trouble, social networking, problem-solving negotiation and compliance, and drug and alcohol refusal—and assignment to a case manager, and (b) continued contact with the case manager for 6 months following release from the institution. The results of this experimental study found short-term improvement in social skills as a result of the cognitive-behavioral skills training.

Three Reviews of the Field

Weinberg, Rahdert, Colliver, and Glantz (1998) highlight a number of areas related to assessment and treatment. Clinically, in-depth information on drug-use history, together with psychiatric and physical examinations, are critical for diagnosis and treatment planning. However, most of the information that is routinely collected in these areas is based on self-reports. Such information has been shown to have limitations, particularly in regard to adolescents reporting their drug use (Dembo et al., 1999). More research is needed on the validity of adolescent self-report data in various contexts. A particular need exists to adapt DSM-IV criteria (American Psychiatric Association, 1994) for adolescents. Recent research has indicated problems in diagnostic classifications and the construct validity of DSM-IV criteria regarding adolescent substance use (Bukstein & Kaminer, 1994).

In regard to treatment, Weinberg et al. (1998) note that, while family-oriented therapies have received considerable attention, other approaches need to be encouraged and evaluated. This is particularly the case for person-centered treatment approaches, adolescent peer therapy (Fisher & Bently, 1996), cognitive-behavioral therapy involving rehearsal and social contracting (Azrin, McMahon, Donohue, Basalel, & Lapinski, 1994), coping skills and problem solving (Hawkins et al., 1991), and relapse-prevention training (Catalano et al., 1990–1991). Further, 12-step programs are frequently used in the field, and they need to be subjected to well-designed process and outcome evaluation studies. Finally, although much is known about the short- and long-term effects of medications, such as methadone, in the detoxification and treatment of adult substance use, few clinical studies have been conducted among adolescents (e.g., Geller, Cooper, Watts, Cosby, & Fox, 1992). This issue is of particular importance due to the fact that many adolescents with substance abuse problems have co-occurring emotional/psychiatric disorders (e.g., attention-deficit/hyperactivity disorders [ADHD]) (Winters, 1998), which require pharmacotherapy while they are undergoing drug abuse treatment. Relatedly, efforts are underway to use buprenorphine in treating heroin addiction among adolescents (Vocci, 1999).

The American Academy of Child and Adolescent Psychiatry (AACAP) report (1999) stressed the importance of in-depth assessments of adolescents experiencing substance abuse problems to explicitly search for any psychiatric disorders commonly found among these youth, such as conduct disorders and ADHD. Like Weinberg et al. (1998), AACAP noted that in-depth interviews with adolescents are often made difficult by their tendency to deny or minimize their drug use and related behavior.

AACAP considered the primary goal of substance-abuse treatment for adolescents to be to achieve and maintain abstinence. Recognizing the chronicity of substance abuse disorders among some adolescents, and the self-limited nature of this problem among others, AACAP recommended that acceptable, interim goals for treatment, such as reduction in use and adverse effects of substances, be adopted. Further, AACAP urged that abstinence not be the only goal of treatment; rehabilitation should target related problems and domains of functioning, such as peer and interpersonal relationships. These interventions should take place in the least restrictive environment (e.g., inpatient, outpatient or community-based care) that is safe and effective.

AACAP noted that while available studies have failed to document the superiority of any one treatment approach over others, some treatment is better than no treatment. Like the Weinberg et al. (1998) report, AACAP recommended controlled study evaluations of other treatment modalities besides family therapy, such as behavioral and cognitive therapies, which case reports and clinical experience suggest have been beneficial. AACAP noted that the use of pharmacological agents to treat the effects of a substance or as aversion agents has received little attention in the literature, and needs to be studied, but that the use of these agents should be reserved for "the most severely dependent adolescents who have been resistant to other treatment" (1999, p. 125). At the same time, AACAP recognized that the high prevalence of comorbid psychiatric disorders among substance-abusing adolescents may require pharmacological agents to address these problems.

In 1999, the Center for Substance-Abuse Treatment published an updated monograph on treating adolescents with substance-abuse disorders (Winters, 1999). The monograph stressed that treatment should address the nuances of each adolescent's experience, "including cognitive, emotional, physical, social, and moral development" (Winters, 1999, xvii). In addition, consideration should be given to age, gender, ethnicity, disability status, readiness to change, cultural background, and delays in cognitive and social-emotional development that are often associated with drug use among adolescents. The report urged treatment programs to involve the adolescents' families in the treatment process, and refrain from using adult programs to treat drug-involved youth. Further, the report argues against explicitly or implicitly coercing adolescents into treatment, asserting that "coercive pressure to seek treatment is not generally sensitive to the behavior change process" (Winters, 1999, xvii). Instead, treatment providers are urged to identify motivational barriers to change, and use various strategies to engage youth reluctant to pursue behavior change. Winters (1999) also suggested that program staff reflect the cultural diversity of the program's clients, and receive intensive continuing education to increase their knowledge of the program's client population and their treatment skills. Program components should include an orientation phase and daily scheduled activities, as well as peer monitoring, conflict resolution, and client behavioral contracts. Programs should address the educational and vocational training needs of the youth. Treatment planning should include a holistic approach reflecting the multiple problems most adolescent substance abusers are experiencing, establish attainable goals, draw on the strengths of adolescents and their families, and, where indicated, link the adolescent with educational, legal, and other external support systems.

MAJOR ISSUES FOR FUTURE RESEARCH

A major issue in research on treatment of adolescents is that there is so little of it. Few programs divert resources from treatment to evaluate outcomes, especially long-term follow-up. Thus, it is not possible to distinguish service or client characteristics associated with good outcomes. One strength of JAC programs is the opportunity to collect and analyze large longitudinal data sets that, over time, provide recidivism information in addition to client intake characteristics and referrals (Dembo, Schmeidler, Pacheco, Cooper, & Williams, 1997). The very large sample sizes and the extensive data collection of the JAC can be used to address other important issues (Dembo et al., 1998b).

It is clear that there are many differences among adolescent drug abusers. However, in the absence of valid in-depth assessment information on their problem areas, a common practice is to refer them to programs that are available, rather then those that address their specific needs. Much more detailed information is needed on these service needs so that more optimal individual treatment program matches can be made. At the same time, almost all treatment studies involve sample sizes that are too small, preventing meaningful comparison among youth subgroups for differential efficacy. If treatment service information were added to a JAC data base, the large sample size would permit exploratory analyses of this important issue.

Integration of treatment program data into the JAC data base could also provide a solution to a major problem in service delivery. Many youth do not enroll in treatment programs to which they are referred or do not remain in treatment. Regular checking of a youth's treatment status on the JAC information system would permit timely intervention to help youth who did not enter treatment or who leave treatment prematurely.

More studies are also needed on treatment integrity (the degree to which a given treatment is implemented in accordance with the critical theoretical and procedural aspects of the model) and differentiation (the degree to which competing treatment conditions differ from one another as intended) (Hogue et al., 1998). Knowledge here is critical to valid evaluations of interventions and to inform their potential implementation in new sites.

In this vein, it seems extraordinarily wasteful of public resources for funded treatment implementation and outcome studies, which demonstrate efficacy, to not be disseminated to other sites. However, we need more knowledge as to how this knowledge transfer process can be successfully achieved.

Finally, the identification of drug use is a critical initial step in the treatment of an abuser. Biological testing provides a more objective evaluation of recent use than a youth's self-report. Thus, it may be used to validate the self-reported use, or may indicate additional drugs of use that are not reported—since youth are reluctant to report the use of more socially proscribed drugs like cocaine (Dembo et al., 1999). Biological testing (urine, hair, and/or saliva) for drug use should be incorporated into the preliminary screening and in-depth assessment processes.

CONCLUSIONS

Our review of the state of treatment for drug-abusing youth involved in the juvenile justice system showed significant developments in the past 10 years, as well as challenges to the field. Addressing these challenges holds promise of improving the quality and effectiveness of care for these youth, and increasing the quality of life in our communities.

Given the limited resources that are currently directed to troubled youth, we believe a national commitment to help them continues to be needed if we are to reduce their substance abuse, delinquency, and associated problems, as well as the personal, familial, community, and social costs that are related to them. Drug-involved youth in the justice system continue to consume a large and growing amount of public health and justice system resources. Beyond these economic estimates is the poignancy of young lives lost to useful purpose and the pain and tragedy this failure causes these youth, their families, and the community. Rates of recidivism among juvenile offenders remain unacceptable For example, a study in Maricopa County (in Phoenix, Arizona), involving 150,000 youth born between 1962 and 1977 who reached age 18 between 1980 and 1995, found that 46% of the males referred to juvenile-court intake for the first time, and 27% of the females, were referred at least one more time—with 19% of the males eventually receiving four or more referrals (Snyder & Sickmund, 1999). Further, many middle-aged prisoners in state prisons traced their criminal careers to adolescence (U.S. Department of Justice, 1983)—stressing the importance of remediating the problems of juvenile offenders early in life. The issues are clear. Do we have the dedication of purpose to rise to the challenge they present? It would be unfair to expect researchers to establish the necessary political infrastructure. We can, however, continue to educate political leaders to gain their commitment to this conceptually based, research-grounded blueprint for improving the quality of life of their constituencies.

ACKNOWLEDGMENT

Preparation of this chapter was supported by Grant # 1-R01-DA08707, funded by the National Institute on Drug Abuse. We are grateful for their support. However, the results reported and the views expressed in the chapter do not necessarily imply any policy or research endorsement by our funding agency.

IV

Effectiveness

19

Probation and Parole Interventions

Timothy W. Kinlock
and Thomas E. Hanlon

This chapter reviews clinical studies of the effectiveness of drug treatment programs that involve application of judicial authority derived from the criminal justice system in the provision of services in the community. Moving beyond the emphasis on specialized caseloads, it highlights clinical approaches, staffing, and settings. With regard to the drug-abusing offender populations served, the present focus is on heroin and/or cocaine abusers. In contrast to the use of other illicit drugs, increased use of these particular substances typically results in an increase in criminal activity (Nurco, Hanlon, & Kinlock, 1991).

Initially in the review, historical influences and pertinent issues with respect to drug and correctional policies are presented. Next, the topic of probation and parole interventions is defined. The subsequent focus is on evaluations of the effectiveness of various interventions, including formal civil commitment programs and, in particular, more recently developed approaches that emphasize community-based treatment as an alternative to incarceration or as a condition of probation or parole. Conceptual and methodological issues are highlighted, in order to illustrate the extent of knowledge regarding both the appropriateness and effectiveness of these approaches. Following a summary of the current status of probation and parole interventions, the chapter concludes by presenting questions that remain unanswered and suggestions for future research.

HISTORICAL PERSPECTIVES AND PERTINENT ISSUES

Since the passage of the Harrison Act in 1914, which prohibited the over-the-counter sale of narcotics and cocaine in the United States, the history of public responses to drug abuse in our nation has been cyclic. Criminal justice sanctions have dominated during periods in which the social and political climate was conservative, whereas treatment and rehabilitation were emphasized during more liberal periods. Since the 1960s, the pattern of the changing social and political climate of the United States, along with other factors, has contributed to dramatic shifts in correctional policies with respect to drug abuse. During the 1960s, many formal referral programs addressing the needs of drug abusers under correctional supervision were established, and a policy of rehabilitation predominated. Such a policy, based on the medical model, prescribed that professionals, typically psychologists and psychiatrists on parole boards, be responsible for determining the nature of the offender's problem, the most appropriate treatment addressing that problem, and the point at which the problem was sufficiently alleviated so the offender could be released from supervision.

Several events led to a change in the above approach in the 1970s (Lilly, Cullen, & Ball, 1995; Musto, 1987; Stojkovic & Lovell, 1997). Literature reviews (e.g., Martinson, 1974) on the effectiveness of rehabilitation during this period were interpreted as "nothing works." Also, following a chaotic decade that experienced widespread prison and urban riots, the violence associated with anti-Vietnam War protests and protest of the civil rights movement, and public perceptions of increasing crime, many Americans sought new directions in correctional policies (Stojkovic & Lovell, 1997). Thus, the emphasis in corrections moved from that of rehabilitation to a policy of retribution, incapacitation, and deterrence. Parole boards were given less discretionary power and influence. Formal treatment-referral programs for drug-involved probationers and parolees were deemphasized.

As 1980 approached, increased alarm experienced by parent groups over adolescent drug use, as well as public and political concern over the criminogenic effects of heroin and cocaine, contributed to the perception that American society was too permissive (Lilly et al., 1995; Musto, 1987). The 1980s also ushered in a period of rising conservatism, which stressed the notion that drug use and criminal behavior were caused by individual deficiencies, rather than being the result of adverse social and economic circumstances (Lilly et al., 1995). Such views prompted an increased emphasis on arrest and incarceration as intervention approaches (Inciardi, 1992; Lilly et al., 1995), as well as an increased prison population and related drug use (Beck & Mumola, 1999).

The above-noted policies also contributed to dramatic increases in probation and parole populations in the United States during the same period. The number of adults on parole and probation increased annually, from 1.2 million in 1980 to a total of 4.2 million on December 31, 1998, the latest published estimate (Bonczar & Glaze, 1999). The escalation in probationer and parolee populations has contributed to larger supervision caseloads, making it more difficult for probation and parole agents to effectively monitor their clients' behavior (Petersilia, 1995). Since a disproportionately high number of these individuals have been drug abusers, an increasingly large number of offenders are being required to participate in community-based drug abuse treatment as a condition of probation or parole (Farabee, Prendergast, & Anglin, 1998). Unfortunately, growing deficits in community corrections' budgets have led to reduced availability of drug treatment for probationers and parolees (Duffie & Carlson, 1996; Petersilia, 1995), and have lowered community corrections staffing patterns that provided the manpower for the coordination of drug treatment and criminal justice agencies (Duffie & Carlson, 1996).

As in the 1970s and 1980s (Leukefeld & Tims, 1988), drug-free outpatient and residential treatment modalities served the most criminal justice clients in the 1990s, with methadone maintenance comprising few of the criminal justice referrals (Simpson & Knight, 1998). Reflecting the need for more effective treatment approaches, the past decade has witnessed the development of several new probation and parole interventions for drug-abusing offenders. Some of these new approaches, including intensive supervision parole/probation (ISP), drug courts, home detention, and electronic monitoring, were employed as alternatives to incarceration. Other recent interventions include case management, social support, residential treatment, and motivational enhancements, some of which, in addition to their use as primary care, are offered as aftercare services associated with interventions that began in prison. Consistent with the requirements of correctional supervision, these newly developed interventions generally involve the use of sanctions for deviant and/or noncompliant behavior.

DEFINITION OF THE TOPIC

In this chapter, the definition of probation and parole interventions is grounded in the approach used by Leukefeld and Tims (1988), who defined compulsory treatment as "activities that increase the likelihood that drug abusers will enter and remain in treatment, change their behavior in a socially desirable way, and sustain that change" (p. 1). They emphasize that such activities focus on the influence of judicial authority aimed at drug abusers who are unwilling to enter treatment voluntarily, particularly addicts responsible for committing many crimes. These authors also stress that such interventions target intravenous drug users at risk for contracting and transmitting AIDS. They further note that such activities, including the supervision involved in parole and probation, were designed to both rehabilitate and control addicts by providing drug abuse treatment combined with urine monitoring and reasonable sanctions for program infractions.

The following review of the effectiveness of probation and parole interventions stresses outcomes emphasized by Leukefeld and Tims (1988). Thus, the extent to which drug-involved offenders enter and remain in treatment is examined, as well as the degree to which heroin use, cocaine use, criminal activity, and AIDS risk behaviors are reduced. Because Leukefeld and Tims (1988) focused on the intent of compulsory treatment to not only change clients' behavior, but to sustain such change, and because the greatest risk of relapse occurs within the first 3 months of treatment (Nurco, Kinlock, & Hanlon, 1994), longer term treatment-evaluation studies are emphasized in the present review.

RESEARCH FINDINGS ON PROBATION AND PAROLE INTERVENTIONS

Formal Referral Programs

Evaluations of formal referral programs have provided evidence that drug abuse treatment, combined with criminal justice sanctions, can be effective in retaining offenders in treatment and reducing drug abuse and crime. Research on the Treatment Alternatives to Street Crimes (TASC) programs found that clients who were legally induced to enter drug abuse treatment remained in treatment longer than those who were not (Collins & Allison, 1983; Hubbard, Collins, Rachal, & Cavanaugh, 1988; Hubbard, Rachal,

Craddock, & Cavanaugh, 1984). Additionally, clients under correctional supervision improved as much as clients with no criminal justice involvement with regard to substance abuse, criminal activity, and employment during the first 6 months of treatment. Positive results were also reported in the evaluations of California's Civil Addict Program for narcotic (principally heroin) addicts. In these evaluations (Anglin, 1988; Anglin & McGlothlin, 1984; McGlothlin, Anglin, & Wilson, 1978), court-ordered outpatient treatment that incorporated urine testing and parole supervision was associated with significant reductions in narcotic drug use, self-reported crime, and arrests.

Intensive Supervision Parole/Probation

Of interventions considered as alternatives to incarceration, ISP has been the most frequently evaluated. Although there is no standard ISP program nationwide, this type of intervention typically involves smaller caseloads and more frequent contacts and drug testing than are required for traditional probation and parole. The rationale behind ISP is that closer surveillance of offenders and smaller caseloads will reduce drug use and crime. This rationale is also based on findings, noted above, that the effectiveness of drug abuse treatment can be enhanced by mandatory supervision.

Probably the most ambitious, rigorous evaluation of ISP involved 569 probationers in five jurisdictions (Turner, Petersilia, & Deschenes, 1992, 1994). Offenders at each site were randomly assigned to either ISP or to traditional supervision. Results at 1-year follow-up indicated that, as planned, ISP probationers received significantly more urine tests, drug counseling, and supervision contacts than controls. However, over the same period, ISP subjects in four sites had significantly more technical violations for drug use than control subjects. Additionally, although ISP and control offenders did not differ with respect to arrests or drug-related arrests, ISP subjects were more likely than controls to be incarcerated, primarily for technical violations for drug use. At 1-year follow-up, 39% of ISP subjects, compared with 28% of controls (routine supervision offenders), had been jailed, and 13% of ISP subjects, compared with 10% of controls, were sent to prison. ISP probationers also spent more time incarcerated during the follow-up period (73 days) than controls (56 days).

In a review of the above and other less precise research evaluating the ISP approach, Deschenes, Turner, and Petersilia (1995) indicated that such interventions have not markedly diminished drug use or prison crowding.

Furthermore, they noted that, because of considerable variations across jurisdictions in sanctions and program implementation, questions remained concerning the effectiveness of ISP, either as a prison diversion or supervision-enhancement program. In an attempt to address these questions, both types of programs were implemented in Minnesota, and subsequently evaluated in a randomized field experiment involving 300 offenders. Results at 1-year follow-up indicated no difference between experimental and control subjects on either positive tests for drug use or arrests (Deschenes et al., 1995).

Despite the above findings, the effectiveness of ISP in reducing drug use and criminal activity cannot be precisely determined (Petersilia & Turner, 1993). Because of closer surveillance, ISP is associated with more technical violations than routine programs. Responses to technical violations are particularly problematic because they often range from minimal to occasionally harsh sanctions (e.g., imprisonment) to the same type of violation. As a means of alleviating inconsistent sanctioning, also typical of routine supervision, Kleiman (1996) has proposed a program of coerced abstinence, yet to be rigorously evaluated, that involves twice weekly urine testing and consistent, mild sanctions (2 days jail time), which should have a positive bearing on continuity of treatment in intensive monitoring situations.

Drug Courts

Severe prosecution delays in our nation's criminal courts have been partially attributable to growing numbers of drug-related cases (Belenko, 1998). This circumstance, together with vast increases in the number of drug abusers in our nation's prisons, has contributed to the proliferation of drug-court programs over the past 10 years. The rationale underlying drug-court models is that by mandating drug-involved offenders to interventions combining strict parole/probation supervision, frequent urine testing, and drug abuse treatment, reductions can be made in addiction, crime, and prison crowding (see Belenko, this volume).

Other Alternatives to Incarceration

Rigorous evaluations of the effectiveness of other alternative sanctions to reduce drug abuse, such as home detention and electronic monitoring, are particularly lacking. These interventions may be used as either part of, or together with, other approaches, such as ISP (Turner et al., 1994). However, when more than one intervention is used, disentangling the effects of one type of surveillance from another is difficult. More extensive study, including random assignment of a considerable number of offenders to combined approaches, is needed in order to provide more definite evidence for the single and combined effectiveness of such interventions.

Case Management/Social Support

Case management and social support approaches, including aftercare components of interventions begun in prison, focus on factors that influence the community adjustment of newly released parolees with histories of drug abuse. There are several reasons why these interventions are especially suitable during the transitional period following incarceration. First, prisoners with histories of heroin and/or cocaine dependence typically have urgent needs for housing and legitimate employment upon release (Martin & Inciardi, 1993). Second, there is a crucial need for such individuals to link with and draw upon the resources of a constructive, positive social-support system in the community (Martin & Inciardi, 1993), particularly since renewed association with drug abusers is a major contributor to early relapse to addiction (Nurco et al., 1991). Third, prisoners with histories of heroin addiction commonly relapse within 1 month of release, and readdiction is typically accompanied by increased criminal activity (Nurco et al., 1994). Finally, overburdened caseloads and scarce resources make it more difficult for corrections officials to ensure that employment and stable residences have been secured for prospective parolees prior to their release.

Recently completed research on a social-support intervention effort involved the development of one such approach for Baltimore parolees with a history of narcotic (principally heroin) and/or cocaine dependence. This approach included weekly counseling, urine monitoring, and the enhancement of the parolee's positive social-support system using client advocacy and case management (Hanlon, Nurco, Bateman, & O'Grady, 1998, 1999). Services provided to offenders over a 1-year period coinciding with their period of parole supervision were compared with a urine-monitoring program alone and routine parole (i.e., no involvement in social-support treatment and little to no urine monitoring).

Analyses of 1-year parole outcomes for 504 subjects provide some evidence for the effectiveness of the social-support approach (Hanlon et al.,

1999). Of these subjects, 270 had been randomly assigned to social support plus urine monitoring, 99 to urine monitoring only, and 135 to routine parole. Results indicated that social-support subjects were significantly more likely than urine-monitoring subjects to remain in treatment longer. They were also less likely than subjects in the other groups to receive a major infraction (parole violation/revocation, warrant, arrest, conviction, incarceration) during the 1-year period. However, drug use (both urinalysis results and self-reported) for routine parole subjects was significantly lower than that for both the social-support or urine-monitoring groups. Hanlon et al. (1999) noted that these latter findings were consistent with those of Petersilia and Turner (1993), described earlier, who reported an increase in the recorded number of transgressions with more intense supervision, and with those of Anglin, Hser, and Chou (1993), who observed that there is a greater admission of self-reported drug use when urinalysis results are concurrently available.

Additional analyses conducted on 237 subjects, who were randomly assigned to the social-support approach, distinguished 119 subjects who received a major infraction during the year of parole from 118 who did not. Individuals with earlier onsets of drug abuse and crime, more deviant family members, and more school-adjustment problems during their formative years tended to have poor outcomes. In contrast, individuals with a lesser predisposition toward deviance and more stable employment prior to their incarceration generally had more favorable outcomes (Hanlon et al., 1998).

In their examination of the setting of the interventions, Hanlon and colleagues (1998) noted that their social-support and urinalysis interventions, although compared with routine parole, were not compared with a no-treatment condition, in view of the fact that 64% of routine parole subjects had become involved in other drug treatment programs during the course of the study. The authors indicated that because all of their subjects were initially determined to be in need of drug treatment, for ethical reasons, they could not prohibit routine parole subjects from applying for substance-abuse treatment elsewhere. Their concerns in this regard were justified inasmuch as complementary analyses revealed that within the control (routine parole) sample, drug-abuse treatment involvement by control subjects was associated with more favorable outcomes in terms of number of infractions, drug use, and employment during the 1-year study period.

Another recently evaluated case-management intervention, Assertive Community Treatment (ACT), focused on the transitional period encompassing both prison treatment and community-based aftercare. In this approach, involving Delaware parolees whose drug-abusing behavior had placed them at risk for HIV infection, intervention was provided in stages, the last stage occurring approximately 6 months postrelease. In succession, the ACT approach involved evaluation and assessment; intensive drug treatment, including individual and group counseling, AIDS education, and family therapy; life skills planning, with an emphasis on educational and vocational training; relapse prevention; and, finally, case management designed to support the client's transition into the community.

Analyses of 6-month (Martin & Inciardi, 1993) and 18-month (Martin & Inciardi, 1997) outcomes suggested limited support for the effectiveness of ACT. Results for 258 offenders (114 randomly assigned to ACT and 144 randomly assigned to standard parole supervision) at 6-month follow-up indicated modest reductions in the probability of relapse to both illicit drug use (assessed by urinalysis and self-report) and drug injection among ACT clients when contrasted with standard parole clients. However, ACT clients were more likely to be arrested than standard parole clients during the study period. Lack of substantial ACT effects was also observed at 18 months on 304 subjects when the analyses controlled for the effects of demographic variables; drug use, drug treatment, and arrest history; and variability in the time between baseline and subsequent assessments. However, a multivariate path model suggested that ACT assignment had indirect positive effects on subsequent illegal drug use in that ACT increased treatment retention (defined as the longest time in a single program, not only ACT) and self-esteem, which, in turn, were related to reduced alcohol intoxication—the strongest predictor of drug use.

Interestingly, Martin and Inciardi (1997) made valuable comments on the setting and staffing of ACT, which paralleled the observations of Hanlon and coworkers (1998) in their research. First, they contended that retention was adversely affected because the project was bound by the requirements of a research-demonstration effort. Under these circumstances, clients could not be offered treatment either as a means for early parole or as a condition of parole. Second, they concluded that random assignment, while being valuable for evaluating outcome, compromised the treatment initiative, since in "real world" settings, program staff often select the clients they believe are ready for treatment and appropriate for a certain modality. In contrast, random assignment, at times, resulted in the assignment of clients to treatment that was inappropriate for them and for which they had little or no commitment. As a consequence, Martin and Inciardi (1997) point out that conclusions made about treatment offered in a research setting may not necessarily apply to a treatment setting unencumbered by the requirements of a research design. Also, with regard to staffing issues, they noted in their process findings that the intervention was less "assertive" than planned. ACT counselors initially were less willing to reach out to clients who, because of the random selection, were not always actively seeking treatment. The investigators were also of the opinion that combining the roles of treatment counselor and case manager produced an intervention that was too generic, and thus worked against the separate tailoring of roles to the individual case.

Motivational Enhancements

Interventions designed to enhance offenders' motivation are considered crucial components of correctional drug treatment. A client's internal motivation to change at the time of program admission has been found to be significantly related to increased retention and engagement in treatment (Joe, Simpson, & Broome, 1998) and to long-term posttreatment outcomes across modalities (Simpson, Joe, & Brown, 1997). Evaluations of correctional and other drug treatment (Nurco et al., 1994; Simpson et al., 1997) indicate that positive posttreatment outcome was significantly related to time in treatment, with retention for at least 3 months crucial for the appearance of behavior change. As emphasized by Farabee et al. (1998), lack of internal motivation may be a particularly severe problem in settings in which offenders are required to enter drug abuse treatment as a condition of probation or parole before they are personally ready to become involved in treatment. Farabee and colleagues (1998) cite the work of Miller (1989), who noted that a client entering treatment before he or she recognizes that drug abuse is a problem is unlikely to benefit from a drug-abuse intervention.

Although there is considerable evidence for the effectiveness of motivational enhancements in alcoholism treatment (Miller, 1996), the use of such techniques has not been extensively evaluated for drug-offending probationers and parolees. One such effort by Blankenship, Dansereau, and Simpson (1999) consisted of a four-session treatment-readiness program that incorporated various cognitive engagement strategies. In this study, probationers in a mandated 4-month residential program were randomly assigned to receive either a standard program induction ($N = 244$) or an enhanced ($N = 249$) treatment-readiness program. The standard program involved lecture and discussion, whereas the enhanced program, specifically designed for probationers with less education, consisted of instructional games, demonstrations, and group activities. Activities for the enhanced program were selected because individuals with the most serious drug problems tend to have less education and gain fewer benefits from standard drug treatment, in part because of problems in communication through traditional verbal channels (Blankenship et al., 1999).

Results of the study showed that, at 8 weeks, probationers in the enhanced program reported significantly greater treatment motivation and confidence in treatment than those in the standard condition. For probationers in the enhanced condition, positive effects were significantly greater in those with less education (10 years or below) than in those with more education. Blankenship et al. (1999) noted that, because their intervention is able to be implemented in a group setting, it is more feasible than traditional, individual motivational interviewing in settings with high client to counselor ratios.

CONCEPTUAL AND METHODOLOGICAL ISSUES

Several important conceptual and methodological issues concerning the evaluation of probation and parole interventions involve the lack of standardization of disciplinary procedures within the criminal justice system. Researchers of ISP and intensive urine-monitoring programs have observed considerable variations, both within and across jurisdictions and among probation and parole agents, in response to drug-use infractions (Hanlon et al., 1998, 1999). Sites and agents tend to vary extensively with respect to the type and severity of sanctions imposed on evidence of drug use among offenders. Also, surveillance-oriented interventions typically increase the amount of deviance brought to the attention of probation and parole agents (Hanlon et al., 1998, 1999; Turner et al., 1992). As a result, the number of technical violations increases. Such an outcome invariably contributes to an artifactual negative evaluation of treatment effectiveness, compared with that associated with less stringent control-monitoring conditions. Moreover, depending on the type of sanctions, such conditions may significantly increase the number of offenders who are incarcerated because of technical violations of probation and parole (Turner et al., 1992).

Caution is also advised in interpreting a number of evaluations of probation and parole interventions in view of other limitations in frequently used outcome measures. Exclusive reliance on arrest and incarceration as indicators of offending can be problematic because such measures are gross underestimates of the degree of criminal activity, including illicit drug use. Self-report studies, in which confidentiality and immunity from prosecution have been assured, have consistently found that less than 1% of crime reported by heroin- and/or cocaine-dependent offenders results in arrest (Kinlock, Hanlon, & Nurco, 1999; Nurco et al., 1991). Although confidential self-reports of drug use and crime are generally valid and reliable when obtained for research purposes from offenders who are entering treatment programs in the community or who are already incarcerated, they are far less likely to be valid for individuals whose probation or parole status would be jeopardized by admission of criminal activity (Kinlock et al., 1999; Nurco et al., 1991). Further, probationers and parolees are more likely to deny participation in drug abuse and crime if they know that urine testing is not required or if they identify researchers as extensions of the criminal justice system. Because of these circumstances, urine monitoring is increasingly being recommended as the most feasible and accurate method of determining the extent of drug abuse among such individuals (Kinlock et al., 1999).

Despite the initial work of Blankenship et al. (1999), little attention has been paid to internal motivation in evaluations of coerced treatment for drug-involved offenders. Farabee et al. (1998) reported that the emphasis on external pressure to enter treatment and its relative success has overshadowed the potential role of internal motivation. As Leukefeld and Tims (1988) emphasized, long-term recovery from drug abuse cannot result from external (legal) pressure alone; motivation and commitment to remain productively involved in treatment must come from internal pressure, with the role of external pressure influencing one to enter treatment.

Unfortunately, individual differences in response to probation and parole interventions have rarely been explored. The studies by Blankenship et al. (1999), Hanlon et al. (1998), and Hiller, Knight, and Simpson (1999) were among the first to examine heterogeneity in response to such interventions. Given the considerable individual variations among drug-involved offenders with regard to criminality, psychological functioning, and motivation for treatment, among other relevant dimensions (Hanlon et al., 1998; Kinlock et al., 1999), a single type of treatment approach is not likely to be effective for all individuals.

Because past evaluations typically have examined treatment without regard to its various components, greater focus needs to be placed on identifying essential components of the treatment process and in examining how these can be enhanced to improve outcomes (Hiller et al., 1999). This is particularly important because many aspects of treatment implemented within corrections, including alternatives to incarceration, are often used in combination, and disentangling the effectiveness of each component, generally and for different types of offenders, has rarely been accomplished. Finally, the actual delivery of correctional drug-treatment services is often different from that originally planned. Even within seemingly similar programs, variations in implementation are common. All too frequently, poor communication between treatment and correctional agencies results in inappropriate, inconsistent, and/or ineffective sanctions and, ultimately, in a failure on the part of clients to receive crucial services for which they have been referred (Farabee et al., 1998).

CURRENT STATUS OF PROBATION AND PAROLE INTERVENTIONS

As noted above, there is evidence that drug abuse treatment, combined with criminal justice sanctions, can be effective in recruiting many drug-involved offenders into treatment, retaining them in treatment, and reducing addiction, criminal activity, and arrest. These findings are particularly significant in view of the growing number of drug-involved offenders in the criminal justice system, the large caseloads of parole and probation agents, and reduced availability of drug treatment for offenders resulting from budget cuts for community corrections. Results pertaining to the effectiveness of probation and parole interventions reflect DATOS findings, which indicate reductions in addiction and crime occur despite reductions in crucial community services, such as health care and child care (Etheridge, Hubbard, Anderson, Craddock, & Flynn, 1997). And, as Etheridge and colleagues (1997) noted in the DATOS study, the overall success of probation and parole interventions in the face of scarce community resources points to the skill of counselors, supervision agents, and other front-line personnel who work directly with drug-involved offenders.

Despite the above positive findings, parole and probation interventions need further improvement. In addition to low client motivation, relapse to deviant behavior in outpatient drug-treatment programs, although significantly lower than in control, or comparison, conditions, is disappointingly high. For example, in Martin and Inciardi's (1997) study, approximately 50% of ACT clients relapsed to the use of illicit drugs 6 to 18 months following baseline assessment. Similarly, Hanlon et al. (1999) found that 50% of subjects receiving social-support treatment received a major sanction during their 1-year parole period. Obviously, new approaches need to be considered to increase the likelihood of positive outcomes among such a recalcitrant population.

UNANSWERED QUESTIONS AND FUTURE DIRECTIONS

Several researchers (Hanlon et al., 1999; Kleiman, 1996; Leukefeld & Tims, 1988; Martin & Inciardi, 1997) have emphasized the need for correctional treatment-outcome studies to incorporate standardized protocols with regard to surveillance and sanctions. Use of a generally accepted strategy would allow for clear understanding for replication (Leukefeld & Tims, 1988). For example, because of extensive variations, both within and across jurisdictions and among probation and parole agents in their response to noncompliance with treatment, there is a strong need for the implementation and evaluation of systematically applied supervisory routines (Hanlon et al., 1999; Martin & Inciardi, 1997). Such a routine needs to involve graduated sanctions and/or treatment referrals that are enforced or mandated and that are clearly understood at the outset by offenders, probation and parole agents, and treatment staff.

Similarly, as Kleiman (1996) emphasized, probation and parole urine-monitoring routines are often problematic because of infrequent testing, and even more infrequent but severe sanctioning (such as several months in prison for a missed or positive test). Kleiman posited that coerced abstinence, involving more frequent (twice weekly) urine testing and automatic, mild sanctions, such as 2 days jail time, would be more effective in deterring heroin and cocaine use than standard parole procedures. As Kleiman recommended, controlled evaluations of coerced abstinence versus standard parole need to be conducted. Further, coerced abstinence routines, if implemented properly and consistently, could provide clinical staff with valuable valid, longitudinal data on the type(s), frequency, and persistence of client drug use and motivation for program participation. Such information could help clinicians make more timely referrals of clients to appropriate services.

Correctional treatment programs need to be frequently and rigorously evaluated to determine their level of effectiveness, both generally and for different types of clients. Outcome measures, in addition to arrest and incarceration, need to include urinalysis results for illicit drug use and objective community-adjustment criteria, along with confidential self-reports of deviant behavior. Analyses of urine-test results need to be conducted separately by type of drug(s) because frequent use of heroin and/

or cocaine is more likely than other drug-use patterns to be related to increased criminal activity and adverse health consequences. Standard measures of the internal motivation of clients also need to be obtained to assess the extent of readiness for treatment and the role this plays in the determination of outcome. Further, in order to better ensure program fidelity and to examine the effectiveness of various components of correctional treatment, detailed process evaluations are needed to capture the nature and number of services received; attendance and compliance with treatment, supervision, and urinalysis requirements; reasons for absence/lateness with regard to required contacts; reasons for noncompliance and termination; and the nature of interactions between criminal justice and treatment agencies. In effect, more attention should be paid to the functional relationships between process measures and treatment outcome if we are to identify the essential components and correlates of successful treatment.

In view of the above findings linking greater levels of internal motivation to improved treatment engagement and retention, and the fact that many offenders are not ready for coerced treatment, the development and evaluation of motivational enhancement in correctional treatment has surfaced as a crucial need. Miller (1999) has indicated that counselors who deliver motivational interviewing interventions have received many requests for training in the procedure from probation and parole departments. He emphasizes that such interventions are urgently needed, given the large number of substance abusers in the criminal justice system and the widespread success of motivational interviewing in other settings.

Increasing the breadth of treatment availability is also an important consideration. More than 10 years ago, Leukefeld and Tims (1988) reported that relatively few probationers and parolees were referred to methadone-maintenance treatment. These authors further noted a consensus among researchers in recommending that the effectiveness of methadone treatment be more persuasively presented to criminal justice personnel. Unfortunately, despite considerable evidence regarding the effectiveness of this approach in reducing addiction, crime, and HIV-risk behavior (Platt, Widman, Lidz, & Marlowe, 1998), the nationwide DATOS study found that only 2% of outpatient methadone slots were filled with referrals from the criminal justice system (Simpson & Knight, 1998). In view of the adverse consequences of heroin addiction, increases in the purity and availability of heroin, and in the number of heroin addicts in the United States (Kinlock, Hanlon, & Nurco, 1998), rigorous research is urgently needed with regard to determination of the effectiveness of methadone and LAAM maintenance in the treatment of addicted probationers and parolees.

In conclusion, researchers and policymakers need to recognize the diversity among drug-involved offenders, and that no single approach is likely to be effective for all individuals. In recognition of this diversity, more research is needed to determine the types of interventions that are most effective for different types of clients. Such a view contrasts sharply with the historical account of public responses to drug abuse in the United States, which have alternated between a reliance on criminal justice sanctions and an emphasis on treatment and rehabilitation. From an historical perspective, drug-abuse policy has been more a function of the prevailing social and political climate than a reaction to research findings. Finally, in order to avoid unproductive confrontations characteristic of the past, both researchers and policymakers need to ensure that law enforcement and treatment agencies work in concert, rather than in competition, with one another.

ACKNOWLEDGMENT

We greatly appreciate the assistance of Barry Brown, PhD, who provided valuable comments on earlier drafts of our manuscript.

20

Screening and Referral for Substance-Abuse Treatment in the Criminal Justice System

Kevin Knight, D. Dwayne Simpson, and Matthew L. Hiller

ccording to the Bureau of Justice Statistics (BJS), the U.S. adult prison and jail inmate population is rapidly approaching the 2 million mark, with drug-involved offenders comprising the majority of the incarcerated population (BJS, 2000). In a 1997 BJS survey, approximately 50% of all state and federal inmates reported that they had used drugs in the month before their offense, and more than 75% indicated that they had used drugs during their lifetime (BJS, 1999).

By providing therapeutic intervention, however, criminal justice agencies have a unique opportunity to identify and rehabilitate (or habilitate) drug-involved offenders who are likely, if untreated, to return to a personally and socially destructive pattern of drug use and criminal activity following release from prison. Indeed, research has shown that focused rehabilitation-oriented treatment services can lead to favorable outcomes following incarceration (Andrews et al., 1990; Gendreau, 1996). Particularly within correctional settings, intensive long-term treatment programs (such as modified in-prison therapeutic communities [TCs]) have been found to reduce postincarceration relapse (i.e., return to drug use) and recidivism (i.e., arrests, reconviction, and reincarceration). For example, recent evaluations of Delaware's Key-Crest, California's Amity, and Texas' Kyle New Vision prison-based TC treatment programs have shown that, compared with their untreated counterparts, drug-involved inmates who complete in-prison drug treatment are significantly less likely to return to a life of drug use and crime following release from prison (Knight, Simpson, & Hiller, 1999; Martin, Butzin, Saum, & Inciardi, 1999; Wexler, Melnick, Lowe, & Peters, 1999). Furthermore, these findings are even more pronounced among those who participate in aftercare treatment (Griffith, Hiller, Knight, & Simpson, 1999; Hiller, Knight, & Simpson, 1999). Nonetheless, the demand for treatment services within the criminal justice system continues to far exceed the supply, with the gap actually getting wider over the past decade.

Therefore, since it is neither possible nor necessary to provide services (particularly intensive residential treatment) to every drug-involved offender, referral decisions must be made regarding whether an offender's drug-related problems are serious enough to warrant treatment. Furthermore, when serious problems are identified, referral decisions must also be made regarding the most appropriate type and intensity of treatment. For example, research suggests that priority for receiving intensive treatment services should be assigned to those with the more severe problems (Knight et al., 1999; Griffith et al., 1999).

Unfortunately, treatment-referral decisions often are based on incomplete and irrelevant information, potentially resulting in unclear or even conflicting objectives (Hepburn, 1994). Inmates who have more severe drug problems may be preempted from being referred to an intensive drug-treatment program because of competing institutional work assignments or education programs. Likewise, political pressures and organizational constraints, such as the need to fill bed space, can result in an individual with either no (or less severe) drug use problems being referred to an intensive residential-treatment program. Similar problems exist when referral is based on subjective criteria, such as an interviewer's judgment about an inmate's need for treatment. For example, a "suspicious" offender may be referred to treatment simply because of an interviewer's unsubstantiated belief that the inmate was lying about drug use. These types of inappropriate referrals needlessly consume valuable staff time and program funds that are better used on inmates who actually have drug problems.

An objective screening and referral protocol, on the other hand, can serve to provide a consistent means of identifying drug-involved offenders most likely to benefit from limited treatment resources. This chapter addresses some of the important factors that correctional agencies should consider when developing a system of screening and referral.

DEVELOPING A SCREENING AND REFERRAL PROTOCOL

The development of an effective and efficient screening and referral protocol requires carefully consideration to three key factors: (a) selecting an instrument appropriate for a specific correctional environment, (b) obtaining truthful responses, and (c) providing suitable treatment options.

Selecting an Appropriate Instrument

Because most correctional agencies do not have the financial and staffing resources to conduct comprehensive assessments of drug problems for every newly admitted inmate, they often rely on the use of a brief screening instrument. As the initial component of a comprehensive screening and referral protocol, a drug-use screen typically is administered as part of a larger battery of assessments given shortly after an inmate is incarcerated. By including the drug screen along with other assessments, decisions regarding the need for treatment can be made in conjunction with other important considerations, such as custody level and educational needs. For example, immediate referral to treatment services for an inmate who self-admits having serious drug problems only can be made when there is an assignment to a custody level where services are available. Also, by administering the screen as soon as possible, the potential for other inmates being able to influence how an inmate responds to the screen is minimized.

The first step in this process is the selection of an appropriate screening instrument. This process should include careful consideration to the instrument's accuracy, length, cost, and window of detection. Other important factors include whether the instrument assesses drug dependence or abuse, is self-administered or given as part of a clinical interview, and whether it requires extensive and continued staff training.

Accuracy

Perhaps the most critical aspect of a screening instrument is its ability to discriminate accurately between those who do and do not have drug problems. Because classification error is inevitable, a decision has to be made regarding whether it is better to select an instrument that is more likely to result in someone being referred to treatment that does not need it, or one that is more likely to result in denying treatment to someone who truly does need it.

Five statistical guidelines can be examined to help inform the decision process (see Cherpitel, 1997, and Peters et al., 2000). First, a measure of overall accuracy is a good general indicator of the instrument's utility. Based on the entire sample of screened offenders, it represents the overall percentage of those who were classified correctly, with higher values being more desirable. However, because a drug screen's overall accuracy is not likely to be 100%, four other statistics also need to be considered, including sensitivity, specificity, positive predictive value, and negative predictive value.

Sensitivity focuses only on offenders who *actually have drug problems* and provides a percentage of those the *screen* accurately identifies as having problems. For agencies that are mandated to identify and provide services to drug-involved offenders, selecting an instrument with high sensitivity can help improve the chances that those with drug problems are detected. An instrument with a high sensitivity score also tends to identify the largest number of treatment-eligible inmates, which may be particularly valuable when treatment slots are empty and need to be filled.

As a counterpart to sensitivity, specificity includes only the offenders who *actually do not have drug problems* and is a percentage of those the *screen* correctly identifies as not having problems. A screen with high specificity decreases the probability that an offender without drug problems will be sent to treatment and may be particularly important for agencies that have few treatment options and a large number of inmates from which to draw. For agencies already having a difficult time filling treatment slots with qualified offenders, a screening instrument with high sensitivity may be more desirable.

Positive predictive value examines only those offenders the *screen* identifies as having drug problems and provides a proportional measure of how many *actually have drug problems*. For agencies that strive to maximize the number of appropriate referrals, positive predictive value deserves special attention. A high value suggests that those the screen identifies as having drug problems actually do have problems and should receive treatment services. This statistic is particularly helpful for agencies with a limited number of treatment options and that want to make sure the distribution of those services is highly efficient.

Based strictly on inmates' self-report the *screen* classifies as not having drug problems, negative predictive value indicates the proportion who *actually do not have drug problems*. In general, a screen with a relatively high positive predictive value will tend to have a relatively low negative predictive value, potentially failing to identify inmates who may be able to benefit from treatment.

Ultimately, the most appropriate instrument is one that has sensitivity and specificity scores, as well as positive and negative predictive values, that correspond with the needs of a specific correctional setting. Under these circumstances, financial and staffing expenditures on inappropriate inmates are minimized.

Length

Another factor to consider when deciding on a drug screen is the amount of time it takes for administration. Correctional systems usually must determine the need for treatment for large numbers of offenders in a short period of time. For example, the Texas Department of Criminal Justice (TDCJ)–Program and Services Division (PSD) coordinates the drug-abuse screening and treatment-referral process of more than 3,300 new inmates each month. They have neither the available staff time nor financial resources to administer lengthy individual interviews with each new admission. Although many popular assessments for drug problems are well designed and serve as broad sorting tools that can be used to assist in making recommendations for general treatment or intervention alternatives, they tend to be fairly lengthy and take more time to administer than correctional agencies can afford.

Cost

Another concern is whether to choose a screen that is in the "public domain" and available for free, or one that is available commercially for a fee. For example, the Substance Abuse Subtle Screening Inventory (SASSI; Fuller, Fishman, Taylor, & Wood, 1994; Miller, 1985; Svanum & McGrew, 1995) is a commercially available drug screen used by several correctional agencies, including the TDCJ–Institutional Division (ID) until recently. By switching to the Texas Christian University Drug Screen (TCUDS; Simpson, Knight, & Broome, 1997)—a public domain instrument—the agency was able to save thousands of dollars annually. For smaller correctional agencies, cost may be less of a concern, particularly if the instrument meets diagnostic needs and is already part of the traditional assessment protocol.

Window of Detection

Another consideration is whether an instrument assesses drug use problems that occurred over the course of several years or during a more recent, restricted time frame. Because there is an increased probability of obtaining valid responses when the diagnostic emphasis is on identifying "current" alcohol or drug problems, a relatively short "window of detection" is usually recommended (Cherpitel, 1997). However, shorter detection windows, such as the past 30 days, may be too restrictive to fill the available treatment services. Furthermore, those who need treatment may be overlooked. For example, a 30-day detection window may fail to detect offenders with drug problems who abstained from recent drug use because of legal pressures or surveillance while waiting for trial. On the other hand, if the instrument assesses the presence of drug use problems at any point during an offender's life, a long waiting list for treatment may result. In this case, those who may not have had serious drug problems recently could be referred to treatment, while those with current drug problems are forced to wait.

Dependence Versus Abuse

Diagnostic criteria can vary considerably across instruments, with some focusing on drug dependence and others on abuse. Screens that are based on highly conservative criteria, such as the *Diagnostic and Statistical Manual of Mental Disorders* (DSM-IV), are designed to detect individuals with serious drug problems (American Psychiatric Association, 1994). These types of instruments are the most likely to identify individuals who could benefit from intensive treatment services. An instrument with diagnostic criteria for abuse, rather than dependence, may be more desirable if an agency's goal is to provide offenders who may have any range of drug-problem severity with less intensive treatment services, such as drug education classes.

Interview or Self-Administered

The way an instrument is delivered also can play an important role in the selection of a screening instrument. For example, the Addiction Severity

Index (ASI) is a comprehensive clinical assessment of drug use problems designed to be administered as part of a face-to-face interview. Other instruments, such as the Simple Screening Instrument (SSI) and the TCUDS, were designed to be brief, self-administered drug screens. Although a lengthy, structured, clinical interview, such as the ASI, may be the preferred choice of many counselors, time and personnel constrains often make shorter self-administered instruments necessary. When a drug-use screen cannot be given as part of a one-on-one interview, research suggests that results can be obtained reliably when self-administered as part of a small-group interview (Broome, Knight, Joe, & Simpson, 1996).

Required Staff Training

Because of high staff turnover, correctional agencies often find that they are deficient in the number of staff who have the clinical experience and credentials necessary to administer certain diagnostic instruments. Even when qualified staff are available, providing extensive and continued training on form administration may be difficult. Therefore, selecting a brief, easily administered screening instrument that requires little staff training can ease this burden greatly. Furthermore, on-going training on some instruments, such as the TCUDS, can be provided by existing correctional staff who have experience administering the screen, eliminating the need to hire an outside "expert" whenever new staff are hired.

Obtaining Truthful Responses

After selecting a screen, a protocol for administration needs to be developed that encourages inmates to respond honestly. Although the accuracy of self-reported drug use with treatment populations can vary considerably across situations, research shows valid drug-use data can be obtained when forms are administered in settings where conditions are favorable for truthful self-disclosure (Wish, 1988).

Perceived Consequences

One of the primary influences on an offender's willingness to self-report drug problems is the perceived consequences of disclosure. Inmates fear that correctional decision-making boards will make custody assignments and postrelease supervision-level decisions based, in part, on what is reported on the drug screen. Unlike community-treatment settings where a client is guaranteed confidentiality, correctional staff cannot provide such guarantees. They can, however, make it clear to an inmate that there are positive consequences for responding honestly, such as getting access to drug treatment services. Likewise, dishonest responding can result in negative consequences. For example, parole decisions are based on whether an inmate poses an unacceptable risk to society if released. This risk may be determined, in part, by whether an inmate has been deceptive while incarcerated, such as failing to self-admit drug use on a screen when there is a criminal record of drug-related offenses. In short, honest responding is more likely to occur when an offender understands that it is in his or her best interest to be honest when completing the screening instrument.

Setting

Obtaining accurate data also is influenced by the setting in which a screening instrument is administered. For example, when a large number of offenders are confined into a small testing area, the overcrowded conditions can lead to offender-management problems that dominate the administrator's time—shifting the focus away from the intent of the screen. In cases where the form can be administered only in a large group setting, proctors can provide invaluable assistance to the interviewer by offering individualized attention to those who may need help, particularly with respect to literacy and behavioral problems. In addition, correctional staff can encourage truthful responding by providing an overview of the instrument, informing inmates why honest responding is important, giving detailed instructions on how to complete the instrument, and encouraging questions. Underreporting is inevitable when the interviewer makes it obvious that the primary goal is to get though the screen as quickly as possible.

Providing Suitable Treatment Options

Appropriate instrument selection and implementation should be followed by referral to appropriate treatment options. Correctional systems that provide two options (e.g., no treatment or intensive TC treatment) do not need elaborate and complex screening and referral protocols that classify inmates into more than two categories of treatment need. Similarly, if multiple treatment options are available, the assessment protocol needs greater precision. For example, those with relatively minor drug problems can be assigned to receive drug education while incarcerated. Those with moderate problems could be required to participate in weekly counseling sessions and encouraged to attend self-help group meetings. Finally, those with the most severe problems could be referred to the most intensive programs available, such as in-prison TC treatment (see Knight et al., 1999). Although this concept of treatment matching has been around for many years, there still is little science to provide detailed guidance in designing the proper protocol.

Other factors, such as co-occurring psychological problems, the length of an inmate's sentence, and the type of current and prior offenses also play a major role in determining which, if any, treatment options are viable. For drug-involved offenders with severe psychological problems, referral is made ideally to a specialized treatment program that provides both substance-abuse treatment and mental health care (Peters & Hills, 1999). When this type of program is not available, correctional officials have to decide whether psychiatric problems are too severe for the offender to be referred to a drug treatment program. In addition, a large percentage of many state correctional populations serve less than a year in confinement, making it impossible for an inmate to complete lengthier residential-treatment programs, such as 9- to 12-month in-prison TC programs. For these offenders, a drug screen may serve only to determine if a short-term, intensive treatment program or drug education program is warranted. Finally, inmates with certain types of offenses also may be excluded from available treatment options. For example, Texas inmates who have committed certain types of aggravated offense are precluded from participating in an in-prison TC program because of their possible disruptive influence. Although intensive treatment programs may not be an option in each of these specific cases, correctional agencies may want to consider at least offering these inmates access to self-help groups and drug education classes.

AVAILABLE SCREENS

Although several screening instruments have been developed over the past few years for use in a variety of community settings (see Cherpitel, 1997; Hepburn, 1994; McPherson & Hersch, 2000), their application within correctional settings has been tested only recently (Peters, Greenbaum, & Edens, 1998; Peters et al., 2000). For example, Peters and his colleagues (2000) conducted a field test of screening instruments with 400 newly admitted male inmates to a Texas prison-transfer facility in 1996. Overall,

51% of the sample indicated a lifetime prevalence of alcohol- or drug-dependence disorders, based on the Structured Clinical Interview for DSM-IV (SCID-IV, Version 2.0, Substance Abuse Disorders module; First, Spitzer, Gibbon, & Williams, 1996). Clinical diagnoses were then compared with seven popular screening instruments, including the TCUDS (Simpson et al., 1997), Alcohol Dependence Scale (ADS; Skinner & Horn, 1984), ASI (Drug Use and Alcohol Use Sections; McLellan et al., 1992), Drug Abuse Screening Test (DAST; Skinner, 1982), Michigan Alcohol Screening Test—Short Version (MAST; Selzer, 1971), SASSI (Miller, 1985), and the SSI (Center for Substance-Abuse Treatment, 1994). Based on their findings, the authors concluded that the TCUDS, the SSI, and a combined instrument (the ADS/ASI) were the most effective in identifying substance abuse and dependence disorders. The SSI and ADS/ASI are described briefly below, followed by a more comprehensive overview of the TCUDS.

Alcohol Dependence Screen/Addiction Severity Index

The ADS (Skinner & Horn, 1984) is a brief screen of 25 items designed to assess alcohol dependency. The ASI (McLellan et al., 1992) was developed as a comprehensive diagnostic interview, and focuses on seven problem areas: alcohol use, medical condition, drug use, employment/support, illegal activity, family/social relations, and psychiatric problems (McLellan et al., 1992). For the purposes of screening, the alcohol- and drug-use sections of the ASI were combined with the ADS to form a single screening instrument. Peters et al. (2000) found that the ADS/ASI screen had high positive predictive value, as well as high sensitivity, providing a high degree of accuracy in excluding nondependent participants and an ability to identify a high proportion of substance-dependent participants. The combined instrument had high overall accuracy (83%), sensitivity (74%), specificity (92%), positive predictive value (89%), and negative predictive value (80%). Although the ADS/ASI combined instrument had good utility within correctional settings, it is important to note that the ADS portion is only available commercially and the ASI alcohol- and drug-use sections were two parts of a lengthier one-on-one interview format and would need to be tested as part of a self-administered, stand-alone component.

Simple Screening Instrument

The SSI is a 16-item public-domain instrument developed by the Center for Substance-Abuse Treatment to assess alcohol and drug dependency

(Center for Substance-Abuse Treatment, 1994). Peters et al. (2000) found that it had relatively high overall accuracy (82%), sensitivity (93%), specificity (73%), positive predictive value (75%), and negative predictive value (92%). It was particularly effective at identifying the largest number of inmates with drug use disorders, although 25% were misclassified as having drug problems. For agencies that are less concerned about sending someone to treatment who does not need it and more concerned about identifying the largest number of treatment-eligible inmates, the SSI may prove useful.

Texas Christian University Drug Screen

The TCUDS (see Appendix) was developed by researchers at the Institute of Behavioral Research at Texas Christian University and has shown promise in meeting the substance-abuse diagnostic needs of large correctional systems (Simpson et al., 1997). It has been used since 1993, originally as part of an earlier version of the instrument called the Brief Background Assessment (BBA). Revised twice since its earlier version as the BBA, the TCUDS includes 15 items that represent key clinical and diagnostic criteria for substance "dependence" as they appear in the Diagnostic and Statistical Manual (DSM; American Psychiatric Association, 1994) and the National Institute of Mental Health (NIMH) Diagnostic Interview Schedule (DIS; Robins, Helzer, Croughan, & Ratcliff, 1981). These criteria were adapted for use within criminal justice settings by rewording "clinical" language to be more appropriate for individuals with 8th-grade reading levels and by using a format that promotes reliable self-administration (Broome et al., 1996). The first part of the TCUDS includes a series of 10 questions about problems related to "drug use," and the second part addresses the frequency of specific drug use prior to prison, as well as a self-assessment of one's readiness for substance-abuse treatment. Based on the first nine items of the TCUDS, a continuous composite score is computed that measures the level of an offender's drug-use severity. Classification criteria for drug use dependency parallels the DSM protocol, based on any combination of three "positive" responses out of the first nine items. The remaining TCUDS items are designed to provide corroborative evidence of potential drug use problems, such as questions pertaining to prior drug treatment.

The TCUDS can be completed as part of an interview or can be self-administered, and prior research shows it elicits information that is highly consistent with other data sources (Broome et al., 1996). Based on the original version of the TCUDS, an article entitled, "Evaluating the drug-abusing probationer: Clinical interview versus self-administered assessment" (Broome et al., 1996), compared probationer responses given under two types of administration—one using an interview format and the other using self-administration—approximately 1 week apart. Overall, there were relatively few differences in item responses between the types of administration, supporting the use of the TCUDS as a self-administered instrument within correctional settings.

Results from the study conducted by Peters and his colleagues indicated that the TCUDS had one of the highest overall accuracy rates (82%; Peters et al., 2000). Furthermore, the TCUDS had high positive predictive value (92%) and specificity (92%). Measures of sensitivity (70%) and negative predictive value (78%) were comparable to the ADS/ASI, yet lower than the SSI. The TCUDS also had good test-retest reliability (0.95).

As part of a grant funded by the National Institute of Justice, Institute for Behavioral Research researchers have been examining the application of the TCUDS within correctional settings more closely. Data include a sample of 18,384 TDCJ inmates (86% male, 14% female) who completed the TCUDS between January 1 and April 30, 1999. Results indicated that 30% of the sample scored at or above the cutoff score of "3." The scale's overall reliability was good (coefficient alpha = 0.89) and was nearly identical across race/ethnic and gender subgroups. Item-total correlations ranged from 0.37 and 0.58, and individual-item positive (i.e., "Yes") responses ranged from 10% to 39%. Based on Item Response Theory analyses (Rasch, 1980), all nine items contributed important and necessary information toward the overall scale score, and the simple summative-scoring scheme was found to be nearly as good as a statistically optimally weighted-scoring algorithm (Knight, Hiller, Broome, & Simpson, 2000).

CONCLUSIONS

Short screening instruments, such as those mentioned in this chapter, can play an important role in the identification of offenders with drug problems. However, the usefulness of brief screens within correctional populations can vary considerably. Among the potential drug-use screens, studies show that the TCUDS, ADS/ASI, and the SSI are highly reliable and valid, and are particularly useful in minimizing inappropriate referrals for more intensive treatment programs, such as in-prison TCs. In addition to the favorable research findings, the brevity of these screens makes them worthy of consideration for use, particularly for larger correctional settings.

Effective screening, however, is contingent on correctional agencies not only being able to identify correctly those offenders with drug problems, but also on being able to refer them to appropriate treatment services. In general, individuals with more severe problems require more intensive treatment (Simpson, Joe, Fletcher, Hubbard, & Anglin, 1999). Studies of intensive prison-based treatment programs have found that they are most effective for high-risk inmates, that is, those with more serious antisocial backgrounds (e.g., history of extensive drug use and criminality) (Knight et al., 1999). On the other hand, individuals with comparatively less serious problems are likely to benefit from a variety of treatment options, regardless of modality or level of intensity (Knight et al., 1999; Simpson et al., 1999). Providing intensive treatment to low-risk offenders (e.g., those not drug dependent and who do not have a history of prior incarcerations), however, is likely to have a limited impact on reincarceration rates and may be wasting valuable taxpayer dollars and scarce treatment resources.

Given that research has demonstrated that community-based aftercare is an essential ingredient of a treatment protocol, referral decisions also need to consider the need for treatment services after an offender is incarcerated. For example, when compared with inmates with drug problems who did not receive treatment or who only completed a prison-treatment program, inmates who completed both the prison-based and aftercare treatment were significantly less likely to reoffend within 3 years of being released from prison (Knight et al., 1999; Martin et al., 1999; Wexler et al., 1999). Failure to provide adequate treatment after releasing offenders from corrections-based programs can undermine any positive changes that occurred during in-prison treatment, and, consequently, severely limit the usefulness of an otherwise effective screening and referral protocol. Better tools and utilization strategies for drug-use assessments are, therefore, crucial for matching needs and resources (Broome et al., 1996).

Because some offenders will fail to disclose drug problems on a drug screen, correctional staff may need to examine other sources of information, such as biological test results and custodial records. For many correctional facilities (such as county jails), urine tests are administered shortly after arrest, and positive results may indicate a need for treatment even when an inmate denies drug use. Urine samples are tested for targeted drugs, such as opiates and cocaine, and are processed typically "in-house" using an immunoassay process with a 2- to 3-day window of detection. Likewise, an indication of drug problems may be found in an offender's criminal record, such as having several arrests for possession of a controlled substance, or in the presentence investigation report that includes an inmate's confession needing help for drug problems. As with self-report measures, biological tests and criminal records also have limitations that need to be considered when making screening and referral decisions. For example, there are several drugs for which there are no biological tests available and, among potentially testable drugs, correctional officials often test for only a few types, such as cocaine and opiates.

Overall, designing an effective and efficient screening and referral protocol requires careful attention to the factors outlined in this chapter. Not only must an instrument be selected that is best suited for a specific correctional environment, but a protocol for administering the screen so that offenders respond honestly also must be developed. In addition, referral decisions need to be based on available treatment options. Failure in any of these areas could undermine the entire screening and referral process, and result in offenders who do not need treatment being referred inappropriately to costly intensive programs, and those who do need treatment remaining untreated—being released into the community with a high probability of reoffending and returning to prison.

ACKNOWLEDGMENTS

This project was supported by Grant No. 99-MU-MU-K008 awarded by the National Institute of Justice, Office of Justice Programs, U.S. Department of Justice. Points of view in this document are those of the authors and do not necessarily represent the official position or policies of the U.S. Department of Justice.

21

Drug-Use Careers

Robert Fiorentine, Maureen P. Hillhouse, and M. Douglas Anglin

In addressing the complexity of the drug-use phenomenon, some investigators have stressed the need to address drug use, criminality, and treatment from a long-term longitudinal, or "careers perspective" (Anglin, Hser, & Grella, 1997; Blumstein & Cohen, 1987; Vaillant, 1992). This chapter describes the career perspective, outlining the advantages of such a research orientation, and summarizing pertinent empirical findings. The emphasis will be on the drug-use career, but its relationship to criminality and treatment will also be discussed. Future research directions will be offered, with recommendations for integrating cognitive-behavioral factors in career research.

THE CAREER PERSPECTIVE

The advantages of a career perspective are that both the progressive and chronic relapsing nature of addiction, characterized as consecutive phases of use and nonuse over the lifecourse, are acknowledged (Anglin et al., 1997; Hser, Anglin, Grella, Longshore, & Prendergast, 1997; Vaillant, 1988). Prospective, longitudinal studies can identify the long-term patterns of drug misuse and recovery, which may not be adequately addressed by cross-sectional studies or short-term longitudinal studies.

The simplest characterization of a drug career is offered by Blumstein and Cohen (1987), describing a criminal career: (a) age of initiation, (b) age of termination, and (c) aspects of use. A drug-use career would begin with the first use of drugs at or above some drug use/addiction threshold, and would end with the last period of drug use (Hanlon, Nurco, Kinlock, & Duszynski, 1990). Noting the nature of drug dependence and the generally high probability of relapse even after an extended period of nonuse, Nurco, Cisin, and Balter (1981a) note that an addiction career may not be over until the addict dies.

DRUG-USE CAREERS

Long-term longitudinal studies reveal that drug misuse often escalates in severity, with repeated cycles of cessation and relapse (Hser et al., 1997). There may be a cyclic pattern of drug use, which Taylor (1994) characterizes as a sequence of "cessation—abstinence—relapse—consumption—secondary cessation . . . ad mortem" (p. 13). Other career patterns of substance misuse have been documented, including: (a) successive episodes of heavy drug use and abstinence over the course of many years (Hunt, 1997), (b) intense use in teens and early adult years, followed by "maturing out" (Winick, 1962), (c) chronic, life-long use (Anglin & Speckart, 1986), and (d) a relatively short addiction career ending with successful treatment (Simpson & Marsh, 1986).

A complete understanding of these patterns does not exist, but several longitudinal studies have identified important aspects of addiction (McGlothlin, Anglin, & Wilson, 1977; Nurco et al., 1981a, 1981b; Simpson, Joe, Lehman, & Sells, 1986; Vaillant & Milosky, 1982). Based on a national sample of substance-abuse treatment clients, Simpson et al. (1986) reported that addiction careers ranged from 1 to 35 years, with a median of 9.5 years. Twenty-seven percent of this sample reported continuous "runs" lasting more than 3 years, and 75% experienced at least one relapse. Nurco, Bonito, Lerner, and Balter (1975), using a sample of Baltimore narcotics users, determined that the mean age of first regular narcotic use was 20.1 years, and the mean period of time between the onset of addiction (regular use) and criminal justice attention was approximately 5 years. Vaillant and Milosky (1980, 1982) and Vaillant and Vaillant (1981) prospectively followed 456 high-risk, inner-city 14-year-old boys until age 47, obtaining complete drinking histories from ages 20 to 47. More than 50% of the men who ever met criteria for alcohol abuse did so by age 31, and one third of these exhibited a progression in severity and increased problems over time. In a study of both heroin addicts and alcoholics, Vaillant (1988) documented the course of addiction as involving multiple relapses, with a duration of addiction often lasting more than 10 years, with some maturing out. At the 18-year follow-up, 35% of the sample were reported as maintaining abstinence, compared with 10% and 23% at 5 and 10 years, respectively.

CAREER PARAMETERS

Although following drug users over their lifetimes may provide important information concerning long-term patterns of use and nonuse, as well as their relationship to criminality and treatment, these studies have several inherent problems: (a) they are lengthy and expensive, (b) it is difficult to track and locate individuals for follow-up interviews, (c) new questions that were not addressed in the original investigation may become more important with time, and (d) activities that have occurred during the previous years, or even decades, are assessed retrospectively—a procedure that may lead to inaccurate or misleading responses. Not surprisingly, few investigations utilizing a longitudinal career approach have been implemented.

Because of the expense and difficulty of conducting prospective, natural history studies, a variety of drug-use history variables have been adopted for use in cross-sectional or short-term longitudinal studies as career parameters (Anglin et al., 1997), including initiation of addictive drug use, type of drug(s) used, and frequency, quantity, duration, and severity of drug use. Results from these studies have determined that age of initiation of drug misuse is related to severity of addiction, involvement in crime, social deviance, and psychopathology (Fergusson, Horwood, & Lynskey, 1994). Age of onset of problem alcohol use is associated with more severe progression of misuse and more negative consequences resulting from this misuse (Babor et al., 1992). Severity of drug use, usually measured as frequency, quantity, and duration of use, has been found to be predictive of treatment outcome and recovery, with higher severity associated with poorer outcomes (Connors, Maisto, & Zywiak, 1996; Gottheil, McLellan, & Druley, 1992).

TREATMENT CAREERS

Recent investigations have applied the careers perspective to treatment (Anglin et al., 1997). Some investigators have noted that the benefit of a single treatment episode may be short-lived, that relapse is common (Leukefeld, Pickens, & Schuster, 1992; Nurco, Balter, & Kinlock, 1994), and that recovery rarely occurs from a single recovery attempt (Hunt, Barnett, & Branch, 1971). Contrary to the conventional view that repeated treatment episodes reflect treatment failure, a treatment-career perspective holds that the effects of treatment are cumulative across treatment episodes; that multiple treatments increase the success of each subsequent treatment episode; and that stable reductions in drug use may occur only after multiple treatment episodes (Hser, Grella, Chou, & Anglin, 1998).

Although research indicates that those with prior treatment experience are more likely to re-enter treatment and stay in treatment longer (Hser et al., 1997; Simpson & Joe, 1993), the findings do not consistently document a positive cumulative effect of multiple treatment episodes (Hser et al., 1998; Hser, Joshi, Anglin, & Fletcher, 1999). Some studies even find that a greater number of previous treatments or hospitalizations for alcohol and drug misuse predict *poorer* outcome, although the effect size is not always large (Hubbard et al., 1989; Ito & Donovan, 1990). Rather than a beneficial cumulative effect as posited by the treatment-careers approach, it may be that multiple treatment episodes more accurately reflect severity of drug and alcohol dependency that, in turn, increases the difficulty of maintaining long-term recovery (Anglin et al., 1997; Hser et al., 1999).

DRUG-USE CAREERS AND TREATMENT OUTCOME

Although recent evidence does not support the main assumptions of the treatment careers perspective, research has demonstrated that single drug-treatment episodes can be effective as measured by lowered relapse and recidivism rates (Tims, Fletcher, & Hubbard, 1991) and desired behavioral change (Tims, 1981). Treatment may be effective even when taking into account repeated cycles of use and nonuse (Hanlon et al., 1990; Simpson & Sells, 1990).

Possibly the most comprehensive natural history study of drug use careers, McGlothlin and colleagues (1977) investigated the long-term patterns of drug use of a population of arrestees in the California Civil Addict Program (CAP). Initiated in 1961 by California legislation recognizing that individuals who engage in criminal activities report extensive use of drugs, CAP was a court-ordered drug treatment program for narcotics-dependent criminal offenders. Following CAP participants since its inception has identified important transitions of use, nonuse, treatment, and imprisonment (Hser, Yamaguchi, Chen, & Anglin, 1995). CAP participants reported lower levels of drug use, higher levels of employment, and less criminal activity than a closely matched comparison group. In support of Winick's (1962) study of maturing out, 12 years after admission to CAP, 40% of the follow-up sample (Anglin & McGlothlin, 1985) had steadily reduced daily narcotic consumption during and after commitment. Other research also demonstrates that drug use, as well as other deviant behaviors, taper off over time (Blumstein & Cohen, 1987); however, maturing out of drug use seems to be inhibited when addicts remain involved in criminal activities (Brecht & Anglin, 1990).

Figure 21.1 presents the results reported by Hser, Anglin, and Powers (1993) for the 24-year CAP follow-up. Although death rates had doubled since the 1974–1975 follow-up (27.7% vs. 13.8%, respectively), 28.6% of the sample in 1974–1975 tested negative for opiates, compared with 25.0% at the 1985–1986 follow-up. Hser et al. (1993) conclude that the eventual cessation of narcotics use is a gradual process, if it occurs at all.

EFFECTIVE TREATMENT

Cessation of drug- and alcohol-dependent behavior may be a gradual process that is not expedited by multiple treatment episodes; however, specific episodes of treatment may be effective for some individuals (McLellan et al., 1997). Why treatment is differentially effective is unclear; however, recent studies have clarified important predictors of treatment success. Research consistently indicates that longer retention in treatment is associated with more positive outcomes (Anglin & Hser, 1990; Hubbard et al., 1989, 1997; Simpson, Joe, Fletcher, Hubbard, & Anglin, 1999; Tims et al., 1991). Long-term programs show more favorable outcomes than short-term programs, particularly for those with higher levels of criminal involvement and psychopathology (Anglin & Hser, 1990; Khalsa & Anglin, 1991).

Several studies have determined that the frequency of counseling-session attendance is associated with favorable treatment outcomes (Fiorentine & Anglin, 1996, 1997; Moos & King, 1997; Simpson, Joe, & Rowen-Szal, 1997a, 1997b). Increasing the opportunity for counseling in outpatient drug treatment programs increases client participation in counseling that,

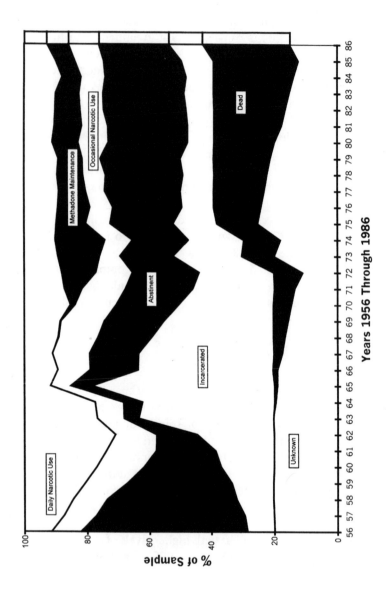

FIGURE 21.1   The natural history of narcotics addiction ($N = 581$).

in turn, enhances overall program effectiveness (Fiorentine & Anglin, 1997). Client-perceived counselor empathy is also associated with frequent counseling attendance and favorable treatment outcomes (Fiorentine, Nakashima, & Anglin, 1999; Luborsky, McLellan, Woody, O'Brien, & Averbach, 1985).

Concurrent participation in outpatient treatment and 12-step programs is associated with higher levels of alcohol and drug abstinence than is participation solely in treatment or in 12-step programs (Fiorentine & Hillhouse, 2000a; Ouimette, Finney, & Moos, 1997). Clients who maintain regular attendance in 12-step programs after treatment report higher levels of abstinence from drug and alcohol use than do those who attend less frequently or not at all (Emrick, 1987; Fiorentine, 1999; Montgomery, Miller, & Tonigan, 1991), and acceptance of 12-step ideology, particularly the view that controlled or nonproblematic drug and alcohol use is impossible for those with histories of substance abuse, is associated with higher levels of posttreatment abstinence (Fiorentine & Hillhouse, 2000b).

Table 21.1 presents the findings from the Los Angeles Target Cities Treatment Enhancement Project (Fiorentine, Gil-Rivas, & Hillhouse, 1998) estimating the probability of maintaining abstinence during the 6 months prior to the 8-month follow-up of an outpatient-treatment sample ($n = 356$).

TABLE 21.1   Logistic Regression Estimates of Abstinence by Participation in Recovery Activities and Frequency of Counseling Attendance

	Mean per week group-counseling session attendance		
Participation in recovery activities	1	3	5
Treatment completion; weekly 12-step attendance ($n = 59$; 16.6%)	0.77	0.83	0.87
Treatment dropout; weekly 12-step attendance ($n = 86$; 24.2%)	0.58	0.66	0.74
Treatment completion; no weekly 12-step attendance ($n = 68$; 19.1%)	0.44	0.53	0.62
Treatment drop out; no weekly 12-step attendance ($n = 143$; 40.2%)	0.25	0.32	0.40

Source: Fiorentine, R., & Hillhouse, M. P. (2000). *Drug treatment, twelve-step attendance, and counseling participation: Revisiting the conclusion that "more is better."* (Manuscript submitted for publication).

The findings indicate that "more is better." The probability of maintaining abstinence for those who complete treatment, maintain weekly or more frequent 12-step attendance, and engage in three group-counseling sessions per week while in treatment is 0.83. By contrast, the probability of abstinence for those who complete treatment and attend three counseling sessions per week, but do not maintain weekly participation in 12-step groups is 0.53. The probability of abstinence of those who drop out of treatment, do not attend 12-step meetings on a regular basis, but attend three counseling sessions per week while in treatment is 0.32.

FUTURE DIRECTIONS

Career research to date has generally been descriptive rather than explanatory. Future research employing a career perspective would benefit from efforts to explain the stability and change of drug misuse and related behaviors over the lifecourse. Whether investigations employ longitudinal or cross-sectional methodologies, gains would occur from identifying the cognitive-behavioral processes underlying addiction and recovery, and how incarceration and participation in recovery activities may influence these processes.

Although this line of inquiry has been initiated, huge gaps remain. Hall, Havassy, and Wasserman (1991) found that cognitive factors, such as a goal of absolute abstinence and greater expected recovery success, predicted a lower risk of lapse in the first 12 weeks after treatment, and suggest that treatment aimed at solidifying abstinence goals may facilitate early abstinence. Jones and McMahon (1996) determined that negative expectancies concerning continued alcohol use predicts favorable treatment outcomes.

Similarly, Fiorentine and Hillhouse (in press) found that cognitive factors, such as low controlled-use self-efficacy, perceived negative consequences associated with continued drug use, and an unconflicted acceptance of abstinence, predicted successful cessation of drug and alcohol use. Results from additional investigations suggest that the frequency of counseling participation and regular attendance of 12-step meetings assist in recovery, in part, because they promote a shift in the cognitions associated with recovery, such as an addict self-concept, perceived future negative consequences of continued drug use, and an unconflicted acceptance of abstinence (Fiorentine & Hillhouse, in press).

CONCLUSIONS

Research indicating that relapse is common and recovery may not occur from a single recovery attempt complicates efforts to understand drug misuse and recovery. To gain a better understanding of addiction, its relationship to criminal activity, and its mediation by treatment, some investigators have stressed the necessity of utilizing a career perspective.

A career perspective acknowledges the dynamic, progressive nature of drug use and recovery. Longitudinal studies utilizing a drug-use careers perspective can determine possible reasons for patterns of use and nonuse, the relationship of these patterns to criminal activity, criminal justice involvement, and treatment participation (Anglin & McGlothlin, 1985; Nurco et al., 1975; Simpson et al., 1986; Vaillant, 1988). Existing careers research, however, involves investigations that describe patterns of use over the lifecourse. Future drug-careers research should extend this focus by explaining why these drug-use patterns occur, and why these patterns of use may be temporarily or permanently influenced by treatment and involvement in the criminal justice system.

Additional studies utilizing a treatment-careers perspective that examine the cumulative effects of treatment, however, do not offer similar promise. The generally contradictory evidence for the notion of a cumulative treatment effect does not justify the time and expense of additional studies. A better use of resources would involve longitudinal investigations with long follow-up periods that explain why specific episodes of treatment are associated with the cessation of addictive behavior for some individuals, but not for others.

Although identifying the social-cognitive processes associated with recovery, and how these processes may be influenced by participation in treatment and 12-step groups, is a promising future frontier in addiction research, the contributions from this effort would be enhanced by utilizing a drug-careers focus. As drug and alcohol addiction is a chronic, relapsing disorder, short-term studies cannot assess the question of stability or permanence of drug use and abstinence. The ability to predict and explain long-term changes in drug and alcohol use would represent a significant advance in addictions research. A drug-use careers approach that follows individuals over the lifecourse offers the best opportunity to achieve this goal.

ACKNOWLEDGMENT

This research was supported by the National Institute of Drug Abuse (NIDA) Research Scientist Development Award (DA00301), and NIDA grants DA11047 and DA11195.

22

Civil Commitment: A Coerced Treatment Model

Faye S. Taxman and Nena P. Messina

C ivil commitment is one of the oldest forms of coerced treatment for compulsive substance abusers. Beginning with the passage of the Harrison Act in 1914, law enforcement officials beckoned the call for a coerced treatment protocol. Civil commitment grew out of the need for a legal remedy to address the chronic behaviors of those who are believed to be a threat to the safety of the community or to themselves. The civil commitment process is often reserved for those involved in the criminal justice system and "nonoffenders" who are unable to control their behavior. It essentially is a form of "coerced treatment" for seemingly deserving people who are unwilling or unable to obtain needed services on their own, even if the target population is not under the control of the criminal justice system. During the last 25 years, the civil commitment process has sparked a continuing debate about the efficacy of coerced treatment, the nature of the coercion felt by the ascribed person, and the adequacy of legal protections for those with their liberties infringed on.

This chapter serves to reframe the discussion about civil commitment procedures from an oddity to a component of a continuum of mandated treatment. In light of recent advancements in jurisprudence, civil commitment procedures have similar qualities as contemporary versions of criminal justice-coerced treatment (see Leukefeld & Tims, 1988). A new theory of jurisprudence raises critical questions about the intention behind the involvement of the legal system to address chronic behaviors that threaten public and individual safety. It also provides a framework for establishing criteria for assessing the necessity of using civil commitment procedures and assessing the adequacy of the state's response to dangerous behaviors. This chapter first reviews the historical description of the civil commitment process. The discussion then describes how therapeutic jurisprudence advances policy and procedure questions about civil commitment and coerced treatment practices. Next, the chapter outlines the issues related to the effectiveness of coerced treatment in many different arenas that can add to discussions about the value and importance of civil commitment procedures. Finally, we outline a future research agenda for understanding how different legal procedures impact addicts and affect the services delivered to addicts.

CIVIL COMMITMENT: A HISTORY OF RESPONSES TO THREATS FROM SUBSTANCE ABUSERS

Civil commitment evolved during the era when the national drug policy was designed and crafted by Harry Anslinger, the grandfather of contemporary law enforcement-focused U.S. drug policy. The major emphasis was placed on using the power of the state to reduce the supply for drugs and to criminalize drug use. A consequence of this approach was also the criminalization of addiction disorder for illicit drug use. The Harrison Act of 1914 began nearly a century of legal remedies to address substance abuse, including the criminalization of illicit drug use behaviors and the increased punitive handling of addicts. While the focus was on increasing the law enforcement powers of the state, law enforcement officials (e.g., the Narcotics Unit of the Treasury Department) requested a program that provided treatment as an alternative to incarceration for certified addicts (Inciardi, 1988; Lindblad, 1988).

The first versions of civil commitment programs were the narcotics farms operated by the U.S. Public Health system in the mid-1930s. Established in the serene rolling hills of Lexington, Kentucky, and Fort Worth, Texas, the narcotic farms housed law breakers, as well as voluntary heroin addicts. The narcotics farms had the same underlying theory of prisons created by the Quakers in the 1800s—serenity and respite care will contribute to the rehabilitation of the individual. The narcotics farms had limited success mainly due to several design flaws, such as: (a) the program lacked mechanisms for holding voluntary patients until they had achieved some level of recovery; and (b) no services were provided after the addict left the farm. The farms were publicly discussed as a failure, although, it was recognized that the programs could be improved with some changes. These changes included providing a mandatory minimum length of stay (even for voluntary cases), coupling intensive residential services with community programming, offering intensive supervision after release, and recognizing a need for coercion with the threat of reinstitutionalization during the aftercare component.

Nearly 30 years later, as a result of the growing number of heroin addicts in the early 1960s, the state of California, followed by New York, and then the federal government—all within a 5-year window—recreated civil commitment programs for substance abusers. The programs in the early 1960s evolved from earlier experiences with the narcotics farms, and sought to address compulsive behaviors of an unmotivated and unwilling addict population. The civil commitment programs were designed to accommodate all types of addicts, including those that were arrested and then diverted from the criminal justice system, and those addicts who were sentenced and then incarcerated for a drug offense. More importantly, the civil commitment process allowed willing addicts to "volunteer" for treatment (without involvement in the criminal or civil justice system) and for addicts to be *involuntarily* admitted for treatment by loved ones or officials who saw self-inflicted harm or potential community danger imminent. The varying types of addicts handled by the same facilities presented some challenges to the civil commitment programs.

The next generation of civil commitment programs emphasized both duration of treatment and community care. The first program, started in California in 1961, included institutionalization for up to 7 years, regardless of whether the addict was convicted of a crime (see Fiorentine, Hillhouse, & Anglin, this volume). The Narcotic Addiction Control Commission was established in 1966 in New York and required addicts to be "judicially certified" for 3 to 5 years. The Federal Narcotics Addict Rehabilitation Act (NARA), also in 1966, provided compulsory treatment for addicts, followed by supervised aftercare in the community. The legal status (e.g., diverted, sentenced, or voluntary admissions) did not affect the minimum committed time period (see Inciardi, 1988; Lindblad, 1988).

The New York and federal NARA programs were plagued with problems from their inception. Public outcry occurred over the cost of the programs, with the New York initiative spending millions of dollars. The success rates of each initiative were also the subject of much concern. Inciardi's (1988) review of the New York program found that the program faltered because: (a) the program had difficulty attracting the nearly 4,500 expected participants; (b) the institutional facilities were old prisons and, therefore, did not offer a therapeutic milieu—instead the environment was controlling and stifling; (c) staff were primarily former custodial staff and administrators were political appointees who lacked clinical experience; and (d) the aftercare component was modeled after traditional supervision without the authority to address noncompliance issues (e.g., failure to appear, absconding behavior, etc.). The federal NARA created a centralized intake procedure that created havoc in the eligibility process, and ultimately contributed to nearly 49% of the addicts being rejected from treatment (Lindblad, 1988). Other issues similar to the New York experience prevailed, including the lack of a therapeutic environment, bureaucratic processes, inattention to treatment issues (e.g., noncompliance of addicts), and the failure to utilize aftercare in the community.

The civil commitment movement, although it was short lived, contributed to a new generation of coerced treatment programs for addicts. The Treatment Alternatives to Street Crime (TASC) program was created as a pretrial diversion program by the Special Action Office for Drug Abuse Prevention (SAODAP) under President Nixon (see Cook, this volume). The concept was to employ the legal carrot of diversion to assist addicts in getting treatment in the community. In 1972, President Nixon also created a federal system of methadone maintenance (MM) centers that contributed to the availability of drug treatment in the community, particularly for veterans. The focus was on the community and using smaller dosages of leverage (e.g., diversion, veterans benefits, etc.) to entice addicts into treatment.

Civil commitment practices fell under suspect in the 1970s with concerns about due process issues related to lengthy stays in commitment facilities. Many civil commitment-type programs operated in correctional environments that created indistinguishable differences between incarceration and therapeutic treatment. Questions were also raised about the nature of the therapeutic environment and the ability of these programs to support the recovery process. From the public perspectives, the civil commitment movement was costly, both in terms of fiscal expenses and constitutional rights. However, the civil commitment concept—detaining public safety risks for an undetermined period of time—remains popular, as evidenced by the recent resurgence in the 1990s of the use of the civil commitment tool for sexual predators and mental health patients (Schopp & Sturgis,

1995) and has been suggested for drug abusers (see Leukefeld & Tims, 1988).

THERAPEUTIC JURISPRUDENCE: DEFINING THE GOALS OF COERCION

Underlying the discussions about the civil commitment process are the procedures that are used to make the determination that commitment is essential to safeguard the individual and/or the community. A series of legal decisions have reinforced the importance of due process before commitment as a means to both protect the civil rights of the accused and as a means to ensure that the state does not wrongly detain individuals, especially for an open-ended duration of time. In *Goldberg v. Kelly* (1970), the Supreme Court found that welfare recipients could not have their benefits terminated without a hearing. Similarly in *Morrissey v. Brewer* (1972), the Court found that a decision to revoke parole could not occur without a hearing. Other examples can be cited where a hearing is deemed necessary to ensure that the inflicted individual is treated properly and that decisions to confine include professional and judicial judgment. The importance of due process rights has been reinforced for many procedures where benefits and rights are being denied to an individual.

Underscoring the emphasis on due process is concern about the violation of the constitutional rights of the individual. Equally important is the realization that the denial of a fair process could be psychologically harmful to the individual and, thus, undermine the rehabilitation efforts intended by the procedure (Tyler, 1996). The psychological harm of experiencing unfair procedures is hypothesized as being antitherapeutic, and, therefore, counterproductive to the goals and intent of coerced treatment. In one discussion, Tyler comments:

> [Courts] recognize the importance of considering the psychological impact of judicial procedures on those experiencing the procedures. The impact is distinct from the desire for a neutral, fact-finding expert, such as judge or a psychiatrist, who is expected to reach accurate decisions. When conceptualized this way, due process involves giving people judicial procedures that they will perceive as fair. (1996, p. 4)

Tyler goes on to discuss:

> Failure to receive due process has a number of negative consequences for people who have personal experience with legal authorities, including

reluctance to accept decisions, diminished respect for the judge, mediator, or other third party, diminished respect for the courts and the legal system, and a diminished willingness to follow legal rules. These effects are completely consistent with the suggestion that experiencing arbitrary procedures leads to social malaise and decreases people's willingness to be integrated into the polity, accepting its authorities and following its rules. [Of] particular relevance to the question of therapeutic implications is the issue of behavior. Enhancing respect for authorities, the willingness to voluntarily accept the decision of authorities and the willingness to follow social rules are core objects of the therapeutic program. Hence, it seems likely that future studies of the therapeutic consequences of judicial hearings will demonstrate that commitment hearings experienced as unfair by those potentially being committed will have strongly antitherapeutic consequences. (1996, p. 13)

Therapeutic jurisdiction identifies how legal process and procedures are therapeutic in nature. The questions that follow are: (a) How are the procedures fair? and (b) How are procedures used to assist the individual in recognizing the problem-behavior? Both interplay to create some form of leverage on the individual to change his/her behavior. The following explores these two dimensions.

What Defines Fairness?

Typically, concerns about fairness apply to the degree to which the decisions are rational and neutral. Fairness is often described in terms of the lack of bias, amount of honesty, and factual nature of the decision making. The use of experts or professionals frequently occurs to ensure objectivity and to ensure that the facts are interpreted from many differing perspectives. Related to the due process qualities of fairness is the perception that an individual has of the process. As a general rule of thumb, individuals perceive situations to be unfair when they have previously been treated differently, or when they know others in like situations have been treated differently (Paternoster, 1987; Taxman, Soule, & Gelb, 1999). The implication is that fair situations are more likely to occur when the individual perceives that his/her behavior is treated similar over time and is similar to how others are treated.

How Can Procedures Be Therapeutic?

An underlying premise of the therapeutic-jurisprudence movement is that legal procedure and settings (e.g., civil commitment, correctional, sentencing, etc.) have a therapeutic quality. The legal and due process procedures can serve as a mechanism to assist the individual in understanding his/her uncontrollable behavior, in recognizing that he/she must take responsibility for that behavior, and in beginning the change process. The legal system can be a catalyst for individuals to change.

Scholars have identified a number of procedural issues that facilitate the therapeutic nature of the intervention. David Wexler raises the question of whether the law, rules, procedures, and roles of lawyers, judges, and legal agencies promote cognitive restructuring in an individual (i.e., fosters the individual to understand the nature of the problem behavior), or denial or minimization of the behavior. Plea bargaining policies and brief sentencing scenarios serve the latter purpose. However, legal processes that require the individual to make a full disclosure of the facts and to acknowledge a role in the behavior are therapeutic. Similarly, getting the individual involved in the negotiation and design of the treatment program contributes to achieving adherence and favorable outcomes. A behavioral-contract process as part of supervised release engages the individual in the definition of the problem behavior, treatment interventions, sanctions and rewards, and timeframe to accomplish certain achievements. In turn, this procedure can increase compliance because it provides both the internal and external motivation needed to address the problem behavior (Wexler, 1996; Taxman et al., 1999).

THE EFFECTIVENESS OF COERCED TREATMENT FOR DIFFERENT TARGET POPULATIONS

Historically, civil commitment programs were considered synonymous with criminal justice-based coerced treatment models. Civil commitment programs before 1970 were defined for addicts of varying legal status (e.g., diverted offenders, sentenced offenders, etc.), volunteers for treatment, and involuntary willingness for treatment. Civil commitment programs since the 1980s have focused on practices for voluntary and involuntary drug dependents with compulsive behaviors that are not involved in the criminal justice system, and very few studies have examined the efficacy of such civil commitment practices. Commensurate with the growth in the arrests since the 1980s, there has been the growing recognition that drug-involved offenders need treatment as part of the criminal justice response (Lipton, 1995; Belenko, 1996; Taxman, 1998). Some experimentation has occurred with different uses of leverage, including conditional release with mandates for treatment, drug courts, in-prison treatment, and in-jail treatment. Similarly for welfare clients, sex offenders, and other target populations, various forms of coerced treatment are employed to motivate the person to address their illicit use of drugs. An examination of the efficacy of drug treatment, particularly for different types of coerced populations, will illuminate the questions that need to be addressed in the next generation of research. A limitation of the current literature on treatment effectiveness is that the impact of different styles of coercion have not been adequately measured and addressed (Young, 1996).

   This review of the literature on coerced treatment concentrates on a number of extant reviews (shown Appendix A) on this topic (De Leon, 1988; Farabee, Prendergast, & Anglin, 1998; Miller & Flaherty, 2000) and some primary studies. Although the term "coercion" typically represents a "range of options of varying degrees of severity across the various stages of criminal justice processing" (Farabee et al., 1998, p. 3), the broader context of coercion refers to addicts that "volunteer" (generally with some informal pressure) or are involuntary subjected to treatment. The definition of coercion ranges from addicts who unwillingly enter treatment due to their uncontrollable behavior, to those who willingly enter treatment as a result of their involvement in social institutions.

Civil Commitment Program

California implemented the first formal civil commitment program in the United States in 1962. Anglin (1988) provides a review of an early evaluation of the California Civil Addict Program (CAP). This CAP evaluation took advantage of a natural experiment that took place during the implementation of the program (see Fiorentine, Hillhouse, & Anglin, this volume). During the first 18 months of the program, almost 50% of the individuals admitted were released after minimal exposure to the program due to procedural mistakes or insufficient desire of the addict. Thus, the study used a quasiexperimental design to compare program admissions that had stayed for at least one inpatient phase and were subsequently released to outpatient treatment or supervision in the community, with those who were admitted and then released without completing the inpatient program. The composition of the comparisons groups, or subsequent analyses, did not include any measures of the degree of motivation of the addicts.

   Hser, Anglin, and Powers (1993) reported findings from a 24-year follow-up of a select sample of CAP admissions ($n = 581$) that entered the program during the years 1962 through 1964 (a subsample from the original sample). The unusually long follow-up period provided a unique opportunity to examine the dynamic changes that occur over the natural history of narcotics addiction. The authors found that there were reductions in daily drug use and incarceration, as well as increased abstinence for some CAP admissions for up to the first 12 years after admission. However, there were no status changes during the next 10-year follow-up period. The results suggested that permanent long-term abstinence from narcotics use is not a common occurrence, and that the civil commitment practice impacted the addict for a short period of time.

The analysis is limited and does not adequately assess the effectiveness of the civil commitment programs. First, it does not compare the findings from those individuals who completed the inpatient period with those who participated in the inpatient program for a minimum period of time, but were released early or were unsuccessfully discharged. The original comparisons were between groups that had vastly different exposure time to inpatient care, which could account for the reported differences. Such comparisons would enhance the understanding of the long-term impact of the CAP program on continued drug use based on the varying length of time involved in the inpatient program. Similarly, the analysis did not look at the differential results of varying types of civil commitment populations, such as those under criminal justice control and those that are involuntary or self-referrals. These comparisons are needed to fully understand whether the type of legal pressure or type of referral had a difference on the reported outcomes.

Impact of Coercion

Farabee et al. (1998) recently provided an overview of the literature regarding the effectiveness of various levels of coerced treatment. Coercion was defined based on the reviewed studies as ranging from low, moderate, and high levels of legal coercion and/or criminal justice pressure. Farabee and associates hypothesized that probation/parole referrals, court-mandated treatment referrals, and TASC referrals were all varied types of legal pressure. The measure of coercion was based on the type of criminal justice referral; the researchers did not have measures of the client's perception of the degree of coercion or the amount of pressure placed on the client. Absent these measures, the studies were ranked based on the nature of the referral, and found that the empirical literature to date largely supported the use of coercion.

Farabee et al. (1998) found that the use of coercive measures not only increased the likelihood of offenders remaining in treatment, but also increased the likelihood of offender's entering treatment early in their substance-abusing careers. Entrance into treatment early has been found to be associated with positive outcomes (Center for Substance-Abuse Treatment, 1994; De Leon & Jainchill, 1986). The majority of the primary studies reviewed reported that coerced clients attended treatment or completed treatment at rates similar to or better than voluntary clients. Furthermore, two studies (both MM programs) reported reductions in drug use and criminality for coerced clients, during and after treatment, similar to those for voluntary clients. The TASC evaluations found that the TASC referrals to treatment were predominately in the early stages of addiction. One TASC evaluation reported that older, long-term, opiate-addicted clients were most likely to benefit (e.g., less arrests and drug use) from the drug-free treatment program, compared with the MM program. Two of the studies reviewed reported that legal pressure was negatively related to retention and outcomes for some clients. For example, older methadone clients and adolescent clients who were referred from probation were retained for shorter periods of time than those who were not on probation. The latter finding again indicates an age-related confound between legal referral and treatment outcomes.

People enter treatment for a variety of reasons, including legal, family, employment, or medical pressures, as well as the desire to terminate addiction and the associated behaviors (De Leon, 1988; Anglin, Farabee, & Prendergast, 1998). Consequences for failure to comply with stipulated treatment requirements can vary as often as reasons for entering treatment. Miller and Flaherty (2000) provide one of the most recent comprehensive reviews of coerced addiction treatment for both criminal justice and non-criminal justice clients, as well as examined the alternative consequences of participation in treatment services. The major findings are:

Criminal Populations: Studies of coerced treatment for convicted substance abusers uniformly reported favorable outcomes. Compliance in treatment programs for criminal justice offenders has resulted in improved psychosocial status, as well as reductions in criminal activity. And, coerced participants appear to comply equally well as those who are not mandated to treatment. In fact, a TASC program evaluation found that criminal justice involvement actually helped retain clients in MM treatment through its leverage in compliance with monitoring during treatment (Brecht, Anglin, & Wang, 1993).

Employed Populations: The Employment Assistance Programs (EAPs) were originated to identify and refer employees for substance-abuse treatment. The literature on coerced treatment for employee populations revealed reduced psychiatric, medical, and legal consequences, and increased productivity in the workplace comparable to volunteer referrals. In addition, coerced participants were more likely to remain in treatment than self-referred participants (Lawental, McLellan, Grissom, Brill, & O'Brien, 1996).

DWI Populations: Miller and Flaherty (2000) cite evidence from two studies in Massachusetts and Ohio that first- and second-time convicted drunken drivers who complied with court-mandated treatment programs had significant reductions in rearrest for drunk-driving offenses, compared with incarcerated DWI offenders. Taxman and Piquero (1998) also found that multiple DWI offenders mandated to treatment have better outcomes than offenders with only punitive conditions (e.g., fine, supervision, etc.).

Child Welfare Populations: Recent use of coerced-treatment models has been employed for parents suspected of or adjudicated for child welfare violations. A 3-year pilot project in California offered alcohol and drug abuse treatment for women to provide an alternative to incarceration or loss of custody sentences. The program also included special training and recruitment of foster parents for the children. An evaluation of the Options for Recovery (OFR) treatment program found that women who were court mandated to the program were more likely to successfully complete treatment than voluntary admissions (Berkowitz, Brindis, Clayton, & Peterson, 1996). In addition, OFR treatment was found to be cost effective compared with the combined costs of incarceration and other substance-abuse treatment programs.

Public Aid Populations: Recent efforts to reform welfare have resulted in a major transition from dependency to employment. As part of this movement, welfare agencies have begun to employ substance-abuse treatment to assist the welfare client in obtaining employment. To ascertain the impact of coercion by a welfare agency on retention in an alcoholism program, Brizer, Maslansky, and Galanter (1990) reviewed the records of 178 consecutive admissions to an inner-city alcoholism clinic. The authors found that there were no differences in the retention rates for clients referred from a public-assistance agency, compared with voluntary admission, for at least nine sessions of treatment. Current studies are being conducted to examine the impact of the required treatment as part of the welfare-to-work reforms.

Within the empirical literature, findings consistently suggest that coerced treatment can be an effective method for reducing substance abuse and criminal behavior, as well as increasing prosocial behavior. The two major findings from this review are as follows: (a) Referred or coerced clients have treatment outcomes similar to voluntary admissions regardless of type of treatment and referral source (e.g., criminal justice, employer, welfare, or public-assistance agency); and (b) referral or coercion is positively associated with retention in treatment for various client populations (e.g., offender, employee, and child-welfare populations). The literature also demonstrated an age-related confound between legal referral and treatment outcomes (e.g., retention in treatment decreases for older and adolescent criminal justice referrals). In addition, criminal justice referrals (particularly diversion clients) tend to be introduced to treatment in the early stages of addiction, and first- and second-time DWI offenders appear to benefit more from treatment than incarceration.

Past and present literature show that the criminal justice system and other social institutions (e.g., welfare, employers, etc.) are useful strategies to get people into a treatment program when they will not enter voluntarily, without adversely affecting their treatment progress and outcomes. The literature is very unclear about the nature of the coercion that contributes to improved outcomes. A number of recent researchers have suggested that the next generation of literature needs to focus on this particular issue in order to identify the substantiate characteristics that define coercion (Young, 1996; Anglin et al., 1998; Hiller, Knight, & Simpson, 1999). The literature has often failed to measure coercion and has frequently relied upon proxy measures to determine the degree of pressure the client experiences entering treatment, or the internal motivation of the client.

DISCUSSION AND RESEARCH AGENDA FOR THE FUTURE

Civil commitment evolved as a tool to allow the state to intervene under two different models: social control (criminal incarceration) or parens patriae (guardianship or protection against harm to self and others). During the last 50 years, civil commitment has waned in popularity due to concerns about the constitutional rights, as well as the need to develop due-process safeguards to ensure that the state does not unjustifiably interfere with the civil liberties of an individual. As civil commitment procedures declined, efforts were made to expand coerced-treatment models under the criminal justice system. However, civil commitment practices have been incorporated as *one* form of coerced treatment due to the large number of addicts involved in the criminal justice system, and renewed interest has occurred regarding civil commitment for mental health and sex offenders (Alexander, 1995). The early civil commitment programs—the narcotics farms of the 1930s and the state and federal civil commitment programs in the 1960s—included addicts involved in the criminal justice system, volunteers, or involuntary admissions. As the criminal justice response heightened, civil commitment processes took a drawback. Constraints about using the civil commitment process evolved from the justification for parens patriae on the part of the state when other vehicles (e.g., criminal) were available.

As shown in the review of the history of civil commitment programs and the findings from the literature on the effectiveness of interventions for addicts with varying forms of coerced pressure, the overriding questions remain: What is coerced treatment? To what degree is the legal process therapeutic in assisting the addict in the behavioral change process? Answers to these questions remain largely unknown and they establish areas where more research is needed.

What Is Coerced Treatment?

One limitation of the above reviews, and treatment outcome studies in general, is that none of the reviewed studies assessed client motivation (or treatment readiness) or measures of the degree to which the addict felt pressure to participate in treatment. Most studies used the referral source as the independent variable to assess the degree to which the client voluntarily engaged in treatment services. While the current literature identifies a trend that coerced clients do as well, if not better, than voluntary or self-referral, more research is clearly needed to understand how different types of pressure affect outcomes.

Further examination is needed of both external and internal motivations to understand the role they play in the treatment and recovery process (Farabee et al., 1998; Taxman, 1998). Internal motivation has been shown to be associated with a client's acceptance of the treatment process, as well as treatment outcomes (Leukefeld & Tims, 1988). Therefore, client's motivation to do well in treatment should be held constant across comparison groups (no coercion vs. various levels of coercion) to avoid bias in treatment outcomes. For example, some coerced clients may be highly motivated to do well in treatment and readily comply with criminal justice stipulations. Thus, their positive treatment outcomes may be due to their internal motivation and not their legal pressure. Or, voluntary clients may be highly motivated to do well in treatment, thus confounding outcomes between voluntary clients and criminal justice clients.

Imbedded in this discussion is the definition of coercion. The traditional research literature utilizes measures of the legal status of the addict (e.g., arrested, diverted, sentenced, or incarcerated). De Leon (1988) observed that "[f]ailure to distinguish among these subgroups of voluntary and non-voluntary clients has introduced unmeasured error associated with the legal referral or legal status variables" (p. 170). Paternoster (1987) views the client's perception of legal pressure as central to affecting behavior. Young (1996) developed a legal-pressure questionnaire that identified different coercive elements, including "the degree of aversiveness" of the consequence for failure, the "discomfort level" associated with the consequences, the immediacy of the response, client contracting, the clarity and consistency of program rules, their enforcement, the point in case processing when diversion to treatment occurs, and the pressure felt by the addict. Young's measure of legal pressure identifies a conglomerate of procedural matters that ensure that the client is informed of the coercive nature of the intervention (e.g., immediacy of responses, behavioral contract, clarity of rules, etc.), as well as the internal pressure felt by the addicted individual.

The lack of a definition for coercion and the impact of varying definitions of coercion on client outcomes are areas where more research is needed. Critically important in this research is the need to develop measures that account for the addict's perception of internal and external motivation and the surrounding procedures that affect these perceptions. The current body of research provides an inadequate foundation of both the processes and procedures that addicts are exposed to in a coercive environment.

Does the Legal Process Assist the Addict in Behavior Change?

From a therapeutic-jurisprudence perspective, the legal system has a distinct role to motivate the addict in the process of contemplating change. First, the legal system must ensure that there are treatment programs available for the addict. And second, the legal system must ensure that these programs are effective in assisting the addict to change his/her behavior. These are two critical issues that the legal system tends to ignore in the application of coerced and civil commitment treatment.

The first concept about availability is particularly disconcerting. In the civil commitment programs of the 1960s, the number of estimated addicts never materialized for the treatment programs. In New York, the program was constantly criticized for being well under the expected population (Inciardi, 1988). In the federal program, the eligibility criteria dwindled down the number of eligible clients, and the selection process deterred many addicts/offenders from entering the program. This is still a common theme today. Many addicts are ineligible for programs due to unclear target-selection criteria or unwillingness of the treatment community to provide services to seemingly undeserving addicts (Duffee & Carlson, 1996).

Availability of adequate treatment services is an ongoing issue for the legal system. Most often, the legal system does not have dedicated funding for treatment services. Rather, the addict/offender must obtain the needed services on his/her own accord. In a recent study, the Center for Substance Abuse at Columbia University estimated that 15% of the offenders received treatment services, and many of these treatment services are educationally oriented and, therefore, insufficient to meet the needs of the target population (Center on Addiction and Substance Abuse, 1998). The national treatment gap is enormous, particularly for intensive, clinically oriented treatment services.

The second critical aspect of therapeutic jurisprudence is the need to ensure that the treatment services provided are capable of changing the behavior of the addict. That is, the programs must be effective. This criteria for the use of civil commitment or coerced treatment is that the legal process should be used only if it protects society and benefits the addict (Wexler, 1996; Alexander, 1995). Recent studies have found that much of our current efforts do not contribute to continued changes in the behavior of offenders (Taxman, 1999). Furthermore, reductions in recidivism tend to be small—usually 10% to 30% (MacKenzie, 1997; Palmer, 1995). The use of coercion methods that infringe on the civil liberties of individuals must be reserved for those situations that are prudent. A mechanism is needed within the context of the legal system to provide better information about the effectiveness of different interventions for different types of addicts.

Future Research

The history of the use of civil commitment and coerced treatment has been paved with many unfulfilled promises. The public has experienced a wave of efforts that continue to repeat the same history—the narcotics farms, the civil commitment programs of the 1960s, and the more recent incarnation of coerced-treatment programs suffer from short-term treatment interventions with varying degrees of coercions or pressure on the addict to become drug free. The legal system has been beset with promises of treatment interventions that are often ill suited to assist the addict in changing his behavior. And the addict in the criminal justice system is presented with treatment interventions that they are ineligible for or are insufficient to meet their behavior needs. Together, the history suggests a revamping of the conditions under which the criminal and civil justice systems are willing to use the powers of the judiciary to coerce addicts to address their seemingly dangerous behavior. The recent surgence of therapeutic jurisprudence raises a number of research questions that future researchers must address to advance our knowledge about the use of coerced treatment on outcomes. These issues are:

1. What are the judicial procedures that encourage addicts to recognize their addictive disorder and to become committed to treatment and recovery?
2. What judicial procedures do different types of addicts respond to that prompt them to change their behavior, while also protecting their civil liberties?
3. What judicial procedures and administrative processes are perceived to be beneficial, yet provide the necessary legal pressure to change behavior?
4. What type of process in the judicial system is needed to inform the judiciary of the benefits and consequences of mandated or coerced treatment?
5. What impact do different types of coerced treatment have on outcomes?

Civil commitment is just one form of coerced treatment. As we have shown, we have a limited understanding of the nature of coercion and a growing need to develop procedures that are more suitable to achieve the desired goals of coerced treatment. The next generation of research should focus on the processes and procedures of coercion that are most likely to generate positive treatment outcomes.

V

Considerations

23

Drug Courts

Steven Belenko

Beginning with the Dade County (Miami, Florida) program in June 1989 (Finn & Newlyn, 1993), the current generation of treatment drug courts has established an important presence in the U.S. criminal court system. In many jurisdictions, drug courts have become the preferred mechanism for linking drug- or alcohol-involved offenders to community-based treatment and related clinical interventions (Office of Justice Programs, 1998), and some jurisdictions are now applying drug-court principles to other types of cases, including domestic violence, DUI, and reentry (National Drug Court Institute, 1999; Tauber & Huddleston, 1999). Although still only serving a relatively small percentage of offenders with substance abuse problems, drug courts have enjoyed considerable positive publicity, government and public encouragement, and special funding.

Drug courts are characterized by a number of philosophical and structural characteristics that distinguish them from traditional judicial structures and court-processing routines. The traditional criminal court focuses on the fair and legal resolution of a criminal case, guided by penal- and criminal-procedure laws (Eisenstein & Jacob, 1976; Kamisar, LaFave, & Israel, 1995), as well as the local legal "culture" (Church, 1982). The individual characteristics of an offender, underlying substance abuse, or other clinical issues are generally not important factors in the adjudication of guilt or innocence in traditional courtroom decisions, except as possible mitigating conditions in a sentencing decision. Cases may proceed through the criminal courts through an individual calendaring system where the entire case is heard by the same judge, or through a multitiered process where different judges may preside over different aspects of the case. In neither case, given the large caseloads typical of modern courts, does the judge or other court staff typically have or seek personal information about the offender.

In contrast, drug courts typically set aside the determination of guilt or imposition of a sentence and, by addressing the offender's substance abuse and related problems, seek to reduce the probability of relapse and new criminal behaviors. The offenders are provided the clinical and social services that are considered necessary to address their specific problems. The key operational components of drug courts typically include (Belenko, 1998; Drug Courts Program Office, 1997):

1. a dedicated courtroom reserved for drug-court participants;
2. judicial supervision of structured community-based treatment;
3. timely screening, assessment, and enrollment of eligible defendants, and referral to treatment and related services as soon as possible after arrest;
4. regular status hearings to monitor treatment progress and program compliance;
5. increasing defendant accountability through a series of graduated sanctions and rewards;
6. mandatory periodic or random drug testing;
7. establishment of specific treatment-program requirements; and
8. dismissal of the case or reduction in sentence upon successful program completion.

Although most treatment drug courts incorporate these core functions, many try to assess and make referrals to address broader clinical issues, including physical and mental health, social service, and employment needs, as well as aftercare and support services following treatment completion to ease successful reentry into the community. A case manager or resource coordinator typically is used to identify service needs, refer clients to services, and monitor progress in treatment and other services.

In the drug-court model, the various components of the criminal justice and substance-abuse treatment systems work together as a team to try and use the coercive power of the court to promote abstinence and prosocial behavior and treatment retention. By comparison, for the types of nonviolent drug offenders generally targeted by drug courts, the typical adjudication process would result in a probation or short jail sentence, with little treatment or close community supervision (Taxman, 1998).

In addition, drug courts often seek to standardize the treatment process by requiring discrete treatment phases, minimum requirements to advance to different program phases, and a minimum length of program involvement. Most drug courts require at least 1 year of participation and incorporate several treatment phases (Cooper, 1997). Phase I usually includes assessment, orientation, development of a treatment plan and treatment readiness, and generally ranges between 30 and 90 days. During this phase, the client typically has 3 to 4 weekly treatment contacts, as well as random urine tests (Cooper, 1998). Phase II is the primary treatment phase, typically lasting 6 months, with treatment contacts and urinalysis similar to those of Phase I. The final Phase III typically includes relapse prevention, discharge planning, vocational and educational training, and lasts between 2 and 4 months. Treatment contacts may be reduced somewhat to 1 to 2 times per week, and urine tests are less frequent. Participants who successfully graduate from the drug-court program either have their charges dismissed (in a diversion or presentence model) or their sentences reduced (in a postsentence model). Some felony drug courts use a postplea, presentence model where, upon successful completion, the participants are allowed to plead guilty to a misdemeanor charge instead of a felony.

Although embodying a nonadversarial approach, the drug-court model incorporates a more central and proactive role for the judge, who in addition to presiding over the legal and procedural issues of the case, seeks to encourage positive client behavior (Marlowe & Kirby, 1999; Satel, 1998). The personality and courtroom style of the judge is often considered a key factor in the court's success (Marlowe & Kirby, 1999; Satel, 1998). Most drug courts have embraced the premise that recovery from addiction is an incremental process, and that small rewards for successes and coordinated sanctions for noncompliance can aid the treatment process.[1] Rewards for compliance might include encouragement or praise from the judge, courtroom ceremonies in which clients are formally advanced to the next treat-

---

[1]Some drug courts resemble contingency-management treatment models (Higgins, Wong, & Badger, 2000), with a point system in which participants must accumulate a certain point total for completing various services before being allowed to advance to the next treatment phase (Bedrick & Skolnick, 1999; Deschenes & Greenwood, 1994), or redeemable vouchers for achieving short-term goals, such as clean urines or attending counseling sessions.

ment stage, or less frequent drug testing or status hearings (Drug Courts Program Office, 1997). Sanctions for noncompliance might range from a judicial warning or admonishment, confinement in the jury box for a period of time, more frequent urine testing, or a short jail stay. Through regular status hearings, the judge strives to demonstrate that he or she cares about the participant treatment, but is also closely monitoring program compliance. Unlike traditional criminal courts, the drug-court judge and offender speak directly to one another.

Drug courts are generally considered "voluntary"; offenders have the right to decline participation and to be prosecuted through regular channels. Some drug courts also allow an initial period during which participants can "opt out" of the program with no loss of rights (Belenko, 1999a). However, some coercive elements (e.g., close judicial supervision and monitoring, regular drug tests, and graduated sanctions) exist in the drug court experience (see Farabee, Prendergast, & Anglin, 1998; Hiller, Knight, & Broome, 1998, for discussions of legal coercion and treatment). Defendants may also feel subtle or overt pressure to participate in drug court because of fears of the consequences of prosecution. The immediacy of sanctions imposed in most drug courts may increase the behavioral impact of judicial responses. Drug-court participants have noted the importance of the certainty, swiftness, and predictability of sanctions for noncompliant behaviors (Harrell & Smith, 1997).

Drug courts employ two basic treatment-delivery models: referral to multiple, existing, community-based programs or the use of dedicated treatment slots that are purchased by the drug court or reserved for drug clients. In the first model, drug-court assessment and referral staff select a treatment provider based on client needs and other factors, such as geographic location or gender. In 1997, 40% of adult drug courts referred clients to two or more treatment providers (Cooper, 1998). In the second model, the drug court uses a single provider, sometimes located at or near the courthouse, to treat all clients regardless of the type or intensity of substance abuse problem. The program might only serve drug-court clients, or might be an existing provider serving the drug court, as well as other constituencies. In a recent survey, 38% of drug courts contracted directly with dedicated treatment providers (Peyton & Gossweiler, 2000). Funding sources for treatment include federal drug court grants, participant fees, local funds, federal block grants, Medicaid, and other third-party insurance reimbursements (Cooper, 1998).

THE GROWTH OF DRUG COURTS

As of June 2000, there were 516 operational drug courts[2]; with an additional 281 being planned (American University, 2000). Drug courts are operating or planned in all 50 states, as well as the District of Columbia, Puerto Rico, Guam, two federal jurisdictions, and 54 Native American Tribal Courts; an estimated 200,000 drug offenders have entered drug-court programs since 1989 and 55,000 have graduated (American University, 2000).

Drug courts have direct antecedents dating back nearly 50 years: special courtrooms dedicated to drug cases existed in Chicago and New York City in the early 1950s (Belenko, 2000; Lindesmith, 1965). Several factors have driven the recent rapid spread of drug courts. One important impetus was the Violent Crime Control and Law Enforcement Act of 1994, which authorized federal funds for the planning, implementation, and enhancement of drug courts for nonviolent drug offenders. Between 1995 and 1999, the U.S. Department of Justice, through its Office of Justice Programs' Drug Courts Program Office (DCPO), provided more than $100 million in funding for the planning, implementation, and enhancement of drug courts. Additionally, the limitations of previous efforts to engage defendants in treatment, such as diversion programs, conditions of pretrial release or probation, or intermediate sanctions, made criminal court systems open for new models of treatment delivery. These earlier efforts were often fragmented, inconsistently or inappropriately used, or not viewed by the criminal justice system as sufficiently effective (Duffee & Carlson, 1996).

Between 1980 and 1998, arrests for drug offenses in the United States rose by 168%, while the number of total arrests increased by only 40% (Federal Bureau of Investigation, 1981, 1999), lending new urgency to find more effective ways to reduce drug-related crime (Belenko, 1990; Goerdt & Martin, 1989). Drug offenses are both the largest category of felony defendants (37%) in large urban courts (Hart & Reaves, 1999), and the most common admission offense (30%) for state prison inmates (Bureau of Justice Statistics, 1999). Drug use is also common among arrestees for nondrug crimes, with a median of 64% of male and 67% of female arrestees testing positive for illegal drugs (National Institute of Justice, 2000). Drug- or alcohol-involved inmates comprise an estimated 80% of the state and

---

[2]Breakdown = 384 adult drug courts, 105 juvenile, 19 family, and 8 combination adult/juvenile/family.

federal prison and local jail populations, which have tripled since 1980 (Belenko & Peugh, 1998).

These trends reflect several policy shifts that began in the early 1980s, including increasing emphasis on the apprehension of low-level street dealers (Kleiman, 1986), the escalation of legislated penalties against drug sale and possession, and the proliferation of mandatory sentencing laws for drug crimes that increase both the likelihood and length of incarceration (Blumstein & Beck, 1999). The emergence of crack cocaine in the mid-1980s, and the punitive antidrug policy response that it triggered, also spurred increasingly punitive policies toward drug crime (Belenko, Fagan, & Chin, 1991). Finally, the high recidivism rates of addicted drug offenders and limited access to substance-abuse treatment have exacerbated the cycle of drug use, arrest, and incarceration (Taxman, 1998).

In the early 1970s, New York City operated special "Narcotics Courts," designed to help ameliorate the anticipated impact on court dockets of the new punitive "Rockefeller" drug laws (Japha, 1978). Beginning in the mid-1980s, some state courts began experiments to provide dedicated courtrooms for drug cases, mainly in order to speed case processing (Cooper & Trotter, 1994). The experience of those early efforts made it clear that without treatment interventions, many offenders would simply recycle through the system, albeit more quickly. Thus, some of these "fast-track" courts began integrating drug treatment into the criminal justice process.

MAJOR CONCEPTUAL AND POLICY ISSUES

The unique structure and philosophy of drug courts provide an opportunity to learn more about the treatment and other health service needs of drug-involved offenders, and to increase access to clinical interventions. The team approach and nonadversarial nature of the court suggest a higher degree of overt cooperation among the key staff. The drug-court approach also assumes that staff have more extensive training about substance abuse and treatment, and share the same overall goal: to assist the participant in succeeding in drug treatment and graduating drug and crime free. The public health system has been reluctant to treat the criminal justice client, leading many drug-court programs to acquire their own services to meet their treatment-delivery needs (Taxman, 1998).

A second unique aspect of drug courts is the nontraditional judicial role, including the rewarding and praising of participants when they do well or achieve specific goals. There is some evidence that drug-court participants also view the judge's role as a key component of the drug court. In a 1997 survey of a nonrepresentative sample of drug-court clients, 75% said that monitoring of treatment progress by a judge was an important difference between the drug court and prior treatment program experience, 82% cited the possibility of sanctions for noncompliance as a very important difference, and 70% of respondents thought that the opportunity to talk about their progress and problems with a judge was a "very important" factor in keeping them in the program (Cooper, 1997).

Basic psychological principles of punishment and rewards suggest the potential power of judicial responses in shaping and changing participant behavior (Marlowe & Kirby, 1999). A large body of behavioral psychology research finds that an intermittent schedule of positive and negative reinforcement (i.e., sanctions and rewards) is the most powerful and lasting shaper of new behaviors (Axelrod & Apsche, 1983). Punishment alone is known to be a poor method of changing behaviors (Azrin & Holz, 1966). The more informal and client-centered atmosphere of the drug court allows these processes to emerge much more freely than in a traditional courtroom setting.

Finally, drug courts typically incorporate formal treatment-delivery structures, funding streams, and interagency relationships that are rarely seen in the criminal justice system. Researchers have noted that the failure to create a stable treatment system has hampered the effectiveness of treatment services (Anglin & Hser, 1990; Schlesinger & Dorwart, 1993). Drug courts may obviate some of the prior problems by offering a more systemic intervention model, providing a continuity of treatment, monitoring and oversight of services and treatment progress, contingencies to maintain compliance, regular information flow between the provider(s) and the court, and client accountability. In addition, drug courts represent an interesting laboratory for studying the organizational, client, and treatment factors that affect the recovery process and desistance from criminal activity.

CURRENT RESEARCH

The rapid expansion of drug courts has occurred in the absence of comprehensive research about their efficacy and impact. Still, there is a growing body of drug-court process and outcome data. In contrast to most other criminal justice innovations, drug courts have undergone considerable scrutiny during their relatively short existence. Although several federal research agencies have recently funded evaluations of various aspects of drug-court operations, the primary sources of information about the operations and impacts of drug courts have been process and outcome evaluations of individual drug courts, and the annual survey of operational drug courts conducted by the American University Drug Court Clearinghouse and Technical Assistance Project (DCCTAP).

In previous reviews of these surveys and approximately 60 drug-court evaluations, Belenko (1998, 1999b) concluded that drug courts provide closer and more frequent offender supervision (e.g., number of required court appearances, drug tests, supervision and treatment contacts) than under the standard probation or pretrial supervision that most nonviolent drug offenders experience, especially earlier in their criminal careers. Second, program retention is substantially longer than typically seen in community-based treatment, regardless of monitoring by the criminal justice system. Third, drug use and criminal behavior are comparatively reduced while drug-court participants are under program supervision. Finally, most evaluations comparing 1-year postprogram recidivism rates for all drug-court participants and a comparison group find a lower rearrest rate for the drug court. However, the effect sizes vary across drug courts, and several evaluations have found no postprogram impact on recidivism. In addition, studies vary in the type and appropriateness of the comparison group. Following is a brief summary of findings from current research on adult drug courts.

The Target Population

Three fourths of adult drug-court clients had had prior drug treatment, and 56% had been in jail or prison (American University, 2000). Seventy-two percent are male, and 74% are 26 or older (37% are over 35); only 19% are married or living with a significant other. Two thirds had been using drugs for at least 6 years. Drug-court clients have fairly extensive criminal histories: 75% of adult drug-court participants nationally had a prior felony conviction, and 43% had three or more prior felonies (American University, 2000). Drugs of choice vary by court and region of the country. For some drug courts on the West Coast, methamphetamine use is common, while in most drug courts in the east or south, cocaine and heroin are the most common drugs of abuse. Several drug courts have a relatively high percentage of participants for whom alcohol is the primary drug: 43% in Cumberland County (Maine) (Anspach & Ferguson, 1999),

27% in Madison County (Illinois) (Godley, Dennis, Funk, Siekmann, & Weisheit, 1998), and 21% in New Castle County (Delaware) (Whillhite & O'Connell, 1998).

Drug courts and other diversion programs have been criticized for carefully screening eligible offenders to admit only "low-risk" individuals to the program (Goldkamp, 2000; Hillsman, 1982). To the extent that such "creaming" takes place, the observed impacts of drug courts might be reduced if drug court capacity were expanded to include more medium- or high-risk offenders. However, there is, at present, little empirical information about how drug courts screen and assess the pool of paper-eligible offenders, or about the number and characteristics of eligible offenders who refuse to participate. However, it is likely that the limits of program capacity (relative to the number of drug cases or substance-involved offenders) allow most drug courts to be relatively selective in their screening and admission process. As drug courts expand and become institutionalized, however, it will be important to document and study the participant screening process to understand how drug-court impacts are likely to be affected by a broadening of the participant population.

Retention

Retention rates for drug courts are much greater than the retention rates typically observed for criminal justice clients specifically and treatment clients in general. An estimated 60% of those who enter drug courts are still in treatment (primarily outpatient drug free) after 1 year, and an estimated 48% graduate (Belenko, 1998; U.S. General Accounting Office, 1997). In contrast, the most recent national evaluation of treatment outcomes found that 50% of those admitted to outpatient drug-free programs stayed less than 3 months (Simpson, Joe, & Brown, 1997).

Much research concludes that retention is a key predictor of positive posttreatment outcomes (Hubbard et al., 1989; Simpson, Joe, & Rowan-Szal, 1997). Accordingly, the positive impacts of drug courts may be increased by strategies that increase the length of participation in treatment. Elements of the drug-court model that may increase retention in treatment (such as graduated sanctions and rewards, judicial supervision, and acceptance of relapse) have not been studied, but merit further research. Several recent drug-court evaluations analyzed the factors associated with program dropout (Bell, 1998; Godley et al., 1998; Denman & Guerin, 1998; Peters, Haas, & Murrin, 1999), and the predictors of dropout (e.g., younger age, more prior polydrug use, less employment) are similar to those found in the broader treatment-retention literature (e.g., Chou, Hser, & Anglin, 1998; Lang & Belenko, 2000).

Drug Use During the Program

Reported positive urinalysis rates are generally low for drug-court partici-pants. For the 13 courts reporting urinalysis test results in a 1998 drug-court survey, an average of 10% of the tests were positive for illegal drugs, compared with an average of 31% for offenders under probation supervision (Cooper, 1998). For example, in the Santa Clara County (California) drug court, only 5.4% of urine tests of drug-court participants tested positive over a 10-month period, compared with 10.2% of tests for nondrug court offenders in electronic monitoring, 13.2% of tests for offenders on Intensive Supervision probation, and 24.5% of tests for probationers under general supervision (Santa Clara County Drug Treatment Court, 1997). In the Second Judicial District Court (New Mexico), 21% of all drug-court clients had a positive drug test compared with 38% of those probation (Denman & Guerin, 1998).

Recidivism During Drug-Court Participation

Several drug-court evaluations have found low rearrest rates during the drug-court program (Belenko, 1998, 1999b). For example, the reported incidence of rearrest was only 3% in Santa Clara County (California) (Santa Clara County Drug Treatment Court, 1997), and 12% in Ventura County (California) (Oberg, 1996). Not surprisingly, given that a new arrest is often a trigger for program termination, in-program rearrest rates are higher for program failures than for graduates. Bell (1998) found 7% of King County (Washington) graduates and 27% of failures had a rearrest during the program, for a combined total of 20%. The percentages of clients rearrested during the program were 32% in Track 1 of the Delaware drug court and 20% in Track 2 (Whillhite & O'Connell, 1998). The average annual number of arrests per person in the Santa Barbara (California) drug court decreased from 2.46 in the year prior to admission to 1.43 during drug-court participation (Cosden, Peerson, & Crothers, 1999).

Treatment Services

Many drug courts recognize that most drug-involved offenders have other service needs in addition to treatment. Most drug-court evaluations that have examined the delivery of ancillary, nontreatment services found that such services were made available and accessed by drug-court clients, although specific data on access to other services are generally not available. Although relatively little is known about the delivery of treatment services to drug-court clients, basic descriptive data have recently been reported. King County (Washington) drug-court participants received an average of 52 sessions of individual counseling, group counseling, or acupuncture (Bell, 1998). Bernalillo County (New Mexico) DWI court clients attended an average of 27.8 group sessions, 10.7 acupuncture sessions, and 24.3 Alcoholics Anonymous (AA)/Narcotics Anonymous (NA) meetings (Guerin et al., 1998). Among Madison County (Illinois) drug-court clients, an average of 6.5 treatment sessions were attended in the first month. This average increased to 9.6 in month 2, then gradually declined to an average of 4 sessions in month 12 (Godley et al., 1998).

Sanctions and Incentives

Although several drug-court evaluations have examined the delivery of sanctions and rewards, little is known about the direct impacts on client compliance or retention (Marlowe & Kirby, 1999), or the styles and behaviors of judges that promote compliance and retention (Satel, 1998). For example, 44% of the sanctions imposed in the Cumberland County (Maine) drug court were time in the "dock," 31% were some time in jail, and 7% were increased AA/NA meetings (Anspach & Ferguson, 1999). Among the incentives, 38% were advancement to the next treatment phase, 30% were other rewards such as gift certificates, and 16% were a reduction in the frequency of court status hearings. Among Washington, DC, drug-court participants, 50% spent 3 days in jail and 22% were at least a week, primarily due to positive drug tests (Harrell, Cavanagh, & Roman, 1999). A jail sanction was imposed for 46% of the graduates (average 0.9 per graduate) and 77% of the nongraduates (1.6 per nongraduate) of the First Judicial District (Florida) (Peters & Murrin, 1998).

However, these findings yield little information about the operational components of a drug court-based sanctions and rewards system that is likely to result in higher compliance and completion rates. According to Marlowe and Kirby (1999), these components include regularity and immediacy of sanctions, predictability, the ability of the drug court to detect undesirable behaviors, and the need for reinforcement structures that will increase the frequency of desirable behaviors.

Economic Impact

An important empirical question about drug courts is whether their added operational costs are lower than the economic benefits that accrue because incarceration time is reduced, or because drug treatment reduces the likelihood of relapse and recidivism. Research on treatment in other criminal justice settings has concluded that investments in treatment generate net economic benefits relative to their costs (e.g., Gerstein, Harwood, Fountain, Siekmann, & Weisheit, 1994; Rajkumar & French, 1996).

Several studies have found drug-court savings in jail costs, especially for pretrial detention (Okamoto, Kassebaum, & Anderson, 1998; Sechrest, Shichor, Artist, & Briceno, 1998). However, studies that have imputed large cost savings by factoring in projected cost savings from the births of drug-free babies (Cooper, 1998; Roehl, 1998) may inflate the real cost savings.[3] Finigan (1999) estimated that a 1-year admissions cohort of Multnomah County (Oregon) drug-court clients yielded net savings of $2,476,760 in criminal justice system costs over 2 years, and $10,223,532 if other cost savings are included (e.g., from reduced victimization, public assistance, and medical claims). The operational costs per client per year in four Los Angeles County drug courts ranged from $3,706 to $8,924 for program graduates and from $1,599 to $3,290 for nongraduates. These figures are much lower than those of prison ($16,500 per year) or residential treatment ($13,000 per year), but higher than probation ($1,200 per year) (Deschenes, Imam, Foster, & Ward, 1999). Harrell et al. (1999) estimated that the graduated sanctions track of the Washington, DC, drug court had much lower costs than incarceration, and yielded a net economic benefit of $713,570, or $2,973 per participant.

Postprogram Recidivism

As criminal justice-based interventions, it is not surprising that most drug courts identify increased public safety as a primary goal. In two previous articles, Belenko (1998, 1999b) reviewed 21 evaluations that had examined

---

[3]Estimates of the long-term economic costs of a drug-exposed baby vary widely (Center for Substance-Abuse Treatment, 1993), and the long-term impacts on child development are uncertain (Zuckerman, 1996). Moreover, attribution of cost savings to the drug court assumes that the babies would have been born addicted had the mother not been in the drug court. But mothers not in drug court can access treatment or may stop using drugs in the late stages of pregnancy without treatment.

postprogram recidivism for all participants and a comparison sample. Drug-court participants had lower postprogram recidivism (generally for a 1-year period, using rearrest as the recidivism measure) than comparison groups in 15 of the 21 studies; in four studies the rates were similar, and in two studies the results were mixed. The different results and varying recidivism rates may reflect the type of comparison group used, the length of the follow-up period, the recidivism measure, differences in the drug-court structure or quality of treatment services, and variations in the target population served.

Only two studies published to date have used an experimental design to test the impact of the drug court on recidivism, and both found reductions in rearrest rates.[4] Eligible drug offenders in Maricopa County (Arizona) were randomly assigned to one of four probation tracks, one of which was the drug court, while the others required varying levels of drug-testing requirements (Deschenes & Greenwood, 1994). Although the drug court had no impact on rearrest rates 12 months after drug court, a significant reduction (33.1% vs. 43.7% for other probation) was found after 36 months (Turner, Greenwood, Fain, & Deschenes, 1999). In the Washington, DC, drug court, rearrest rates 12 months after sentencing were significantly lower for participants in the sanctions track (without treatment requirements) compared with felony defendants randomly assigned to the standard court docket (19% vs. 27%) (Harrell et al., 1999). Unfortunately, neither the Maricopa County postsentence probation nor the Washington, DC, sanctions-only model are generalizable to most drug courts.

Because of resource and staffing constraints, few drug courts provide any formal postprogram supervision or aftercare, yet consistent results from evaluations of prison-based treatment show that long-term outcomes are substantially improved when treatment and related services are continued in the community following release (Knight, Simpson, & Hiller, 1999; Martin, Butzin, Saum, & Inciardi, 1999). Second, Godley et al. (1998) and Peters et al. (1999) found that even for those who fail the drug court, early dropouts tend to have higher recidivism rates than those that drop out later in the program. Accordingly, it is plausible that even if graduation rates remain stable, postprogram recidivism could be reduced further if

---

[4]Other drug-court evaluations have used matched or unmatched comparison groups of varying appropriateness (Belenko, 1998, 1999b). Examples include offenders referred to and eligible for the drug court, but who opted not to participate, matched offenders from standard diversion programs, individually matched offenders sentenced to probation, and drug offenders adjudicated before the drug court was implemented.

drug courts are able to increase the average length of treatment by reducing early dropout.

Other Outcomes

Few studies have examined other postprogram outcomes, such as drug use, employment, family stability, or health. Cosden et al. (1999) compared average Addiction Severity Index (Fureman, Parikh, Bragg, & McLellan, 1990) problem scores at intake and after 12 months in the program in the Santa Barbara County (California) drug court. The severity of drug-court participants' alcohol, drug, medical, legal, family, and psychological problems were significantly lower after 12 months in the drug court. In contrast, after controlling for other defendant characteristics in multivariate analyses, Harrell et al. (1999) found no significant differences in postprogram drug use, employment, or legal income between the drug-court sanctions docket and standard docket cases.[5]

CONCLUSIONS AND FUTURE DIRECTIONS

Drug courts are a relatively new and structurally different approach to engaging offenders in community-based treatment. The encouraging retention rates and relatively low prevalence of drug use and criminal activity during participation and for program graduates suggests that the drug-court model can successfully engage many drug offenders into long-term treatment and related services. Postprogram outcomes are less clear: most studies find lower 1-year postprogram recidivism for drug-court participants, but the size of the difference varies across drug courts, and several evaluations have not found an impact. Moreover, few studies have examined postprogram recidivism beyond 1 year, and the available comparison groups are often problematic (Belenko, 1999b).

    The importance of treatment retention in improving postprogram outcomes suggests that more research is needed on the individual client, clinical, staff, and organizational factors that promote drug-court retention, compliance, and positive outcomes. The judge's explicit personal involve-

---

[5]Because of implementation problems, sufficient treatment services were not available during the evaluation period to allow a valid test of the impact of the treatment track of the Washington, DC, drug court (Harrell et al., 1999).

ment in the offender's treatment outcome and their interactions in court (Satel, 1998), as well as the embrace of the therapeutic-jurisprudence model (Hora, Schma, & Rosenthal, 1999) may be critical. In any event, the unique structure of the drug-court model, its interaction with the offender, and the way in which treatment is integrated into the court process may operate to increase the likelihood of successful program completion. Although a few drug-court studies have begun to examine predictors of retention, there is little extant knowledge to guide the development of new drug-court programs or to modify existing programs to reduce dropout and increase graduation rates.

There may also be important but relatively untapped ancillary public health benefits of drug courts. Given the multiple health services needs of their target populations (Marquart, Merianos, Hebert, & Carroll, 1997), drug courts can provide an important public health intervention role, including reducing HIV-risk behaviors. The screening, assessment, and referral process provides an opportunity to identify health problems and provides linkages to appropriate clinical interventions. The close supervision and case management typical of drug courts can help to assure better access to health services, follow through with clinical interventions, and monitoring of compliance with treatment and medication regimens. But the available research is not yet sufficient to determine how these linkages are facilitated or what barriers exist to achieving more effective linkages. Comprehensive health assessments, access to referral networks, appropriate referrals, and follow-up with participants to assure compliance with health care regimens are all important dimensions for improving the effectiveness of drug court-based health services, and keys to better long-term outcomes for drug-involved offenders.

Improving the Effectiveness of Clinical Services

There are other research and operational issues that warrant attention if the full potential of drug courts is to be realized. First, targeting, eligibility screening, and assessment processes directly drive the number and type of drug-court clients, and thus the types of clinical services needed. Narrow targeting, strict eligibility screening, and program admission procedures that allow higher risk offenders to drop out prior to "formal" enrollment may limit the number of participants, and produce a creaming effect whereby the drug court serves mostly low-risk clients. Such courts may show high levels of compliance and success rates, but may not be cost effective. Clients may have done as well under less intensive adjudication and treatment models. Moreover, the voluntary nature of drug-court participation can result in self-selection bias in which highly motivated or lower-risk offenders are more likely to participate.

As in other criminal justice-supervised treatment, drug courts need to improve staff training in substance abuse and treatment. Although some drug courts offer formal training for judges and staff, others rely more on ad hoc training or the interest and motivation of individual judges. Given the lack of universal training in these areas in standard judicial education, improving and formalizing such training curricula should be a goal of the drug-court movement. The regional training workshops for judges and other drug-court personnel recently implemented by the National Drug Court Institute are an important step toward improving staff knowledge. Given the racial, ethnic, and class disparity between the drug-client population and criminal justice program staff, improving cultural competence and sensitivity should also be an important part of any training curriculum. Cultural and gender issues may be closely related to treatment outcomes (Aponte & Barnes, 1995; Fiorentine & Hillhouse, 1999).

To date, little attention has been given to the role of treatment process or the organization of service delivery on drug-court clients' compliance, retention, or outcomes (Taxman, 1999). Yet recent research notes the importance of treatment process on outcomes in criminal justice-based treatment (Joe, Simpson, & Broome, 1998; Simpson, Joe, Rowan-Szal, & Greener, 1997). Few drug courts have implemented either comprehensive and periodic clinical assessments, or regular systematic monitoring of therapeutic contacts. Also, it may be important for treatment to be theoretically driven to engage the client in the treatment process and ameliorate patient risk factors at intake, to motivate the client to change behavior through the use of incentives and sanctions, and to provide a therapeutic environment that actively involves the client in the treatment process (Palmer, 1995).

The drug-court model incorporates a nonclinical but authoritative figure (the judge) who can and often does make decisions that directly affect the treatment process. Depending upon the drug-court structure, the knowledge and training of the judge and the drug-court staff, and the relationship between the judge and treatment provider(s), judicial behaviors, comments, and decisions can support or undermine the treatment process (Marlowe & Kirby, 1999). In particular, it may be difficult for the judge, other drug-court staff, and clinical treatment staff to reach consensus over the appropriate response to relapse. The philosophical or operational tensions surrounding staff's views and attitudes about addiction and recovery can be difficult to resolve, yet may have a profound effect on drug-court outcomes (Taxman, 1999). Careful preprogram implementation planning, timely and appropriate information exchange between the court and clinical staff, and regular stakeholder meetings may mitigate some of these difficulties (Drug Courts Program Office, 1997).

Minimizing tensions between judge and treatment provider can be difficult but important to resolve. Not only can judicial attitudes or decisions affect the treatment process, but clinical decisions can, in turn, affect the imposition of sanctions, rewards, or phase advancement. The phased-treatment structure of drug courts places an inherent time limit on treatment progress. If a client remains too long in one phase (e.g., due to multiple relapses), then the client might be terminated. Although lack of treatment progress may lead to program termination under other models of criminal justice-based treatment supervision (such as probation or parole), retention time under those models is expected to be shorter than under the drug-court model, where relapse is expected and more acceptable.

Key Research Gaps

Although much research on drug courts has emerged in recent years, there are many gaps in our knowledge about drug-court processes and outcomes. These have been outlined in detail elsewhere (Belenko, 1998, 1999b). Most important are the need for better-controlled studies of the impacts of various drug-court interventions; more research on how the components of the drug-court model (especially the judicial role) affect program and treatment compliance; studies of the factors affecting in-program relapse and criminal activity, as well as postprogram relapse and criminal activity; the importance of experimental designs for program-impact evaluations, or the use of more appropriate comparison groups; the collection and analysis of long-term outcome data; and the improvement of automated drug-court data systems that can support evaluation.

Moreover, data on the effectiveness of different drug-court treatment and operational models are lacking. For example, little is known about the relative efficacy of having a single contracted or court-operated treatment provider compared with referral to multiple community-based programs. The elements of the relationships among drug-court staff, treatment and other service providers, and clients that promote or deter successful outcomes are not well studied. Data are also lacking on the optimum drug court-phase structure, or the impacts of different sanctions and rewards or contingency systems.

Finally, the rapid growth of drug courts and the eventual phasing out of federal funding for implementation raise the question of how institution-alization will affect drug-court operations in the future. Issues such as funding streams, staff burnout, and the shift from committed early drug-court pioneers to use of drug courts as just another judicial assignment merit further study. The history of policy innovations suggests that early program success is common, but maintaining that success as innovations become institutionalized is much more difficult.

24

Mandatory Minimum Sentencing and Drug-Law Violations: Effects on the Criminal Justice System

Duane C. McBride, Curtis J. VanderWaal, Rosalie L. Pacula, Yvonne Terry-McElrath, and Jamie F. Chriqui

Society often seeks to impose simple solutions on complex problems. One such attempted "simple solution" to the problem of drug-law violations has been the creation of mandatory minimum-sentencing laws at both federal and state levels. Essentially, mandatory minimum sentencing involves Congress or a state legislature mandating a specific minimum punishment for a given violation of law. Mandatory minimum sentencing is not a new phenomenon, but it has reemerged as a significant issue in current drug-policy debates. Today, most states, as well as the federal government, have some form of mandatory-sentencing laws for drug violations. Although these laws were designed to eliminate sentencing disparities and toughen violation penalties, many unintended consequences have resulted. This chapter will examine mandatory minimum-sentencing laws using the following framework:

1. Current context of mandatory sentencing,
2. Discussion of expected effects,
3. Description of unanticipated consequences,
4. Evaluation of overall impact, and
5. Proposal of a framework for alternatives.

THE CONTEXT OF CURRENT MANDATORY SENTENCING

In its current manifestation, mandatory sentencing appears to have arisen within the framework of four social currents: (a) the drug revolution of the 1970s, (b) the rapidly increasing crime rates of that era (often associated with increasing drug use), (c) the growing mistrust of the judicial branch of government by federal and state legislators, and (d) the expectations implied by general deterrence theory.

The Drug Revolution

A wide variety of data indicate that during the 1970s, U.S. society experienced a significant increase in drug use. By the end of the decade, the use of marijuana was about as common as tobacco use among high school seniors (Johnston, O'Malley, & Bachman, 1999). At the same time, in many communities, the majority of those arrested for property crimes were illegal drug users (McBride & McCoy, 1992). The apparent "drug–crime connection" provided a major impetus for increased funding in drug research, prevention, and treatment (McBride & McCoy, 1992), and supported the reemergence of mandatory sentences for drug-using criminals.

The Crime Revolution

The 1950s was an era of perceived relative social calm in the United States. The experience of most citizens was one of limited danger from criminal activity. The crime index rate in 1960 was 1,116 per 100,000 population. By 1966, the rate was 1,656, an increase of 48.4% (Federal Bureau of Investigation [FBI], 1967). This rapid increase in crime was well covered in the media, and prompted, coupled with other things, a powerful conservative response culminating in the election of Richard Nixon in 1968.

Legislative Reaction to Judicial Discretion

During the 1960s, mandatory minimum sentencing had largely disappeared, and judges had considerable discretion in sentence imposition. During this time period, the dominant criminal justice philosophy focused on increased mental health treatment, general rehabilitation, and the necessity of changing the social conditions that contributed to criminal and drug-using behaviors (Ryan, 1971). By the early 1970s, there was considerable state-level reaction to what was perceived to be generous and capricious judicial discretion in sentencing application. In the 1970s, New York passed two very strong mandatory-sentencing laws focused primarily on drug violations. These laws have come to be known as Rockefeller's Drug Law and the Second Felony Offender Law. Rockefeller's Drug Law mandated prison terms of at least 15 years (with a maximum of life imprisonment) for those convicted of violating a variety of drug laws. The Second Felony Offender Law likewise mandated specific minimum-sentence lengths for those convicted of a second felony. These laws are widely believed to have influenced the development of other state and federal mandatory minimum-sentencing laws, most of which were directed at drug-law violations. By 1984, Congress had become an enthusiastic initiator of mandatory minimum sentences that superceded previously adopted flexible sentencing guidelines. This congressional support culminated in the passage of the 1984 Federal Sentencing Reform Act, which established the U.S. Sentencing Commission. The Commission's primary responsibilities were to create sentencing guidelines to be applied to offenders in federal court. However, the act also created mandatory minimum sentences for drug offenses committed near schools, provided "sentencing enhancements" for all drug and violent offenses involving possession or use of a firearm, and mandated prison sentences for all serious felonies (United States Sentencing Commission, 1991). Two years later, Congress expanded the scope of mandatory minimum penalties with the passage of the Anti-Drug Abuse Act of 1986. This act included offenses involving crack or powder cocaine found in a defendant's possession (Musto, 1999). By 1997, 26 states and the federal government had enacted laws imposing mandatory sentences and reducing judicial discretion (Austin, Clark, Hardyman, & Henry, 1999).

Deterrence Theory and Mandatory Sentencing

The underlying philosophical rationale for severe mandatory punishment for those who violated specific laws was drawn from general deterrence theory. Deterrence theory assumes that human beings make rational choices based on the benefit to be gained from a choice compared with the potential costs. If the costs are significantly higher than the total benefits, then the behavior is much less likely to occur (Becker, 1968). Criminologists have argued that deterrence is most likely to work if the severity of punishment is coupled with both certainty and swiftness of punishment.

Evaluations of deterrence theory have been mixed. Those who argue against it note that deterrence theory rests on a faulty assumption about the rationality of criminal behavior. In particular, they argue that such a rationally based theory does not apply to drug use, which often involves physical and psychological dependency or addiction. Advocates of deterrence theory maintain that if society would successfully and uniformly increase the severity of consequences for drug-law violations, there would, indeed, be less use and, thus, less crime and violence (Kahan, 1997).

EXPECTED EFFECTS OF MANDATORY SENTENCING

Supporters of mandatory minimums were originally enthusiastic about the potential of the laws. The penalties were expected to accomplish a broad range of objectives, including retribution, incapacitation, elimination of sentencing disparity, inducement of cooperation, and inducement of pleas (United States Sentencing Commission, August 1991, pp. 13–14).

Retribution or "Just Desserts"

Congress primarily created the Anti-Drug Abuse Act of 1986 as a response to public frustration with serious offenders receiving relatively short sentences or not serving full sentences. Proponents argued that longer sentences were generally deserved, but that many judges were reluctant to impose appropriately stiff penalties for reasons that have been discussed. The United States Sentencing Commission estimated that this law more than doubled the average time being served for federal drug offenses at the time (United States Sentencing Commission, August 1991, p. 114).

Deterrence

Proponents claimed that mandatory minimum-sentencing laws would deter drug offenses by discouraging offenders from repeating their crime (specific deterrence) and, by example, preventing others from committing similar offenses (general deterrence) for fear of long prison sentences. Proponents maintained that both certainty and severity of punishment were guaranteed through this more focused approach.

Incapacitation

Supporters of mandatory sentences argued that the laws would increase public safety by incapacitating drug dealers and violent criminals for long periods of time. For example, in the most extreme form of mandated sentencing, convicted drug kingpins would be given a mandatory life sentence without the possibility of parole.

Elimination of Sentencing Disparity

Sentencing guidelines historically allowed judges to choose from a range of penalties, depending on the offense and various individual factors. Proponents of mandatory sentencing argued that criminals convicted of the same sentence could receive vastly different penalties, depending on a judge's leniency and perhaps the defendant's ethnicity or gender. Mandatory sentencing was designed to eliminate this disparity by removing judicial discretion over the lower end of the sentencing range. To a significant extent, mandatory minimum sentencing was seen as guaranteeing "truth in sentencing."[1]

Inducement of Cooperation

Supporters claimed that mandatory minimums could be used in a "carrot and stick" fashion (Caulkins, Rydell, Schwabe, & Chiesa, 1997) to induce

---

[1]First enacted through the Violent Crime Control and Law Enforcement Act of 1994, federal Truth in Sentencing laws require offenders to serve 85% of their prison sentence. Parole eligibility and good-time credits are restricted or eliminated.

the cooperation of offenders in identifying the criminal conduct of others. The "carrot" refers to a judge's discretion to reduce a mandated sentence below the minimum threshold if the offender is determined to have offered "substantial assistance" in the prosecution of another individual. The otherwise mandatory "stick" is viewed as being both a certain and severe enough incentive to induce the offender's cooperation.

Inducement of Pleas

Proponents argued that guilty offenders might wish to plead guilty to a lesser charge in the hopes that they could avoid a conviction that would trigger a mandatory minimum sentence. Such guilty pleas would save trial costs.

Supporters of mandatory minimums point to the dramatic declines of both crime and drug use in the general population during the 1980s and 1990s as evidence of their success (Levitt, 1998). However, while mandatory minimum penalties promised a great deal, critics contend that they have, in many ways, failed to accomplish their intended objectives. In some situations, the laws have had significant unintended consequences. Such consequences have included a dramatic increase in drug arrests, a rising proportion of drug offenders in prison, inappropriate incarceration of many drug offenders, prison overcrowding, a shifting of power from judge to prosecutor, a breakdown of Truth in Sentencing laws, unintended benefits for large-scale dealers, and an unfair and disproportionate effect on female and African American drug offenders.

UNANTICIPATED CONSEQUENCES
OF MANDATORY SENTENCING

Increased Drug Arrests

During the 1980s, the Reagan Administration's "war on drugs" resulted in funding reductions for treatment and research. At the same time, the Administration's demand reduction strategy resulted in a dramatic increase in the number of arrests for drug offenses. At the federal level, a total of 581,000 drug arrests in 1980 nearly tripled to a record high of 1,584,000 in 1997. By this time, 79% of drug arrests were for possession and 21% were for sales (FBI, 1999). Overall, 44% of drug arrests were for marijuana offenses (FBI, 1999) and drug defendants comprised 42% of felony convictions (Bureau of Justice Statistics [BJS], August 1999). Since these arrests have included many low-use users and low-level dealers, critics have argued that the stiff sentences are inappropriate to the level of the offense.

Rising Proportion of Prisoners Who Are Drug Users

State and federal prison inmates also reported high levels of drug use while committing their offenses. In the 1997 Survey of Inmates in State and Federal Correctional Facilities, more than 570,000 of U.S. prisoners (51%) reported the use of alcohol or drugs while committing their offense. Additionally, more than 80% of state and 70% of federal prisoners reported past drug use (Mumola, 1999). Such increases have driven up prison costs since drug-involved offenders generally have poorer health status and higher recidivism rates (Leukefeld, Logan, Martin, Purvis, & Farabee, 1998) than nondrug offenders.

Rising Proportion of Drug Offenders in Prison

As arrest rates have risen, so have incarceration rates. By 1998, overall incarceration rates in federal and state prisons, as well as local jails, were more than three and a half times higher than rates in 1980 (501,900 persons vs. 1,802,496 persons; Brown, Gilliard, Snell, Stephan, & Wilson, 1996; Gilliard, 1999). This figure may have turned the United States into the world leader in per capita prison incarceration rates (The Sentencing Project, 1999a, 1999b). Drug offenses are cited as one of the leading causes for the recent population increases in federal and state prisons. In 1980, there were 19,000 offenders in state prisons for drug offenses and 4,900 in federal prisons, which represented 6% and 25% of all inmates, respectively (Brown et al., 1996). However, by 1997, drug offenders in federal and state prisons had swelled to more than 250,000 persons, now representing 21% of state and 60% of federal prisoners (BJS, April 1999; Mumola, 1999). A similarly rapid increase occurred in jail inmates held for any drug offense, rising from an estimated 20,400 in 1983 to 109,200 in 1996, or 22% of the estimated total jail population (Harlow, 1998).

Prison Overcrowding

A consequence of such high incarceration rates has been prison overcrowding. By the end of 1998, state prisons were operating between 13% and

22% above capacity, whereas federal prisons were operating 27% above capacity (BJS, August 1999). As a result, both state and federal corrections agencies currently contract with local jails, privately operated facilities, and other facilities to incarcerate sentenced inmates. Most states, as well as the federal government also have been rapidly constructing new prisons in an attempt to keep up with the high volume of inmates being sentenced. At the beginning of 1998, more than 1.2 million beds were either planned or under construction in the United States, for a total estimated cost of $3.9 billion (Camp & Camp, 1998).

Shifting of Power from Judges to Prosecutors

Minimum sentencing mandates that a judge can rarely depart from a statutory minimum to take mitigating circumstances into account. Prosecutors, on the other hand, are not required to charge offenders with a count carrying a mandatory minimum penalty if other options are possible. Prosecutors often use this flexibility to convince a defendant to offer "substantial assistance" in the conviction of another person in exchange for a reduced sentence. Some have questioned the wisdom of transferring this power away from the judge (Stewart, 1999), arguing that private deals between prosecutors and defense attorneys do not allow for proper public accountability of sentencing decisions. Others, however, like having a prosecutor who is "tough on crime" and willing to make decisions to seriously punish those who have broken the law.

Breakdown of Truth-in-Sentencing Laws

Perhaps as a result of prison overcrowding, mandatory sentencing has not resulted in truth in sentencing. Estimates from the BJS reveal that the mean prison sentence for drug offenses is 51 months, but the mean time served is only 21 months (Bonczar & Beck, 1997). Further, state definitions of mandatory sentence lengths also vary significantly. Ditton and Wilson (1999) found that state definitions of Truth-in-Sentencing laws range between 50% and 100% of time sentenced.

Unintended Benefits for Large-Scale Dealers

Researchers have concluded that there has been an increase in plea bargaining as a means of circumventing mandatory sentences (Weinstein &

Turner, 1997). It appears that defendants are willing to plea just below a charge that would require a mandatory sentence. At the federal level, the prison sentences for individuals convicted of drug crimes declined significantly between 1992 and 1998—from 86 to 67 months (Transactional Records Access Clearinghouse [TRAC], 2000). This likely occurred because defendants pled to a lesser first-offense drug charge that did not require the imposition of mandatory sentencing (TRAC, 2000). Declines may also have occurred due to the development of "safety valve" provisions,[2] which are used in about 20% of all federal drug cases (United States Sentencing Commission, 1998). Many have argued that this has also reduced the number of sentences that are imposed. Although mandatory sentences may cause an expected behavior in this area (an increased willingness to plea), they may not result in the expected increased consequences for drug law violations. Large-scale, wholesale-level dealers are often able to plea bargain for lower level sentences (Caulkins, Rydell, Schwabe, & Chiesa, 1998). Kane (1995) has argued that this willingness to plead guilty to a lesser offense and prosecutorial willingness to accept such lower pleas may be allowing dangerous individuals to serve less time and avoid treatment interventions than could occur with mandatory sentencing. In contrast, the street-level dealer (who is often unable to offer substantial assistance to prosecutors) is given a mandatory sentence. Such individuals are easily replaced, thus perpetuating the continued arrests of dealers and users with few, if any, high-level convictions.

Differential Impact by Gender

The increases in the numbers of individuals incarcerated were dramatic for both men and women. However, the impact appears to be greater for women. Although the number of males imprisoned for drug offenses rose 48% between 1990 and 1997, the number of female inmates serving time for drug offenses nearly doubled (BJS, August 1999). This increase has resulted in large numbers of both pregnant women in prison, as well as children who are removed from maternal care because their mothers are imprisoned (Alexander, 1997; Raeder, 1995).

---

[2]In 1994, the U.S. Congress adopted a safety valve provision that allows federal judges to sentence offenders below the applicable mandatory minimum penalty if the offender has a minimal prior record, no violence was involved in the offense, and the offender offers substantial assistance to the prosecution.

Disproportionate Effect on African Americans

The Anti-Drug Abuse Act of 1986 established mandatory minimum senten-ces for offenses involving both crack and powder cocaine. However, con-gressional testimony heightened fears of the greater dangers of crack, resulting in the same 5- to 40-year mandatory penalties being given for possession of 5 grams of crack as for 500 grams of powdered cocaine, a 1:100 ratio (Musto, 1999). Further, crack cocaine is the only controlled substance for which a mandatory minimum sentence exists for a first offense of simple possession for personal use versus sale/distribution or trafficking (The Anti-Drug Abuse Act of 1986; Office of National Drug Control Policy, 1999).

The U.S. Sentencing Commission cited several reasons for these differences:

> For example, crack cocaine is more often associated with systemic crime—crime related to its marketing and distribution—particularly the type of violent street crime so often connected with gangs, guns, serious injury and death. In addition, because it is easy to manufacture and use and relatively inexpensive, crack is more widely available on the street and is particularly appealing and accessible to the most vulnerable mem-bers of our society. (April 1997, p. 4)

The Commission also noted that crack cocaine is more addictive than powder cocaine due to its more intense physiological and psychotropic effects.

However, at least at the federal level, these sentencing disparities have had a disproportionate effect on African Americans. For example, although approximately two thirds of crack-cocaine offenders were Caucasian or Hispanic in 1997, African Americans represented 85% of the offenders convicted in federal court for crack-cocaine distribution (United States Sentencing Commission, February 1995, 1998). As a result, members of the African American community have strongly accused the justice system of racial bias in sentencing. Such concerns appear well founded, as sentenc-ing disparities have dramatically increased both incarceration rates and sentencing lengths for African American offenders. For example, between 1990 and 1997, the number of Black inmates serving time for drug viola-tions increased more than 60%, whereas increases for White and Hispanic inmates were up by only 46% and 32%, respectively (Beck & Mumola, 1999). In addition, while safety valve provisions have reduced overall sentence lengths for many drug offenders, crack-cocaine offenders have been the least likely to benefit from this provision (51% of heroin offenders vs. 16% of crack-cocaine offenders; United States Sentencing Commission, 1998).

In response to this appearance of racial bias in drug sentencing, in May 1995, the Sentencing Commission officially recommended to Congress that disparities between sentencing guidelines for crack and powder cocaine be eliminated (United States Sentencing Commission, February 1995). By fall of 1995, however, both Congress and the Clinton Administration rejected these recommendations, arguing that crack was more dangerous due to its greater addictiveness, low price, ease of manufacture, and associated street violence. In April 1997, the commission altered its recommendation to reduce the amount of powder necessary to trigger a mandatory minimum sentence (between 125 and 375 grams), while increasing the amount of crack (between 25 and 75 grams) (United States Sentencing Commission, April 1997).

OVERALL EFFECTIVENESS OF MANDATORY MINIMUMS

Although numerous studies have examined the impact of mandatory minimum sentences and three-strikes laws on courts, local jails, prison populations, and recidivism (Clark, Austin, & Henry, 1997; Meierhoefer, 1992a; Tonry, 1987), few studies have examined their overall effectiveness at achieving the stated objectives described previously. A comprehensive examination of effectiveness should evaluate the impact of these laws across all objectives. However, no studies to date have been that comprehensive. Instead, evaluations have focused on the impact the laws have had on specific objectives, including deterrence (Loftin & McDowall, 1984), retribution (United States Sentencing Commission, 1991), incapacitation (Clark et al., 1997; Greenwood et al., 1994), and elimination of sentencing disparity (Meierhoefer, 1992b). A few more comprehensive studies have evaluated the impact on several of the stated objectives (Austin et al., 1999; Caulkins et al., 1997, 1998; Tonry, 1987; United States Sentencing Commission, August 1991). The more comprehensive studies will be discussed below.

In a review of the early literature on the effects of mandatory minimums on the criminal justice system, Tonry (1987) found that arrest rates for targeted crimes declined soon after the laws took effect and that sentences became longer and more severe. Further, he found that dismissal and diversion rates increased at early stages of court processing after the laws became effective. This suggests that these laws may have been effective at inducing cooperation and/or pleas. However, he found that for defendants whose cases were not dismissed, plea-bargain rates declined and trial rates increased, thereby making it unclear what the overall effect was in terms of meeting these two objectives. The interpretation of these findings was further confused by the fact that officials were able to circumvent these laws when they believed the results were too harsh for the crime committed (such as the use of safety valve provisions noted earlier).

A more recent study examining California's three-strikes law provides additional evidence that prosecutorial discretion reduces the potential deterrent effect of mandatory sentencing laws and may actually increase sentencing disparity (Austin et al., 1999). The authors found significant variation in application of California's three-strikes law by county prosecutors in five large counties, resulting in significant sentencing disparity within the state. These five counties revealed similar changes in pre- and postreform crime rates despite differential application of the law, leading the study's authors to conclude that the law failed to deter or incapacitate so-called high-rate offenders (Austin et al., 1999).

Three problems exist with evaluations such as the two cited above that are based on variation created by natural experiments. First, the evaluations frequently ignore secular trends in crime and punishment that are concurrent with changes in law or do not interpret the results within this broader context. Other evaluations of the California law, for example, note that two of the most commonly used indicators of general deterrence, crime rates and drug use, were falling even before the laws came into effect (Greenwood et al., 1994). Second, when evaluations consider the cost of these laws, they very frequently compare only the partial cost of the law vis-à-vis another program. Third, they do not consider differences in program outcomes when comparing costs, making any cost comparisons difficult to interpret.

A series of RAND studies have tried to overcome these limitations by examining the effects of mandatory minimum laws on general deterrence through simulation analyses. Unlike other evaluations, these are based on models of crime and drug use that enable researchers to control for secular trends and thus identify the incremental impact of the laws. Further, the models can be used to compare the cost and implementation of mandatory minimums with alternative policies that could be used to achieve the same objectives.

In the first study, Greenwood and his colleagues (1994) simulated the costs and benefits of California's three-strikes law. The simulation incorporated several assumptions regarding trends in California crime rates and the impact of the law on deterrence and retribution. Assuming that the law only led to longer sentences and did not have a deterrent effect, the authors projected that the three-strikes law would triple California's prison population over the next 25 years, at an average additional cost of $5.5 billion each year. Partially offsetting this cost, however, they estimated the law would lead to a 28% reduction in serious crime, resulting in a total correctional cost of about $16,300 per crime averted. If the law instead enhanced sentences of only repeat violent offenders (i.e., those whose current crime and prior two offenses were violent, serious crimes), the reduction in crime attributed to the law would be only 18%. However, this alternate policy had a much lower total correctional cost of $12,000 per crime averted, and was therefore more cost effective at reducing crime.

In separate studies, Caulkins and his colleagues (1997, 1998) examined the issue of federal mandatory minimums and their cost effectiveness at reducing cocaine consumption, cocaine expenditures, or drug-related crimes relative to increased conventional enforcement and treatment of heavy users. The authors focused on a strict variant of federal mandatory minimums because the state- and local-level data they employed included all dealers, not just those meeting the triggering conditions necessary for a mandatory minimum sentence.[3] Instead, the authors examined the benefit of spending an additional million dollars on increasing the sentences served by a representative set of drug dealers to 5 or 10 years from an average term of 1 year (the average time served by dealers exiting prison in 1990). Two different approaches were taken to mathematically model the market for cocaine, but the conclusion was the same regardless of method: mandatory minimum sentences were not justifiable on the basis of cost effectiveness at reducing cocaine consumption, cocaine expenditures, or drug-related crime relative to treatment of heavy users or increased enforcement. Mandatory minimums that targeted a specific class of drug dealers (i.e., third-level wholesale dealers) did result in a better cost-effectiveness ratio, but this policy was still less cost effective than expanding the scope of conventional enforcement by arresting and prosecuting more dealers under traditional sentencing laws.

Caulkins et al. (1998) also compared the costs of mandatory minimums with those of drug treatment. The authors concluded that treatment was eight times more cost effective in terms of reducing future drug consump-

---

[3]Typically, dealers only incur longer sentences when some specified amount of cocaine can be associated with their crime.

tion than the use of mandated sentencing requirements. In addition, expanding the use of treatment was estimated to reduce drug-related crime up to 15 times more that mandatory sentencing.

It is important to keep in mind the limitations of policy simulations in evaluating mandatory minimum legislation. First, all of these simulations are based on underlying assumptions of baseline rates of criminal activity and drug use. If these rates change, then the models need to be re-evaluated. Second, the models hold other factors constant when evaluating the impact of particular policies. While this is necessary to identify the incremental impact of the particular policies, it does not mean that the outcome from the simulations would actually be observed.

FUTURE DIRECTIONS

The implementation of mandatory sentencing has resulted in serious unanticipated consequences. A reversal of this policy to total judicial discretion, with a primary focus on individual rehabilitation or societal restructuring, would likely encounter significant public resistance. As noted previously, mandatory minimum-sentencing practices have been based on general deterrence theory: severity, certainty, and swiftness of punishment.

New Deterrence Theory

In a 1997 article, Kahan describes the new deterrence scholarship as seeking to integrate social norms into conventional economic conceptions of deterrence. The approach "aims to enrich economics by identifying social phenomena important enough to be worth regulating but malleable enough to be regulated efficiently" (p. 2). According to Kahan (1997), the goal of the new deterrence theory is to create a feasible middle ground. This public health-based, risk-reduction approach[4] would support the development of a policy environment that does not seek to encourage strictly dichotomous policy approaches (either continuing to increase the cost of crime on a solely economic deterrence basis, or to focus entirely on sociological concerns within the context of structural and cultural conditions). Instead,

---

[4]The central feature of harm reduction is " . . . the attempt to ameliorate the adverse health, social, or economic consequences associated with the use of mood-altering substances without necessarily requiring a reduction in the consumption of these substances" (Inciardi & Harrison, 2000).

the goal would be to "identify morally and politically acceptable law-enforcement strategies that themselves ameliorate the social conditions that cause crime" (Kahan, 1997, p. 10).

Ecological Systems Theory

The new deterrence approach suggests methods to successfully combine appropriate sanction severity within the context of social issues. However, it can perhaps be argued that such methods will not be successful unless implemented within an understanding of how they can be transferred from macro to mezzo and micro levels. Ecological systems theory presents guidance on such implementation issues. Ecological systems theory posits that transactions are constantly occurring between individuals and other humans, as well as environmental systems, resulting in reciprocal change (Hepworth, Rooney, & Larson, 1997). In the case of sentencing-reform issues, ecological systems theory encourages approaches, such as multisystem collaboratives, that can act as intermediaries between macrolevel policy initiatives and local agency implementation efforts. The theory also supports the use of mezzolevel, cross-systems case management to assist individual offenders in accessing and successfully completing needed programs and services in areas such as treatment, supervision, and community reintegration (Terry, VanderWaal, McBride, & VanBuren, 2000). At the microlevel, the theory supports those interventions that show the greatest ability to integrate the multiple needs of offenders within the context of their unique family, employment, and peer environments. Such interventions can occur in a wide range of supervision settings. For example, therapeutic communities have shown success in reducing drug-use rates among prisoners in prison and jail settings. Diversion programs, such as Treatment Alternatives to Street Crimes (TASC), provide individuals with drug treatment services while still under the close supervision of a parole or probation officer. Finally, community-based interventions, such as multisystemic therapy, have demonstrated reduced recidivism and drug use rates with serious juvenile offenders (McBride, VanderWaal, Terry, & VanBuren, 1999b).

Concrete Strategies Based on Theory and Research

Current experiments within the justice system are beginning to incorporate both of these perspectives. Specifically, policy and case processing for drug offenses are increasingly using a public health approach acknowledging the findings that (a) treatment works and is cost effective (Centers for Substance-Abuse Treatment, 2000), and (b) a public health approach coupled with increased attention to the need for economic development and opportunities may provide the best foundation on which to base national drug policy (McBride, Terry, & Inciardi, 1999a). In a recent review of the most promising programs and services to break the cycle of drug use and crime within the juvenile justice system, McBride and his colleagues (1999b) described a potentially successful model. Model components reported as being most likely to be successful included the following: comprehensive assessment, empirically valid treatment modalities integrated into the offender's natural environment, and adequate supervision within a graduated sanctions framework. This model would be coordinated using a case-management approach within multisystem collaboratives, with an emphasis on public safety, rehabilitation, and community reintegration. Such an approach emphasizes social organization and moral credibility through careful respect of the need for adequate supervision and public safety, while also incorporating community buy-in and support through multisystem collaboration. Deterrence is implemented through the graduated sanctions process of assigning penalties based on the offender's progress in treatment and other activities. Finally, social influence is acknowledged by giving attention to community reintegration supervision and program involvement. Concrete examples of programs that may incorporate these types of approaches include drug courts and TASC (McBride et al., 1999b).

SUMMARY

The expected outcomes of mandatory minimum sentencing have not been realized. Their implementation has resulted in prison overcrowding, differential impacts by gender and ethnicity, continued sentencing disparities, and relatively low measures of cost effectiveness. However, current efforts to develop specific alternative approaches to sentencing procedures show promise in combining the important lessons learned from both mandatory minimum sentencing, as well as the problems encountered using a purely sociocultural context approach to dealing with criminal behavior. Within a framework of the new deterrence scholarship, as well as recognition of the reality of systemic environmental conditions, it may be possible to find a middle ground. The goal of such efforts should be to balance both the moral concerns and safety fears of communities searching for ways to reduce crime and drug use, and the needs of the justice system to design and enforce penalties while still meeting the rehabilitation needs of offenders.

25

Health Services in Correctional Settings: Emerging Issues and Model Strategies

Angela Hegamin, Douglas Longshore, and Genevieve Monahan

Over the past two decades, growth in the U.S. prison population has taxed the capacity of correctional systems to manage their inmate populations, and has given rise to overcrowded conditions conducive to the spread of illness. Moreover, mandatory- and fixed-sentencing policies have increased the number of elderly and terminally ill inmates whose lives will end in prison. Hence, prisons today face a host of new challenges, including the management and control of infectious disease, prevention of smoking-related disease, provision of end-of-life care, service to inmates with a history of exposure to violence or trauma, and increased demand for psychiatric services. At the same time, inmates released from prison are bringing these health problems back into the community, thus raising the importance of coordinating health services between correctional and public health care systems. In this paper, we review emerging challenges in correctional health care and discuss three new strategies—telemedicine, managed care, and continuity of care—to address these challenges. Citing particular reasons for concern regarding the effect of managed care on correctional health services, we argue that research on the health-related outcomes of managed care is urgently needed.

BACKGROUND

Before the 1970s, prison health services were substandard at best and inhumane in many scenarios (McDonald, 1999). Since then, the U.S. correctional system has undergone a dramatic transformation in the manner in which health services are delivered to its inmate populations. This transformation was fueled, in large part, by federal court intervention. In the landmark case *Estelle v. Gamble* (1976), the U.S. Supreme Court established what came to be known as the prisoner's constitutional right to health care. Although not the first case of its kind, *Estelle v. Gamble* gave birth to an unprecedented standard for judging the adequacy of medical services provided to prison inmates, namely, the standard of deliberate indifference.[1] Various sets of guidelines for the provision of health care to inmates in U.S. prisons (e.g., the American Correctional Association *Certification Standards for Health Care Programs,* the American Public Health Association *Standards for Health Services in Correctional Institutions,* and the National Commission on Correctional Health Care *Standards for Health Services in Prisons*) all take their cue from this legal standard.

Efforts to develop correctional health care guidelines in the 1980s paralleled the nation's worsening drug problem. By 1989, the federal government was implementing the National Drug Control Strategy, which, among other things, called for mandatory minimum sentences[2] for drug-related crimes. From 1990 to 1997, the number of inmates confined in both state and federal prisons skyrocketed to slightly more than 1.1 million (U.S. Department of Justice, Bureau of Justice Statistics [BJS], 1999d). By 1998, nearly 60% of the federal prison population had been sentenced for drug offenses, compared with 16% in 1970, 25% in 1980, and 52% in 1990 (U.S. Department of Justice, BJS, 1999d). This increase paralleled implementation of mandatory minimum-sentencing policies (see McBride, Vander-Waal, Pa-

---

[1]*Deliberate indifference* as defined by the U.S. Supreme Court is the intentional failure to address the medical needs of a prisoner, an action proscribed by the Eighth Amendment's prohibition of torture.

[2]*Mandatory minimum sentences* are statutorily mandated penalties that carry a range of sanctions for specific offenses and require minimum stays with no possibility for early release for good behavior (Thorburn, 1995).

cula, Terry-McElrath, & Chriqui, this volume). Many believe this approach is related to the severe overcrowding of prisons in the 1990s (Glaser & Greifinger, 1993; Thorburn, 1995; Weiner & Anno, 1992).

Coupled with funding cuts for community mental health services, de-institutionalization in the 1970s gave rise to a growing number of prison inmates with psychiatric disorders who previously had been handled in the mental health system (Thorburn, 1995). Inmates of the 1990s were increasingly more likely than those of earlier decades to have a substance abuse problem or to have acute or chronic medical conditions as a result of substance abuse (Glaser & Greifinger, 1993; Glaser, Warchol, D'Angelo, & Guterman, 1990; U.S. Department of Justice, BJS, 1999d). In addition, the 1990s were characterized by an increase in the practice of fixed sentencing,[3] which led to longer periods of incarceration for many inmates (Weiner & Anno, 1992). As a result, the number of elderly and terminally ill inmates in U.S. prisons has increased dramatically.

Both the rapid expansion of the prison population during the 1990s and the emergence of a new generation of chronic and infectious diseases now place tremendous financial burdens on the correctional health system. From 1982 to 1989, per capita expenditures for correctional health more than doubled, from $906 to $1,848 per year, totaling approximately $25 million in 1989 (Thorburn, 1995). By 1999, the annual per capita cost for inmate health care grew to $2,248, constituting 9.8% of the overall prison budget for that year, with some states spending as much as $4,150 per inmate per year. Much of the increase has been attributed to rising demands for HIV treatment and mental health services, as well as increased medication costs (American Correctional Association, 1999a, 1999b). By the end of the 1990s, prisons were thus confronted with the challenge of managing a broad array of health care needs in severely overcrowded facilities.

EMERGING CHALLENGES

In this section, we review new health challenges faced by correctional systems as a result of the developments cited above. These challenges include controlling and treating HIV/AIDS, hepatitis C virus (HCV), and smoking-related disease; providing end-of-life care to elderly and terminally

---

[3]The term *fixed sentence* refers to a sentence in which the length of time served in a correctional facility is established by law (Weiner & Anno, 1992).

ill inmates; treating inmates with histories of exposure to violence; and addressing mental health needs.

HIV and AIDS

By the end of 1997, an estimated 2.1% of state and federal inmates were infected with HIV. Female inmates were more likely than male inmates to be HIV positive (3.4% vs. 2.2%, respectively). Inmates charged with drug-related offenses had the highest prevalence of HIV infection (2.9%), compared with inmates with other charges. Among inmates infected with HIV, 26% were confirmed AIDS cases, more than five times the rate of AIDS in the general population. Moreover, AIDS-related mortality was three times higher among inmates than the general population (ages 15 to 54). In 1997, approximately 19% of inmate deaths were related to AIDS versus 6% among the general population (U.S. Department of Justice, BJS, 1999a).

Hepatitis C Virus

One of the most significant problems faced by the correctional health system has been the epidemic of HCV among inmates, particularly those with a history of injection drug use (Reindollar, 1999). Of 5,000 inmates screened in the California Department of Corrections, 53.5% of women and 39.4% of men were HCV positive (Horowitz, 1999). Apart from this study, information regarding the prevalence of HCV in prisons is very limited (Spaulding, Greene, Davidson, Schneidermann, & Rich, 1999).

The absence of standardized HCV screening and treatment protocols in correctional settings of most states has hampered efforts to control the spread of HCV within inmate populations (Spaulding et al., 1999). While screening and treatment of inmates who are already infected is an important goal for correctional health systems, preventive education is equally important to protect those inmates not yet infected, as well as the communities to which they will be released (Braithwaite, Hammett, & Mayberry, 1996; Reindollar, 1999).

Smoking-Related Disease

The prohibition of smoking in many correctional institutions signals the emergence of another important issue in correctional health. Smoking bans have been imposed as other public institutions and agencies have initiated no-smoking policies, as well as in response to inmate-initiated lawsuits charging that exposure to secondhand smoke is "cruel and unusual punishment" and violates their right to live in a healthy environment. Other concerns that have contributed to smoking bans in prisons and jails include the growing awareness of the potential health hazards of smoking and the high cost of smoking-related disease (e.g., asthma, coronary heart disease, cancer) requiring treatment by correctional medical staff. According to the American Correctional Association (1999a, 1999b), 10 state corrections departments have imposed comprehensive smoking bans and 36 have instituted partial bans. In many cases, smoking-cessation programs and treatment (e.g., nicotine patches) are offered to inmates and employees in conjunction with these bans (Stashenko, 1999).

End-of-Life Care

Mandatory- and fixed-sentencing policies have resulted in a "graying" of the correctional population. This trend has given rise to the need for specialized services for inmates who are elderly or terminally ill (Dubler, 1998). A 1997 survey of corrections departments found that 27 of them had specialized services for these populations (National Institute of Corrections, 1998).

Like elderly persons in the general population, elderly inmates are likely to experience health problems, including heart disease, stroke, diabetes, and chronic respiratory conditions, among many others (Dubler, 1998; Glaser et al., 1990). Specialized services for elderly inmates should address chronic health problems such as these.

By 1997, nearly 50% of all state correctional systems were providing formal or informal hospice care funded through a variety of public and private sources (National Institute of Corrections, 1998). More generally, however, the correctional environment presents numerous challenges for providing competent end-of-life care for elderly and terminally ill inmates. The lack of advocacy services within the corrections system, the underlying distrust of the criminal justice system by inmates, and the need for security measures (e.g., shackling dying inmates to their beds) continue to interfere with the provision of compassionate care by medical staff (Dubler, 1998; Maull, 1998).

Exposure to Violence

Exposure to violence and abuse is widespread among correctional populations. A national survey of inmates conducted by the BJS found that female inmates were more likely to have a history of abuse than women in the general population (U.S. Department of Justice, BJS, 1999c). Approximately 50% of the female inmates surveyed reported histories of physical and/or sexual abuse. Additionally, 25% of the female inmates in jails and one third of those in state prisons reported being raped prior to incarceration, compared with 3% to 15% of women in the general population, depending upon the study (Acierno, Resnick, & Kilpatrick, 1997). The prevalence of previous physical or sexual abuse among male inmates surveyed was approximately 10%, with 3% reporting a history of rape (U.S. Department of Justice, BJS, 1999c). The comparable figures for males in the general population are 10% to 19% and 1%, for physical/sexual abuse and rape, respectively (Acierno et al., 1997).

Histories of abuse and neglect are also common among adolescents in the juvenile justice system. The prevalence of posttraumatic stress disorder is higher among incarcerated juvenile females than among incarcerated males or female adolescents in the general population (Cauffman, Feldman, Waterman, & Steiner, 1998). Chronic exposure to abuse and violence frequently results in physical, psychological, and emotional problems often left untreated in the period preceding incarceration. These problems are exacerbated for many women who, as a result of their incarceration, are isolated from their children and families. Correctional medical staff are often inadequately prepared to meet the complex needs of inmates suffering from these problems (National Commission on Correctional Health Care, 1997; Young, 1998).

Mental Health

A recent survey of the adult prison and jail populations found that approximately 16% of inmates had emotional or mental health problems or had been hospitalized for such problems in the past (U.S. Department of Justice, BJS, 1999b). The majority of mentally ill inmates (nearly 75%) had a history of prior incarceration. Mentally ill inmates were more likely to have a history of violence and to serve longer sentences than other inmates (U.S. Department of Justice, BJS, 1999b). Some studies have demonstrated the rates of mental illness among inmate populations to be at least twice the rates found in the general population.

The prevalence of mental illness among incarcerated adolescents is reported to be higher than that of the general adolescent population, and incarcerated female adolescents are more likely that their male counterparts to have a mental health problem (Pliszka, Sherman, Barrow, & Irick, 2000; Timmons-Mitchell et al., 1997). Posttraumatic stress disorder and other psychopathology have been correlated with poor impulse control and threat of violent behavior among incarcerated juvenile females compared with males (Cauffman et al., 1998).

National guidelines require initial mental health screening and referral by qualified staff for every inmate entering the correctional system, and most institutions comply with these guidelines (Metzner, Miller, & Kleinsasser, 1994; Morrissey, Swanson, Goldstrom, Rudolph, & Manderscheid, 1993; U.S. Department of Justice, BJS, 1999b). Sixty-one percent of the mentally ill inmates identified in the BJS survey reported receiving treatment or counseling since their current admission to the criminal justice system. Mental health services were provided within institutions, within community-based agencies, or a mix of both (U.S. Department of Justice, BJS, 1999b).

STRATEGIES FOR HEALTH CARE DELIVERY

In this section we highlight three new strategies—telemedicine, managed care, and continuity of care—adopted to address these challenges. Telemedicine and continuity of care appear to be promising, if limited in scope. However, managed care is typically implemented at the institution or system-wide level and, therefore, has tremendous potential to influence how correctional health services are delivered. We comment at some length on the possible effect of managed care on correctional health.

Telemedicine

In recent years, a number of correctional systems have begun to implement telemedicine programs (health care delivery via telecommunication), with a majority of state prisons now operating programs or planning programs in the future (National Institute on Corrections, 1998). Telemedicine has made it possible to expand access to highly qualified medical specialists for inmates in correctional facilities located in remote, sparsely populated areas. Correctional facilities under court order to provide a minimum standard of care to inmates from specialists (e.g., psychiatrists) have found telemedicine to be one way to meet these legal mandates (Martin, 1999).

The driving force behind the increased use of telemedicine in the correctional health system is the expectation that it will reduce the cost of providing care. Cost savings reported in telemedicine pilots are between $14 to $107 per inmate encounter (Brunicardi, 1998; McCue et al., 1998; National Institute of Justice, 1999). As the cost of setting up telemedicine capabilities decreases over time, the savings associated with this new technology is expected to increase (National Institute of Justice, 1999).

While telemedicine apparently improves inmate access to health services, there are other potential benefits as well. It may provide greater continuity of care and better quality of care for inmates (e.g., shorter waiting times), and may reduce injuries to correctional staff during inmate transfers for medical care off-site (McDonald, Hassol, & Carlson, 1999; Martin, 1999; National Institute of Justice, 1999).

Managed Care

As a result of rising expenditures for inmate health care, many corrections systems have turned to managed care strategies, that is, " . . . processes or techniques to control or influence the quality, accessibility, utilization, costs and prices or outcomes [of health services] provided to a defined population" (American Medical Association, 1999). Under these strategies, costs may be contained by, for example, limiting services to those deemed "medically necessary" according to legal and professional standards; employing "utilization management" procedures and disincentives such as copayments to control access to services; reducing the use of costly or unnecessary medications (often replaced by generic medications); and expansion of screening to detect conditions that, if left undetected, have the potential to be costly (McDonald, 1999). Like telemedicine, managed care may well succeed in containing health care costs while sustaining, or even improving, the quality of care in correctional settings, but there are reasons for concern.

First, access to and quality of health services for inmates of correctional institutions may depend largely on whether competition among contractors willing to deliver services in those settings is strong enough to enable governments to negotiate from a position of strength by, for example, stipulating high standards of care, requiring evidence of favorable outcomes, or requiring accreditation (Camp & Gaes, 1998; Moore, 1998). But there is no assurance that competition is always strong, especially with respect to provision of care in large maximum-security facilities. Pollack, Khoshnood, and Altice (1999) have cited the "thinness" of the correctional health care marketplace as an obstacle to competition. If few providers are willing and qualified to do the work, government may have little leverage (Bowditch & Everett, 1987). On the other hand, stronger competition does not necessarily translate into high service quality. Rather, it may result in lower bids, and governments tend to choose the low bidders. Contractors who win business with "bare bones" budgets may provide less care to begin with or may reduce the level of care as it becomes clear that a profit cannot be generated from providing more comprehensive care. In short, the extent to which competition actually exists in correctional health is unclear, as is the degree to which its presence or absence will affect health service access and quality.

Second, it is not clear how the medically necessary standard of care will be applied within correctional settings. Any number of services available in the free world (e.g., organ replacement, artificial joints, life support, and expensive diagnostic procedures) may not be deemed medically necessary for inmates, especially those serving long-term or life sentences. Other cost-containment strategies may curtail access to services that are unequivocally medically necessary even in correctional settings. Copayments, for example, may represent a greater barrier to access in prison because correctional health patients are drawn from populations of low socioeconomic status that typically cannot afford to pay for health services in the community (Conklin, Lincoln, & Flanigan, 1998; Glasser & Greifinger, 1993).

Third, costs in correctional settings are often reduced by hiring health care staff who are willing to work for less, and by devoting insufficient resources to training or staff development (Bowditch & Everett, 1987; McDonald, 1992, 1999; Pollack et al., 1999). Pollack et al. (1999) reported that physicians found guilty of ethical or criminal abuses can be issued restricted licenses, allowing them to practice in jails or prisons but not in the community. Quality of care may suffer as a result of cost-containment strategies such as these.

Compliance monitoring and case review are widely seen as mechanisms by which government can ensure satisfactory delivery of care, but it is not clear that government auditors can be effective in this aim. Gelber (1999b) has described the very limited extent of oversight of managed care in correctional facilities. Bowditch and Everett (1987) cite adverse factors in other industries (e.g., contractors can weaken the government's oversight function by lobbying for particular regulatory policies) and "see no reason to expect that these factors would not influence the regulation of prisons" (p. 449). Pollack et al. (1999) note the absence of an effective lobby or strong public sentiment for enforcing quality health care standards for criminal offenders. If the correctional health care marketplace remains thin, government may simply have no alternative to a contractor who underperforms.

Concerns regarding managed health care in corrections take on increasing importance in the context of a broader trend toward privatization of all aspects of correctional-facilities management. In fact, use of managed care in correctional health may be an important precursor to privatization (Gelber, 1999b), and both managed care and privatization are driven by the same interests, namely, cost control and profit making. In 1997, there were more than 120 privately managed prisons in 27 states (Moore, 1998). Privatization is not new, especially in correctional facilities for juveniles and low-risk adults (McDonald, 1992), but it has rapidly expanded in recent years—a trend likely to continue (Gelber, 1999a; Moore, 1998)—and has begun to work its way into facilities housing higher-risk adults. Privatization may lead to lower costs and improved management of correctional facilities (McDonald, 1992, 1999; Camp & Gaes, 1998; U.S. General Accounting Office, 1996), but, as with managed health care, it is not clear that access to and quality of health services will be sustained or enhanced under privatization (Logan, 1992). First, if privatization does lead to lower costs, the better part of that reduction may be due to containment of expenditures for health care (Camp & Gaes, 1998). Thus, privatization raises the same set of issues noted earlier regarding managed care. Second, higher-risk and adult populations are likely to have health care problems more extensive than those seen among lower-risk and juvenile populations, and chronically ill inmates serving long-term sentences will need long-term care. Hence, as privatization moves into maximum-security facilities or takes over entire correctional systems, pressures to control health care costs can only increase.

Continuity of Care

Coordination of health services during the inmate's term of incarceration and upon his/her return to the community is increasingly recognized as essential. The National Commission on Correctional Health Care (1997) recommends that efforts be made to obtain medical information on inmates' prior health histories and to incorporate this information into ongoing care, that discharge planning be undertaken to assess inmates' postrelease medical needs, and that collaborative efforts be forged between the public health and correctional health systems.

Over the past decade, a growing number of innovative programs, designed to enhance collaboration between correctional and public health systems, have emerged. These programs seek to deliver high-quality, cost-effective health care services to prison inmates and parolees. The Hampden County Correctional Center in Ludlow, Massachusetts, operates one of the nation's most comprehensive, community-based correctional health care systems, emphasizing early detection, effective treatment, prevention, and continuity of care (Conklin et al., 1998). The Center houses approximately 1,800 jail and prison inmates, an estimated 90% of whom resided in the surrounding metropolitan area prior to their incarceration. Inmates are assigned to one of four health teams responsible for covering their residential catchment area. Each health team consists of a supervising physician, a full-time primary nurse, two full-time nurse practitioners, and a case manager who works both in the correctional facility and in the community. Community health services are provided at one of four contracted local health care centers. Hospice and ophthalmological care are provided by a local hospital, and dental care is provided by the dental school of a local university. During their incarceration, inmates are assigned to a physician who, upon the inmate's release, continues to be responsible for the care of the now-paroled inmates as they reenter the community. Although outcome studies demonstrating the effectiveness of this model have not been conducted, the program appears to have achieved some cost savings. The daily cost of operating the program is about $6 per inmate, an amount less than the cost of other prison health care programs (Skolnick, 1998).

Rhode Island provides comprehensive care to HIV-positive female inmates at an adult correctional institution in Cranston both during and following their incarceration (Skolnick, 1998). The model is the product of a collaboration between the Rhode Island Department of Corrections, the Rhode Island Health Department, and the Brown University AIDS Program. Female inmates who test positive for HIV receive follow-up medical care, drug-rehabilitation services, and housing and other support following their release to the community (Skolnick, 1998). Recidivism among the HIV-positive inmates participating in this program is considerably lower than among HIV-positive inmates released from the prison in the year preceding implementation of the program (12% vs. 27% at 6 months postrelease and 17% vs. 39% at 12 months postrelease). In addition, participants appeared to be more likely to keep follow-up medical appointments, thereby potentially enhancing the effectiveness of their HIV-treatment regimens. Sixty-eight percent of participants with histories of drug abuse were enrolled in drug treatment during the postrelease period (Skolnick, 1998).

Health Link is a program sponsored by the Hunter College Center on AIDS, Drugs and Community Health in New York City, with funding from the Robert Wood Johnson Foundation (Freudenberg, 1998; Freudenberg, Wilets, Greene, & Richie, 1998; National Institute of Justice, 1999). The program targets drug-using female and adolescent inmates to reduce drug use and recidivism, as well as to assist with reintegration into the community upon parole. Health Link has developed collaborative relationships with several community organizations to provide comprehensive services to participants. The caseworker component of the program includes case management, discharge planning, counseling, and health education during incarceration and for 1 year following parole. The program provides direct funding, training, and other assistance to their collaborating community-based organizations to develop the capacity of these organizations to serve Health Link participants and to advocate on behalf of ex-offenders by working directly with local and state policy makers. Recidivism among women participating in the program is considerably lower than among women inmates not participating in the program (38% vs. 59%, respectively). The intervention is effective in reducing drug use as well, in part because program staff and inmates have developed during- and after-prison relationships that enhance follow-up on service referrals.

Continuity of care may be especially important for ensuring the health of paroling inmates with histories of mental illness. One program involving a federal prison and community-based mental health center uses an interdisciplinary team from both agencies to ensure that inmates receive psychiatric, medical, substance-abuse treatment and residential services (Roskes & Feldman, 1999). Ventura, Cassel, Jacoby, and Huang (1998) found significantly less recidivism among mentally ill inmates receiving similar case-management services following their release to parole.

CONCLUSIONS

The rapid growth in the U.S. prison population has exceeded the capacity of the correctional system to manage its inmate populations and has given rise to overcrowded conditions conducive to the spread of illness. Mandatory- and fixed-sentencing policies have contributed to the growth in the number of elderly and terminally ill inmates who will serve terms to the end of their lives. For these reasons, correctional health faces new challenges, including the management and control of infectious disease, prevention of smoking-related disease, provision of end-of-life care, inmates exposed to violence or trauma, and increased demand for psychiatric services. At the same time, inmates released from prison are bringing these health problems back into the community, thus raising the importance of coordinating health services between correctional and public health care systems.

Among the strategies adopted to address these needs are telemedicine, managed care, and programs to promote continuity of care between prison and community. There is limited but encouraging evidence for the effectiveness of telemedicine and continuity of care. There is potential for improvement in correctional health services under managed care as well. However, we have cited several reasons for concern regarding the effects of managed care on the delivery of health services to inmates. Because managed care is typically implemented at the institution or system-wide level, it may have the greatest influence on the future of correctional health.

26

Federal Drug-Abuse Treatment Research Priorities

Robert J. Battjes and Steven B. Carswell

For the past three decades, the federal government has supported numerous research projects to examine the effectiveness of drug-abuse treatment for drug-abusing offenders. This chapter will review past research efforts, highlighting what has been learned, consider recent research initiatives, identify major issues to be addressed, and recommend future research directions.

PAST WORK

Federally supported research on drug-abuse treatment for offenders has largely been supported by the National Institute on Drug Abuse (NIDA). This review of past research will focus largely on NIDA-supported research, although selected studies supported by other federal agencies are included. This review focuses on studies that exemplify major research themes and should not be considered exhaustive. Some federally supported research is addressed in other chapters of this volume and will only be mentioned briefly here. An early emphasis of federally supported research and the initial focus of this review will be on research regarding the effects of legal coercion on treatment. Other areas that will be covered include therapeutic community (TC) and other residential treatment, pharmacotherapies, counseling approaches, treatment for women, and family-oriented treatment for adolescents. Finally, a report of meta-analyses of treatment approaches for incarcerated offenders is also included.

LEGAL COERCION AND TREATMENT

Experience with the treatment of heroin addicts through the early 1960s revealed that retention of clients in treatment was problematic. Based on clinical and criminal justice system experience, three treatment strategies were developed incorporating coercion into treatment: civil commitment, the Treatment Alternatives to Street Crimes (TASC) program, and drug courts. Federally supported research has examined all three of these approaches, as well as less formalized approaches to treating drug-abusing offenders.

McGlothlin, Anglin, and Wilson (1977) evaluated the California Civil Addict Program (CAP), the prototype for subsequent interventions that combined criminal justice system sanctions with drug abuse treatment in order to rehabilitate drug-abusing offenders. CAP was a state-wide civil commitment program initiated in California in 1962 for narcotic addicts (McGlothlin et al., 1977), which provided inpatient treatment followed by extended outpatient treatment combined with rigorous parole supervision. Compared with those released on writ due to procedural errors, the civil commitment group substantially reduced their daily narcotic drug use, criminal activity, and arrests, and modestly increased employment over 7 years following institutional release (Anglin, 1988).

TASC was a federally funded program, operating under state or local auspices, that provided systematic linkages between the criminal justice system and drug-abuse treatment, including identifying drug abusers who came into contact with the criminal justice system, screening and referral for treatment, monitoring treatment progress, and returning violators to the criminal justice system (see Cook, this volume, for a review). Briefly, Hubbard, Collins, Rachal, and Cavanaugh (1988), in a study of TASC and other legal coercion, found that criminal justice system involvement was associated with longer retention in outpatient drug-free and residential treatment and with reduced use of the primary problem drug in the first year after treatment. More recently, in a study of five TASC programs, Anglin, Longshore, and Turner (1999) found that TASC subjects had superior drug-use outcome at three sites, while there were no significant differences in the remaining two sites. Favorable outcomes on self-reported crime were found in two sites. However, TASC subjects were more likely to be arrested or to commit a technical violation in two sites, perhaps reflecting more intensive supervision. Analyses indicated that TASC was more effective with hard-core offenders, rather than those with less criminal involvement.

The most recent formalized-linkage approach is drug courts that are characterized by mandatory treatment, frequent and random urinalysis, and regular, frequent court appearances (Office of Justice Programs, unpublished). While research on drug courts is in its early stages, the Office of Justice Programs (unpublished), U.S. Department of Justice, reports that drug courts have now been established in 48 states and the District of Columbia, that retention rates of more than 70% are substantially higher than found generally with treatment programs for offenders, that recidivism rates of 5% to 28% are lower, and that drug-free urinalyses rates of more than 90% are higher.

In their studies of treatment careers, Anglin and his colleagues (1999) have also studied the effects of less formalized forms of legal coercion. A study of drug abusers actively seeking referral to drug abuse treatment found that those who actually entered treatment were much more likely to report legal coercion as a reason for seeking treatment than those who did not enter treatment. Additionally, those who entered treatment were also more likely to report being on probation or parole or to be awaiting charges, trial, or sentencing (Hser, Maglione, Polinsky, & Anglin, 1998). In a study of methadone maintenance treatment, subjects with low, moderate, and high levels of coercion had similar retention rates, and there were few differences among these groups in treatment outcome, with all groups improving substantially in narcotic use and crime during treatment (Brecht, Anglin, & Wang, 1993). In another study of legal coercion and methadone maintenance treatment, legal supervision was associated with decreased narcotic use and crime only when the supervision was frequent and included urine testing (Brecht, Hser, & Anglin, 1991). Based on a number of studies on coercion and treatment, Anglin and Perrochet (1998) concluded that legal supervision and treatment needed to be linked strategies— coercion resulting from legal supervision encourages treatment entry, retention, and program compliance, enhancing treatment's ability to reduce drug use.

Finally, Simpson and his colleagues (Hiller, Knight, Broome, & Simpson, 1998; Knight, Hiller, Broome, & Simpson, in press) have reported on the effects of legal pressure among clients admitted between 1991 and 1993 to 18 long-term residential treatment programs included in the Drug Abuse Treatment Outcome Study (DATOS). Clients with moderate to high levels of legal pressure were significantly more likely than those with low levels of legal pressure to remain in treatment for at least 90 days, while high levels of pressure did not increase retention over moderate pressure. Also, the effects of legal pressure increased as the proportion of clients under legal supervision within a treatment program increased (Hiller et al., 1998). Examining the effects of legal pressure and treatment readiness (i.e., internal motivation), Knight and his colleagues (in press) found that both legal pressure and treatment readiness contributed independently to retention in treatment at least 90 days, with treatment readiness having the stronger effect on retention. Treatment readiness was also found to be associated with engagement in treatment, whereas legal pressure was not, suggesting the need for motivational interventions to increase engagement of those criminal justice clients who have low motivation for treatment.

THERAPEUTIC COMMUNITY AND OTHER RESIDENTIAL TREATMENT

Therapeutic community treatment is reviewed extensively elsewhere in this volume (see Deitch, Carleton, Koutsenok, & Marsolais; De Leon, Saccks, & Wexler; and Inciardi, Surratt, Martin, & Hooper). Important federally supported studies include the Stay 'N Out Therapeutic Community evaluation in which Wexler, Falkin, Lipton, and Rosenblum (1992) found that participants in a jail-based TC were less likely to be rearrested during parole than those receiving alternative treatment or no treatment. Another important study, the KEY/CREST Therapeutic Community Treatment evaluation of prison-based and work-release TC treatment (Martin, Butzin, Saum, & Inciardi, 1999), found that combining prison-based and work-release TC treatment was more effective than work-release TC treatment alone in reducing arrests and drug use 1-year posttreatment, while TC treatment in prison alone resulted in no better outcomes than no TC treatment. While the 1-year treatment effects had been largely attenuated at 3-year follow-up, treatment effects were extended for those who had also received aftercare services.

A third study, the Amity Prison Therapeutic Community evaluation, found that prison-based TC participants had significantly lower reincarceration rates 1 and 2 years posttreatment compared with an untreated control group (Wexler, De Leon, Thomas, Kressel, & Peters, 1999a), while the difference between groups at 3 years was no longer statistically significant (Wexler, Melnick, Lowe, & Peters, 1999b). Prison-based TC participants who also completed aftercare TC remained significantly less likely to have been reincarcerated at the 3-year followup.

The last federally supported TC evaluation to be reported here, the Kyle New Vision Treatment Program (Knight, Simpson, & Hiller, 1999), funded by the National Institute of Justice (NIJ), studied a continuum of care, including prison-based TC followed by 3 months of community-based TC aftercare and up to 12 months of outpatient counseling. This treatment continuum was effective only with offenders having high criminal severity, but not among those with low severity, and aftercare TC treatment was essential to a sustained treatment effect in the high severity group. Thus, the Key/Crest, Amity Prison, and Kyle New Vision studies all point to the importance of postrelease treatment in order to sustain the effects of prison-based TC treatment.

Finally, an evaluation of a non-TC residential program operating within 20 federal prisons, the Triad Drug Treatment Evaluation, was conducted by the Federal Bureau of Prisons, with funding from NIDA. Program participants resided in special housing units and engaged in standard treatment modules for half of each day, while participating in typical institutional activities during the remainder of the day. Residential treat-ment typically lasted 9 months, following which participants returned to the general prison population, receiving relapse-prevention counseling until release. Following release, graduates received transitional services that consisted of counseling and, for the majority, residence in a correctional half-way house. Comparing program participants with nonparticipants, while controlling for background differences and selection bias, partici-pants were less likely to be rearrested (3.3% vs. 12.1%) or have evidence of drug use (20.5% vs. 36.7%) during the 6 months following release from prison (Bureau of Prisons, unpublished report).

PHARMACOTHERAPIES

Methadone Maintenance. Although methadone maintenance is widely used in the treatment of heroin addiction, the criminal justice system seldom refers heroin-addicted offenders to this treatment modality, and related research is largely absent. An exception to this is research conducted on the Key Extended Entry Program (KEEP), which enabled heroin addicts who entered the New York City central jail facility on Rikers Island to be maintained on a stable dose of methadone during their stay and to be referred upon release to a dedicated methadone treatment slot in the community (Magura, Rosenblum, Lewis, & Joseph, 1993). KEEP permitted continuation of medication for those already in maintenance treatment at arrest and induction on medication and linkage to treatment for those not already in maintenance treatment. Outpatient KEEP clinics, providing treatment upon release, operated as 180-day detoxification programs, during which time the need for longer-term maintenance was assessed, resulting in transfer to maintenance treatment or discharge. The KEEP evaluation, conducted on 1988-1990 admissions, found that 53% of male and 47% of female KEEP participants showed up for treatment following release from jail. Retention rates for those who showed up for treatment were 70% after 1 month and 40% after 5 months, with no gender differences. Reinterviewed an average of 6.5 months postrelease from jail, KEEP participants were 27 times more likely to have applied for treatment during the follow-up period and nearly seven times more likely to be in treatment at follow-up, compared with non-KEEP participants who were detoxified in jail (controlling for baseline differences). While KEEP participation per se was not associated with decreased drug use, injection frequency, and property offenses, these outcomes were all related to current drug-treatment status, which was strongly related to KEEP participation. Maintenance programs providing community treatment to KEEP patients tended to see these patients as more severely disabled than their other patients, suggesting that the program served a hard-to-reach population.

Naltrexone. Naltrexone is a narcotic antagonist medication that blocks opioid effects and, thus, has potential utility in the treatment of opioid addiction. However, naltrexone's utility with general opioid-addict populations has been limited by poor patient acceptance. Cornish and his colleagues (1997) examined its effectiveness with federal probationers and parolees, hypothesizing that patient acceptance and response might be greater among individuals under correctional supervision. Of probationers and parolees recruited to participate in the study, 23% were willing to participate, a considerably higher acceptance rate than that found with noncorrectional populations. Of those randomly assigned to receive naltrexone, 52% remained in treatment for the full 6-month treatment. Compared with subjects who received correctional supervision and counseling only, naltrexone subjects were less likely to have urinalyses positive for opioids (8% vs. 30%) and to have their probation status revoked, resulting in return to prison (26% vs. 56%). Thus, it appears that naltrexone may be a viable treatment option for correctional populations. In spite of close correctional supervision and frequent urinalyses, rates of cocaine use were high in both the naltrexone and comparison groups. Cornish and his colleagues (1997) concluded that coercion and naltrexone with low-intensity counseling provided in this study were insufficient to impact nonopioid drug use, and suggest that impact on such drug use might have been improved with more intensive counseling.

COUNSELING APPROACHES

Social Support. Hanlon, Nurco, Batemen, and O'Grady (1999) tested the effectiveness of a drug abuse treatment program, social support, specifically designed for parolees with a history of heroin and/or cocaine abuse who were required to participate in treatment as a condition of parole. The intervention included weekly individual counseling that emphasized case management (i.e., assertively linking clients to available services) and relapse-prevention strategies, combined with weekly urine monitoring. Subjects were randomly assigned to three conditions during their 1-year parole period: social support with urine monitoring (SSU), weekly urine monitoring with routine parole supervision (UM), and routine parole supervision without regular urine monitoring. Subjects receiving SSU were retained in their assigned intervention an average of 7.6 months, significantly longer than the 5.3 months for the UM group. At 1-year follow-up, SSU subjects were significantly less likely to incur major infractions than the UM subjects or those on routine parole, and there was little difference between the latter two conditions. Self-reported cocaine and heroin use did not differ among the three groups, while the SSU and UM groups, which were tested regularly, were more likely to have positive urinalyses than the routine parole subjects who were rarely tested. There were no differences across groups in employment. However, the routine parole-supervision condition was not a no-treatment condition in that 64% of these subjects received other drug abuse treatment during their year on parole. Thus, for the total sample, subjects who received treatment were compared with those who did not, with treated subjects less likely to have parole violations, revocation of parole, warrants for arrest, convictions for new offenses, or incarceration. Treated subjects in the routine parole condition were also less likely to report narcotic addiction or heavy cocaine use, and more likely to have been employed based on parole officer records, than were the untreated subjects. Linking of social support with urine monitoring proved problematic in that many subjects stopped attending counseling sessions that were linked with urine testing, and many participants requested transfers to other drug treatment programs that did not have such stringent urine-testing requirements and, hence, presented less risk for parole violation.

Motivational Enhancement. A treatment-induction intervention to enhance client motivation and confidence regarding treatment outcomes and processes was tested with probationers who had been mandated to a 16-week, modified TC program located at a county correctional facility (Blankenship, Dansereau, & Simpson, 1999). The intervention, specifically designed for persons with low education and limited cognitive functioning, uses experiential exercises or games to help individuals who have difficulty communicating through traditional verbal channels. TC program admissions in 1996–1997 were assigned sequentially to 16 "communities," which were then randomly assigned to the enhanced induction program or standard treatment. The induction program occurred during the fourth and fifth weeks of treatment, since earlier research indicated that clients needed to first acclimate to the treatment environment. Program evaluation, measured at 8 weeks of treatment, examined a treatment by educational-level interaction, since it was hypothesized that the intervention would be effective with individuals having low educational attainment. As hypothesized, the less educated subjects receiving the enhanced intervention reported higher motivation than the other four groups. Similarly, they reported greater confidence in treatment than either high- or low-education subjects receiving the standard intervention. Regarding motivation to resist alcohol and drugs following treatment, the less educated subjects receiving the enhanced intervention reported higher motivation than the less educated subjects receiving the standard intervention. Additionally, the less educated subjects in the enhanced intervention reported more confidence in their ability to resist drugs and alcohol than the other three groups.

Node-Link Mapping. Another counseling approach, node-link mapping, is a cognitive-behavioral treatment technique originally developed for use with methadone maintenance clients and applied to probationers in the modified TC program, described above (Pitre, Dansereau, Newbern, & Simpson, 1998; Newbern, Dansereau, & Pitre, 1999). It is a visual graphic technique conducted in groups, which helps participants process and communicate ideas. Probationers admitted to the TC in 1995 were assigned to newly formed communities of approximately 35 participants. Twelve communities formed during the study period were randomly assigned to mapping-enhanced or standard counseling. Participants were assessed at midterm and at the end of the 16-week TC program. The mapping participants participated more actively in group sessions, reported better progress toward treatment goals, and greater treatment engagement than did clients in the control communities (Pitre et al., 1998). Mapping participants also had significantly higher scores for both their motivation to and self-efficacy for communicating with others at both midterm and the end of treatment, and they had significantly higher scores on motivation to control their emotions at both times, while their self-efficacy ratings for emotional control were higher at midterm, but not at the end of treatment (Newbern et al., 1999). These findings suggest that node-link mapping can contribute to recovery by positively impacting treatment engagement and by enhancing basic cognitive and emotional skills that contribute to recovery.

TREATMENT FOR WOMEN

In Project WORTH (Women's Options for Recovery, Treatment, and Health), Strauss and Falkin (in press) are currently studying eight treatment programs for drug-abusing women offenders in New York City and Portland, Oregon, including prison- and jail-based, community-residential, and outpatient programs, using both quantitative and qualitative research approaches. In a study of treatment retention in a prison-based residential program, retention was related to higher initial motivation and treatment readiness, favorable perceptions of program staff, and feeling empowered by the treatment experience in dealing with their feelings, while termination was related to conflict over program rules, such as the feeling that rules were unfair (Strauss & Falkin, in press). In another study of drug use immediately following outpatient and residential treatment, primary reasons given for drug use during the first week posttreatment included using drugs to cope with emotional distress, social influences, and simply wanting or feeling the need to get high. Referral to posttreatment services, notably self-help support groups and transitional housing, was associated with abstinence (Strauss & Falkin, unpublished manuscript).

ADOLESCENT TREATMENT

Adolescent treatment is reviewed extensively elsewhere in this volume (see Dembo, Livingston, & Schmeidler). Important federally supported studies include Multisystemic Therapy (MST) (Henggeler, Pickrel, & Brondino, 1999) and Family Empowerment Intervention (FEI) (Dembo et al., in press). Both are intensive, family-systems interventions targeting juvenile offenders, and are typically delivered in the home. At treatment completion, MST treatment was associated with decreased self-reported alcohol, marijuana, and other drug use, with these effects limited largely to females and younger adolescents, and with reduction in days in out-of-home placement. These effects were not maintained at follow-up 6 months posttreatment. These modest program effects contrasted with strong MST program effects found in earlier research with other delinquent populations (which nonetheless included, but were not limited, to substance abusing/dependent youth) and may be accounted for by poor fidelity of program implementation (Henggeler et al., 1999). In an evaluation of FEI compared with a low-intensity intervention (monthly phone contacts with referral to community services), FEI subjects reported fewer drug sales, getting high or drunk on alcohol less often, and less marijuana use, and had lower rates of positive hair tests for marijuana (Dembo, Seeberger, Shemwell, Schmeidler, et al., unpublished manuscript), but there were no differences between groups in the total numbers of either arrest charges or arrests at 12-month follow-up (Dembo et al., in press). Comparisons of FEI completers with non-completers found that youth whose families completed the FEI intervention had better outcomes that those whose families did not.

META-ANALYSES OF TREATMENT STRATEGIES

Correctional Drug Abuse Treatment Effectiveness Project (CDATE). Pearson and Lipton (1999) reported on meta-analyses of correctional drug abuse treatment research conducted between 1968 and 1996. Of 1,606 studies or substudies that were identified and coded, analyses published to date are limited to 30 studies of treatment for incarcerated drug abusers. All included studies had treatment and comparison groups. Pearson and Lipton (1999) rated the research methods of these studies largely as poor (14) or fair (15), with only one study rated as good, the only study utilizing a true randomized experimental design. Of various types of corrections-based drug abuse treatment, only three types had sufficient studies to permit meaningful meta-analyses, boot camps, TCs, and group-counseling programs. Meta-analysis of each of these treatment approaches found evidence of effectiveness in reducing recidivism only for TC treatment. Ex post facto exploratory analyses of the six boot camp studies found two studies with negative effects and four with positive effects. However, the four positive studies are actually separate comparisons within the same larger study, involving the same program environment and same research team, and, thus, are not independent replications. All six boot camp studies were rated as methodologically poor. Exploratory analyses of the seven TC studies indicated substantial positive effects in six of the studies. The one study reporting negative effects was rated as methodologically poor, whereas the studies finding positive effects included one good, three fair, and two poor methodological ratings. The seven drug-focused counseling studies largely provided only vague information on the interventions, suggesting that there was probably considerable variability in approach. Only two of the seven studies found positive effects. The remaining treatment modalities for incarcerated drug abusers included in the CDATE project—methadone maintenance, substance abuse education, other substance-abuse treatment, and 12-step—did not have sufficient studies to reach any firm conclusions about effectiveness. However, Pearson and Lipton (1999) noted that the effectiveness of methadone maintenance is supported by meta-analysis of studies involving nonincarcerated criminal justice populations, yet to be published. The conclusion from these meta-analyses is that, except for TC treatment, insufficient quality research has been conducted to permit conclusions regarding effectiveness.

RECENT INITIATIVES

A number of federally supported studies are ongoing, and published findings are not yet available. Themes emerging in these studies will be briefly summarized to indicate recent directions in federally supported research. Undoubtedly, the largest recent initiative targeting offender populations has been research on drug courts, reflecting the growing popularity of this intervention approach. In 1999, NIDA solicited applications to study drug courts and funded six new studies, in addition to two ongoing studies previously funded. In 2000, NIJ also solicited research applications on drug courts. Counseling approaches under study include cognitive-behavioral therapy, social support (including one project specifically focused on women), skills building for female offenders, and cognitive treatment for youthful offenders. Other interventions currently under study include after-care following the conclusion of formal outpatient treatment, case management, community-based TC treatment as an alternative to incarceration, TC treatment for mentally ill chemical-abusing offenders, vocational skills training, HIV-prevention interventions, and comprehensive treatment including health care, housing, and vocational training.

MAJOR ISSUES

Federally supported research on drug abuse treatment for offender populations has largely been focused around a central theme, namely the interrelationship of coercion and treatment. The initial issue faced by the drug abuse treatment and corrections fields was whether coercion and treatment were antithetical or complementary. The initial questions were: Can drug abuse treatment reduce criminal recidivism among drug-abusing offenders? Can individuals coerced to enter treatment derive benefit from it? Can coercion contribute to treatment effectiveness? Affirmative answers to these questions gave rise to the next issue, namely, how to coordinate the treatment and corrections systems so that they mutually contribute to offender rehabilitation. The response to this issue was the development of structured collaborative programs, including civil commitment and TASC. The recent emergence and rapid expansion of drug courts, and the solicitations of research on this topic by NIDA and NIJ, indicate the ongoing importance of this issue, the challenges in effectively coordinating the treatment and corrections systems, and the need for more effective approaches to bridging these systems.

The next major issue that emerged and was addressed by federally funded research was how to effectively treat drug-abusing offenders within correctional institutions. The response was to turn to the most intensive treatment approach, namely TCs, which had been designed to resocialize the most deviant drug abusers. Research indicated that TCs were effective in reducing drug use and criminal recidivism, but that treatment effects diminished rather quickly following release. This finding gave rise to the next major issue, namely, how to maintain the effects of treatment following return to the community. This led to federally supported research on postinstitutional treatment in the community, including both TC and outpatient treatment, which demonstrated that the benefits of institutional TC treatment could be extended with postinstitutional treatment. More recently, attention has been focused on adaptation of TC treatment for mentally ill chemical-abusing offenders.

Other major issues in the treatment of drug-abusing offenders have received considerably less attention than the above issues. One issue is how to improve the treatment of offenders, including modifying existing community-based treatment strategies for offenders and developing new treatment strategies. Included in this issue is the development of effective treatments for specific subgroups of offenders. Another question is how to treat offenders in the least restrictive environment. Yet another major issue that has received little attention to date is the area of diagnosis/treatment matching, that is, what types and intensities of service are needed by individual drug-abusing offenders.

CONCLUSIONS

Federally supported research has confirmed that coercion from the corrections system is effective in bringing drug-abusing offenders into and retaining them in treatment. This research also confirms that treatment combined with coercion is effective in reducing drug abuse, criminal activity, and arrests. Coordination of the treatment and corrections systems is essential to treatment effectiveness, yet such coordination is not easily achieved. Structured programs to achieve systems coordination, including civil commitment and TASC, have demonstrated positive effects, and another highly structured approach, drug courts, is being examined currently. Federally supported research also confirms that institutional treatment, even intensive TC treatment within prisons, is of limited value if not combined with postinstitutional treatment that helps offenders establish themselves in the community. Federally supported research also demonstrates that treatment effects erode over time, indicating that sustained or repeated treatment will be required for many drug-abusing offenders. Further research is clearly needed to improve the effectiveness of drug abuse treatment, including the development of new treatment approaches for those who are not responding to current treatment approaches and to achieve more sustained effects with those who initially respond positively to existing treatments, but relapse over time.

FUTURE DIRECTIONS

Over the past decade, public policy has emphasized incarceration of drug-abusing offenders, and the numbers of such offenders in prisons and jails has increased dramatically. Institutional treatment programs have also expanded. Considering the costs of incarceration and institutional treatment, and considering past federally supported research indicating the limited value of institutional treatment by itself, future federally supported research must address the issue of who requires institutional treatment and who can be treated more effectively in the community. Related to this is the question of whether comprehensive community services in conjunction with treatment can reduce the number of persons requiring incarceration. For those exiting institutions, an important research question is what services are needed to facilitate this transition and sustain recovery.

While methadone maintenance has emerged as a major, effective treatment approach for heroin addiction, it is noteworthy that the corrections system makes little use of this modality, and relatively little federally supported research has addressed this topic. Opportunities for research that would explore the potential contribution of methadone maintenance to offender rehabilitation should be pursued.

Federally supported research has largely focused on adult offenders, with relatively little attention paid to reaching juvenile offenders before their criminal involvement becomes entrenched. Additional research on juvenile offenders should be a priority.

Prior federally supported research regarding adult offenders has failed largely to look within the "black box" of treatment to determine what contributes to effectiveness and how treatment can be improved. Recent work, particularly by Simpson and his colleagues (see Hiller et al., this volume) to develop motivational and cognitive strategies, reflects progress in this area, but much more attention needs to be focused on this research area. Enhancing motivation to engage in treatment for clients coerced to enter and remain in treatment is a particularly important focus. Additional attention also needs to be focused on specific subgroups of offenders, such as women, distinct cultural groups, offenders with co-occurring mental disorders, HIV-infected offenders, and violent offenders and others whose criminality is largely independent of their drug use. While expanding the range of treatment options, research is also needed to improve diagnosis and matching of offenders to treatments. Finally, research needs to focus on the cost effectiveness of treatment approaches, compared with no treatment and also compared with alternative treatment approaches.

ACKNOWLEDGMENTS

We want to thank the federally supported researchers who helped us identify major research findings. We also wish to acknowledge the helpful review comments of Dr. Peter Delany, National Institute on Drug Abuse, and Dr. Timothy Kinlock, Social Research Center, Friends Research Institute. Manuscript preparation was supported in part under NIDA Grant No. R01 DA 10180.

27

Looking to the Future: Substance Abuse and Corrections

Frank M. Tims, Carl G. Leukefeld, and David Farabee

S ince 1979, incarcerated populations in the United States have increased dramatically. State prison populations have more than tripled,
and there has been a similar increase in federal prison populations.
We have also seen dramatic increases in the proportion of prisoners who
are addicts or who were significantly involved with drugs and/or alcohol
at the time of their offenses. The Bureau of Justice Statistics (1999) estimates
there are about 1.6 million prisoners held by jails and prisons in the United
States, and more than 5 million persons under court supervision as of 1996.

This chapter addresses selected issues facing the criminal justice system,
as well as community substance abuse and addiction treatment providers,
and offers recommendations for policy and research. Themes focus on
lessons learned from U.S. research, underserved populations, and the need
for commitment to system improvement and system change. From our
point of view, there is a clear need to integrate policy and research. A
clear example of how science and technology can reduce costs is in-home

monitoring, although many treatment improvements will not have such concrete and obvious benefits. Improvements may have higher immediate costs (such as making treatments more comprehensive), just as computers have front-loaded costs to improve productivity. Integrating policy and research suggests that a partnership must be established between policymakers in the criminal justice system and researchers. Just as results of policy changes may not be immediately apparent, researchers cannot provide instant findings, although they can advise based on what is known at the time. Cooperation must be viewed as a long-term enterprise. For the relationship to work, researchers must be forthcoming with information, as well as the benefit of their own judgment.

In our opinion, service systems dealing with substance abuse and dependence are usually fragmented, and drug abusers are just as likely to receive services in the criminal justice system as in other systems (Weisner & Schmidt, 1995). The fragmentation also extends to the mental health system, and the lack of continuity between substance-abuse treatment and mental health services is a frequent problem for the criminal justice system, which has become a de facto provider of mental health, as well as general health services (see Hegamin, Longshore, & Monahan, this volume). The range of health issues covered in an integrated system must also include infectious diseases, such as hepatitis and HIV/AIDS (see Farabee & Leukefeld, this volume).

Effective approaches to offender populations call for the coordination of the criminal justice system with treatment, effective supervision, and drug testing (see DuPont, this volume). Resources must be available to integrate appropriate assessment, prevention, treatment, supervision, and aftercare. Integrating seamless service systems and technological resources have the potential to increase effectiveness and reduce offender treatment costs (see Prendergast & Burdon, this volume). Requirements, resources, and strategies will vary in prisons (see Inciardi, Surratt, Martin, & Hooper, this volume; Deitch, Carleton, Koutsenok, & Marsolais, this volume; Weinman & Dignam, this volume), jails (Peters & Matthews, this volume), and in probation and parole (see Kinlock & Hanlon, this volume).

FUTURE RESEARCH

Future research for drug offenders should address a range of issues, but focus on continuously improving assessment, therapies, service delivery, and the continuum of care. To make the case for services, estimates of costs and benefits must be included (see McCollister & French, this volume). Needs assessment should focus on the epidemiology of substance abuse and related problems in different parts of the justice system. Effective prevention strategies and early intervention should be identified and tested for those youth who have their first contact with the justice system. Examining addiction careers and treatment careers will help understand the effects of treatment and need for multiple treatment episodes. In addition, longerterm therapeutic relationships should be studied to understand the impact of relapse on recidivism and recovery (Anglin, Hser, & Grella, 1997). Research from a careers perspective and how biological and psychosocial maturation affects behavior of addicted probationers and parolees is recommended, as well as how technology (e.g., information systems, electronic monitoring, diagnostic instrumentation, drug testing) can be used to study salient aspects of these changes.

Appropriate Responses to Drug Offenses

Responding to drug offenses and drug-involved offenders can be difficult. For example, at one extreme, judges and prosecutors have little doubt about what to do in major trafficking cases, those who commit violent offenses, or patterns of sociopathy. Less clear cut can be users who make bad decisions in their personal lives from addiction-driven behavior. In the cases of those less culpable or addicts guilty of possessing a small amount of a controlled substance, diversion can be a preferred course. Judges sometimes believe that their hands are tied by sentencing mandatory minimum requirements (see McBride, VanderWaal, Pacula, Terry-McGrath, & Chrique, this volume). Since the area of sentencing discretion is a subject of public debate, it is recommended that policy studies focus on the outcomes of different sentencing options over time. Many opportunities present themselves for examination in the policy arena, such as the impact of California's recently approved proposition 36 (treatment in lieu of prosecution for many addicts).

Costs and System Improvement

Further research on costs and cost offsets should distinguish among identifiable populations, and take into account how cost-benefit estimates can be examined by integrating treatment into probation, parole, and incarceration (see McCollister & French, this volume). Research needs to focus on improved outcomes for corrections clients who are substance abusers by examining (a) alternatives to incarceration, (b) prevention, community policing, and drug courts, (c) screening and assessment to identify treatment needs and risks, (d) systematically applied supervisory routines, (e) standardized protocols for research regarding surveillance and sanctions for replication, (f) the heterogeneity of drug-involved offenders, and targeting interventions to enhance outcomes, (g) improving access and treatment utilization, (h) motivational enhancement, (i) treatment combined with coercion as effective in reducing drug use, criminality, and arrests, and (j) system coordination.

Transition from Institution to Society

Because addiction is a chronic, relapsing condition with biological, psychological, and social aspects, a continuum of care is needed. For example, the point of transition from incarceration to community reentry is high risk. Not only are the individual's coping skills and motivation tested, but also numerous pressures are encountered. In addition to prerelease treatment, effective transitional and aftercare programs as exemplified by programs like CREST (Lockwood, Inciardi, & Surratt, 1997) must be provided. Continuing research on transition to the community, effective models for transition for short- and long-term inmates, and the effect of different models of supervision on drug use and criminal behavior is suggested.

Community Policing

Street-level interventions, such as community policing, could document "best practices" for identifying and diverting young drug abusers, and building rapport with families. For example, studies to address training of police in the area of substance-abuse treatment should be implemented. Other studies can focus on improving communication and factual information on substance dependence and treatment in one-on-one, small group, and town meetings.

Drug Courts and Diversion

Drug courts (see Belenko, this volume) and other diversion models like Treatment Alternative to Street Crime (TASC) (see Cook, this volume) should be studied to develop models for replication, and to improve outcomes. In particular, attention should be given to: (a) levels of care, (b) comprehensiveness of treatment, (c) roles of judges and court staff, (d) assessing and enhancing client motivation, (e) therapeutic approaches, (f) length of treatment and aftercare arrangements, (g) characteristics of effective drug-court judges, and (h) criteria for continuing deferred sentencing.

Special Risk Populations

Studies of effective intervention strategies with targeted risk populations should be conducted. Although the case for treatment effectiveness has been made (Hubbard, Craddock, Flynn, Anderson, & Etheridge, 1997), there are knowledge gaps related to, for example, the therapeutic relationship, matching clients to treatment, and treatment models for special-risk populations who contact the criminal justice system.

Three "special-population" groups are highlighted for research and policy focus because of the urgent need for services and the problematic nature of service programming, access, and delivery: (a) Adolescents are a high-priority population because of the paucity of knowledge regarding their needs and effective strategies for identifying, engaging, treating, and diverting adolescents early in their substance abuse careers; (b) women have particular needs relating to treatment access, utilization, and service needs. Special issues that are gender specific must be addressed by treatment, and high-risk behaviors and comorbidity should be taken into account; (c) substance abusers with psychiatric comorbidity: Mentally ill addicts have service needs that go beyond substance-abuse treatment (see De Leon, Sacks, & Wexler, this volume). The first need is to properly assess and diagnose the comorbidity. Since the criminal justice system has become a de facto provider of both substance abuse and mental health services on a large scale, those offenders who have both problems present a challenge and an opportunity. Integrated treatment models and appropriate medications need to be examined in corrections to improve outcomes.

Adolescents

Dembo, Livingston, and Schmeidler (this volume) report that, "A major issue in research on treatment of adolescents is that there is so little of it." They highlight the absence of long-term treatment outcome studies of adolescents. Major developmental issues should be examined as they are affected by drugs and contact with the juvenile or criminal justice systems. Resources such as juvenile-assessment centers can be valuable, particularly if they are linked to service providers in a way that makes appropriate care (including levels of care) available. Placing adolescents in adult facilities may exacerbate already existing but undiagnosed mental illness, in addition to other actual risks to health. However, there is very limited data. While those arrested for relatively minor drug offenses may appear otherwise "normal" to law enforcement personnel, recent work has shown that adolescents referred to outpatient treatment with marijuana abuse and dependence diagnoses as their primary presenting problem often manifest clinically significant mental and emotional problems (Tims, Hamilton, Dennis, Godley, & Funk, 2000). This underscores the risks to both youth and society of failing to provide adequate assessment and appropriate care.

Effective treatment models are needed for adolescents who are early in their careers. Available databases, which include adolescent substance abusers, both with and without criminal justice system involvement, should be extensively analyzed to identify treatment issues and subtypes. Issues to be examined include; (a) understanding juvenile assessment centers (JACs) and their linkages to treatment; (b) brief interventions in JACs to improve treatment entry; (c) developing and testing effective treatment models; (d) strategies for engagement and involvement of the family in treatment; (e) analysis of client and parent characteristics that increase potential for family involvement to enhance outcomes; (f) enhancing motivation (both internal and external) for treatment, including motivational therapies and court pressures; (g) improving treatment retention; (h) analyses of the therapeutic relationship between adolescents and therapists, including studies of effective therapists and client response; (i) long-term treatment outcome studies of adolescents, including cessation of drug use versus maintenance of drug-use patterns, criminal behavior, and drug-use careers; (j) effects of substance-abuse treatment and other health services on criminal behavior in adolescents and young adults; (k) determinants and mitigating influences in the progression (or nonprogression) of conduct disorder to antisocial personality disorder in young adults; (l) impact of differing types of criminal justice system experience on outcomes; (m) influence of peers, parents, and authority figures on outcomes, including studies of influence processes; and (n) influence of media and aspiration on drug use and criminal behavior.

Women

The justice system may respond quite differently to women addicts and their illegal activities. Women's service needs may not be apparent, and gender issues may not be well understood by providers (see Staton, Leukefeld, & Logan, this volume). Issues such as poverty, dependency, victimization, domestic violence, and reproduction may complicate treatment, especially in the community where such factors are continuing parts of everyday life for some clients. Psychiatric illness and chronic powerlessness may have led to patterns of adaptation that frustrate treatment, and may have led to enmeshment in both dysfunctional relationships and self defeating behavior. Child custody and maternal issues may also be areas presenting problems and service needs. The unique service needs of women may also provide insight into opportunities for engagement and motivation. For example, pregnant and postpartum women have very clear health care needs, both for themselves and their infants. Integrating prenatal care, child care, and parenting-skill development can not only address service needs, but also remove treatment barriers. A clear example is the PAR village demonstration project in Florida, in which addicted women kept their infants and small children in a day care facility in their residential-treatment program, with the result that retention improved dramatically (Hughes et al., 1994). Regaining child custody can be a powerful motivator and can be linked to successful participation in treatment. Comprehensiveness and focus of properly designed treatment regimes need to be examined further, since they can also effectively address areas such as sexual-risk behavior, relationships, self-esteem, assertiveness, and general health, in addition to substance abuse (Simpson, Dansereau, & Joe, 1997).

Research is needed to (a) effectively target at-risk women prior to incarceration; (b) better understand service needs of women; (c) identify and overcome barriers to services; (d) examine strategies to improve access to treatment and treatment comprehensiveness; (e) develop and test treatment models that address gender issues, such as sexual trauma, custody and parenting, and substance abuse in community and institutional settings; (f) examine, where appropriate, how pharmacological agents should be included in treatment for managing craving and co-occurring disorders; (g) integrate behavior therapies with improving parental fitness and drug abstinence; and (h) assess aftercare programming, including case management.

Dually Diagnosed

Co-occurring disorders present a major treatment challenge, both in institutions and the community, regardless of criminal justice status. It is commonplace for persons with mental illness to be locked up in jails and prisons for varying periods of time, with their conditions not sufficiently understood to be recognized. The linkage between substance abuse and mental illness is complex, and models that integrate treatment need to be examined.

Research is needed to: (a) clarify the interrelationship between addiction and other mental health conditions; (b) incorporate screening and assessment of mental disorders into processing persons charged with substance abuse-related offenses, including dimensional measures to identify subclinical levels of symptomatology; (c) develop strategies to coordinate assessing mental disorders with public defenders and other officers of the court, and to ensure that judges and corrections staff have complete information to provide for treatment; (d) develop guidelines that will help correctional personnel understand appropriate responses to subclinical levels of psychopathology and conditions in partial remission but that have a high likelihood of recurring; and (e) develop validated training modules for nonclinical corrections staff to enable them to better understand the nature of substance abuse and associated comorbidity.

Building Public Support for Treatment

Greater public understanding of the treatment of drug-involved offenders is needed. The stigma of addiction and its prevalence among the powerless makes it difficult to support treatment, and yet, for many, treatment can reduce both drug use and crime. The task of science is to provide decision makers with sound information (e.g., making a sound case for treatment is a better investment than warehousing offenders). To this end, the public must learn more about the nature of addiction. The "nothing works" mentality is the simple way out. There is a strong case that treatment, combined with regimens of testing, monitoring, and accountability, can work and that it does return benefits to society. The key to successful treatment is to keep trying, even in the face of denial and resistance.

CONCLUSIONS

A stronger partnership is suggested between the criminal justice system, substance-abuse treatment, and research. The potential research agenda may be long, but it should be viewed in an integrated way, with research informing policy and practice. The ultimate beneficiaries of an effective partnership will be society and the offenders themselves, as we move toward a safer and more just society. Research must be responsive to needs of the criminal justice system, judges, administrators, and treatment providers. The accumulated evidence from several decades of research refutes the nothing works argument. We now see that research has a great deal to offer the justice system, and that real partnership works. However, creativity, diligence, and a regular process of communication need to be maintained. Policymakers must constantly be reminded that the stakes are high and the investment is worthwhile.

Appendices

Texas Christian University Drug Screen

During the *last 6 months* before prison . . .

	Circle Answer

1. Did you often use *larger amounts of drugs* (including alcohol) or use them *for a longer time* than you had planned or intended?   0 = No   1 = Yes

2. Did you *try to cut down on drugs* and were *unable* to do it?   0 = No   1 = Yes

3. Did you *spend a lot of time* getting drugs, using them, or recovering from their use?   0 = No   1 = Yes

4. Did you often *get so high or sick* from drugs that it—
   a. *kept you from* doing work, going to school, or caring for children?   0 = No   1 = Yes
   b. *caused an accident* or became a danger to yourself or others?   0 = No   1 = Yes

5. Did you often *spend less time at work, school, or with friends* so that you could use drugs?   0 = No   1 = Yes

6. In the last 6 months before prison, did your drug use often *cause—*
   a. *emotional or psychological* problems?   0 = No   1 = Yes
   b. problems with *family, friends, work, or police?*   0 = No   1 = Yes
   c. *physical health or medical* problems?   0 = No   1 = Yes

7. Did you *increase the amount* of a drug you were taking so that you could get the same effects as before?   0 = No   1 = Yes

8. Did you ever keep taking a drug to *avoid withdrawal* or keep from *getting sick?*   0 = No   1 = Yes

9. Did you *get sick or have withdrawal* when you quit or missed taking a drug?   0 = No   1 = Yes

10. Which *drugs* caused you the *MOST serious problems* in the last 6 months before prison? [SEE LIST BELOW]

    Worst: _____ DRUG NUMBER
    Next: _____ DRUG NUMBER
    Next: _____ DRUG NUMBER

Choose Drug Numbers from This List:

0. None   3. Marijuana   6. Tranquilizers or sedatives
1. Alcohol   4. Cocaine or crack   7. Hallucinogens
2. Inhalants   5. Other stimulants   8. Opiates

11. How often did you use each type of drug during the *last 6 months* before prison?

Drug Use in Last 6 Months

		Never	Only a few times	1–3 times a month	1–5 times a week	About every day
a.	*Alcohol*	0	1	2	3	4
b.	*Marijuana/* Hashish	0	1	2	3	4

c.	Hallucinogens/ LSD/ Psychedelics/ PCP/ Mushrooms/ Peyote	0	1	2	3	4
d.	Crack/ Freebase	0	1	2	3	4
e.	Heroin and Cocaine (mixed together as speedball)	0	1	2	3	4
f.	Cocaine (by itself)	0	1	2	3	4
g.	Heroin (by itself)	0	1	2	3	4
h.	Street Methadone (nonprescription)	0	1	2	3	4
i.	Other Opiates/ Opium/ Morphine/ Demerol	0	1	2	3	4
j.	Methamphetamine/ Speed/Ice/ Other Uppers	0	1	2	3	4
k.	Tranquilizers/ Barbiturates/ Sedatives	0	1	2	3	4
l.	Other (specify)	0	1	2	3	4

12. In the 6 months before entering prison, how often did you *inject drugs* with a needle?
    0. Never
    1. Only a few times
    2. 1–3 times a month
    3. 1–5 times a week
    4. About every day

13. *How serious* do you thing your drug problems are?

    0.   Not at all
    1.   Slightly
    2.   Moderately
    3.   Considerably
    4.   Extremely

14. How many times *before now* have you ever   ____   NUMBER
     been in a *drug or alcohol treatment program*?   OF TIMES
     [DO NOT INCLUDE AA/NA/CA MEETINGS]

15. Do you think you *need treatment* for   0 = No   1 = Yes*
     your drug use now?

*IF YES
    a. *How important to you* is it that you get into some type of
        treatment program now?
        0.   Not at all
        1.   Slightly
        2.   Moderately
        3.   Considerably
        4.   Extremely

SCORING FOR THE TEXAS CHRISTIAN UNIVERSITY DRUG SCREEN

The TCU Drug-Dependence Screen is scored as follows:

1. Give 1 point to each "yes" response to questions 1 to 9. (Questions
    4 and 6 are worth 1 point each if a respondent answers "yes" to
    any portion.)
2. The total score can range from 0 to 9; score *values of 3 or greater*
    indicate relatively severe drug-related problems, and correspond
    approximately to DSM drug dependence diagnosis.
3. Responses to question 10 indicate which drug (or drugs) the respon-
    dent feels is primarily responsible for his or her drug-related
    problems.

There have been no composite score protocols developed for questions 11
to 15 on pages 374–376.

B

State of Maryland Executive Order

OFFENDER EMPLOYMENT COORDINATING COUNCIL

WHEREAS,   Maryland has experienced both an increased demand for a trained and skilled labor force and, an increased offender population seeking an employment opportunity;

WHEREAS,   Pilot projects in other states and cities have led to the creation of public-private partnerships that are focused on employment as a tool to long-term change in offender behavior;

WHEREAS,   Reductions in recidivism are dramatically increased depending on the degree of well-designed employment initiatives with comprehensive workforce issues that include job preparation and skill-development components, along with placement and retention efforts; and,

WHEREAS,   There is a need to establish employment-related efforts that span the correctional system—prison to community.

NOW, THERE-FORE,   I, PARRIS N. GLENDENING, GOVERNOR OF THE STATE OF MARYLAND, BY VIRTUE OF THE AUTHORITY VESTED IN ME BY THE CONSTITUTION AND

LAWS OF MARYLAND, HEREBY PROCLAIM THE FOL-
LOWING EXECUTIVE ORDER EFFECTIVE IMMEDI-
ATELY:

A. Established. There is an Offender Employment Coordinating
Council.

B. Membership and Procedures.

(1) The Council shall consist of:

(A) The Secretary of Department of Public Safety and
Correctional Services;

(B) The State Superintendent of Education;

(C) Five representatives of the business community appointed by the Governor;

(D) One representative from Baltimore City appointed
by the Mayor of Baltimore City;

(E) One member of the House of Delegates appointed
by the Speaker of the House of Delegates;

(F) One member of the Senate appointed by the President
of the Senate;

(G) One representative from the faith-based community
appointed by the Governor; and,

(H) Two representatives of the Judicial Branch appointed
by the Chief Judge of the Maryland Court of Appeals.

(2) The Governor shall appoint the chairperson from among
the business members of the Council;

(3) The members of the Council may not receive compensation for their services. Members may be reimbursed for
their reasonable expenses incurred in the performance of
their duties in accordance with the standard travel regulation as provided in law;

(4) The term of the members shall expire December 2004;
and

(5) The Department of Public Safety and Correctional Services
shall provide a full-time Executive Director, staff support,
and technical assistance to the Council through December
2004.

C. Duties of the Council. The Offender Employment Coordinating
Council shall:

(1) Develop transitional supports for offenders, including employment opportunities and expand the linkage of current

programs to include new career options for offenders, both in institutional and community setting to:

   (a) increase employment opportunities available to offenders in both institutional and community-based setting;

   (b) provide employment counseling for every offender under correctional control;

   (c) transfer successful institutional programs and services to the community setting, including job preparedness and employment opportunities;

   (d) increase both job-placement and job-retention rates for all offenders under correctional control; and,

   (e) improve the overall coordination of employment services for offenders.

(2) Develop and implement a business-mentoring program.

(3) Expand the current Maryland prison-to-work program to include offenders under community supervision.

(4) Establish Mock Job Fairs within institutions and in the community.

(5) Develop a Maryland plan for transitional employment.

(6) Provide support and direction to the Executive Director.

D. Information. All State agencies shall provide information as requested by the Council.

E. Reports to the Governor. The Council shall provide an interim report to the Governor by August 30, 2002 on its activities and recommendations; and, a final report to the Governor by August 30, 2004.

References

Abramson, M. (1972). The criminalization of mentally disordered behavior: Possible side-effect of a new mental health law. *Hospital and Community Psychiatry, 23,* 101–107.

Acierno, R., Resnick, H. S., & Kilpatrick, D. G. (1997). Prevalence rates, case identification, and risk factors for sexual assault, physical assault, and domestic violence in men and women, part 1 (Health impact of interpersonal violence). *Behavioral Medicine, 23,* 53–64.

Alexander, C. (1997). Crushing equality: Gender equal sentencing in America. *American University Journal of Gender & Law, 6,* 199.

Alexander, J. F., & Parsons, B. V. (1982). *Functional family therapy: Principles and procedures.* Carmel, CA: Brooks/Cole.

Alexander, R. (1995). Employing the mental health system to control sex offenders after penal incarceration. *Law & Policy, 17*(1), 111–130.

Altschuler, D. M., & Armstrong, T. L. (1991). *Intensive community-based aftercare prototype: Policies and procedures* (Report prepared for the Office of Juvenile Justice and Delinquency Prevention, U.S. Department of Justice.). Johns Hopkins University, Institute for Policy Studies, Baltimore.

Amen, D. (1998). *Firestorms in the brain—An inside look at violent behavior.* Fairfield, CA: MindWorks Press.

American Academy of Child and Adolescent Psychiatry. (1998). Summary of the practice parameters for the assessment and treatment of children and adolescents with substance use disorders. *Journal of the American Academy of Child and Adolescent Psychiatry, 37,* 122–126.

American Correctional Association. (1989). *Certification standards for health care programs.* Chicago: Author.

American Correctional Association. (1999a). Inmate health, part I: Survey summary. *Corrections Compendium, 24*(10), 8–17.

American Correctional Association. (1999b). Inmate health, part II: Survey summary. *Corrections Compendium, 24*(11), 12–20.

American Medical Association. (1999). *Principles of managed care.* Chicago, IL: AMA Council on Medical Science.

American Psychiatric Association. (1994). *Diagnostic and statistical manual of mental disorders* (4th ed.). Washington, DC: Author.

American Psychiatric Association. (1996). *American psychiatric association practice guidelines.* Washington, DC: Author.

American Public Health Association, Jails and Prisons Task Force. (1976). *Standards for health services in correctional institutions.* Washington, DC: Author.

American Society of Addiction Medicine. (1996). *Patient placement criteria for the treatment of substance-related disorders* (2nd ed.). Chevy Chase, MD: Author.

American University. (2000). *Drug court activity update: Summary.* Washington, DC: U.S. Department of Justice, Office of Justice Programs, Drug Court Clearinghouse.

Andrews, D. A. (1998). *The psychology of criminal conduct* (2nd ed.). Cincinnati, OH: Anderson Publishing Co.

Andrews, D. A., Zinger, I., Hoge, R. D., Bonta, J., Gendreau, P., & Cullen, F. T. (1990). Does correctional treatment work? A clinically relevant and psychologically informed meta-analysis. *Criminology, 28,* 369–404.

Anglin, D. M. (1988). The efficacy of civil commitment in treating narcotic addiction. In C. G. Leukefeld & F. M. Tims (Eds.), *Compulsory treatment of drug abuse: Research and clinical practice.* National Institute On Drug Abuse Monograph 86 (pp. 8–34). Washington, DC: National Institute of Drug Abuse.

Anglin, D. M., Longshore, D., & Turner, S. (1999). Treatment alternatives to street crime. *Criminal Justice and Behavior, 26,* 168–195.

Anglin, M., Farabee, D., & Prendergast, M. (1998). *The role of coercion in offender drug treatment.* A report to the Physician Leadership on National Drug Policy. Washington, DC: Physician Leadership Group.

Anglin, M. D., & Fisher, D. G. (1987). Survival analysis in drug program evaluation: II. Partitioning treatment effects. *International Journal of the Addictions, 22,* 377–387.

Anglin, M. D., & Hser, Y. I. (1990). Treatment of drug abuse. In M. Tonry & J. Wilson (Eds.), *Drugs and crime* (pp. 393–460). Chicago: University of Chicago Press.

Anglin, M. D., Hser, Y., & Chou, C. (1993). Reliability and validity of retrospective behavioral self-report by narcotics addicts. *Evaluation Review, 17,* 91–108.

Anglin, M. D., Hser, Y. I., & Grella, C. E. (1997). Drug addiction and treatment careers among clients in the Drug Abuse Treatment Outcome Study (DATOS). *Psychology of Addictive Behaviors, 11,* 308–323.

Anglin, M. D., Longshore, D., & Turner, S. (1999). Treatment alternatives to street crime: An evaluation of five programs. *Criminal Justice and Behavior, 26,* 168–195.

Anglin, M. D., Longshore, D., Turner, S., McBride, D., Inciardi, J., & Prendergast, M. (1996). *Studies of the functioning and effectiveness of treatment alternatives to street crime (TASC) programs* [Final report]. Los Angeles: UCLA Drug Abuse Research Center.

Anglin, M. D., & Maugh, T. H. (1992). Ensuring success in interventions with drug using offenders. *Annals of the American Academy of Political and Social Sciences, 521,* 66–90.

Anglin, M. D., & McGlothlin, W. H. (1984). Outcome of narcotic addict treatment in California. In F. M. Tims & J. P. Ludford (Eds.), *Drug abuse treatment evaluation: Strategies, progress, and prospects* (pp. 106–128). Washington, DC: U.S. Government Printing Office.

Anglin, M. D., & McGlothlin, W. H. (1985). Methadone maintenance in California. In L. Brill & C. Winick (Eds.), *The yearbook of substance abuses* (pp. 219–280). New York: Human Sciences Press.

Anglin, M. D., & Perrochet, B. (1998). Drug use and crime: A historical review of research conducted by the UCLA drug abuse research center. *Substance Use and Misuse, 33,* 1871–1914.

Anglin, M. D., & Speckart, G. (1988). Narcotics use and crime: A multisample, multimethod analysis. *Criminology, 26,* 197–233.

Anglin, M. D., & Speckart, M. W. (1986). Narcotics use, property crime and dealing: Structural dynamics across the addiction career. *Journal of Quantitative Criminology, 2*(4), 355–375.

Anspach, D. F., & Ferguson, A. S. (1999). *Cumberland County's drug court program: An evaluation report of Project Exodus.* Portland, ME: University of Southern Maine.

Aos, S., Phipps, P., Barnoski, R., & Lieb, R. (1999). *The comparative costs and benefits of programs to reduce crime: A review of national research findings with implications for Washington State.* Washington State Institute for Public Policy.

Aponte, J. F., & Barnes, J. M. (1995). Impact of acculturation and moderator variables on the intervention and treatment of ethnic groups. In J. F. Aponte, R. Y. Rivers, & J. Wohl (Eds.), *Psychological interventions and cultural diversity.* Needam Heights, MA: Allyn & Bacon.

Arella, L. R., Deren, S., Randell, J., & Brewington, V. (1990). Vocational functioning of clients in drug treatment: Exploring some myths and realities. *Journal of Applied Rehabilitation Counseling, 21*(2), 7–18.

Armstrong, T. L. (Ed.). (1991). *Intensive interventions with high-risk youths: Promising approaches in juvenile probation and parole.* Monsey, NY: Criminal Justice Press.

Armstrong, T. L., & Altschuler, D. M. (1998). Recent developments in juvenile aftercare: Assessment, findings, and promising programs. In A. R. Roberts (Ed.), *Juvenile justice* (2nd ed.). Chicago: Nelson-Hall.

Austin, J., Clark, J., Hardyman, P., & Henry, A. D. (1999). The impact of 'three strikes and you're out.' *Punishment and Society, 1,* 131–162.

Axelrod, S., & Apsche, J. (Eds.). (1983). *The effects of punishment on human behavior.* New York: Academic Press.

Azrin, N. H., & Holz, W. C. (1966). Punishment. In W. K. Honig (Ed.), *Operant behavior: Areas of research and application* (pp. 380–447). New York: Appleton-Century-Crofts.

Azrin, N., McMahon, P., Donohue, B., Basalel, V. A., & Lapinski, K. J. (1994). Behavior therapy for drug abuse: A controlled treatment outcome study. *Behavioral Residential Therapy, 32,* 857–866.

Babor, T. F., Hofman, M., Delboca, F. K., Hesselbrock, V., Meyer, R. E., Dolinsky, Z. S., & Rounsaville, B. (1992). Types of alcoholics, I: Evidence for an empirically derived typology based on indicators of vulnerability and severity. *Archives of General Psychiatry, 49,* 599–608.

Ball, J. C., Shaffer, J. W., & Nurco, D. N. (1983). The day-to-day criminality of heroin addicts in Baltimore: A study in the continuity of offense rates. *Drug and Alcohol Dependence, 12,* 119–142.

Bander, K. W., Goldman, D. S., Schwartz, M. A., Rabinowitz, E., et al. (1987). Survey of attitudes among three specialties in a teaching hospital toward alcoholics. *Journal of Medical Education, 62*(1), 17–24.

Bandura, A. (1977). *Social learning theory.* Englewood Cliffs, NJ: Prentice-Hall.

Bandura, A. (1994). Social cognitive theory and exercise of control over HIV infection. In R. J. DiClemente & J. Peterson (Eds.), *Preventing AIDS* (pp. 25–59). New York: Plenum.

Barton, W. (1982). Drug histories and criminality of inmates of local jails in the United States (1978): Implications for treatment and rehabilitation of the drug abuser in a jail setting. *The International Journal of the Addictions, 17,* 417–444.

Battjes, R. J., Onken, L. S., & Delany, P. J. (1999). Drug abuse treatment entry and engagement: Report of a meeting on treatment readiness. *Journal of Clinical Psychology, 55,* 643–657.

Beck, A. J. (1999). *Prisoners in 1998.* Bureau of Justice Statistics Bulletin. Washington, DC: U.S. Department of Justice.

Beck, A. J., & Mumola, C. J. (1999). Prisoners in 1998. *Bureau of Justice Statistics Bulletin.* Washington, DC: Department of Justice, Office of Justice Programs.

Beck, A. J., & Mumola, C. J. (1999, August). *Prisoners in 1998. Bureau of Justice Statistics Bulletin* (NCJ 175687). Washington, DC: U.S. Department of Justice, Office of Justice Programs, http://www.ojp.usdoj.gov/bjs/abstract/p98.htm.

Becker, G. (1968). Crime and punishment: An economic approach. *Journal of Political Economy, 76,* 191–193.

Becker, R. (1997). The privatization of prisons. In J. M. Pollock (Ed.), *Prisons: Today and tomorrow.* Gathersburg, MD: Aspen Publishers.

Bedrick, B., & Skolnick, J. H. (1999). From 'treatment' to 'justice' in Oakland, California. In W. C. Terry (Ed.), *The early drug courts—Case studies in judicial innovation* (pp. 43–76). Thousand Oaks, CA: Sage.

Belenko, S. (1990). The impact of drug offenders on the criminal justice system. In R. Weisheit (Ed.), *Drugs, crime, and the criminal justice system.* Cincinnati, OH: Anderson Publishing.

Belenko, S. (1996). *Comparative models of treatment delivery in drug courts.* Prepared for the Sentencing Project. New York: New York City Justice Agency.

Belenko, S. (1998). Research on drug courts: A critical review. *National Court Institute Review, 1,* 1–30.

Belenko, S. (1998, June). Research on drug courts: A critical review. *National Center on Addiction and Substance Abuse at Columbia University, 1*(1), 1–42.

Belenko, S. (1999a). Diverting drug offenders to treatment courts: The Portland experience. In C. Terry (Ed.), *The early drug courts: Case studies in judicial innovation* (pp. 108–138). Newbury Park, CA: Sage.

Belenko, S. (1999b). Research on drug courts: A critical review. 1999 update. *National Drug Court Institute Review, 2*(2), 1–58.

Belenko, S. (2000). The challenges of integrating drug treatment into the criminal justice process. *Albany Law Review, 63*, 833–876.

Belenko, S., Fagan, J., & Chin, K. L. (1991). Criminal justice responses to crack. *Journal of Research in Crime and Delinquency, 28*(1), 55–74.

Belenko, S., & Peugh, J. (1998). Fighting crime by treating substance abuse. *Issues in Science and Technology, 15*(1), 53–60.

Belenko, S., Peugh, J., Califano, J. A., Jr., Usdansky, M., & Foster, S. E. (1998, October). Substance-abuse and the prison population: A three-year study by Columbia University reveals widespread substance-abuse among offender population. *Corrections Today, 60*, 82–154.

Benson, H. (with Scriber, M. S.). (1997). *Timeless healing: The power and biology of belief.* New York: Simon and Schuster.

Berkowitz, G., Brindis, C., Clayton, Z., & Peterson, S. (1996). Options for recovery: Promoting success among women mandated to treatment. *Journal of Psychoactive Drugs, 28*(1), 31–38.

Blanchard, C. (1999). Drugs, crime, prison, and treatment. *Spectrum: The Journal of State Government, 72*(1), 26–28.

Blankenship, J., Dansereau, D. F., & Simpson, D. D. (1999). Cognitive enhancements of readiness for corrections-based treatment for drug abuse. *Prison Journal, 79*, 431–445.

Blume, S. B. (1998). Addiction in women. In *Textbook of substance-abuse treatment* (2nd ed., pp. 485–490). Washington, DC: American Psychiatric Press.

Blumstein, A., & Beck, A. J. (1997). Population growth in U.S. prisons, 1980–1996. In M. Tonry & J. Petersilia (Eds.), *Prisons, crime and justice, annual review* (Vol. 26, pp. 17–61). Chicago; University of Chicago Press.

Blumstein, A., & Cohen, J. (1987). Characterizing criminal careers. *Science, 237*, 985–991.

Bonczar, T. P., & Beck, A. J. (1997, March). Lifetime likelihood of going to state or federal prison. Bureau of Justice Statistics (NCJ 160092). Washington, DC: U.S. Department of Justice, Office of Justice Programs, http://www.ojp.usdoj.gov/bjs/abstract/llgsfp.htm.

Bonczar, T., & Glaze, L. (1999). *Probation and parole in the United States.* Washington, DC: U.S. Department of Justice.

Bond, L., & Semaan, S. (1996). At risk for HIV infection: Incarcerated women in a county jail in Philadelphia. *Women & Health, 24*(4), 27–45.

Bowditch, C., & Everett, R. S. (1987). Private prisons: Problems within the solution. *Justice Quarterly, 4*, 441–453.

Braithwaite, R. L., Hammett, T., & Mayberry, R. M. (1996). *Prisons and AIDS: A public health challenge.* San Francisco: Jossey-Bass Publishers.

Brecht, M. L., Hser, Y. I., & Anglin, M. D. (1991). A multimethod assessment of social intervention effects of narcotics use and property crime. *International Journal of the Addictions, 25,* 1317–1340.

Brecht, M., & Anglin, M. D. (1990). Conditional factors of maturing out: Legal supervision and treatment. *International Journal of the Addictions, 25,* 393–407.

Brecht, M., Anglin, M., & Wang, J. (1993). Treatment effectiveness for legally coerced versus voluntary methadone maintenance clients. *American Journal of Drug and Alcohol Abuse, 19*(1), 89–106.

Brewer, V. E., Marquart, J. W., Mullings, J. L., & Crouch, B. N. (1998). AIDS-related risk behaviors among female prisoners with histories of mental impairment. *Prison Journal, 78,* 101–118.

Brewington, V., Arella, L., Deren, S., & Randell, J. (1987). Obstacles to the utilization of vocational services: An analysis of the literature. *International Journal of the Addictions, 22,* 1091–1118.

Brindis, C. D., & Theidon, K. S. (1997). The role of case management in substance-abuse treatment services for women and children. *Journal of Psychoactive Drugs, 29*(1), 79–88.

Brizer, D. A., Maslansky, R., & Galanter, M. (1990). Treatment retention of patients referred by public assistance to an alcoholism clinic. *American Journal of Drug and Alcohol Abuse, 16,* 259–264.

Broome, K. M., Flynn, P. M., & Simpson, D. D. (1999). Psychiatric comorbidity measures as predictors of retention in drug abuse treatment programs. *Health Services Research, 34,* 791–806.

Broome, K. M., Hiller, M. L., & Simpson, D. D. (2000, March). *During-treatment changes in psychosocial functioning for probationers.* Paper presented at the annual meeting of the Academy of Criminal Justice Sciences (ACJS), New Orleans, LA.

Broome, K. M., Knight, K., Hiller, M. L., & Simpson, D. D. (1996). Drug treatment process indicators for probationers and prediction of recidivism. *Journal of Substance-Abuse Treatment, 13,* 487–491.

Broome, K. M., Knight, D. K., Knight, K., Hiller, M. L., & Simpson, D. D. (1997). Peer, family, and motivational influences on drug treatment process and recidivism for probationers. *Journal of Clinical Psychology, 53,* 387–397.

Broome, K. M., Knight, K., Joe, G. W., & Simpson, D. D. (1996). Evaluating the drug-abusing probationer: Clinical interview versus self-administered assessment. *Criminal Justice and Behavior, 23,* 593–606.

Brown, B. S. (1997). Staffing patterns and services for the war on drugs. In J. A. Egertson, D. M. Fox, & A. I. Leshner (Eds.), *Treating drug abusers effectively* (pp. 99–124). Malden, MA: Blackwell.

Brown, B. S., & Ashery, R. S. (1979). Aftercare in drug abuse programming. In R. L. Dupont, A. Goldstein, & J. O'Donnell (Eds.), *Handbook on drug abuse* (pp. 165–173). Washington, DC: U.S. Government Printing Office.

Brown, J. M., Gilliard, D. K., Snell, T. L, Stephan, J. J., & Wilson, D. J. (1996, June). *Correctional populations in the United States, 1994* (NCJ 160091). Washington, DC: U.S. Department of Justice, Office of Justice Programs, http://www.ojp.usdoj.gov/bjs/abstract/cpius94.htm.

Brunicardi, B. O. (1998). Financial analysis of savings from telemedicine in Ohio's prison system. *Telemedicine Journal, 4,* 49–54.

Bukstein, O., & Kaminer, Y. (1994). The nosology of adolescent substance abuse. *American Journal of Addiction, 3,* 1–13.

Bureau of Justice Assistance. (1992). *Treatment alternatives to street crime: Program brief.* Washington, DC: U.S. Department of Justice, Office of Justice Programs.

Bureau of Justice Statistics. (1991). *Survey of state prison inmates, 1991* (NCJ 136949). Rockville, MD: U.S. Department of Justice.

Bureau of Justice Statistics. (1992). *Drugs, crime, and the justice system.* Washington, DC: U.S. Department of Justice.

Bureau of Justice Statistics. (1994). *State and federal prison population tops one million.* October 17, 1994 press release. Washington, DC: U.S. Department of Justice.

Bureau of Justice Statistics. (1994). Bureau of Justice Statistics Special Report: Survey of state prison inmates, 1991, women in prison. Washington, DC: Author.

Bureau of Justice Statistics. (1995). *Drugs and crime facts.* Rockville, MD: U.S. Department of Justice.

Bureau of Justice Statistics. (1996). *HIV in prisons, 1994* (NCJ 158020). Rockville, MD: U.S. Department of Justice.

Bureau of Justice Statistics. (1997, December). *Characteristics of adults on probation, 1995* (Bureau of Justice Statistics Special Report). Washington, DC: Author.

Bureau of Justice Statistics. (1998). *Sourcebook of criminal justice statistics.* Washington, DC: U.S. Department of Justice.

Bureau of Justice Statistics. (1998, March). *Substance abuse and treatment of adults on probation, 1995* (Bureau of Justice Statistics Special Report). Washington, DC: Author.

Bureau of Justice Statistics. (1999). *Correctional populations in the United States, 1996* (NCJ 171684). Rockville, MD: U.S. Department of Justice.

Bureau of Justice Statistics (BJS). (1999). *Correctional populations in the United States, 1996* (Report NCJ 170013). Available through BJS website http//www.ojp.usdoj.gov/bjs/abstract/cplus96.htm.

Bureau of Justice Statistics. (1999). *Special report: Substance abuse and treatment, state and federal prisoners.* Washington, DC: U.S. Department of Justice, Office of Justice Programs.

Bureau of Justice Statistics. (1999). Prisoners in 1998. Bureau of Justice Statistics Bulletin. Washington, DC: Author.

Bureau of Justice Statistics. (1999). U.S. Department of Justice Web site. Available: http://www.ojp.usdoj.gov/bjs/correct.htm

Bureau of Justice Statistics. (1999, April). *Correctional populations in the United States, 1996* (NCJ 170013). Washington, DC: U.S. Department of Justice, Office of Justice Programs, http://www.ojp.usdoj.gov/bjs/abstract/cpius96.htm.

Bureau of Justice Statistics. (1999, August). *Federal criminal case processing, 1998* (NCJ 169277). Washington, DC: U.S. Department of Justice, Office of Justice Programs, http://www.ojp.usdoj.gov/bjs/abstract/pjim98.htm.

Bureau of Justice Statistics. (1999, January). *Substance abuse and treatment, state and federal prisoners, 1997* (NCJ-172871). Washington, DC: U.S. Department of Justice.

Bureau of Justice Statistics. (2000). *Special report: Drug use, testing, and treatment in jails.* Washington, DC: U.S. Department of Justice.

Bureau of Justice Statistics. (2000). *State court sentencing of convicted felons, 1996* (NCJ 175708). Rockville, MD: U.S. Department of Justice.

Bureau of Justice Statistics Bulletin. (2000, April). *Prison and jail inmates at midyear 1999* (NCJ-181643). Washington, DC: U.S. Department of Justice.

Bureau of Prisons. (unpublished report). Triad drug treatment evaluation—Six-month report. Available: www.bop.gov.

Burtless, G. T. (1997). Welfare recipients' job skills and employment prospects. *Future of Children, 7*(1), 39–51.

Butts, J. A., & Harrell, A. V. (1998). *Delinquents or criminals: Policy options for young offenders.* Washington, DC: The Urban League.

Camp, G. C., & Camp, G. M. (1996). *The corrections yearbook, 1995.* South Salem, NY: Criminal Justice Institute.

Camp, C. G., & Camp, G. M. (1997). *The 1997 corrections yearbook.* South Salem, NY: Criminal Justice Institute.

Camp, C. G., & Camp, G. M. (1998). *The corrections yearbook, 1998.* Middletown, CT: Criminal Justice Institute.

Camp, S. D., & Gaes, G. G. (1998). *Private adult prisons: What do we really know and why don't we know more?* Unpublished manuscript.

Carlson, B. (1998). Addiction and treatment in the criminal justice system. Principles of addiction (2nd ed.). In B. Wilford (Ed.), *American Society of Addiction Medicine.* Chevy Chase, MD.

CASA—Center on Addiction and Substance Abuse. (1998, January). Behind bars: Substance abuse and America's prison population. New York: Columbia University.

Catalano, R. F., Hawkins, J. D., Wells, E. A., Miller, J., & Brewer, D. (1990–1991). Evaluation of the effectiveness of adolescent drug abuse treatment, assessment of risks for relapse, and promising approaches for relapse prevention. *The International Journal of the Addictions, 25,* 1085–1140.

Catalano, R. F., Wells, E. A., Jenson, J. M., & Hawkins, J. D. (1989). Aftercare services for drug-using adjudicated youth in residential settings. *Social Service Review, 63,* 553–577.

Cauffman, E., Feldman, S. S., Waterman, J., & Steiner, H. (1998). Posttraumatic stress disorder among female juvenile offenders. *Journal of the American Academy of Child and Adolescent Psychiatry, 37,* 1209–1216.

Caulkins, J., Rydell, C., Schwabe, W., & Chiesa, J. (1997). *Mandatory minimum drug sentences: Throwing away the key or the taxpayers' money?* (MR-826-DPRC). Santa Monica, CA: RAND.

Caulkins, J., Rydell, C., Schwabe, W., & Chiesa, J. (1998). Are mandatory minimum drug sentences cost-effective? *Corrections Management Quarterly, 2*(1), 62–73.

Cavanagh, D. P., & Harrell, A. (1995). Evaluation of the Multnomah County drug testing and evaluation program. Final report to the National Institute of Justice. Cambridge, MA: BOTEC Analysis Corporation.

Center for Substance Abuse Research. (1992). Washington county explores a structure for success. *CESAR Reports, 2*(2), 1, 5.

Center for Substance-Abuse Treatment. (1993). *Improving treatment for drug-exposed infants* (TIP No. 5). Rockville, MD: U.S. Department of Health and Human Services, Author.

Center for Substance-Abuse Treatment. (1994). *Combining substance-abuse treatment with intermediate sanctions for adults in the criminal justice system* (Treatment Improvement Protocol [TIP] Series 12). Washington, DC: Substance Abuse and Mental Health Services Administration, Department of Health and Human Services.

Center for Substance-Abuse Treatment. (1994). *Simple screening instrument for outreach for alcohol and other drug abuse and infections diseases* (Treatment improvement protocol (TIP) Series, No. 11). Rockville, MD: U.S. Department of Health and Human Services.

Center for Substance-Abuse Treatment. (1995a). *Developing state outcomes monitoring systems for alcohol and other drug abuse treatment* (Treatment Improvement Protocol [TIP] Series 14). Washington, DC: Substance Abuse and Mental Health Services Administration, Department of Health and Human Services.

Center for Substance-Abuse Treatment. (1995b). *Planning for alcohol and other drug abuse treatment for adults in the criminal justice system* (Treatment Improvement Protocol [TIP)] Series 17). Washington, DC: Substance Abuse and Mental Health Services Administration, Department of Health and Human Services.

Center for Substance-Abuse Treatment. (1998). *Continuity of offender treatment for substance use disorders from institution to community* (Treatment Improvement Protocol [TIP] Series 30). Washington, DC: Substance Abuse and Mental Health Services Administration, Department of Health and Human Services.

Center for Substance Abuser Treatment. (1994). *Screening and assessment for alcohol and other drug abuse among adults in the criminal justice system.* Washington, DC: U.S. Government Printing Office.

Center on Addiction and Substance Abuse. (1998). Behind bars: Substance abuse and America's prisons—Executive Summary. Available from the world wide web, URL: www.Casacolumbia.org/pubs/jan98/summary.htm.

Centers for Disease Control and Prevention. (1998a). Assessment of sexually transmitted disease services in city and county jails—United States. *MMWR, 47,* 429–431.

Centers for Disease Control and Prevention. (1999). *HIV/AIDS surveillance report, 11*(1).

Centers for Substance-Abuse Treatment (CSAT). (2000). *Savings exceed costs of substance-abuse treatment three to one.* CSAT by fax 5 (3), 12 April.

Chaiken, J. M., & Chaiken, M. R. (1990). Drugs and predatory crime. In M. Tonry & J. Q. Wilson (Eds.), *Drugs and crime* (pp. 203–239). Chicago: University of Chicago Press.

Chaiken, M. R. (1986). Crime rates and substance abuse among types of offenders. In B. D. Johnson & E. Wish (Eds.), *Crime rates among drug-abusing offenders. Final report to the National Institute of Justice.* New York: Narcotic and Drug Research.

Cherpitel, C. J. (1997). Brief screening instruments for alcoholism. *Alcohol Health & Research World, 21,* 348–351.

Chou, C. P., Hser, Y. I., & Anglin, M. D. (1998). Interaction effects of client and treatment program characteristics on retention: An exploratory analysis using hierarchical linear models. *Substance Use & Misuse, 33*(11), 2281–2301.

Church, T. (1982). *Examining local legal culture: Practitioner attitudes in four criminal courts.* Washington, DC: National Institute of Justice.

Churchman, C. W. (1968). *The systems approach.* New York: Delacorte Press.

Churchman, C. W. (1979). *The systems approach and its enemies.* New York: Basic Books.

Clark, J., Austin, J., & Henry, D. A. (1997, September). *Three strikes and you're out: A review of state legislation.* Washington, DC: U.S. Department of Justice, National Institute of Justice. U.S. Department of Justice, National Institute of Justice.

Cloninger, C. R. (1999). Genetics of substance abuse. In M. Galanter & H. D. Kleber (Eds.), *Textbook of substance-abuse treatment* (2nd ed., pp. 59–66). Washington, DC: American Psychiatric Association.

Coll, C. G., Surrey, J. L., Buccio-Notaro, P., & Molla, B. (1998). Incarcerated mothers: Crimes and punishment. In C. G. Coll, J. L. Surrey, & K. Weingarten (Eds.), *Mothering against the odds: Diverse voices of contemporary mothers* (pp. 255–274). New York: Guilford Press.

Collins, J. J., & Allison, M. (1983). Legal coercion and retention in drug abuse treatment. *Hospital and Community Psychiatry, 34,* 1145–1149.

Comerford, A. W. (1999). Work dysfunction and addiction. *Journal of Substance-Abuse Treatment, 16,* 247–253.

Condelli, W. S., & Hubbard, R. L. (1994). Relationship between time spent in treatment and client outcomes from therapeutic communities. *Journal of Substance-Abuse Treatment, 11*(1), 25–33.

Conklin, T. J., Lincoln, T., & Flanigan, T. P. (1998). A public health model to connect correctional health care with communities. *American Journal of Public Health, 88,* 1249–1250.

Connors, G. J., Maisto, S. A., & Zywiak, W. H. (1996). Understanding relapse in the broader context of post-treatment functioning. *Addiction, 91,* S173–S189.

Conrad, H. T. (1972). NIMH Clinical Research Center Lexington, Kentucky: Current Status. In L. Brill & L. Lieberman (Eds.), *Major modalities in the treatment of drug abuse.* New York: Behavioral Publications.

Cook, L. F. (1992). TASC: Case management models linking criminal justice and treatment. In R. S. Ashery (Ed.), *Progress and issues in case management* (National Institute on Drug Abuse Research Monograph 127). Washington, DC: U.S. Government Printing Office.

Cook, L. F., & Weinman, B. A. (1988). Treatment alternatives to street crime. In C. G. Leukefeld & F. M. Tims (Eds.), *Compulsory treatment of drug abuse: Research and clinical practice.* National Institute on Drug Abuse Research Monograph 86 (pp. 99–105). Washington, DC: National Institute of Drug Abuse.

Cooper, C. (1997). *1997 Drug court survey report: Executive summary.* Washington, DC: Drug Court Clearinghouse and Technical Assistance Project, American University.

Cooper, C. (1998). *1998 Drug court survey report.* Washington, DC: Drug Court Clearinghouse and Technical Assistance Project, American University.

Cooper, C. S., & Trotter, J. (1994). Recent developments in drug case management: Re-engineering the judicial process. *The Justice System Journal, 17*(1), 83–98.

Cooper, C. S., & Trotter, J. A. (1994). *Case management and treatment intervention strategies in state and local courts.* Washington, DC: Bureau of Justice Assistance Drug Court Resource Center, U.S. Department of Justice.

Cornish, J. W., Metzger, D., Woody, G. E., Wilson, D., McLellan, A. T., Vandergrift, B., & O'Brien, C. P. (1997). Naltrexone pharmacotherapy for opioid dependent federal probationers. *Journal of Substance-Abuse Treatment, 14,* 529–534.

Corrigan, P. W. (1995). Wanted: Champions of psychiatric rehabilitation. *American Psychologist, 50,* 514–521.

Cosden, M., Peerson, S., & Crothers, L. (1999). Evaluation report of the Santa Barbara County substance-abuse treatment courts' first graduates. University of California, Santa Barbara.

Cotton-Oldenburg, N. U., Jordan, K., Martin, S. L., & Kupper, L. (1999). Women inmates' risky sex and drug behaviors: are they related? *American Journal of Drug and Alcohol Abuse, 25*(1), 129–149.

Cotton-Oldenburg, N. U., Martin, S. L., Jordan, B. K., Sadowski, S. L., & Kupper, L. (1997). Preincarceration risky behaviors among women inmates: Opportunities for prevention. *Prison Journal, 77,* 281–294.

Covington, S. S. (1998). Women in prison: Approaches in the treatment of our most invisible population. *Breaking the Rules: Women in Prison and the Feminist Theory, 21*(1), 141–155.

Craddock, S. G., Rounds-Bryant, J. L., Flynn, P. M., & Hubbard, R. L. (1997). Characteristics and pretreatment behaviors of clients entering drug abuse treatment: 1969 to 1993. *American Journal of Drug and Alcohol Abuse, 23*(1), 43–59.

De Jong, P., & Miller, S. D. (1995). How to interview for client strengths. *Social Work, 40,* 729–736.

De Leon, G. (1984). *The therapeutic community: Study of effectiveness* (NIDA Research Monograph Series, DHHS Publication No. ADM 84-1286). Rockville, MD: National Institute on Drug Abuse.

De Leon, G. (1988). Legal pressure in therapeutic communities. *Journal of Drug Issues, 18,* 625–640.

De Leon, G. (1989). Psychopathology and substance abuse: What we are learning from research in therapeutic communities. *Journal of Psychoactive Drugs, 21,* 177–188.

De Leon, G. (1990–1991). Aftercare in therapeutic communities. *International Journal of the Addictions, 25*(9A-10A), 1229–1241.

De Leon, G. (1991). Retention in drug-free therapeutic communities. In R. W. Pickens, C. G. Leukefeld, & C. R. Schuster (Eds.), *Improving drug abuse treatment* (NIDA Research Monograph 106, DHHS Publication No. ADM 91-1754). Rockville, MD: National Institute on Drug Abuse.

De Leon, G. (1997). *Community as method: Therapeutic communities for special populations and special settings.* Westport, CT: Greenwood Publishing.

De Leon, G. (2000). *The therapeutic community: Theory, model & method.* New York: Springer Publishing Co.

De Leon, G., & Deitch, D. (1987). Treatment of the adolescent substance abuser in a therapeutic community. In A. S. Friedman & G. M. Beschner (Eds.), *Treatment services for adolescent substance abusers.* Rockville, MD: National Institute on Drug Abuse.

De Leon, G., Inciardi, J. A., & Martin, S. S. (1995). Residential drug treatment research: Are conventional control designs appropriate for assessing treatment effectiveness? *Journal of Psychoactive Drugs, 27,* 85–91.

De Leon, G., & Jainchill, N. (1986). Circumstances, motivation, readiness, and suitability as correlates of treatment tenure. *Journal of Psychoactive Drugs, 18,* 203–208.

De Leon, G., Melnick, G., Kressel, D., & Jainchill, N. (1994). Circumstances, motivation, readiness, and suitability (the CMRS scales): Predicting retention in therapeutic community treatment. *American Journal of Drug and Alcohol Abuse, 20,* 495–515.

De Leon, G., Melnick, G., Schoket, D., & Jainchill, N. (1993). Is the therapeutic community culturally relevant? Findings on race/ethnic differences in retention in treatment. *Journal of Psychoactive Drugs, 25*(1), 77–86.

De Leon, G., Melnick, G., Thomas, G., Kressel, D., & Wexler, H. K. (2000). Motivation for treatment in a prison-based therapeutic community. *American Journal of Drug and Alcohol Abuse, 26*(1), 33–46.

De Leon, G., & Rosenthal, M. S. (1989). Treatment in residential therapeutic communities. In T. Karasu (Vol. Ed.), *Treatments of psychiatric disorders* (Vol. 2, pp. 1380–1398). Washington, DC: American Psychiatric Press.

De Leon, G., Sacks, S., Staines, G., & McKendrick, K. (1999). Modified therapeutic community for homeless MICAs (MICAs): Emerging subtypes. *American Journal of Drug and Alcohol Abuse, 25,* 493–513.

De Leon, G., Sacks, S., Staines, G., & McKendrick, K. (2000). Modified therapeutic community for homeless MICAs: Treatment outcomes. *American Journal of Drug Alcohol Abuse, 26,* 461–480.

De Leon, G., & Schwartz, S. (1984). Therapeutic communities: What are the retention rates. *American Journal of Drug and Alcohol Abuse, 10,* 267–284.

Dean-Gaitor, H. D., & Fleming, P. L. (1999). Epidemiology of AIDS in incarcerated persons in the United States, 1994–1996. *AIDS, 13,* 2429–2435.

Dees, S. M., Dansereau, D. F., Peel, J. L., Boatler, J. G., & Knight, K. (1991). Using conceptual matrices, knowledge maps, and scripted cooperation to improve personal management strategies. *Journal of Drug Education, 2,* 211–228.

Dees, S. M., Dansereau, D. F., & Simpson, D. D. (1999). *Implementing a readiness program for mandated substance-abuse treatment.* Manuscript submitted for publication.

Deitch, D. (1973). Treatment of drug abuse in the therapeutic community: Historical influences, current considerations and future outlook. In *The technical papers of the second report of the National Commission on Marihuana and Drug Abuse (Vol. 4): Treatment and rehabilitation* (pp. 158–175).

Deitch, D., Koutsenok, I., Burgener, M. L., Marsolais, K., & Cartier, J. (2000). *In-custody therapeutic community substance-abuse treatment: Does it make a difference to custody personnel?* Manuscript submitted for publication.

Deitch, D., Koutsenok, I., McGrath, P., Ratelle, J., & Carleton, S. (1998). *Outcome findings regarding in-custody adverse behavior between therapeutic community treatment and non-treatment populations.* Consensus meeting on drug treatment in criminal justice system. Washington, DC.

Deitch, D., & Solit, R. (1993). Training drug abuse treatment personnel in therapeutic community methodologies. *Psychotherapy, 30,* 305–316.

Dembo, R., & Brown, R. (1994). The Hillsborough County juvenile assessment center. *Journal of Child and Adolescent Substance Abuse, 3,* 25–43.

Dembo, R., Ramirez-Garnica, G., Rollie, M., Schmeidler, J., Livingston, S., & Hartsfield, A. (2000). Youth recidivism 12 months after a family empowerment intervention: Final report. *Journal of Offender Rehabilitation, 31,* 29–65.

Dembo, R., Schmeidler, J., Nini-Gough, B., Chin Sue, C., Borden, P., & Manning, D. (1998b). Predictors of recidivism to a juvenile assessment center: A three year study. *Journal of Child and Adolescent Substance Abuse, 7,* 57–77.

Dembo, R., Schmeidler, J., Nini-Gough, B., & Manning, D. (1998a). Sociodemographic, delinquency-abuse history, and psychosocial functioning differences among juvenile offenders of various ages. *Journal of Child and Adolescent Substance Abuse, 8,* 63–78.

Dembo, R., Schmeidler, J., Pacheco, K., Cooper, S., & Williams, L. (1997). The relationships between youths' identified substance use, mental health or other problems at a juvenile assessment center and their referrals to needed services. *Journal of Child and Adolescent Substance Abuse, 6,* 23–54.

Dembo, R., Shemwell, M., Guida, J., Schmeidler, J., Baumgartner, W., Ramirez-Garnica, G., & Seeberger, W. (1999). Comparison of self-report, urine sample, and hair testing for drug use: A longitudinal study. In T. Mieczkowski (Ed.), *Drug testing methods: Assessment and evaluation.* New York: CRC Press.

Dembo, R., & Seeberger, W. (1999, April). The need for innovative approaches to meet the substance abuse and mental health service needs of inner-city, African-American male youth involved with the juvenile justice system. Paper presented before the U.S. Commission on Civil Rights, Washington, DC.

Dembo, R., Seeberger, W., Shemwell, M., Schmeidler, J., Klein, L., Rollie, M., Pacheco, K., Hartsfield, A., & Wothke, W. (in press). Psychosocial functioning among juvenile offenders 12 months after family empowerment intervention. *Journal of Offender Rehabilitation*.

Dembo, R., Washburn, M., Wish, E. D., Schmeidler, J., Getreu, A., Berry, E., Williams, L., & Blount, W. R. (1987). Further examination of the association between heavy marijuana use and crime among youths entering a juvenile detention center. *Journal of Psychoactive Drugs, 19*, 361–373.

Dembo, R., Williams, L., & Schmeidler, J. (1993). Addressing the problems of substance abuse in juvenile corrections. In J. A. Inciardi (Ed.), *Drug treatment in criminal justice settings*. Newbury Park, CA: Sage.

Dembo, R., Williams, L., & Schmeidler, J. (1998). Key findings from the Tampa longitudinal study of juvenile detainees: Contributions to a theory of drug use and delinquency among high risk youths. In A. R. Roberts (Ed.), *Juvenile justice* (2nd ed.). Chicago: Nelson-Hall.

Dembo, R., Williams, L., Wothke, W., Schmeidler, J., & Brown, C. H. (1992). The role of family factors, physical abuse and sexual victimization experiences in high risk youths' alcohol and other drug use and delinquency: A longitudinal model. *Violence and Victims, 7*, 245– 266.

Denman, K., & Guerin, P. (1998). *Status report: An analysis of Second Judicial District Court drug court client data*. Albuquerque, NM: University of New Mexico, Institute for Social Research.

Department of Health and Human Services. (1999). *Treatment episode data set (TEDS) 1992–1997*. Washington, DC: Author.

Deren, S., & Randell, J. (1990). The vocational rehabilitation of substance abusers. *Journal of Applied Rehabilitation Counseling, 21*(2), 4–6.

Deschenes, E. P., & Greenwood, P. W. (1994). Maricopa County's drug court: An innovative program for first-time drug offenders on probation. *Justice System Journal, 17*(1), 99–116.

Deschenes, E. P., Imam, I., Foster, T., & Ward, D. (1999). *Evaluation of Los Angeles County drug courts*. Long Beach, CA: Center for Applied Local Research, UC Long Beach.

Deschenes, E. P., Turner, S., & Greenwood, P. (1995). Drug court or probation?: An experimental evaluation of Maricopa County's drug court. *Justice System Journal, 18*, 55–73.

Deschenes, E. P., Turner, S., & Petersilia, J. (1995). A dual experiment in intensive community supervision: Minnesota's prison diversion and enhanced supervised release programs. *Prison Journal, 75*, 330–356.

DiClemente, C. C., & Prochaska, J. O. (1998). Toward a comprehensive, transtheoretical model of change: Stages of change and addictive behaviors. In W. R.

Miller & N. Heather (Eds.), *Treating addictive behaviors: Applied clinical psychology* (2nd ed.). New York: Plenum Press.

Ditton, P. M. (1999). *Mental health and treatment of inmates and probationers.* Bureau of Justice Statistics Special Report. Washington, DC: U.S. Department of Justice, Office of Justice Programs.

Ditton, P. M., & Wilson, D. J. (1999, January). *Truth in sentencing in state prisons. Bureau of Justice Statistics Special Report* (NCJ 170032). Washington, DC: Department of Justice, Office of Justice Programs, http://www.ojp.usdoj.gov/bjs/abstract/tssp.htm.

Dolan, B. (1994). Therapeutic communities for offenders. *Therapeutic Communities, 15,* 4.

Dolan, B. (1996). *Perspectives on the Henderson Hospital.* Henderson Hospital, 2 Homeland Drive, Sutton, Surrey, UK SM2 5LT.

Dolan, K., Wodak, A., & Penny, R. (1995). AIDS behind bars: Preventing HIV spread among incarcerated drug users. *AIDS, 9,* 825–832.

Donaldson, S. (1995). *Rape of incarcerated Americans: A preliminary statistical look* (7th ed.). Available World Wide Web: www.spr.org/docs/stats.html.

Downes, E. A., & Shaening, M. A. (1993, Spring). Linking state AOD and justice systems. *Center for Substance-Abuse Treatment TIE Communique,* 8–9.

Drake, R., & Mueser, K. (2000). Psychosocial approaches to dual diagnosis. *Schizophrenia Bulletin, 26,* 105–118.

Drug Courts Program Office. (1997). *Defining drug courts: The key components.* Washington, DC: U.S. Department of Justice.

Drug Courts Program Office. (1998). *Drug court activity: Summary information.* Washington, DC: Office of Justice Programs, U.S. Department of Justice.

Drummond, M. F., O'Brien, B., Stoddart, G. L., & Torrance, G. W. (1997). *Methods for the economic evaluation of health care programmes* (2nd ed.). New York: Oxford University Press.

Dubler, N. N. (1998). The collision of confinement and care: End-of-life care in prisons and jails. *Medicine & Ethics, 26,* 149–156.

Duffee, D. E., & Carlson, B. E. (1996). Competing value premises for the provision of drug treatment to probationers. *Crime and Delinquency, 42,* 574–592.

Dugan, J. R., & Everett, R. S. (1998). An experimental test of chemical dependency therapy for jail inmates. *International Journal of Offender Therapy and Comparative Criminology, 42,* 360–368.

DuPont, R. (2000, October 9). Drug wars [Interview published on-line from Frontline series]. Available: PBS.org.D.Fanning (Producer). WGBH. Boston, MA, and Alexandria, VA (Distributor).

Du Pont, R. L., Goldstein, A., & O'Donnel, J. (1978). *Handbook on drug abuse,* Rockville, MD: National Institute on Drug Abuse.

Du Pont, R. L., & McGovern, J. P. (1994). *A bridge to recovery—An introduction to 12-step programs.* Washington, DC: American Psychiatric Press.

DuPont, R. L. (1972). Heroin addiction treatment and crime reduction. *American Journal of Psychiatry, 128,* 856–860.

DuPont, R. L. (1997). *The selfish brain: Learning from addiction.* Washington, DC: American Psychiatric Press.

DuPont, R. L. (1998). Addiction: A new paradigm. *Bull Menninger Clin 62,* 231–242.

DuPont, R. L. (in press). Heroin addiction in the nation's capital (1966–1973). In D. F. Musto (Ed.), *One hundred years of heroin.* New Haven, CT: Yale University Press.

DuPont, R. L., & Katon, R. N. (1971). Development of a heroin addiction treatment program: Effect on urban crime. *Journal of the American Medical Association, 216,* 1320–1324.

DuPont, R. L., & MacKenzie, D. L. (1994). Narcotics and drug abuse: An unforseen tidal wave. In J. A. Conley (Ed.), *The 1967 President's crime commission report: Its impact 25 years later* (pp. 121–144). Cincinnati, OH: Anderson Publishing.

DuPont, R. L., & Wish, E. D. (1992). Operation tripwire revisited. *Annals of The American Academy of Political and Social Science, 521,* 91–111.

Eddy, N. B. (1973). *The national research council involvement in the opiate problem: 1928–1971.* Washington, DC: National Academy of Sciences.

Edens, J., Peters, R., & Hills, H. (1997). Treating prison inmates with co-occurring disorders: An integrative review of existing programs. *Behavioral Sciences and the Law, 15,* 439–457.

Edlin, B. R., Irwin, K. L., Ludwig, D. D., McCoy, V., Serrano, Y., Word, C., Bowser, B., Faruque, S., McCoy, C., Schilling, R., & Holmbeg, S. (1992). High-risk sex behavior among young street-recruited crack cocaine smokers in three American cities: An interim report. *Journal of Psychoactive Drugs, 24,* 363–371.

Eisenstein, J., & Jacob, H. (1976). *Felony justice: An organizational analysis of criminal courts.* Boston: Little Brown.

Emrick, C. (1987). Alcoholics anonymous: Affiliation processes and effectiveness as treatment. *Alcoholism: Clinical & Experimental Research, 11,* 416–423.

Englehart, P. F., Robinson, F., & Kates, H. (1997). The workplace. In J. H. Lowinson, P. Ruiz, R. B. Millman, & J. G. Langrod (Eds.), *Substance abuse: A comprehensive textbook* (3rd ed., pp. 874–884). Baltimore: Williams & Wilkins.

Etheridge, R., Hubbard, R., Anderson, J., Craddock, S., & Flynn, P. (1997). Treatment structure and program services in DATOS. *Psychology of Addictive Behavior, 11,* 244–260.

Falck, R. S., Siegal, H. A., & Carlson, R. G. (1992). Case management to enhance AIDS risk reduction for injection drug users and crack cocaine: Practical and philosophical considerations. In R. S. Ashery (Ed.), *Progress and issues in case management* (National Institute on Drug Abuse Research Monograph 127, pp. 167–180). Washington, DC: U.S. Government Printing Office.

Falkin, G. (1993). Coordinating drug treatment for offenders: A case study. Unpublished report to the National Institute of Justice. New York: National Development Research Institution.

Farabee, D., & Leukefeld, C. G. (1999). Opportunities for AIDS prevention in a rural state in criminal justice and drug treatment settings. *Substance Use and Misuse, 34,* 617–631.

Farabee, D., Prendergast, M., & Anglin, M. D. (1998). The effectiveness of coerced treatment for drug-abusing offenders. *Federal Probation, 62*(1), 3–10.

Farabee, D., Prendergast, M., Cartier, J., Wexler, H., Knight, K., & Anglin, M. D. (1999). Barriers to implementing effective correctional drug treatment programs. *The Prison Journal, 79*(2), 150–162.

Farabee, D. J., Simpson, D. D., Dansereau, D. F., & Knight, K. (1995). Cognitive inductions into treatment among drug users on probation. *Journal of Drug Issues, 25,* 669–682.

Farrington, D. P., & West, D. J. (1990). The Cambridge study in delinquent development: A long-term follow-up of 411 London males. In H. J. Kerner & G. Kaiser (Eds.), *Criminality: Personality, behavior and life history.* New York: Springer-Verlag.

Federal Bureau of Investigation. (1967). *Crime in the United States. Uniform Crime Reports—1966.* Washington, DC: U.S. Department of Justice.

Federal Bureau of Investigation. (1981). *Crime in the United States, 1980.* Washington, DC: U.S. Department of Justice, Author.

Federal Bureau of Investigations. (1991). *Crime in the United States.* Washington, DC: Government Printing Office.

Federal Bureau of Investigation. (1999). *Crime in the United States, 1998.* Washington, DC: U.S. Department of Justice, Author.

Fergusson, D. M., Horwood, L. J., & Lynskey, M. T. (1994). The childhoods of multiple problem adolescents: A 15-year longitudinal study. *Journal of Child Psychology and Psychiatry and Allied Disciplines, 35,* 1123–1140.

Field, G. (1985). The cornerstone program: A client outcome study. *Federal Probation, 49,* 50–55.

Field, G. (1995). *Turning point alcohol and drug program (women's unit) outcome study.* Salem, OR: Oregon Department of Corrections.

Field, G. (1998). From the institution to the community. *Corrections Today, 60*(6), 94–97, 113.

Field, G. D. (1989). A study of the effects of intensive treatment on reducing the criminal recidivism of addicted offenders. *Federal Probation, 53*(10), 51–56.

Finigan, M. (1998). An outcome program evaluation of the Multnomah County S.T.O.P. Drug diversion program. Report to the State Justice Institute and the Multnomah County Department of Community Corrections. West Linn, OR: Northwest Professional Consortium.

Finigan, M. (1999). Assessing cost off-sets in a drug court setting. *National Drug Court Institute Review, 2*(2), 59–92.

Finkelstein, N., Kennedy, C., Thomas, K., & Kearns, M. (1997). *Gender specific substance-abuse treatment* (CSAP Contract No. 277-94-3009). Rockville, MD: Center for Substance Abuse Prevention.

Finn, P. (1998). Successful job placement for ex-offenders: The center for employment opportunities. *Successful job placement for ex-offenders: The center for employment opportunities. Program focus* (NCJ 168102). Washington, DC: National Institute of Justice, Office of Correctional Education, National Institute of Corrections.

Finn, P., & Newlyn, A. K. (1993). *Miami's "drug court:" A different approach.* Washington, DC: U.S. Department of Justice, National Institute of Justice.

Fiorentine, R. (1999). After drug treatment: Are 12-step programs effective in maintaining abstinence? *American Journal of Drug and Alcohol Abuse, 25*, 93–116.

Fiorentine, R., & Anglin, M. D. (1996). More is better: Counseling participation and the effectiveness of outpatient drug treatment. *Journal of Substance-Abuse Treatment, 13,* 341–348.

Fiorentine, R., & Anglin, M. D. (1997). Does increasing the opportunity for counseling increase the effectiveness of outpatient drug treatment? *American Journal of Drug and Alcohol Abuse, 23,* 369–382.

Fiorentine, R., Gil-Rivas, V., & Hillhouse, M. P. (1998). *Enhancing drug treatment: Evaluation of the Los Angeles target cities project (Years 4–5).* Manuscript submitted to the Center for Substance-Abuse Treatment.

Fiorentine, R., & Hillhouse, M. P. (1999). Drug treatment effectiveness and client-counselor empathy: Exploring the effects of gender and ethnic congruency. *Journal of Drug Issues, 29*(1), 59–74.

Fiorentine, R., & Hillhouse, M. P. (2000a). Drug treatment and 12-step program participation: The additive effects of integrated recovery activities. *Journal of Substance-Abuse Treatment, 18,* 65–74.

Fiorentine, R., & Hillhouse, M. P. (2000b). Exploring the additive effects of drug treatment and twelve-step involvement: Does twelve-step ideology matter? *Substance Use and Misuse, 35,* 367–397.

Fiorentine, R., & Hillhouse, M. P. (in press). Self-efficacy, expectancies, motivation and abstinence acceptance: Further evidence for the Addicted-Self Model of cessation of alcohol and drug dependent behavior. *American Journal of Drug and Alcohol Abuse.*

Fiorentine, R., Nakashima, J., & Anglin, M. D. (1999). Client engagement in treatment. *Journal of Substance-Abuse Treatment, 17,* 199–206.

First, M. B., Spitzer, R. L., Gibbon, M., & Williams, J. B. W. (1996). *Structured clinical interview for DSM-IV Axis 1 disorders—Patient edition (SCID-I/P, Version 2.0).* New York: Biometrics Research Department.

Fisher, M., & Bently, K. (1996). Two group therapy models for clients with a dual diagnosis of substance abuse and personality disorder. *Psychiatric Service, 47,* 1244–1250.

Flanigan, T. P., Kim, J. Y., Zierler, S., Rich, J., Vigilante, K., & Bury-Maynard, D. (1996). A prison release program for HIV-positive women: Linking them to health services and community follow up. *American Journal of Public Health, 86,* 886–887.

Fletcher, B. W., Inciardi, J. A., & Horton, A. M. (Eds.). (1994). *Drug abuse treatment: The implementation of innovative approaches to drug abuse treatment.* Westport, CT: Greenwood Press.

Fortney, J., Booth, B., Zhang, M., Humphrey, J., & Wiseman, E. (1998). Controlling for selection bias in the evaluation of Alcoholics Anonymous as aftercare treatment. *Journal of Studies on Alcohol, 59,* 690–697.

French, M. T. (1999a). *Drug abuse treatment cost analysis program (DATCAP): Program version user's manual* (4th ed.). Coral Gables, FL: University of Miami.

French, M. T. (1999b). *Drug abuse treatment cost analysis program (DATCAP): Program version* (6th ed.). Coral Gables, FL: University of Miami.

French, M. T. (2000). Economic evaluation of alcohol treatment services. *Evaluation and Program Planning, 23*(1), 27–39.

French, M. T., Dennis, M. I., McDougal, G. L., Karuntzos, G. T., & Hubbard, R. L. (1992). Training and employment programs in methadone treatment: Client needs and desires. *Journal of Substance-Abuse Treatment, 9,* 293–303.

French, M. T., Dunlap, L. J., Zarkin, G. A., McGeary, K. A., & McLellan, A. T. (1997). A structured instrument for estimating the economic cost of drug abuse treatment: The drug abuse treatment cost analysis program (DATCAP). *Journal of Substance-Abuse Treatment, 14,* 1–11.

French, M. T., McCollister, K. E., Sacks, S., McKendrick, K., & De Leon, G. (2000a). *Benefit-cost analysis of a modified therapeutic community for mentally ill chemical abusers.* Manuscript submitted for publication.

French, M. T., McGeary, K. A., Chitwood, D. D., McCoy, C. B., Inciardi, J. A., & McBride, D. (2000c). Chronic drug use and crime. *Substance Abuse, 21*(2), 95–109.

French, M. T., Roebuck, M. C., Dennis, M. L., Diamond, G., Godley, S. H., Tims, F., Webb, C., & Herrell, J. M. (in press). The economic cost of outpatient marijuana treatment for adolescents: Findings from a multisite field experiment. *Journal of Substance-Abuse Treatment.*

French, M. T., Salomè, H. J., Sindelar, J. L., & McLellan, A. T. (2000b). *Benefit-cost analysis of substance-abuse treatment: Methodological guidelines and application using the DATCAP and ASI.* Manuscript submitted for publication.

French, M. T., Zarkin, G. A., Bray, J. W., & Hartwell, T. D. (1999). Costs of employee assistance programs: Comparison of national estimates from 1993 and 1995. *Journal of Behavioral Health Services and Research, 26*(1), 95–103.

French, M. T., Zarkin, G. A., Hubbard, R. L., & Rachal, J. V. (1991). The impact of time in treatment on the employment and earnings of drug abusers. *American Journal of Public Health, 81*(7), 904–907.

Freudenberg, N. (1998, November). *Barriers to implementing promising systemic and programmatic approaches for working with substance-abusing youthful offenders.* Paper presented at the Juvenile Justice & Substance Abuse National Planning meeting, Annapolis, MD.

Freudenberg, N., Wilets, I., Greene, M. B., & Richie, B. E. (1998). Linking women in jail to community services: Factors associated with rearrest and retention of drug-using women following release from jail. *JAMWA, 53,* 89–93.

Fuller, M. G., Fishman, E., Taylor, C. A., & Wood, R. B. (1994). Screening patients with traumatic brain injuries for substance abuse. *Journal of Neuropsychiatry and Clinical Neuroscience, 6,* 143–146.

Fureman, B., Parikh, G., Bragg, A., & McLellan, A. T. (1990). *Addiction Severity Index* (5th ed.). Philadelphia: University of Pennsylvania Center for the Studies of Addiction.

Galanter, M., Egelko, S., De Leon, G., & Rohrs, C. (1993). A general hospital day program combining peer-led and professional treatment of cocaine abusers. *Hospital and Community Psychiatry, 44,* 644–649.

Gandossy, R. P., Williams, J. R., Cohen, J., & Harwood, H. J. (1980). *Drugs and crime: A survey and analysis of the literature.* Washington, DC: U.S. Department of Justice.

Gelber, S. (1999a, November). *Adult and juvenile justice: Creating organized systems of care using care management organizations (CMO's).* Paper presented at the meeting of the Schneider Institute for Health Policy, Heller School, Brandeis University, New York.

Gelber, S. (1999b, February). *Public sector managed care reform: The unfolding challenge for substance abuse, criminal justice, child welfare and welfare reform populations.* Paper presented at the meeting of the Brown Bag Session, CASA/Columbia.

Geller, B., Cooper, T., Watts, H., Cosby, C., & Fox, L. (1992). Early findings from a pharmokinetically designed double-blind and placebo-controlled study of lithium for adolescents comorbid with bipolar and substance dependency disorders. *Progress in Neuropsychopharmacology, Biology and Psychiatry, 16,* 281–299.

Gendreau, P. (1996). Offender rehabilitation: What we know and what needs to be done. *Criminal Justice and Behavior, 23,* 144–161.

Gendreau, P., Goggin, C., & Law, M. A. (1996). Predicting prison misconducts. *Criminal Justice and Behavior, 24,* 414–431.

Gendreau, P., Little, T., & Goggin, C. (1996). A meta-analysis of the predictors of adult offender recidivism: What works! *Criminology, 34,* 575–607.

Gendreau, P., & Ross, R. R. (1979). Effectiveness of correctional treatment: Bibliotherapy for cynics. *Crime and Delinquency, 25,* 463–489.

General Accounting Office. (1991). *Despite new strategy, few federal inmates receive treatment.* Washington, DC: Author.

General Accounting Office. (1997). *Drug courts: Overview of growth, characteristics, and results.* Washington, DC: United States General Accounting Office.

Gerstein, D. R. (1999). Outcome research: Drug abuse. In *Textbook of substance-abuse treatment* (2nd ed., pp. 135–147). Washington, DC: American Psychiatric Press.

Gerstein, D. R., & Harwood, H. J. (1990). *Treating drug problems. Vol. I (Summary): A study of the evolution and financing of public and private drug treatment systems.* Washington, DC: National Academy Press.

Gerstein, D. R., Harwood, H., Fountain, D., Suter, N., & Malloy, K. (1994). *Evaluating recovery services: The California drug and alcohol treatment assessment.* Washington, DC: National Opinion Research Center.

Gilliard, D. K. (1999). *Prison and jail inmates at midyear 1998.* Bureau of Justice Statistics Bulletin. Washington, DC: U.S. Department of Justice.

Gilliard, G. (1999, March). *Prison and jail inmates at midyear 1998. Bureau of Justice Statistics Bulletin* (NCJ 173414). Washington, DC: U.S. Department of Justice, Office of Justice Programs, http://www.ojp.usdoj.gov/bjs/abstract/pjim98.htm.

Glaser, J. B. (1990). From theory to practice: The planned treatment of drug users [Interview]. *International Journal of the Addictions, 25,* 307–343.

Glaser, J. B., & Greifinger, R. B. (1993). Correctional health care: A public health opportunity. *Annals of Internal Medicine, 118,* 139–145.

Glaser, J. B., Warchol, A., D'Angelo, J. T., & Guterman, H. (1990). Infectious diseases of geriatric inmates. *Reviews of Infectious Diseases, 12,* 683–692.

Godley, M. D., Dennis, M. L., Funk, R., Siekmann, M., & Weisheit, R. (1998). *Madison County assessment and treatment alternative court—Final evaluation report.* Bloomington, IL: Chestnut Health Systems.

Goerdt, J. S., & Martin, J. A. (1989, Fall). The impact of drug cases on case processing in urban trial courts. *State Court Journal,* pp. 4–12.

Gold, M. R., Siegel, J. E., Russell, L. B., & Weinstein, M. C. (1996). *Cost-effectiveness in health and medicine.* New York: Oxford University Press.

Goldkamp, J. (1993). The relative risk of implementing a treatment-oriented 'drug court': Findings from Dade County. Presented at the 45th annual meetings of the American Society of Criminology, Phoenix.

Goldkamp, J. S. (2000). The drug court response: Issues and implications for justice change. *Albany Law Review, 63*(3).

Goldkamp, J. S., & Weiland, D. (1993). Assessing the impact of Dade County's felony drug court. Research in brief. Washington, DC: U.S. Department of Justice, National Institute of Justice.

Gorsuch, R. L. (1995). Religious aspects of substance abuse and recovery. *Journal of Social Issues, 51*(2), 86–83.

Gottfredson, D. C., & Exum, M. L. (2000). *The Baltimore city drug treatment court: First evaluation report.* College Park, MD: Department of Criminology and Criminal Justice, University of Maryland.

Gottfredson, M., & Hirschi, T. (1990). *A general theory of crime.* Palo Alto, CA: Stanford University Press.

Gottheil, E., McLellan, T., & Druley, K. A. (1992). Length of stay, patient severity and treatment outcome: Sample data from the field of alcoholism. *Journal of Studies on Alcohol, 53,* 69–75.

Graham, W. F., & Wexler, H. K. (1997). The Amity therapeutic community program at Donovan prison: Program description and approach. In G. De Leon (Ed.), *Community as method* (pp. 69–86). Westport, CT: Praeger.

Granfield, R., & Eby, C. (1997). An evaluation of the Denver drug court: The impact of a treatment oriented drug offender system. Denver, CO: Department of Sociology, University of Denver.

Grant, B. (2000). Estimates of U.S. children exposed to alcohol abuse and dependence in the family. *American Journal of Public Health, 90,* 113–115.

Greenley, J. R. (1992). Neglected organizational and management issues in mental health systems development. *Community Mental Health Journal, 28,* 371–384.

Greenwood, P. W. (1995). Strategies for improving coordination between enforcement and treatment efforts in controlling illegal drug use. *Journal of Drug Issues, 25,* 73–89.

Greenwood, P., Rydell, C., Abrahamse, A., Caulkins, J., Chiesa, J., Model, K. E., & Klein, S. P. (1994). *Three strikes and you're out: Estimated benefits and costs of California's new mandatory sentencing law* (MR-509-RC). Santa Monica, CA: RAND.

Greenwood, P. W., & Zimring, F. E. (1985). *One more chance: The pursuit of promising intervention strategies for chronic delinquent offenders.* Santa Monica, CA: Rand.

Grella, C. E., Polinsky, M. L., Hser, Y. I., & Perry, S. M. (1999). Characteristics of women-only and mixed-gender drug abuse treatment programs. *Journal of Substance-Abuse Treatment, 17*(1–2), 37–44.

Griffith, J. D., Hiller, M. L., Knight, K., & Simpson, D. D. (1999). A cost-effectiveness analysis of in-prison therapeutic community treatment and risk classification. *Prison Journal, 79*(3), 352–368.

Grinstead, O. A., Zack, B., Faigeles, B., Grossman, N., & Blea, L. (1999). Reducing post-release HIV risk among male prison inmates: A peer-led intervention. *Criminal Justice and Behavior, 26,* 453–465.

Groah, C., Goodall, P., Kreutzer, J. S., Sherron, P., & Wehman, P. H. (1990). Addressing substance abuse issues in the context of a supported employment program. *Cognitive Rehabilitation, 8,* 8–12.

Guerin, P., Hyde, R., Carrier, L., Denman, K., Frerichs, R., Halsted, J., Kurhajetz, S., & Neely, J. (1998). *Final report—Process evaluation of the administrative office of the courts drug court programs: First Judicial District Court, Third Judicial District Court, and Bernalillo County Metropolitan Court.* Albuquerque, NM: Institute for Social Research, University of New Mexico.

Haapanen, R. (2000). Does drug testing matter? *National Institute of Justice Journal,* p. 28.

Hall, S. (1998). Drug abuse treatment. In E. A. Blechman & K. D. Brownell (Eds.), *Behavioral medicine & women: A comprehensive handbook* (pp. 420–424). York, PA: Guilford Press.

Hall, S. M., Havassy, B. E., & Wasserman, D. A. (1991). Effects of commitment to abstinence, positive moods, stress, and coping on relapse to cocaine use. *Journal of Consulting and Clinical Psychology, 59,* 526–532.

Hall, S. M., Loeb, P., Coyne, K., & Cooper, J. (1981). Increasing employment in ex-heroin addicts: I. Criminal justice sample. *Behavior Therapy, 12,* 443–452.

Hammett, T. M. (1998). *Public health/corrections collaborations: Prevention and treatment of HIV/AIDS, STDs, and TB.* Washington, DC: U.S. Department of Justice.

Hammett, T. M., & Harmon, P. (1999). Sexually transmitted diseases and hepatitis: Burden of disease among inmates. In *1996–1997 Update: HIV/AIDS, STDs, and*

TB in correctional facilities (National Institute of Justice, NCJ 157642). Washington, DC: U.S. Department of Justice.

Hammett, T. M., Harmon, P., & Maruschak, L. M. (1999). *1996–1997 Update: HIV/AIDS, STDs, and TB in correctional facilities* (NCJ 176344). Washington, DC: U.S. Department of Justice.

Hanlon, T. E., Nurco, D. N., Bateman, R. W., & O'Grady, K. E. (1998). The response of drug abuser parolees to a combination of treatment and intensive supervision. *Prison Journal, 78,* 31–44.

Hanlon, T. E., Nurco, D. N., Bateman, R. W., & O'Grady, K. E. (1999). The relative effects of three approaches to the parole supervision of narcotic addicts and cocaine abusers. *Prison Journal, 79,* 163–181.

Hanlon, T. E., Nurco, D. N., Kinlock, T. W., & Duszynski, K. R. (1990). Trends in criminal activity and drug use over an addiction career. *American Journal of Drug and Alcohol Abuse, 16,* 223–238.

Harlow, C. W. (1998). *Profile of jail inmates 1996. Bureau of Justice Statistics Special Report* (NCJ172871). Washington, DC: Department of Justice, Office of Justice Programs, http://www.ojp.usdoj.gov/bjs/abstract/pji96.htm.

Harm, N. J., Thompson, P. J., & Chambers, H. (1998). The effectiveness of parent education for substance abusing women offenders. *Alcoholism Treatment Quarterly, 16*(3), 63–77.

Harrell, A. (2000). Unpublished findings from the Evaluation of Breaking the Cycle.

Harrell, A., Cavanagh, S., & Roman, J. (1999). *Final report: Findings from the evaluation of the District of Columbia Superior Court drug intervention program.* Washington, DC: The Urban Institute.

Harrell, A., Cook, F., & Carver, J. (1998, July). Breaking the cycle of drug abuse Birmingham. *National Institute of Justice Journal* (pp. 9–13). Washington, DC: U.S. Department of Justice.

Harrell, A., & Smith, B. (1996). Evaluation of the District of Columbia Superior Court drug intervention program: Focus group interviews. Report to the National Institute of Justice. Washington, DC: The Urban Institute.

Harrison, L. D., Butzin, C. A., Inciardi, J. A., & Martin, S. S. (1998). Integrating HIV-prevention strategies in a therapeutic community work-release program for criminal offenders. *Prison Journal, 78,* 232–244.

Hart, T. C., & Reaves, B. A. (1999). *Felony defendants in large urban counties, 1996.* Washington, DC: U.S. Department of Justice, Bureau of Justice Statistics.

Harwood, H. J., Hubbard, R. L., Collins, J. J., & Rachal, J. V. (1988). The costs of crime and the benefits of drug abuse treatment: A cost-benefit analysis using TOPS data. In C. G. Leukefeld & F. M Tims (Eds.), *Compulsory treatment of drug abuse: Research and clinical practice.* [Research monograph series 86]. Rockville, MD: National Institute on Drug Abuse.

Hawkins, J. D., Catalano, R. F., & Miller, J. Y. (1992). Risk and protective factors for alcohol and other drug problems in adolescence and early adulthood: Implications for substance abuse prevention. *Psychological Bulletin, 112*(1), 64–105.

Hawkins, J. D., Jenson, J. M., Catalano, R. F., & Wells, E. A. (1991). Effects of a skills training intervention with juvenile delinquents. *Research on Social Work Practice, 1,* 107–121.

Henderson, D. J. (1998). Drug abuse and incarcerated women. *Journal of Substance-Abuse Treatment, 15*(6), 579–587.

Henggeler, S. W. (1997). The development of effective drug-abuse services for youth. In J. A. Egertson, D. M. Fox, & A. I. Leshner (Eds.), *Treating drug abuse effectively.* Williston, VT: Blackwell Publishers.

Henggeler, S. W., Pickrel, S. G., & Brondino, M. J. (1999). Multisystemic treatment of substance-abusing and dependent delinquents: Outcomes, treatment, fidelity, and transportability. *Mental Health Services Research, 1,* 171–184.

Henggeler, S. W., Pickrel, S. G., Brondino, M. J., & Crouch, J. L. (1996). Eliminating (almost) treatment dropout of substance abusing or dependent delinquents through home-based multisystemic therapy. *American Journal of Psychiatry, 153,* 427–428.

Henggeler, S. W., Schoenwald, S. K., Pickrel, S. G., Brondino, M. J., Borduin, C. M., & Hall, J. A. (1994). *Treatment manual for family preservation using multisystemic therapy.* Charleston, SC: Medical University of South Carolina.

Henry, D. A., & Clark, J. (1990). Pretrial drug testing: An overview of issues and practices. Washington, DC: U.S. Department of Justice, Office of Justice Programs, Bureau of Justice Assistance.

Hepburn, J. (1996). *User accountability and long-term recidivism.* A report submitted to The National Institute of Justice. Washington, DC: U.S. Department of Justice.

Hepburn, J. R. (1994). Classifying drug offenders for treatment. In D. L. MacKenzie & C. D. Uchida (Eds.), *Drug and crime: Evaluating public policy initiatives* (pp. 172–187). Thousand Oaks, CA: Sage.

Hepworth, D. H., Rooney, R. H., & Larson, J. A. (1997). *Direct social work practice: Theory and skills* (3rd ed.). Pacific Grove, CA: Brooks/Cole.

Hermalin, J. A., Steer, R. A., Platt, J. J., & Mettzger, D. S. (1990). Risk characteristics associated with chronic unemployment in methadone clients. *Drug and Alcohol Dependence, 26,* 117–125.

Higgins, S. T., & Budney, A. L. (1997). From the initial clinic contact to aftercare: A brief review of effective strategies for retaining cocaine abusers in treatment. In L. Onken, J. Blaine, & J. Boren (Eds.), *Beyond the therapeutic alliance: Keeping the drug-dependent individual in treatment* (NIH Publication No. 97-4142, NIDA Research Monograph 165, pp. 25–43). Rockville, MD: National Institute on Drug Abuse, U.S. Department of Health and Human Services.

Higgins, S., Wong, C., & Badger, G. (2000). Contingent reinforcement increases cocaine abstinence during outpatient treatment and one year of follow-up. *Journal of Consulting & Clinical Psychology, 68*(1), 64–72.

Hiller, M. L., Knight, K., Broome, K. M., & Simpson, D. D. (1998). Legal pressure and treatment retention in a national sample of long-term residential programs. *Criminal Justice and Behavior, 25*(4), 463–481.

Hiller, M. L., Knight, K., & Simpson, D. D. (1999). Prison-based substance-abuse treatment, residential aftercare, and recidivism. *Addiction, 94*(6), 833–842.

Hiller, M. L., Knight, K., & Simpson, D. D. (1999). Risk factors that predict dropout from corrections-based treatment for drug abuse. *Prison Journal, 79*, 411–430.

Hiller, M. L., Knight, K., & Simpson, D. D. (2000, March). *Psychosocial and motivational influences on early engagement and the treatment process.* Paper presented at the annual meeting of the Academy of Criminal Justice Sciences (ACJS), New Orleans, LA.

Hills, H. (2000). *Creating effective treatment programs for persons with co-occurring disorders in the justice system.* Delmar, NY: The National GAINS Center.

Hillsman, S. T. (1982). Pretrial diversion of youthful adults: A decade of reform and research. *Justice System Journal, 7*, 361–387.

Hitchcock, H. C., Stainback, R. D., & Roque, G. M. (1995). Effects of halfway house placement on retention of patients in substance abuse aftercare. *American Journal of Drug and Alcohol Abuse, 21*(3), 379–390.

Hogue, A., Liddle, H., Rowe, C., Turner, R., Dakof, G., & LaPann, K. (1998). Treatment adherence and differentiation in individual versus family therapy for adolescent substance abuse. *Journal of Counseling Psychology, 45*, 104–114.

Holden, G. H., Wakefield, P., & Shapiro, S. J. (1990). *Treatment options for drug-dependent offenders: A review of the literature for state and local decision-makers.* Washington, DC: National Criminal Justice Association.

Hooper, R. M., Lockwood, D., & Inciardi, J. A. (1993). Treatment techniques in corrections-based therapeutic communities. *Prison Journal, 73*, 290–306.

Hora, P. F., Schma, W. G., & Rosenthal, J. (1999). Therapeutic jurisprudence and the drug treatment court movement: Revolutionizing the criminal justice system's response to drug abuse and crime in America. *Notre Dame Law Review, 74*(2), 439–537.

Horowitz, E. (1999, November). *Hepatitis C: Current concepts by the California Department of Corrections.* Paper presented at the National Conference on Correctional Health Care meeting, Fort Lauderdale, FL.

Horsburgh, C. R., Jarvis, J. Q., McArthur, T., Ignacio, T., & Stock, P. (1990). Seroconversion to HIV in prison inmates. *American Journal of Public Health, 80*, 209–210.

Hosmer, D. W., & Lemeshow, S. (1989). *Applied logistic regression.* New York: John Wiley & Sons.

Hser, Y. I., & Anglin, M. D. (1991). Criminal justice and the drug-abusing offender: Policy issues of coerced treatment. *Behavioral Sciences and the Law, 9*, 243–267.

Hser, Y.-I., Anglin, M. D., Grella, C., Longshore, D., & Prendergast, M. L. (1997). Drug treatment careers: A conceptual framework and existing research findings. *Journal of Substance-Abuse Treatment, 14*, 543–558.

Hser, Y.-I., Anglin, M. D., & Powers, K. (1993). A 24-year follow-up of California narcotics addicts. *Archives of General Psychiatry, 50*, 577–584.

Hser, Y.-I., Grella, C., Chou, C., & Anglin, M. D. (1998). Relationships between drug treatment careers and outcomes: Findings from the National Drug Abuse Treatment Outcome Study. *Evaluation Review, 22*, 496–519.

Hser, Y.-I., Joshi, V., Anglin, M. D., & Fletcher, B. (1999). Predicting posttreatment cocaine abstinence for first-time admissions and treatment repeaters. *American Journal of Public Health, 89,* 666–671.

Hser, Y. I., Maglione, M., Polinsky, M. L., & Anglin, M. D. (1998). Predicting drug treatment entry among treatment-seeking individuals. *Journal of Substance-Abuse Treatment, 15,* 213–220.

Hser, Y.-I., Yamaguchi, K., Chen, J., & Anglin, M. D. (1995). Effects of interventions on relapse to narcotics addiction: An event history analysis. *Evaluation Review, 19,* 123–140.

Hubbard, R. L. (1997). Evaluation and outcome of treatment. In J. H. Lowinson, P. Ruiz, R. B. Millman, & J. G. Langrod (Eds.), *Substance abuse: A comprehensive textbook* (3rd ed., pp. 499–511). Baltimore: Williams & Wilkins.

Hubbard, R. L., Collins, J. J., Rachal, J. V., & Cavanaugh, E. R. (1988). The criminal justice client in drug abuse treatment. In C. G. Leukefeld & F. M. Tims (Eds.), *Compulsory treatment of drug abuse: Research and clinical practice* (NIDA Research Monograph 86, pp. 57–80). Rockville, MD: National Institute on Drug Abuse.

Hubbard, R. L., Craddock, S. G., Flynn, P. M., Anderson, J., & Etheridge, R. M. (1997). Overview of 1-year follow-up outcomes in the Drug Abuse Treatment Outcome Study (DATOS). *Psychology of Addictive Behaviors, 11,* 261–278.

Hubbard, R., & Harwood, H. (1981). *Employment related services in drug treatment programs* (DHHS Publication No. ADM 81-1144). National Institute on Drug Abuse Treatment Research Report. Rockville, MD: U.S. Department of Health and Human Services.

Hubbard, R. L., Marsden, M. E., Rachal, J. V., Harwood, H. J., Cavanaugh, E. R., & Ginzburg, H. M. (1989). *Drug abuse treatment: A national study of effectiveness.* Chapel Hill, NC: University of North Carolina Press.

Hubbard, R. L., Rachal, J. V., Craddock, S. G., & Cavanaugh, E. R. (1984). Treatment outcome prospective study (TOPS): Client characteristics and behaviors before, during, and after treatment. In F. M. Tims & J. P. Ludford (Eds.), *Drug abuse treatment evaluation: Strategies, process and prospects.* National Institute on Drug Abuse Monograph 51 (pp. 42–68). Washington, DC: National Institute of Drug Abuse.

Hughes, P. H., Coletti, S. D., Neri, R. L., Stahl, S., Urmann, C. F., Sicilian, D. M., & Anthony, J. C. (1994). Retention of cocaine abusing women in residential treatment. In L. S. Harris (Ed.), *Problems of drug dependence 1993* (NIDA Research Monograph). Washington, DC: National Institutes of Health.

Hughey, R., & Klemke, L. W. (1996). Evaluation of a jail-based substance-abuse treatment program. *Federal Probation, 60*(4), 40–44.

Hunt, D. E. (1997). A selected bibliography on the drug use(r) "career." *Substance Use & Misuse, 32,* 283–291.

Hunt, W. A., Barnett, L. W., & Branch, L. G. (1971). Relapse rates in addiction programs. *Journal of Clinical Psychology, 22,* 11–17.

Hutchins, E. (1995). Psychosocial risk factors associated with drug use during pregnancy. Unpublished doctoral dissertation, Johns Hopkins University, Baltimore.

Iguchi, M. Y. (1998). Drug abuse treatment as HIV risk prevention: Changes in social drug use patterns might also reduce risk. *Journal of Addictive Diseases, 17,* 9–32.

Inciardi, J. A. (1988). Compulsory treatment in New York: A brief narrative history of misjudgment, mismanagement, and misrepresentation. *Journal of Drug Issues, 18,* 547–560.

Inciardi, J. A. (1988). Some consideration on the clinical efficacy of compulsory treatment: Reviewing the New York experience. In C. Leukefeld & F. Timms (Eds.), *Compulsory treatment of drug abuse: Research and clinical practice* (NIDA Research Monograph 86, DHHS Publication No. ADM 89-1578, 126–138). Washington, DC: U.S. Government Printing Office.

Inciardi, J. A. (1992). *The war on drugs II: The continuing epic of heroin, cocaine, crack, crime, AIDS, and public policy.* Mountain View, CA: Mayfield.

Inciardi, J. A. (1993). *Drug treatment and criminal justice.* Newbury Park, CA: Sage.

Inciardi, J. A. (1994). *Screening and assessment for alcohol and other drug abuse among adults in the criminal justice system* (DHHS Publication No. SMA 94-2076). Rockville, MD: U.S. Department of Health and Human Services.

Inciardi, J. A. (1996). HIV risk reduction and service delivery strategies in criminal justice settings. *Journal of Substance-Abuse Treatment, 13,* 421–428.

Inciardi, J. A., & Harrison, L. D. (2000). *Harm reduction: National and international perspectives.* Thousand Oaks, CA: Sage.

Inciardi, J. A., Lockwood, D. A., & Martin, S. S. (1991, May). *Therapeutic communities in corrections and work release.* Paper presented at the National Institute on Drug Abuse Technical Review Meeting on Therapeutic Community Research, Bethesda, MD.

Inciardi, J. A., Lockwood, D., & Quinlan, J. A. (1993). Drug use in prison: Patterns, processes, and implications for treatment. *Journal of Drug Issues, 23*(1), 119–129.

Inciardi, J. A., Martin, S. S., Butzin, C. A., Hooper, R. M., & Harrison, L. D. (1997, Spring). An effective model of prison-based treatment for drug-involved offenders. *Journal of Drug Issues, 27,* 261–278.

Inciardi, J. A., & McBride, D. C. (1991). *Treatment alternatives to street crime: History, experiences, and issues.* National Institute on Drug Abuse (DHHS Pub. No. ADM 91-1749). Washington, DC: U.S. Government Printing Office.

Inciardi, J. A., McBride, D. C., & Rivers, J. E. (1996). *Drug control and the courts.* Thousand Oaks, CA: Sage.

Inciardi, J. A., & Pottieger, A. E. (1991). Kids, crack, and crime. *Journal of Drug Issues, 21,* 257–270.

Inciardi, J., & Pottegier, A. (1998). Drug use and street crime in Miami: An (almost) twenty-year retrospective. *Substance Use & Misuse, 33,* 1839–1870.

Indermaur, D. (1999). Situational prevention of violent crime: Theory and practice in Australia. *Studies on Crime and Crime Prevention, 8,* 71–87.

Ingram-Fogel, C. (1991). Health problems and needs of incarcerated women. *Journal of Prison & Jail Health, 10*(1), 43–57.

Innes, C. (1997). Patterns of misconduct in the federal prisons system. *Criminal Justice Review, 22,*157–174.

Innes, C. A. (1988). *Special report: Profiles of state prison inmates, 1986.* Washington, DC: U.S. Department of Justice, Bureau of Justice Statistics.

Institute of Medicine. (1996). *Pathways of addiction: Opportunities in drug abuse research.* Washington, DC: National Academy Press.

Intagliata, J. (1982). Improving the quality of community care for the chronically mentally disabled: The role of case management. *Schizophrenia Bulletin, 8,* 655–674.

Ito, J. R., & Donovan, D. M. (1990). Predicting drinking outcome: Demography, chronicity, coping, and aftercare. *Addictive Behaviors, 15,* 553–559.

Jainchill, N., Hawke, J., DeLeon, G., & Yagelka, J. (2000). Adolescents in TCs: One-year post-treatment outcomes. *Journal of Psychoactive Drugs, 32,* 81–94.

James, A. L., Bottomley, A. K., Liebling, A., & Clare, E. (1997). *Privatizing prisons: Rhetoric and reality.* Thousand Oaks, CA: Sage.

Jameson, R., & Peterson, N. A. (1995). Evaluation of the first year of operation of the Jackson County drug court. Kansas City, MO: Ewing Marion Kauffman Foundation.

Japha, A. (1978). The nation's toughest drug law: Final report of the Joint Committee on the NY drug law evaluation. Washington, DC: National Institute of Law Enforcement and Criminal Justice.

Joe, G. W., Brown, B., & Simpson, D. D. (1995). Psychological problems and client engagement in methadone treatment. *Journal of Nervous and Mental Diseases, 183,* 704–710.

Joe, G. W., Chastain, R. L., & Simpson, D. (1990). Relapse. In D. D. Simpson & S. B. Sells (Eds.), *Opioid addiction and treatment: A 12-year follow-up* (pp. 121–136). Malabar, FL: Krieger.

Joe, G. W., Knezek, L. D., Watson, D. D., & Simpson, D. D. (1991). Depression and decision-making among intravenous drug users. *Psychological Reports, 68,* 339–347.

Joe, G. W., Simpson, D. D., & Broome, K. M. (1998). Effects of readiness for drug abuse treatment on client retention and assessment of process. *Addiction, 93,* 1177–1190.

Johnson, B. D., Williams, T., Dei, K. A., & Sanabria, H. (1990). Drug abuse in the inner city: Impact on hard-drug users and the community. In M. Tonry & J. Q. Wilson (Eds.), *Drugs and crime* (pp. 9–67). Chicago: University of Chicago Press.

Johnston, L., O'Malley, P., & Bachman, J. G. (1999). *National survey results on drug use from The Monitoring The Future Study, 1975–1997.* Rockville, MD: U.S. Department of Health and Human Services. National Institute on Drug Abuse.

Jones, B. T., & McMahon, J. (1996). Changes in alcohol expectancies during treatment relate to subsequent abstinence survivorship. *British Journal of Clinical Psychology, 35,* 221–234.

Jones, C. C., Waskin, H., Gerety, B., Skipper, B. J., Hull, H. F., & Mertz, G. J. (1987). Persistence of high-risk sexual activity among homosexual men in an area of low incidence of the acquired immunodeficiency syndrome. *Sexually Transmitted Diseases, 14,* 79–82.

Jones, M. (1953). *Therapeutic community: A new treatment method in psychiatry.* New York: Basic Books.

Jordan, B. K., Schlenger, W. E., Fairbank, J. A., & Caddell, J. M. (1996). Prevalence of psychiatric disorders among incarcerated women. *Archives of General Psychiatry, 53,* 513–519.

Kahan, D. (1997). Between economics and sociology: The new path of deterrence. *Michigan Law Review, 95*(8), 2477–2498.

Kamisar, Y., LaFave, W., & Israel, J. (1995). *Modern criminal procedure.* St. Paul, MN: West Publishing.

Kane, R. (1995). A sentencing model for the 21st century. *Federal Probation, 59*(3), 10–16.

Kanter, J. (1996). Case management with long-term patients: A comprehensive approach. In S. Soreff (Ed.), *Handbook for the treatment of the seriously mentally ill* (pp. 171–189). Seattle, WA: Hogrefe & Huber.

Kenkel, D. (1997). On valuing morbidity, cost-effectiveness analysis, and being rude. *Journal of Health Economics, 16,* 749–757.

Kennedy, D., Nair, G., Elliot, L., & Ditton, J. (1991). Drug misuse and sharing of needles in Scottish prisons. *British Medical Journal, 301,* 1507.

Kessler, R. C., McGonagle, K. A., Zhao, S., Nelson, C. B., Hughes, M., Eshleman, Wit, H. U., & Kendler, K. S. (1994). Lifetime and 12-month prevalence of DSM-III-R Psychiatric Disorders in the United States: Results from the national comorbidity survey. *Archives of General Psychiatry, 51,* 8–19.

Khalsa, H., & Anglin, M. D. (1991). *Treatment effectiveness for cocaine abuse: Cocaine today and its effects on the individual and society.* United Nations Interregional Crime and Research Institute Monograph (UNICRI Pub. No. 44, pp. 89–98). New York: United Nations.

King, R. (1972). *The drug hang-up: America's fifty-year folly.* New York: W. W. Norton.

Kinlock, T. W., Hanlon, T. E., & Nurco, D. N. (1998). Heroin use in the United States: History and present developments. In J. A. Inciardi & L. Harrison (Eds.), *Heroin in the age of crack-cocaine* (pp. 1–30). Thousand Oaks, CA: Sage.

Kinlock, T. W., Hanlon, T. E., & Nurco, D. N. (1999). Criminal justice responses to adult substance abuse. In R. E. Tarter, R. T. Ammerman, & P. J. Ott (Eds.), *Prevention and societal impact of drug and alcohol abuse* (pp. 202–220). Mahwah, NJ: Erlbaum.

Kitchener, H. L., & Teitelbaum, H. (1986). *A review of research on implementation of NARA title II in the bureau of prisons.* Washington, DC: Federal Bureau of Prisons.

Kleiman, M. (1992). *Against excess: Drug policy for results.* New York: Basic Books.

Kleiman, M. (1996, Spring). Coerced abstinence for drug-involved offenders on probation and parole: A proposed experiment. *On Balance*, pp. 4–6.

Kleiman, M. A. R. (1986). *Bringing back street-level heroin enforcement.* Presented at Workshop on Drugs and Crime, Atlanta, GA: National Research Council and National Institute of Justice.

Kleiman, M. A. R. (1997). Coerced abstinence: A neo-paternalistic drug policy initiative. In L. A. Mead (Ed.), *The new paternalism.* Washington, DC: Brookings Institution Press.

Klitzner, M., Fisher, D., Stewart, K., & Gilbert, S. (1991). *Report to the Robert Wood Johnson Foundation on strategies for early intervention with children and youth to avoid abuse of addictive substances.* Bethesda, MD: Pacific Institute for Research and Evaluation.

Knibb, M. A. (1987). *The Qumran Community Cambridge commentaries on writings of the inter-testament period 200BC to 200AD* (Vol. 2). London: Cambridge University Press.

Knight, K., & Hiller, M. L. (1997). Community-based substance-abuse treatment for probationers: 1-year outcome evaluation of the Dallas County Judicial Treatment Center. *Federal Probation, 61*(2), 61–68.

Knight, K., Hiller, M. L., Broome, K. M., & Simpson, D. D. (2000, March). *Screening offenders for substance use problems.* Paper presented at the annual meeting of the Academy of Criminal Justice Sciences (ACJS), New Orleans, LA.

Knight, K., Hiller, M. L., Broome, K. M., & Simpson, D. D. (in press). Legal pressure, treatment readiness, and engagement in long-term residential programs. *Journal of Offender Rehabilitation.*

Knight, K., Simpson, D. D., Chatham, L. R., & Camacho, L. M. (1997). An assessment of prison-based drug treatment: Texas' in-prison therapeutic community program. *Journal of Offender Rehabilitation, 24*(3/4), 75–100.

Knight, K., Simpson, D. D., & Hiller, M. L. (1996). Evaluation of prison-based treatment and aftercare. Paper presented at the annual meeting of the American Psychological Association, Toronto, Canada.

Knight, K., Simpson, D. D., & Hiller, M. L. (1999). Three-year reincarceration outcomes for in-prison therapeutic community treatment in Texas. *Prison Journal, 79*(3), 337–351.

Krueger, S. (1997). Five-year recidivism study of MRT-treated offenders in a county jail. *Cognitive-Behavioral Treatment Review, 6,* 3.

Kumpfer, K., & Alvarado, R. (1998). *Effective family strengthening interventions.* Washington, DC: U.S. Department of Justice.

Lake, E. (1993). An exploration of the violent victim experiences of female offenders. *Violence and Victims, 8,* 41–51.

Lang, M., & Belenko, S. (2000). Predicting retention in a residential drug treatment alternative to prison program. *Journal of Substance-Abuse Treatment, 19,* 145–160.

Langeland, W., & Hartgers, C. (1998). Child sexual abuse and alcoholism: A review. *Journal of Studies on Alcohol, 59,* 336–348.

Lanier, M. M., Pack, R. P., & DiClemente, R. J. (1999). Changes in incarcerated adolescents' human immunodeficiency virus knowledge and selected behaviors from 1988 to 1996. *Journal of Adolescent Health, 25,* 182–186.

Lash, S. J. (1998). Increasing participation in substance abuse aftercare treatment. *American Journal of Drug and Alcohol Abuse, 24*(1), 31–37.

Lawental, E., McLellan, A., Grissom, G., Brill, P., & O'Brien, C. (1996). Coerced treatment for substance abuse problems detected through workplace urine surveillance: Is it effective? *Journal of Substance Abuse, 8*(1), 115–128.

Lazar Institute. (1976). *Phase I report, treatment alternatives to street crime (TASC) national evaluation program.* Washington, DC: Law Enforcement Assistance Administration.

Lees, J., Manning, N., Menzies, D., & Morant, N. (Eds.). (in press). *Researching therapeutic communities.* London: Kingsley Publishers.

Leshner, A. E. (1997). Addiction is a brain disease, and it matters. *Science, 278,* 45–47.

Leukefeld, C. G. (1985). The clinical connection: Drugs and crime. *International Journal of the Addictions, 20,* 1049–1064.

Leukefeld, C. G. (1990, Fall). Opportunities for strengthening community corrections with coerced drug abuse treatment. *Perspectives: Journal of the American Probation and Parole Association,* pp. 6–9.

Leukefeld, C. G., & Leukefeld, S. (1999). Primary socialization theory and a bio/psycho/social/spiritual practice model for substance use. *Substance Use/Misuse, 34,* 983–991.

Leukefeld, C. G., Logan, T. K., Martin, S. S., Purvis, R. T., & Farabee, D. (1998). A health services use framework for drug-abusing offenders. *American Behavioral Scientist, 41*(8), 1123–1135.

Leukefeld, C. G., Pickens, R. W., & Schuster, C. R. (1992). Recommendations for improving drug treatment. *International Journal of the Addictions, 27,* 1223–1239.

Leukefeld, C. G., & Tims, F. M. (Eds.). (1988). *Compulsory treatment for drug abuse; Research and clinical practice* (NIDA Research Monograph 86). Washington, DC: U.S. Government Printing Office.

Leukefeld, C. G., & Tims, F. R. (1988). Compulsory treatment: A review of the findings. In C. G. Leukefeld & F. M. Tims (Eds.), *Compulsory treatment of drug abuse: Research and clinical practice* (NIDA Research Monograph 86. DHHS Publication No. ADM 88-1578, pp. 236–251). Washington, DC: U.S. Government Printing Office.

Leukefeld, C. G., & Tims, F. M. (1992). *Drug treatment in prisons and jails* (NIDA Research Monograph 118). Washington, DC: U.S. Government Printing Office.

Leung, S. A. (1995). Career development and counseling: A multicultural perspective. In J. G. Ponterotto, J. M. Casa, L. A. Suzuki, & C. M. Alexander (Eds.), *Handbook of multicultural counseling.* Thousand Oaks, CA: Sage.

Levitt, S. (1998). Juvenile crime and punishment. *Journal of Political Economy, 106*(6), 1156–1185.

Lidz, V., Bux, D. A., Platt, J. J., & Iguchi, M. Y. (1992). Transitional case management: A service model for AIDS outreach projects. In R. S. Ashery (Ed.), *Progress and issues in case management* (pp. 112–144). Rockville, MD: National Institute on Drug Abuse.

Liebling, A. (1994). Suicide amongst women prisoners. *Howard Journal, 33*(1), 1–9.

Liese, B. S., & Najavits, L. M. (1997). Cognitive and behavioral therapies. In J. H. Lowinson, P. Ruiz, R. B. Millman, & J. G. Langrod (Eds.), *Substance abuse: A comprehensive textbook* (3rd ed., pp. 467–478). Baltimore: Williams & Wilkins.

Lilly, J. R., Cullen, F. T., & Ball, R. A. (1995). *Criminological theory: Context and consequences* (2nd ed.). Thousand Oaks, CA: Sage.

Lindblad, R. (1988). Civil commitment under the Federal Narcotic Addict Rehabilitation Act. *Journal of Drug Issues, 18,* 595–624.

Lindesmith, A. R. (1965). *The addict and the law.* Bloomington, IN: Indiana University Press.

Lipsey, M. W., & Wilson, D. B. (1998). Effective intervention for serious juvenile offenders: A synthesis of research. In R. Loeber & D. Farrington (Eds.), *Serious and violent juvenile offenders: Risk factors and successful interventions.* London: Sage.

Lipton, D. S. (1994). The correctional opportunity: Pathways to drug treatment for offenders. *Journal of Drug Issues, 24,* 331–348.

Lipton, D. S. (1995, November). *The effectiveness of treatment for drug abusers under criminal justice supervision* (National Institute of Justice Research Report, NCJ 157642). Washington, DC: U.S. Department of Justice.

Lipton, D. S., & Wexler, H. K. (1988). The drug-crime connection: Rehabilitation shows promise. *Corrections Today, 50,* 144–147.

Litwak, E., & Rothman, J. (1970). Towards the theory and practice of coordination between formal organizations. In W. R. Lofton & M. Rosengren (Eds.), *Organizations and clients: Essays—the sociology of service.* Columbus, OH: Charles E. Merrill.

Lockwood, D., Inciardi, J. A., & Surratt, H. L. (1997). CREST outreach center: A model for blending treatment and corrections. In F. M. Tims, J. A. Inciardi, B. W. Fletcher, & A. M. Horton (Eds.), *The effectiveness of innovative approaches in the treatment of drug abuse* (pp. 70–82). Westport, CT: Greenwood Press.

Lockwood, D., McCorkel, J., & Inciardi, J. A. (1998). Developing comprehensive prison-based therapeutic community treatment for women. *Drugs & Society, 13*(1/2), 193–212.

Loftin, C., & McDowall, D. (1984). The deterrent effects of the Florida felony firearm law. *Journal of Criminal Law and Criminology, 75,* 250–259.

Logan, C. H. (1992). Well kept: Comparing quality of confinement in private and public prisons. *Journal of Criminal Law and Criminology, 83,* 577–613.

Logan, C. H., & Rausch, S. P. (1985, September). Punish and profit: The emergence of private enterprise prisons. *Justice Quarterly, 2,* 303–318.

Logan, T. K., Leukefeld, C., & Williams, K. (1999). *Fayette drug court program process evaluation.* Lexington, KY: University of Kentucky, Center on Drug and Alcohol Research.

Longshore, D., Taxman, F., Turner, S., Harrell A., & Bryne, J. (2000). *Operation drug test evaluation.* Draft Report to the National Institute of Justice. Santa Monica, CA: UCLA Drug Abuse Research Group.

Longshore, D., Turner, S., & Anglin, M. D. (1998). Effects of case management on drug user's risky sex. *Prison Journal, 78*(1), 6–30.

Lowe, L., Wexler, H. K., & Peters, J. (1998). *The R. J. Donovan in-prison and community substance abuse program: Three-year return to custody data.* Sacramento, CA: Office of Substance Programs, California Department of Corrections.

Luborsky, L., McLellan, A. T., Woody, G. E., O'Brien, C. P., & Auerbach, A. (1985). Therapist success and its determinants. *Archives of General Psychiatry, 42,* 602–611.

Luengo, M. A., Carrillo-de-la-Pena, M. T., Otero, J. M., & Romero, E. (1994). A short-term longitudinal study of impulsivity and antisocial behavior. *Journal of Personality and Social Psychology, 66,* 542–548.

Lurigio, A. J., & Swartz, J. A. (1994). Life at the interface: Issues related to the implementation and evaluation of a multiphased, multiagency, jail-based, substance-abuse treatment program. *Evaluation Program Planning, 17,* 205–216.

MacKenzie, D. L. (1997). *Preventing crime: What works, what doesn't, what's promising. A report to the United States Congress.* Prepared for the National Institute of Justice.

MacKenzie, D. L. (1997). Criminal justice and crime prevention. In L. W. Sherman, D. Gottfredson, D. MacKenzie, J. Eck, P. Reuter, & S. Bushway (Eds.), *Preventing crime: What works, what doesn't, what's promising.* College Park, MD: University of Maryland.

MacKenzie, D. L., & Hebert, E. E. (1996). *Correctional boot camps: A tough intermediate sanction.* National Institute of Justice Research Report. Washington, DC: U.S. Department of Justice.

MacKenzie, D. L., & Souryal, C. (1994). *Multisite evaluation of shock incarceration.* National Institute of Justice Research Report. Washington, DC: U.S. Department of Justice.

Maddux, J. F. (1978). Drug addiction and the U.S. public health service 1935–1974. In *History of the hospital treatment programs.* Washington, DC: U.S. Government Printing Office.

Magura, S., Rosenblum, A., Lewis, C., & Joseph, H. (1993). The effectiveness of in-jail methadone maintenance. *The Journal of Drug Issues, 23,* 75–99.

Mahon, N. (1996). New York inmates' HIV risk behaviors: The implications for prevention and programs. *American Journal of Public Health, 86,* 1211–1215.

Mahon, N. (1997). Treatment in prisons and jails. In P. Lowinson (Ed.), *Substance abuse: A comprehensive textbook.* Baltimore: Williams & Wilkins.

Mark, M. M., Henry, G. T., & Julnes, G. (1999). Toward an integrative framework for evaluation practice. *American Journal of Evaluation, 20,* 177–198.

Marlowe, D. B., & Kirby, K. C. (1999). Effective use of sanctions in drug courts: Lessons from behavioral research. *National Drug Court Institute Review, 2*(1), 1–32.

Marquart, J. W., Brewer, V. E., & Mullings, J. L. (1999). Health risk as an emerging field within the new penology. *Journal of Criminal Justice, 27,* 143–154.

Marquart, J., Merianos, D., Hebert, J., & Carroll, L. (1997). Health conditions and prisoners: A review of research and emerging areas of inquiry. *Prison Journal,* 77, 184–208.

Marsh, K. L., & Simpson, D. D. (1986). Sex differences in opioid addiction careers. *American Journal of Drug and Alcohol Abuse,* 12, 309–329.

Martin, C. (1999, November). *Maximizing the use of telemedicine in the correctional setting.* Presentation given to the National Conference on Correctional Health Care Annual Meeting, Fort Lauderdale, FL.

Martin, S. S., Butzin, C. A., Saum, C. A., & Inciardi, J. A. (1999). Three-year outcomes of therapeutic community treatment for drug-involved offenders in Delaware: From prison to work release to aftercare. *Prison Journal,* 79(3), 294–320.

Martin, S. S., & Inciardi, J. A. (1993). A case management treatment program for drug-involved prison releasees. *Prison Journal,* 73, 319–331.

Martin, S. S., & Inciardi, J. A. (1997). Case management outcomes for drug-involved offenders. *Prison Journal,* 77, 168–182.

Martin, S. S., & Scarpitti, F. R. (1993). An intensive case management approach for paroled iv drug users. *Journal of Drug Issues,* 23(1), 43–59.

Martinson, R. (1974). What works? Questions and answers about prison reform. *The Public Interest,* 35, 22–54.

Martinson, R. (1979). New findings, new views: A note of caution regarding sentencing reform. *Hofstra Law Review,* 7, 252–254.

Maruschak, L. M. (1999). HIV in prisons and jails, 1996. In *1996–1997 Update: HIV/AIDS, STDs, and TB in correctional facilities* (National Institute of Justice, NCJ 157642). Washington, DC: U.S. Department of Justice.

Massing, M. (1998). *The fix.* New York: Simon and Schuster.

Maull, F. W. (1998). Issues in prison hospice: Toward a model for the delivery of hospice care in a correctional setting. *Hospice Journal,* 13, 57–82.

Mauser, E., Van Stelle, K. R., & Moberg, D. P. (1994). The economic impact of diverting substance abusing offenders into treatment. *Crime and Delinquency,* 40(4), 568–588.

McBride, D., & McCoy, C. B. (1992). The drugs-crime relationship: An analytical framework. *Prison Journal,* 73, 257–278.

McBride, D., Terry, Y., & Inciardi, J. A. (1999a). Alternative perspectives on the drug policy debate. In J. Incardi (Ed.), *The drug legalization debate* (pp. 9–54). Thousand Oaks, CA: Sage.

McBride, D., VanderWaal, C., Terry, Y., & VanBuren, H. (1999b). *Breaking the cycle of drug use among juvenile offenders* (NCJ 179273). Trans. Washington, DC: National Institute of Justice. Web-only document.

McCorkel, J. A., Butzin, C. A., Martin, S. S., & Inciardi, J. A. (1998). Use of health care services in a sample of drug-involved offenders: A comparison with national norms. *American Behavioral Scientist,* 41, 1079–1089.

McCorkel, J., Harrison, L. D., & Inciardi, J. A. (1998). How treatment is constructed among graduates and dropouts in a prison therapeutic community for women. *Journal of Offender Rehabilitation,* 27, 37–59.

McCue, M. J., Mazmanian, P. E., Hampton, C., Marks, T. K., Fisher, E., Parpart, F., Malloy, W. N., & Fisk, K. J. (1998). Cost-minimization analysis: A follow-up study of a telemedicine program. *Telemedicine Journal, 4*, 323–327.

McDonald, D. C. (1992). Private penal institutions. In M. Tonry (Ed.), *Crime and justice: A review of research, Vol. 16* (pp. 361–419). Chicago: The University of Chicago Press.

McDonald, D. C. (1999). Medical care in prison. In M. Tonry & J. Petersilia (Eds.), *Prisons* (pp. 427–478). Chicago and London: University of Chicago Press.

McDonald, D., Hassol, A., & Carlson, K. (1999, April). Can telemedicine reduce spending and improve prisoner health care? *National Institute of Justice Journal,* pp. 20–25.

McGlothlin, W. H., & Anglin, M. D. (1981). Shutting off methadone: Costs and benefits. *Archives of General Psychiatry, 38*, 885–892.

McGlothlin, W. H., Anglin, M. D., & Wilson, B. D. (1977). A follow-up of admissions to the California Civil Addict Program. *American Journal of Drug Alcohol Abuse, 4*, 179–199.

McGlothlin, W. H., Anglin, M. D., & Wilson, B. D. (1977). An evaluation of the California Civil Addict Program [Monograph Series]. Washington, DC: U.S. Government Printing Office.

McGlothlin, W. H., Anglin, M. D., & Wilson, B. D. (1978). Narcotic addiction and crime. *Criminology, 16*, 293–316.

McKay, J. R., McLellan, T. A., Alterman, A. I., Cacciola, J. S., Rutherford, M. J., & O'Brien, C. P. (1998). Predictors of participation in aftercare sessions and self-help groups following completion of intensive outpatient treatment for substance abuse. *Journal of Studies on Alcohol, 59*(2), 152–162.

McLellan, A. T. (1983). Patient characteristics associated with outcomes. In J. R. Cooper, F. Altman, B. S. Brown, & D. Czechowicz (Eds.), *Research on the treatment of narcotic addiction: State of the art* (DHHS Publication No. ADM 87-1281, pp. 500–529). Rockville, MD: U.S. Department of Health and Human Services.

McLellan, A. T., Alterman, A. I., Metzger, D. S., Grissom, G. R., Woody, G. F., Luborsky, L., & O'Brien, C. P. (1994). Similarity of outcome predictors across opiate, cocaine, and alcohol treatment: Role of treatment services. *Journal of Counseling and Clinical Psychology, 62*, 1141–1158.

McLellan, A. T., Alterman, A. I., Metzger, D. S., Grissom, G. R., Woody, G. E., Luborsky, L., & O'Brien, C. P. (1997). Similarity of outcome predictors across opiate, cocaine, and alcohol treatments: Role of treatment services. In G. A. Marlatt & G. R. VandenBos (Eds.), *Addictive behavior: Readings on etiology, prevention, and treatment.* Washington, DC: American Psychological Association.

McLellan, A. T., & Dembo, R. (1993). *Screening and assessment of alcohol- and other drug-abusing adolescents.* Rockville, MD: Center for Substance-Abuse Treatment.

McLellan, A. T., Kushner, H., Metzger, D., Peters, R. H., Smith, I., Grissom, G., Pettinati, H., & Argeriou, M. (1992). The fifth edition of the addiction severity index. *Journal of Substance-Abuse Treatment, 9*, 199–213.

McLellan, A. T., & McKay, J. R. (1998). Components of successful treatment programs. Lessons from the research literature. In A. W. Graham & T. K. Schultz (Eds.), *Principles of addiction medicine.* Chevy Chase, MD: American Society of Addiction Medicine.

McPherson, T. L., & Hersch, R. K. (2000). Brief substance use screening instruments for primary care settings. *Journal of Substance-Abuse Treatment, 18,* 193–202.

Meierhoefer, B. (1992a). *General effect of mandatory minimum prison terms: A longitudinal study of federal sentence imposed.* Washington, DC: Federal Judicial Center.

Meierhoefer, B. (1992b). Role of offense and offender characteristics in federal sentencing. *Southern California Law Review, 66*(1), 367–404.

Mejta, C., Bokos, P., Maslar, E. M., Mickenberg, J. H., & Senay, E. C. (1997). The effectiveness of case management in working with intravenous drug users. In F. M. Tims, J. A. Inciardi, B. W. Fletcher, & A. M. Horton (Eds.), *The effectiveness of innovative approaches in the treatment of drug abuse* (pp. 101–114). Westport, CT: Greenwood Press.

Metzner, J. L., Miller, R. D., & Kleinsasser, D. (1994). Mental health screening and evaluation within prisons. *Bulletin of the American Academy of Psychiatry Law, 22,* 451–457.

Michaels, D., Zoloth, S. R., Alcabes, P., Braslow, C. A., & Safyer, S. (1992). Homelessness and indicators of mental illness among inmates in New York City's correctional system. *Hospital and Community Psychiatry, 43,* 150–155.

Miller, G. A. (1985). *The substance abuse subtle screening inventory (SASSI) manual.* Bloomington, IN: SASSI Institute.

Miller, N. S., & Gold, M. S. (1994). Criminal activity and crack addiction. *International Journal of Addictions, 29,* 1069–1078.

Miller, N., & Flaherty, J. (2000). Effectiveness of coerced addition treatment (alternative consequences): A review of the clinical research. *Journal of Substance-Abuse Treatment, 18,* 9–16.

Miller, W. R. (1989). Increasing motivation for change. In R. K. Hester & W. R. Miller (Ed.), *Handbook of alcoholism treatment approaches* (pp. 67–80). New York: Pergamon.

Miller, W. R. (1996). Motivational interviewing: Research, practice, and puzzles. *Addictive Behaviors, 21,* 835–842.

Miller, W. R. (1999). Pros and cons: Reflections on motivational interviewing in correctional settings. *Minuet, 6,* 2–3.

Miller, W. R., & Rollnick, S. (1991). *Motivational interviewing.* New York: Guilford Press.

Minkoff, K., & Drake, R. (Ed.). (1991). *Dual diagnosis of major mental illness and substance disorder.* San Francisco: Jossey-Bass.

Modrcin, M., Rapp, C., & Chamberlain, R. (1985). *Case management with physically disabled individuals: Curriculum and training program.* Lawrence, KS: University of Kansas School of Social Welfare.

Moffitt, T. (1993). Adolescent-limited and life-course-persistent antisocial behavior: A developmental taxonomy. *Psychological Review, 100,* 674–701.

Montgomery, H. A., Miller, W. R., & Tonigan, J. S. (1991). Differences among AA groups: Implications for research. *Journal of Studies on Alcohol, 54,* 502–504.

Monti, P. M., Abrams, D. B., Kadden, R. M., & Cooney, N. L. (1989). *Treating alcohol dependence.* New York: Guilford Press.

Moore, A. T. (1998). *Private prisons: Quality corrections at lower cost* (Policy Study No. 240). Los Angeles: Reason Public Policy Institute.

Moos, R. H., & King, M. J. (1997). Participation in community residential treatment and substance abuse patients' outcomes at discharge. *Journal of Substance-Abuse Treatment, 14,* 71–80.

Morash, M., Haarr, R. N., & Rucker, L. (1994). A comparison of programming for women and men in U.S. prisons in the 1980s. *Crime & Delinquency, 40,* 197–221.

Morrissey, J. P., Swanson, J. W., Goldstrom, I., Rudolph, L., & Manderscheid, R. W. (1993). *Overview of mental health services provided by state adult correctional facilities: United States, 1998. Mental Health Statistical Note.* Washington, DC: U.S. Department of Health & Human Services, Public Health Service, Substance Abuse and Mental Health Services Administration.

Mostashari, F., Riley, E., Selwyn, P. A., & Altice, F. L. (1998). Acceptance and adherence with antiviral therapy among HIV-infected women in a correctional facility. *Journal of Acquired Immune Deficiency Syndromes and Human Retrovirology, 18,* 341–348.

Mueser, K. T., Drake, R. E., Clark, R. E., McHugo, G. J., Mercer-McFadden, C., & Ackerson, T. H. (1995). *Evaluating substance abuse in persons with severe mental illness.* Cambridge, MA: Human Services Research Institute.

Mumola, C. J. (1998). Substance-abuse and treatment of adults on probation, 1995. Bureau of Justice Statistics Special Report. Washington, DC: U.S. Department of Justice.

Mumola, C. (1999, January). *Substance abuse and treatment, state and federal prisoners, 1997.* Bureau of Justice Statistics Special Report (NCJ172871). Washington, DC: U.S. Department of Justice, Office of Justice Programs, http://www.ojp.usdoj.gov/bjs/abstract/satsfp97.htm.

Murray, D. W. (1992). Drug abuse treatment programs in the federal bureau of prisons: Initiatives for the 1990s. In C. G. Leukefeld & F. M. Tims (Eds.), *Drug abuse treatment in prisons and jails* (National Institute of Drug Abuse Research Monograph 118). Washington, DC: U.S. Government Printing Office.

Musto, D. F. (1987). *The American disease—Origins of narcotic control.* New York: Oxford University Press.

Musto, D. (1999). *The American disease: Origins of narcotic control* (3rd ed.). New York: Oxford University Press.

Nacci, P. L., & Kane, T. R. (1983). The incidence of sex and sexual aggression in federal prisons. *Federal Probation, 48*(1), 31–36.

National Association of Social Work. (1992). *NASW Standards for Social Work Case Management.* Washington, DC: Author.

National Center on Addiction and Substance Abuse (CASA). (1998). *Behind bars: Substance abuse and America's prison population*. New York: Columbia University.

National Certification Reciprocity Consortium/Alcohol and Other Drug Abuse. (1993). *Standards for Certification*. Atkinson, NH: Author.

National Commission on Correctional Health Care. (1997). *Standards for health services in prisons*. Chicago: Author.

National Drug Court Institute. (1999). *Reentry drug courts*. Alexandria, VA: Author.

National GAINS Center. (1997). The prevalence of co-occurring mental and substance-abuse disorders in the criminal justice system. *Just the facts*. Delmar, NY: Author.

National Institute of Corrections. (1997). *Prison medical care: Special needs populations and cost control*. Longmont, CO: U.S. Department of Justice.

National Institute of Corrections. (1998). *Hospice and palliative care in prisons: Special issues in corrections*. Longmont, CO: U.S. Department of Justice.

National Institute of Corrections. (1998, September). Current issues in the operation of women's prisons (J1C0-110).

National Institute of Justice. (1998). *The Delaware department of correction life skills program: Program focus*. Washington, DC: Author.

National Institute of Justice. (1998). Annual report: Drug use among adult and juvenile arrestees (p. 3, April 1999). Washington, DC: U.S. Department of Justice.

National Institute of Justice. (1999). *1998 Annual report on drug use among adult and juvenile arrestees*. Washington, DC: Author.

National Institute of Justice. (1999). *Telemedicine can reduce correctional health care costs: An evaluation of a prison telemedicine network*. Washington, DC: U.S. Department of Justice.

National Institute of Justice. (2000). *1999 Annual report on drug use among adult and juvenile arrestees*. Washington, DC: National Institute of Justice.

National Institute on Drug Abuse. (1986). *Drug abuse treatment evaluation: Strategies, progress, and prospects* (NTIS Publication #85-150365/AS). Rockville, MD.

National Institute on Drug Abuse. (1997). *Treatment of drug-dependent individuals with Comorbid mental disorders* (National Institute of Health Publication 97-4172). Rockville, MD.

National Institute on Drug Abuse. (2000) Second Annual NIDA/NDRI Research to Practice Meeting. *Drug abuse treatment in the correctional system*. Bethesda, MD: Author.

Nelles, J., & Fuhrer, A. (1995). *Drug and HIV prevention at the Hindelbank penitentiary: Abridged report of the evaluation results*. Bern, Switzerland: Swiss Office of Public Health.

Newbern, D., Dansereau, D. F., & Pitre, U. (1999). Positive effects on life skills motivation and self-efficacy: Node-link maps in a modified therapeutic community. *American Journal of Drug and Alcohol Abuse, 25*, 407–423.

Nurco, D. N., Balter, M. B., & Kinlock, T. (1994). Vulnerability to narcotic addiction: Preliminary findings. *Journal of Drug Issues, 24*, 293–314.

Nurco, D. N., Bonito, A. J., Lerner, M., & Balter, M. B. (1975). Studying addicts over time: Methodology and preliminary findings. *American Journal of Drug and Alcohol Abuse, 2,* 183–196.

Nurco, D. N., Cisin, I. H., & Balter, M. B. (1981a). Addict careers I: A new typology. *International Journal of the Addictions, 16,* 1305–1325.

Nurco, D. N., Cisin, I. H., & Balter, M. B. (1981b). Addict careers II: The first ten years. *International Journal of the Addictions, 16,* 1327–1356.

Nurco, D. N., Hanlon, T. E., & Kinlock, T. W. (1991). Recent research on the relationship between illicit drug use and crime. *Behavioral Sciences and the Law, 9,* 221–242.

Nurco, D. N., Hanlon, T. E., Kinlock, T. W., & Duszynski, K. R. (1988). Differential criminal patterns of narcotic addicts over an addiction career. *Criminology, 25,* 407–423.

Nurco, D. N., Kinlock, T. W., & Hanlon, T. E. (1994). The nature and status of drug abuse treatment. *Maryland Medical Journal, 9,* 51–57.

Oberg, J. C. (1996). *An initial evaluation and analysis of the Ventura County drug court program.* Ventura, CAL: Ventura Drug Court.

O'Donnell, J. A., & Ball, J. C. (1966). *Narcotic addiction.* New York: Harper & Row.

Office of Applied Studies. (2000). *Substance-abuse treatment in adult and juvenile correctional facilities: Findings from the uniform facility data set 1997 survey of correctional facilities* (Drug and Alcohol Services Information System Series: S-9). Rockville, MD: Author.

Office of Justice Programs, U.S. Department of Justice. (1998). *Looking at a decade of drug courts.* Prepared by the drug court clearinghouse and technical assistance project. Washington, DC: American University.

Office of Justice Programs. (unpublished report). Looking at a decade of drug courts. U.S. Department of Justice report available at www.ojp.usdoj.gov/depo/decade98.htm.

Office of National Drug Control Policy. (1996). Treatment protocol effectiveness study. Washington, DC: Author, Executive Office of the President.

Office of National Drug Control Policy. (1997). *What America's users spend on illegal drugs, 1988–1995.* Washington, DC: Author.

Office of National Drug Control Policy. (1998). Drug treatment in the criminal justice system. *ONDCP Drug policy information clearinghouse fact sheet.* Washington, DC: U.S. Government Printing Office.

Office of National Drug Control Policy. (1999). *National drug control strategy* (NCJ174469). Washington, DC: The White House.

Okamoto, D., Kassebaum, G., & Anderson, M. (1998). *Evaluation of the Hawaii drug court: Final report for the judiciary.* Honolulu, HI: Okamoto Consulting Group.

Onken, L. S., Blaine, J. D., & Boren, J. J. (Eds.). (1997). *Beyond the therapeutic alliance: Keeping the drug-dependent individual in treatment* (National Institute on Drug Abuse Research Monograph Series, Vol. 165). Washington, DC: U.S. Government Printing Office.

Ossmann, J. (1999). *Evolution of continuing care in California.* Bidder's Conference Presentation. Sacramento, CA: Office of Substance Abuse, California Department of Corrections.

Ouimette, P. C., Finney, J. W., & Moos, R. H. (1997). Twelve-step and cognitive-behavioral treatment for substance abuse: A comparison of treatment effectiveness. *Journal of Consulting and Clinical Psychology, 65,* 230–240.

Pacific Southwest Addiction Technology Transfer Center. (1999). *Clinical assessment of substance abusers in custody settings: Bridging the gap.* Proceedings of the research to practice symposium, La Jolla, CA: Author.

Palmer, T. (1995). Programmatic and nonprogrammatic aspects of successful intervention: New directions for research. *Crime and Delinquency, 41*(1), 100–131.

Paone, D., Des Jarlais, D. C., & Shi, Q. (1998). Syringe exchange use and HIV risk reduction over time. *AIDS, 12,* 121–122.

Parent, D. G. (1990). *Day reporting centers for criminal—a descriptive analysis of existing programs.* National Institute of Justice Issues and Practices. Washington, DC: U.S. Department of Justice.

Paternoster, R. (1987). The deterrent effect of the perceived certainty and severity of punishment: A review of the evidence and issues. *Justice Quarterly, 4,* 173–217.

Pearlin, L. I., & Schooler, C. (1978). The structure of coping. *Journal of Health and Social Behavior, 19,* 2–21.

Pearson, F. S., & Lipton, D. S. (1999). A meta-analytic review of the effectiveness of corrections-based treatments for drug abuse. *Prison Journal, 79,* 384–410.

Pelissier, B., Rhodes, W., Gaes, G., Camp, S., O'Neil, J., Wallace, S., & Saylor, W. (1998). *Alternative solutions to the problem of selection bias in an analysis of federal residential drug treatment programs.* Washington, DC: Federal Bureau of Prisons.

Pelissier, M. M., Gaes, G., Rhodes, W., Camp, S., O'Neil, J., Wallace, S., & Saylor, W. (1998, January). *TRIAD drug treatment evaluation project six month interim report.* Washington, DC: Federal Bureau of Prisons, Office of Research and Evaluation.

Pepper, B., & Massaro, J. (1992). Trans-institutionalization: Substance abuse and mental illness in the criminal justice system. *Ties Lines, 92,* 1–4.

Peters, R. H. (1993). Drug treatment in jails and detention settings. In J. Inciardi (Ed.), *Drug treatment and criminal justice* (pp. 44–80). Newbury Park CA: Sage.

Peters, R. H., Greenbaum, P. E., Edens, J. F., Carter, C. R., & Ortiz, M. M. (1998). Prevalence of DSM-IV substance abuse and dependence disorders among prison inmates. *American Journal of Drug and Alcohol Abuse, 24,* 573–587.

Peters, R. H., Greenbaum, P. E., Steinberg, M. L., Carter, C. R., Ortiz, M. M., Fry, B. C., & Valle, S. K. (2000). Effectiveness of screening instruments in detecting substance use disorders among prisoners. *Journal of Substance-Abuse Treatment, 18,* 349–358.

Peters, R. H., Haas, A. L., & Murrin, M. R. (1999). Predictors of retention and arrest in drug courts. *National Drug Court Institute Review, 2*(1), 33–60.

Peters, R. H., & Hills, H. A. (1993). Inmates with co-occurring substance abuse and mental health disorders. In H. J. Steadman & J. J. Cocozza (Eds.), *Mental illness in America's prison* (pp. 159–212). Seattle, WA: National Coalition for the Mentally Ill in the Criminal Justice System.

Peters, R. H., & Hills, H. A. (1997). *Intervention strategies for offenders with co-occurring disorders: What works?* Delmar, NY: Policy Research.

Peters, R. H., & Hills, H. A. (1999). Community treatment and supervision strategies for offenders with co-occurring disorders: What works? In E. Latessa (Ed.), *Strategic solutions: The international community corrections association examines substance abuse* (pp. 81–137). Lanham, MD: American Correctional Association.

Peters, R. H., Kearns, W. D., Murrin, M. R., Dolente, A. S., & May, R. L. II. (1993). Examining the effectiveness of in-jail substance-abuse treatment. *Journal of Offender Rehabilitation, 19*(3/4), 1–39.

Peters, R. H., May, R. L., & Kearns, W. D. (1992). Drug treatment in jails: Results of nationwide survey. *Journal of Criminal Justice, 20*, 283–297.

Peters, R. H., & Murrin, M. R. (1998). *Evaluation of treatment-based drug courts in Florida's first judicial circuit.* Tampa, FL: Department of Mental Health, Law and Policy, Louis de la Parte Florida Mental Health Institute, University of South Florida.

Peters, R. H., & Steinberg, M. L. (2000). Substance-abuse treatment services in U.S. prisons. In D. Shewan & J. Davies (Eds.), *Drugs and prisons* (pp. 89–116). London: Harwood Academic Publishers.

Peters, R. H., Strozier, A. L., Murrin, M. R., & Kearns, W. D. (1997). Treatment of substance-abusing jail inmates: Examination of gender differences. *Journal of Substance-Abuse Treatment, 14*, 339–349.

Petersilia, J. (1995). A crime control rationale for reinvesting in community corrections. *Prison Journal, 75*, 479–496.

Petersilia, J. (1997). Probation in the United States. In M. Tonry (Ed.), *Crime and justice: A review of research* (vol. 22, pp. 149–200). Chicago: University of Chicago Press.

Petersilia, J., & Turner, S. (1993). Evaluating intensive supervision probation and parole: Results of a nationwide experiment. *Research in brief.* Washington, DC: National Institute of Justice.

Petersilia, J., & Turner, S. (1993). Intensive probation and parole. *Crime and Justice: A review of Research, 17*, 281–336.

Petersilia, J., Turner, S., & Deschenes, E. P. (1992). The costs and effects of intensive supervision for drug offenders. *Federal Probation, 56*, 12–17.

Peterson, M., & Johnstone, B. M. (1995). The Atwood Hall Health Promotion Program: Federal Medical Center, Lexington, KY: Effect on drug-involved federal offenders. *Journal of Substance-Abuse Treatment, 12*, 43–48.

Peyton, E. A. (in press). *TASC in the 21st century: A guide for practitioners and policymakers.* Prepared for National TASC. Rockville, MD: Center for Substance-Abuse Treatment.

Peyton, E. A., & Gossweiler, R. (2000). *Treatment services in adult drug courts: Report on the 1999 national drug court treatment survey.* Prepared for National TASC. Washington, DC: U.S. Department of Justice, Drug Courts Program Office.

Pickens, R. W., Leukefeld, C. G., & Schuster, C. R. (Eds.). (1991). *Improving drug abuse treatment* (NIDA Research Monograph 106). Washington, DC: U.S. Government Printing Office.

Pinkerton, S., & Abramson, P. R. (1995). Decision making and personality factors in sexual risk-taking for HIV/AIDS: A theoretical integration. *Personality & Individual Differences, 19,* 713–723.

Pitre, U., Dansereau, D. F., Newbern, D., & Simpson, D. D. (1998). Residential drug abuse treatment for probationers: Use of node-link mapping to enhance participation and progress. *Journal of Substance-Abuse Treatment, 15,* 535–543.

Platt, J. J. (1986). *Heroin addiction: Theory, research and treatment. Vol. 1* (2nd ed.). Melbourne, FL: Krieger.

Platt, J. (1995). Vocational rehabilitation of drug abusers. *Psychological Bulletin, 117,* 416–433.

Platt, J. J. (1997). Vocational rehabilitation of drug abusers. In G. A. Marlatt & G. R. VandenBos (Eds.), *Addictive behaviors: Readings on etiology, prevention, and treatment* (pp. 759–801). Washington, DC: American Psychological Association.

Platt, J. J., Burhringer, G., Kaplan, C. D., Brown, B. S., & Taube, D. O. (1988). The prospects and limitations of compulsory treatment for drug addiction. *Journal of Drug Issues, 18,* 595–525.

Platt, J. J., Husband, S. D., Hermalin, J., Cater, J., & Metzger, D. S. (1993). Cognitive problem-solving employment readiness intervention for methadone clients. *Journal of Cognitive Psychotherapy, 7,* 21–23.

Platt, J., Widman, M., Lidz, V., & Marlowe, D. (1998). Methadone maintenance treatment: Its development and effectiveness after 30 years. In J. A. Inciardi & L. Harrison (Eds.), *Heroin in the age of crack-cocaine* (pp. 160–187). Thousand Oaks, CA: Sage.

Pliszka, S. R., Sherman, J. O., Barrow, M. V., & Irick, S. (2000). Affective disorder in juvenile offenders: A preliminary study. *American Journal of Psychiatry, 150,* 130–132.

Pollack, H., Khoshnood, K., & Altice, F. (1999). Health care delivery strategies for criminal offenders. *Journal of Health Care Finance, 26,* 63–77.

Prendergast, M., Wellisch, J., & Wong, M. (1996a). Residential treatment for women parolees following prison drug treatment: Treatment experiences, needs and services, outcomes. *Prison Journal, 76,* 253–274.

Prendergast, M., Wellisch, J., & Wong, M. (1996b). *A study of women on parole who graduated from the forever free substance abuse program: Treatment experiences, needs and services, outcomes* (Final Report, California Department of Corrections Contract C94.217). Los Angeles: UCLA Drug Abuse Research Center.

Raeder, M. (1995). The forgotten offender: The effect of the sentencing guidelines and mandatory minimums on women and their children. *Federal Sentencing Review, 8,* 157.

Rahdert, E. (Ed.). (1991). *The adolescent assessment/referral system.* Rockville, MD: National Institute on Drug Abuse.

Rahdert, E., & Czechowicz, D. (Eds.). (1995). *Adolescent drug abuse: Clinical assessment and therapeutic interventions.* Rockville, MD: National Institute on Drug Abuse.

Rajkumar, A. S., & French, M. T. (1997). Drug abuse, crime costs, and the economic benefits of treatment. *Journal of Quantitative Criminology, 13,* 291–323.

Rapaport, R. N. (1960). *Community as doctor.* London: Tavistock Publications.

Rapp, R. C. (1998). *Outcomes associated with a strengths-based approach to substance-abuse treatment. Issues of substance.* Washington, DC: National Association of Social Work.

Rapp, R. C., Kelliher, C. W., Fisher, J. H., & Hall, F. J. (1994). A role in addressing denial in substance-abuse treatment. *Journal of Case Management, 3*(4), 139–144.

Rasch, G. (1980). *Probabilistic models for some intelligence and attainment tests.* Chicago: University of Chicago Press.

Rawlings, B., & Yates, R. (Eds.). (in press). *Therapeutic communities for drug abuse.* London: Jessica Kingsley.

Regier, D. A., Farmer, M. E., Rae, D. S., Locke, B. S., Keith, S. J., Judd, L. L., & Goodwin, F. K. (1990). Comorbidity of mental disorders with alcohol and other drug abuse. *Journal of American Medical Association, 264,* 2511–2518.

Reindollar, R. W. (1999). Hepatitis C and the correctional population. *American Journal of Medicine, 107,* 100S–103S.

Reuter, P. (1992). *Hawks ascendant: The punitive trend of American drug policy.* Santa Monica, CA: RAND.

Reuter, P. (1997). Can we make prohibition work better? Some consequences of avoiding the unattractive. *Proceedings of the American Philosophical Society, 141,* 262–275.

Rhodes, W., Hyatt, R., & Scheiman, P. (1996). Predicting pretrial misconduct with drug tests of arrestees: evidence from six sites. *Research in brief.* Washington, DC: U.S. Department of Justice, National Institute of Justice.

Robins, L. N., Helzer, J. E., Croughan, J., & Ratcliff, K. S. (1981). National institute of mental health diagnostic interview schedule: Its history, characteristics, and validity. *Archives of General Psychiatry, 38,* 381–389.

Roehl, J. (1998). *Monterey County drug court evaluation report #1.* Alexandria, VA: Justice Research Center.

Room, J. A. (1998). Work and identity in substance abuse recovery. *Journal of Substance-Abuse Treatment, 15,* 65–74.

Rose, S. J., Zweben, A., & Stoffel, V. (1999). Interfaces between substance-abuse treatment and other health and social systems. In B. S. McCrady & E. B. Epstein (Eds.), *Addictions: A comprehensive guidebook.* New York: Oxford UP.

Roskes, E., & Feldman, R. (1999). A collaborative community-based treatment program for offenders with mental illness. *Psychiatric Services, 50,* 1614–1619.

Ross, H. E., Glaser, F. B., & Germanson, T. (1988). The prevalence of psychiatric disorders in patients with alcohol and other drug problems. *Archives of General Psychiatry, 45,* 1023–1031.

Ross, H. L. (1992). *Confronting drunk driving: Social policy for saving lives.* New Haven, CT: Yale University Press.

Ross, H. L. (1993). Confronting drunk driving: Social policy for saving lives. *Journal of the American Medical Association, 270,* 100.

Ross, M. W., & Darke, S. (1992). Mad, bad and dangerous to know: Dimensions and measurement of attitudes toward drug abusers. *Drug and Alcohol Dependence, 30*(1), 71–74.

Ross, P. H., & Lawrence, J. E. (1998). Health care for women offenders. *Corrections Today, 60,* 122–127.

Rounsaville, B. J., Anton, S. F., Carroll, K., Budde, D., Prusoff, B. A., & Gawin, F. (1991). Psychiatric diagnoses of treatment-seeking cocaine abusers. *Archives of General Psychiatry, 48,* 43–51.

Rowan-Szal, G. A., Chatham, L. R., & Simpson, D. D. (2000). Importance of identifying cocaine and alcohol dependent methadone clients. *American Journal on Addictions, 9*(1), 38–50.

Rubin, S. E., & Roessler, R. T. (1995). *Foundations of the vocational rehabilitation process* (4th ed.). Austin, TX: Pro-Ed.

Ruiz, J. D., Molitor, F., Sun, R., Mikanda, J., Facer, M., Colford, J. M., Rutherford, G. W., & Ascher, M. S. (1999). Prevalence and correlates of hepatitis C virus infection among inmates entering the California Correctional System. *Western Journal of Medicine, 170,* 156–160.

Ryan, W. (1971). *Blaming the victim.* New York: Pantheon Books.

Rychtarik, R. G., Prue, D. M., Rapp, S. R., & King, A. C. (1992). Self-efficacy, aftercare and relapse in a treatment program for alcoholics. *Journal of Studies on Alcohol, 53*(5), 435–440.

Sacks, S., De Leon, G., Bernhardt, A. I., & Sacks, J. Y. (1997). A modified therapeutic community for homeless MICA clients. In G. De Leon (Ed.), *Community-as-method: Therapeutic communities for special populations and special settings* (pp. 19–38). Westport, CT: Greenwood Publishing.

Sacks, S., Wexler, H., Peters, J., & Sacks, J. (2000). *Modified TC for MICA inmates in correctional settings.* Unpublished manuscript.

Saleeby, D. (1996). The strengths perspective in social work practice: Extensions and cautions. *Social Work, 41,* 295–305.

Salomè, H. J., & French, M. T. (in press). Using cost and financing instruments for economic evaluation of substance-abuse treatment services. In M. Galanter (Ed.), *Recent developments in alcoholism, Volume XIV, services research in the era of managed care, Section 3.* New York: Kluwar Academic/Plenum Press.

Santa Clara County Drug Treatment Court. (1997). *Drug treatment court: Third progress report, March 1, 1996–March 31, 1997.* Santa Clara, CA: Author.

Santiago, L., Beauford, J., Campt, D., & Kim, S. (1996). *SISTER project final evaluation report: Sisters in sober treatment empowered in recovery, San Francisco County Sheriff's Office Department*. Clearinghouse for Drug Exposed Children, University of California, San Francisco.

Satel, S. (1998). Observational study of courtroom dynamics in selected drug courts. *National Drug Court Institute Review, 1*(1), 43–72.

Schinka, J. A., Hughes, P. H., Coletti, S. D., Hamilton, N. L., Urmann, C. F., Neri, R. L., & Renard, C. G. (1999). Changes in personality characteristics in women treated in a therapeutic community. *Journal of Substance-Abuse Treatment, 16*, 137–142.

Schopp, R. F., & Sturgis, B. J. (1995). Sexual predators and legal mental illness for civil commitment. *Behavior Sciences and the Law, 13*, 437–458.

Schottenfeld, R. S., Pascale, R., & Sokolowski, S. (1992). Matching services to needs: Vocational services for substance abusers. *Journal of Substance-Abuse Treatment, 9*(1), 3–8.

Seal, D. W., & Agostinelli, G. (1994). Individual differences associated with high-risk sexual behaviour: Implications for intervention programs. *AIDS Care, 6*, 393–397.

Sechrest, D. K., Shichor, D., Artist, K., & Briceno, G. (1998). *The Riverside County drug court: Final research report*. San Bernardino, CA: California State University, Criminal Justice Department.

Sells, S. B. (Ed.). (1974). *The effectiveness of drug abuse treatment: I and II*. Cambridge, MA: Ballinger.

Selzer, M. L. (1971). The Michigan alcoholism screening test: The quest for a new diagnostic instrument. *American Journal of Psychiatry, 127*, 89–94.

Sheridan, M. J. (1996). Comparison of the life experiences and personal functioning of men and women in prison. *Families in Society: The Journal of Contemporary Human Services, 77*, 423–434.

Sherman, L. W. (2000). *The defiant imagination: Conscience and the science of sanctions*. Albert M. Greenfield Memorial lecture: University of Pennsylvania, Philadelphia.

Shine, J. (Ed.). (2000). *A compilation of Grendon research*. Aylesbury, England: HM Prison Grendon, Grendon Underwood.

Siegal, H. A. (1998). *Comprehensive case management for substance-abuse treatment* (DHHS Publication No. SMA 98-3222). Rockville, MD: Center for Substance-Abuse Treatment, U.S. Department of Health and Human Services.

Siegal, H. A., Fisher, J., Rapp, R. C., Wagner, J. H., Forney, M. A., & Callejo, V. (1995). Presenting problems of substance abusers in treatment: Implications for service delivery and attrition. *American Journal of Drug and Alcohol Abuse, 21*(1), 17–26.

Siegal, H. A., Rapp, R. C., Li, L., Saha, P., & Kirk, K. (1997). The role of case management in retaining clients in substance-abuse treatment: An exploratory analysis. *Journal of Drug Issues, 27*, 821–831.

Silverman, I. (1985). Addiction intervention: Treatment models and public policy. *International Journal of the Addictions, 20*(1), 183–201.

Simon, L. (1997). Do criminal offenders specialize in crime types? *Applied and Preventive Psychology, 6,* 35–53.

Simpson, D. D. (1984). National treatment system based on the drug abuse reporting program (DARP) follow up research. In F. M. Tims & J. P. Ludford (Eds.), *Drug abuse treatment evaluation: Strategies, process, and prospects.* National Institute on Drug Abuse Monograph 51 (pp. 29–41). Washington, DC: National Institute of Drug Abuse.

Simpson, D. D., Camacho, L. M., Vogtsberger, K. N., Williams, M. L., Stephens, R. C., Jones, A., & Watson, D. D. (1994). Reducing AIDS risks through community outreach interventions for drug injectors. *Psychology of Addictive Behaviors, 8,* 86–101.

Simpson, D. D., Chatham, L. R., & Joe, G. W. (1993). Cognitive enhancements to treatment in DATAR: Drug abuse treatment for AIDS risks reduction. In J. Inciardi, F. Tims, & B. Fletcher (Eds.), *Innovative approaches to the treatment of drug abuse: Program models and strategies* (pp. 161–177). Westport, CT: Greenwood Press.

Simpson, D. D., Chatham, L. R., & Knight, K. (1997). *Research summary, April, 1997.* Fort Worth, TX: Texas Christian University, Institute of Behavioral Research.

Simpson, D. D., & Curry, S. J. (Eds.). (1997). Drug abuse treatment outcome study (DATOS) [Special issue]. *Psychology of Addictive Behavior, 11*(4).

Simpson, D. D., Dansereau, D. F., & Joe, G. W. (1997). The DATAR project: Cognitive and behavioral enhancements to community-based treatments. In F. M. Tims, J. A. Inciardi, B. W. Fletcher, & A. M. Horton, Jr. (Eds.), *The effectiveness of innovative approaches in the treatment of drug abuse* (pp. 182–203). Westport, CT: Greenwood Press.

Simpson, D. D., & Joe, G. W. (1993). Motivation as a predictor of early dropout from drug abuse treatment. *Psychotherapy, 30,* 357–368.

Simpson, D. D., Joe, G. W., & Brown, B. S. (1997). Treatment retention and follow-up outcomes in the drug abuse treatment outcome study (DATOS). *Psychology of Addictive Behaviors, 11*(4), 294–307.

Simpson, D. D., Joe, G. W., Fletcher, B. W., Hubbard, R. L., & Anglin, M. D. (1999). A national evaluation of treatment outcomes for cocaine dependence. *Archives of General Psychiatry, 56,* 507–514.

Simpson, D. D., Joe, G. W., Greener, J. M., & Rowan-Szal, G. A. (in press). Modeling year 1 outcomes with treatment process and posttreatment social influences. *Substance Use and Misuse.*

Simpson, D. D., Joe, G. W., Lehman, W. E. K., & Sells, S. B. (1986). Addiction careers: Etiology, treatment, and 12-year follow-up outcomes. *Journal of Drug Issues, 16,* 107–121.

Simpson, D. D., Joe, G. W., & Rowan-Szal, G. A. (1997). Drug abuse treatment retention and process effects on follow-up outcomes. *Drug and Alcohol Dependence, 47,* 227–235.

Simpson, D. D., Joe, G. W., Rowan-Szal, G. A., & Greener, J. (1995). Client engagement and change during drug abuse treatment. *Journal of Substance Abuse, 7,* 117–134.

Simpson, D. D., Joe, G. W., Rowan-Szal, G. A., & Greener, J. M. (1997). Drug abuse treatment process components that improve retention. *Journal of Substance-Abuse Treatment, 14*(6), 565–572.

Simpson, D. D., & Knight, K. (1998, November). *Health, addiction treatment, and the criminal justice system* [Report to Physician Leadership on National Drug Policy]. Providence, RI: Brown University Center for Alcohol and Addiction Studies.

Simpson, D. D., & Knight, K. (1999). *Research summary, December, 1999.* Fort Worth, TX: Texas Christian University, Institute of Behavioral Research.

Simpson, D. D., Knight, K., & Broome, K. M. (1997). *TCU/CJ forms manual: Drug dependence screen and initial assessment.* Fort Worth, TX: Texas Christian University, Institute of Behavioral Research.

Simpson, D. D., Knight K., & Hiller, M. L. (1997, January). *TCU/DCJTC forms manual: Intake and during-treatment assessments.* Fort Worth: Texas Christian University, Institute of Behavioral Research. [On-line]. Available: www.ibr.tcu.edu

Simpson, D. D., & Marsh, K. L. (1986). Relapse and recovery among opioid addicts 12 years after treatment. In F. M. Tims & C. G. Leukefeld (Eds.), *Relapse and recovery in drug abuse* (NIDA Research Monograph No. 72 DHHS Pub. ADM 86-1473). Washington, DC: U.S. Government Printing Office.

Simpson, D. D., & Sells, S. B. (1990). *Opioid addiction and treatment: A 12-year follow-up.* Malabar, FL: Krieger Publishing Company.

Simpson, D. D., Wexler, H. K., & Inciardi, J. A. (1999). Introduction. *Prison Journal, 79*, 291–293.

Simpson, D. D., Wexler, H. K., & Inciardi, J. A. (Eds.). (1999a). Drug treatment outcomes for correctional settings, Part 1 [Special issue]: *Prison Journal, 79*(3).

Simpson, D. D., Wexler, H. K., & Inciardi, J. A. (Eds.). (1999b). Drug treatment outcomes for correctional settings, Part 2 [Special issue]. *Prison Journal, 79*(4).

Sindelar, J. L., Jofre-Bonet, M., French, M. T., & McLellan, A. T. (2000). Cost-effectiveness analysis of treatments for illicit drug dependence: Paradoxes with multivariate outcomes. Unpublished manuscript, Yale University, New Haven, CT.

Singer, M. I., Bussey, J., Song, L. Y., & Lunghofer, L. (1995). The psychosocial issues of women serving time in jail. *Social Work, 40*, 103–113.

Skinner, H. A. (1982). The drug abuse screening test. *Addictive Behaviors, 7*, 363–371.

Skinner, H. A., & Horn, J. L. (1984). *Alcohol dependence scale: Users guide.* Toronto, Canada: Addiction Research Foundation.

Skolnick, A. (1998). Correctional and community health care collaborations. *Journal of the American Medical Association, 279*, 98–99.

Slayton, J. (2000). *Establishing and maintaining interagency information sharing.* Juvenile Accountability Incentive Block Grants Program Bulletin, March 2000. Washington, DC: Office of Juvenile Justice and Delinquency Programs, U.S. Department of Justice.

Slobogin, D. (1995). Therapeutic jurisprudence: Five dilemmas to ponder. *Public Policy and Law*, 193–196.

Smith, B., Davis, R. C., & Goretsky, S. R. (1997). *Strategies for courts to cope with the caseload pressure of drug cases—Draft*. American Bar Association, Criminal Justice Section.

Smith, B., & Dillard, C. (1994). Female prisoners and AIDS: On the margins of public health and social justice. *AIDS & Public Policy Journal, 9*(2), 78–85.

Snyder, H., & Sickmund, M. (1995). *Juvenile offenders and victims: A national report*. Washington, DC: Office of Juvenile Justice and Delinquency Prevention.

Snyder, H., & Sickmund, M. (1999). *Juvenile offenders and victims: 1999 national report*. Washington, DC: Office of Juvenile Justice and Delinquency Prevention.

Solursh, L. P., Solursh, D. S., & Meyer, C. A. (1993). Is there sex after the prison door slams shut? *Medicine and Law, 12*, 439–443.

Spaulding, A., Greene, C., Davidson, K., Schneidermann, M., & Rich, J., (1999). Hepatitis C in state correctional facilities. *Preventive Medicine, 28*, 92–100.

St. Lawrence, J. S., Eldridge, G. D., Shelby, M. C., Little, C. E., Brasfield, T. L., & O'Bannon, R. E. (1997). HIV risk reduction for incarcerated women: A comparison of brief interventions based on two theoretical models. *Journal of Consulting and Clinical Psychology, 65*, 504–509.

Stashenko, J. (1999). State outlines timetable for ban on smoking in prisons. *Associated Press*, July 21, 1999.

Staton, M., Leukefeld, C., & Logan, T. K. (in press). Health service utilization and victimization among incarcerated female substance abusers. *Substance Use & Misuse*.

Staton, M., Leukefeld, C., Logan, T. K., & Purvis, R. (2000). Process evaluation for prison based treatment program. Unpublished manuscript, University of Kentucky.

Steadman, H. J., Cocozza, J. J., & Melick, M. E. (1987). Explaining the increased arrest rates among mental patients: The changing clientele of state hospital. *American Journal of Psychiatry, 135*, 816–820.

Stein, L. I., & Santos, A. B. (1998). *Assertive community treatment of persons with severe mental illness*. New York: W. W. Norton.

Stein, L. I., & Test, M. A. (1980). Alternative to mental hospital treatment. *Archives of General Psychiatry, 37*, 392–397.

Stewart, J. (1999). Sentencing law symposium: The effects of mandatory minimums on families and society. *T. M. Cooley Law Review, 16*, 37.

Stojkovic, S., & Lovell, R. (1997). *Corrections: An introduction* (Rev. ed.). Cincinnati, OH: Anderson.

Strauss, S. M., & Falkin, G. P. (in press). The relationship between the quality of drug user treatment and program completion: Understanding the perceptions of women in a prison-based program. *Substance Use and Misuse*.

Strauss, S. M., & Falkin, G. P. (unpublished manuscript). The first week after drug treatment: The influence of treatment on drug use among women offenders.

Svanum, S., & McGrew, J. (1995). Prospective screenings of substance dependence: The advantages of directness. *Addictive Behaviors, 20,* 205–213.

Swartz, J. A., & Lurigio, A. J. (1999). Psychiatric illness and comorbidity among adult male jail detainees in drug treatment. *Psychiatric Services, 50,* 1628–1630.

Swartz, J. A., Lurigio, A. J., & Slomka, S. A. (1996). The impact of IMPACT: An assessment of the effectiveness of a jail-based treatment program. *Crime and Delinquency, 42,* 553–573.

System Sciences. (1979). *Evaluation of treatment alternatives to street crime: National evaluation program, phase II report.* Washington, DC: National Institute of Law Enforcement and Criminal Justice.

Talboy, E. S. (1998). *Therapeutic community experiential training: Facilitator guide.* Kansas City, MO: Mid-America Addiction Technology Transfer Center [www.mattc.org].

Tauber, J., & Huddleston, C. W. (1999). *DUI/Drug courts: Defining a national strategy.* Alexandria, VA: National Drug Court Institute.

Taxman, F. S. (1998a). *Reducing recidivism through a seamless system of care: Components of effective treatment, supervision, and transition services in the community.* (Prepared for Office of National Drug Control Policy Treatment and Criminal Justice System Conference). Greenbelt, MD: University of Maryland, College Park.

Taxman, F. S. (1998b). 12 steps to improved offender outcomes. *Corrections Today, 60*(6), 114–117.

Taxman, F. (1999). Unraveling "what works" for offenders in substance-abuse treatment services. *National Drug Court Institute Review, 2*(2), 93–132.

Taxman, F. S. (1999, Summer). Substance-abuse treatment within the criminal justice system: An analysis of conflicting needs and implications. *Perspectives: Journal of the American Probation and Parole Association,* pp. 18–26.

Taxman, F., & Bouffard, J. (2000, in press). Understanding the therapeutic integrity of therapeutic communities in jails for drug-involved offenders. *Justice Research and Policy.*

Taxman, F., & Piquero, A. (1998). On preventing drunk driving: Rehabilitation vs. punishment approaches. *Journal of Criminal Justice, 26,* 129–144.

Taxman, F. S., Soule, D., & Gelb, A. (1999). Graduated sanctions: Stepping into accountable systems and offenders. *Prison Journal, 79,* 182–204.

Taxman, F. S., & Spinner, D. L. (1996). *The jail addiction services (JAS) project in Montgomery County, Maryland: Overview of results from a 24 month follow-up study.* University of Maryland at College Park.

Taylor, C. (1994). Alcohol, drug, and tobacco dependence: Charting and comparing the likelihood and time-course of relapse and recovery. In G. Edwards & M. Lader (Eds.), *Addiction: Processes of change* (Society for the Study of Addiction Monograph No. 3). Oxford, England: Oxford University Press.

Tepin, L. (1990). Detecting disorder: The treatment of mental illness among jail detainees. *Journal of Consulting and Clinical Psychology, 58,* 233–236.

Teplin, L. A., Abram, K. M., & McClelland, G. M. (1997). Mental disorders women in jail: Who receives services? *American Journal of Public Health, 87,* 604–609.

Terkel, S. (1972). *Working: People talk about what they do all say and how they feel about what they do.* New York: Ballantine Books.

Terry, Y., VanderWaal, C., McBride, D., & VanBuren, H. (2000). Provision of drug treatment services in the juvenile justice system: A system reform. *Journal of Behavioral Health Services and Research, 27,* 194–214.

The Anti-Drug Abuse Act of 1986. 100 Stat. 1 Publ. L. No.99-570:3207.

The Sentencing Project. (1999a). *Americans behind bars: U.S. and international use of incarceration 1995.* The Sentencing Project Publications. http://www.sentencingproject.org/policy/9030data.html.

The Sentencing Project. (1999b). *National inmate population of two million projected in 2000.* The Sentencing Project Publications. http://www.sentencingproject.org/pubs/tsppubs/prison~1.htm.

Therapeutic Communities of America (TCA) Criminal Justice Committee. (1999). *Therapeutic communities in correctional settings: The prison-based TC standards development project, Final report of phase II.* (Prepared for the White House Office of National Drug Control Policy [ONDCP], NCJ179365). Available at http://www.whitehousedrugpolicy.gov or from the National Drug Clearinghouse, 1-800-666-3332.

Thorburn, K. M. (1995). Health care in correctional facilities. *Western Journal of Medicine, 163,* 560–564.

Timmons-Mitchell, J., Brown, C., Schulz, S. C., Webster, S. E., Underwood, L. A., & Semple, W. E. (1997). Comparing the mental health needs of female and male incarcerated juvenile delinquents. *Behavioral Science and the Law, 15,* 195–202.

Tims, F. M. (1981). *Effectiveness of drug abuse treatment programs* (DHHS Publication ADM 84-1143). Rockville, MD: National Institute on Drug Abuse.

Tims, F. M., Fletcher, B. W., & Hubbard, R. L. (1991). Treatment outcomes for drug abuse clients. In R. W. Pickens, C. G. Leukefeld, & C. R. Schuster (Eds.), *Improving drug abuse treatment* (NIDA Research Monograph 106, pp. 93–113). Washington, DC: U.S. Government Printing Office.

Tims, F. M., Hamilton, N., Dennis, M. L., Godley, S., & Funk, R. (2000). Characteristics, problems, and HIV risk behavior of 600 adolescents admitted to drug abuse treatment. Paper presented at the annual meeting of the American Psychological Association, Washington, DC.

Tonry, M. (1987). *Sentencing reform impacts.* Washington, DC: U.S. Department of Justice, National Institute of Justice.

Tonry, M. (1990). Research on drugs and crime. In M. Tonry & J. Wilson (Eds.), *Drugs and crime.* Chicago: The University of Chicago Press.

Torborg, M. A., Bellassai, J. P., Yezer, A. M. J., & Trost, R. P. (1999). *Assessment of pre-trial urine-testing in the District of Columbia: Summary report.* Washington, DC: U.S.Department of Justice, National Institute of Justice.

Transactional Records Access Clearinghouse (TRAC). (2000). *New findings—Overall: Federal drug sentences substantially down*. http://trac.syr.edu/tracdea/findings/aboutDEA/newFindings.html.

Tucker, T. C. (1998). *Outcome evaluation of the Detroit target cities jail based substance-abuse treatment program*. Detroit, MI: Wayne County Department of Community Justice.

Tunis, S., Austin, J., Morris, M., Hardyman, P., & Bolyard, M. (1996). *Evaluation of drug treatment in local corrections*. Washington, DC: National Institute of Justice.

Turner, S., Greenwood, P., Fain, T., & Deschenes, E. (1999). Perceptions of drug court: How offenders view ease of program completion, strengths and weaknesses, and the impact on their lives. *National Drug Court Institute Review, 2*(1), 1–58.

Turner, S., Petersilia, J., & Deschenes, E. (1992). Evaluating intensive probation/parole (ISP) for drug offenders. *Crime and Delinquency, 38*, 539–556.

Turner, S., Petersilia, J., & Deschenes, E. P. (1994). The implementation and effectiveness of drug testing in community supervision: Results of an experimental evaluation. In D. L. MacKenzie & C. D. Uchida (Eds.), *Drugs and crime: Evaluating public policy initiatives* (pp. 231–252). Thousand Oaks, CA: Sage.

Tyler, T. R. (1996). The psychological consequences of judicial procedures: Implications for civil commitment hearings. In D. B. Wexler & B. J. Winick (Eds.), *Law in a therapeutic key: Developments in therapeutic jurisprudence* (pp. 3–16). Durham, NC: Carolina Academic Press.

U.S. Department of Justice. (1983). *Career patterns in crime* (NCJ-88672). Washington, DC: Bureau of Justice Statistics Bulletin.

U.S. Department of Justice. (1996). *Prison and jail inmates, 1995*. Washington, DC: Author.

U.S. Department of Justice, Bureau of Justice Statistics. (1999a). *HIV in prisons 1997* (NCJ-178284). Washington, DC: U.S. Department of Justice.

U.S. Department of Justice, Bureau of Justice Statistics. (1999b). *Mental health and treatment of inmates and probationers* (NCJ-174463). Washington, DC: U.S. Department of Justice.

U.S. Department of Justice, Bureau of Justice Statistics. (1999c). *Prior abuse reported by inmates and probationers* (NCJ-172879). Washington, DC: U.S. Department of Justice.

U.S. Department of Justice, Bureau of Justice Statistics. (1999d). *Sourcebook of criminal justice statistics, 1998*. Washington, DC: U.S. Government Printing Office.

U.S. Department of Justice. (2000). *Correctional populations 1999*. Bureau of Justice Statistics. Washington, DC: U.S. Government Printing Office.

U.S. General Accounting Office. (1996). *Private and public prisons: Studies comparing operational costs and/or quality of service*. Washington, DC: U.S. General Accounting Office.

U.S. General Accounting Office. (1997). *Drug courts: Overview of growth, characteristics, and results*. Washington, DC: U.S. General Accounting Office.

United States Department of Health and Human Services. (1994). Assessment and treatment of patients with coexisting mental illness and alcohol and other drug abuse. *Center for Substance-Abuse Treatment: Treatment Improvement Protocol.* Rockville, MD: Author.

United States Sentencing Commission. (1991). *Federal sentencing guidelines: A report on the operation of the guidelines system and short-term impacts on disparity in sentencing, use of incarceration, and prosecutorial discretion and plea bargaining.* Washington, DC: Author.

United States Sentencing Commission. (August 1991). *Special report to the Congress: Mandatory minimum penalties in the federal criminal justice system.* Washington, DC: Author. http://www.ussc.gov/legist.htm.

United States Sentencing Commission. (February 1995). *Special report to the Congress: Cocaine and federal sentencing policy.* Washington, DC: Author. http://www.ussc.gov/crack/exec.htm.

United States Sentencing Commission. (April 1997). *Special report to the Congress: Cocaine and federal sentencing policy.* Washington, DC: Author. http://www.ussc.gov/legist.htm.

United States Sentencing Commission. (1998). *1998 Sourcebook of federal sentencing guidelines.* Washington, DC: Author. http://www.ussc.gov/research.htm.

University of California, San Diego. (1999). *Mixing of sex offenders in custodial drug treatment therapeutic community units: Problems and potential solutions.* Proceedings of the symposium conducted at University of California, San Diego.

Vaillant, G. E. (1988). What can long-term follow-up teach us about relapse and prevention of relapse in addiction? *British Journal of Addiction, 83,* 1147–1157.

Vaillant, G. E. (1992). The beginning of wisdom is never calling a patient a borderline, or the clinical management of immature defenses in the treatment of individuals with personality disorders. *Journal of Psychotherapy Practice and Research, 1,* 117–134.

Vaillant, G. E., & Milosky, E. S. (1980). Natural history of male psychological health, IX: Empirical evidence for Erikson's model of the lifecycle. *American Journal of Psychiatry, 137,* 1348–1359.

Vaillant, G. E., & Milosky, E. S. (1982). Natural history of male alcoholism, IV: Paths to recovery. *Archives of General Psychiatry, 39,* 127–133.

Vaillant, G. E., & Vaillant, C. O. (1981). Natural history of male psychological health, X: Work as a predictor of positive mental health. *American Journal of Psychiatry, 138,* 1433–1440.

Van Stelle, K., Mauser, E., & Moberg, D. P. (1994). Recidivism to the criminal justice system of substance-abusing offenders diverted into treatment. *Crime and Delinquency, 40,* 175–196.

Vanicelli, M. (1978). Impact of aftercare in the treatment of alcoholics. *Journal of Studies on Alcohol, 39,* 1875–1886.

Ventura, L. A., Cassel, C. A., Jacoby, J. E., & Huang, B. (1998). Case management and recidivism of mentally ill persons released from jail. *Psychiatric Services, 49,* 1330–1337.

Vigdal, G. L., & Stadler, D. W. (1989). Controlling inmate drug use: Cut consumption by reducing demand. *Corrections Today, 51,* 96–98.

Vigilante, K. C., Flynn, M. M., Affleck, P. C., Stunkle, J. C., Merriman, N. A., Flanigan, T. P., Mitty, J. A., & Rich, J. D. (1999). Reduction in recidivism of incarcerated women through primary care, peer counseling, and discharge planning. *Journal of Women's Health, 8,* 409–415.

Visher, C. A. (1992a). Pretrial drug testing: Panacea or pandora's box. *Annals, AAPSS, 521,* 112–131.

Visher, C. A. (1992b). Pretrial drug testing. *Research in brief.* Washington, DC: U.S. Department of Justice, National Institute of Justice.

Vito, G. F. (1989). The Kentucky substance abuse program: A private program to treat probationers and parolees. *Federal Probation, 53,* 65–72.

Vocci, F. J. (1999, June). Buprenorphine and buprenorphine with naloxone: Briefing paper and current data. Paper presented at the National Association of State Alcohol and Drug Abuse Directors Annual Meeting, Clearwater Beach, FL.

von Sternberg, K. (1997). *Project check-in summary report.* Houston, TX: Change Assessment Research Project, University of Houston.

Walters, G. D. (1990). *The criminal lifestyle: Patterns of serious criminal conduct.* Newbury Park, CA: Sage.

Walters, G. D. (1996). The psychological inventory of criminal thinking styles: Part III. Predictive validity. *International Journal of Offender Therapy and Comparative Criminology, 40,* 105–112.

Walters, G. D. (1998). The lifestyle criminality screening form: Psychometric properties and practical utility. *Journal of Offender Rehabilitation, 27,* 9–23.

Walters, G. D., & Elliott, W. N. (1999). Predicting release and disciplinary outcome with the psychological inventory of criminal thinking styles: Female data. *Legal and Criminological Psychology, 4*(1), 15–21.

Walters, G. D., & McDonough, J. R. (1998). The lifestyle criminality screening form as a predictor of federal parole/probation/supervised release outcome: A 3-year follow-up. *Legal and Criminological Psychology, 3,* 173–181.

Walters, G. D., White, T. W., & Denny, D. (1991). The lifestyle criminality screening form: Preliminary data. *Criminal Justice and Behavior, 18,* 406–418.

Wanberg, K. W., & Milkman, H. B. (1998). *Criminal conduct and substance-abuse treatment: Strategies for self-improvement and change.* Thousand Oaks, CA: Sage.

Weinberg, N., Rahdert, E., Colliver, J., & Glantz, M. (1998). Adolescent substance abuse: A review of the past 10 years. *Journal of the American Academy of Child and Adolescent Psychiatry, 37,* 252–261.

Weiner, J., & Anno, B. J. (1992). The crisis in correctional health care: The impact of the National Drug Control Strategy on correctional health services. *Annals of Internal Medicine, 117,* 71–77.

Weinstein, J., & Turner, N. R. (1997). The cost of avoiding injustice by guideline circumventions. *Federal Sentencing Review, 9,* 298.

Weisner, C., & Schmidt, L. A. (1995). Expanding the frame of health services research in the drug abuse field. *Health Service Research, 30,* 707–726.

Weisz, J. R, Weiss, B., Han, S. S., Granger, D. A., & Norton, J. (1995). Effects of psychotherapy with children and adolescents revisited: A meta-analysis of treatment outcome studies.*Psychological Bulletin, 117*, 450–468.

Wellisch, J., Anglin, M. D., & Prendergast, M. (1993). Treatment strategies for drug-abusing women offenders. In J. Inciardi (Ed.), *Drug treatment and criminal justice* (pp. 5–29). Newbury Park, CA: Sage.

Wellisch, J., Prendergast, M. L., & Anglin, M. D. (1995). Toward a drug abuse treatment system. *Journal of Drug Issues, 25*, 759–782.

Wexler, D. B. (1996). Therapeutic jurisprudence and the criminal courts. In D. B. Wexler & B. J. Winick (Eds.), *Law in a therapeutic key: Developments in therapeutic jurisprudence* (pp. 157–170). Durham, NC: Carolina Academic Press.

Wexler, D. B., & Winick, B. J. (1996). *Law in a therapeutic key: Developments in therapeutic jurisprudence.* Durham, NC: Carolina Academic Press.

Wexler, H. (1986). Therapeutic communities within prisons. In G. De Leon & J. Zeigenfuss (Eds.), *Therapeutic communities for addictions: Readings in theory, research and practice* (pp. 227–238). Springfield, IL: Charles C Thomas.

Wexler, H. K. (1995). The success of therapeutic communities for substance abusers in American prisons. *Journal of Psychoactive Drugs, 27*(7), 57–66.

Wexler, H. K. (1997). Therapeutic communities in American prisons. In E. Cullen, L. Jones, & R. Woodward (Eds.), *Therapeutic communities in prisons.* New York: Wiley.

Wexler, H. K. (2000). *Co-occurring mental health and substance abuse programs in American prison planning meeting.* Washington, DC: Author.

Wexler, H. K. (in press). Criminal justice aftercare: An integrated approach. *Counselor.*

Wexler, H. K., De Leon, G., Thomas, G., Kressel, D., & Peters, J. (1999a). The Amity prison TC evaluation: Reincarceration outcomes. *Criminal Justice and Behavior, 26*, 147–167.

Wexler, H. K., Falkin, G. P., & Lipton, D. S. (1990). Outcome evaluation of a prison therapeutic community for substance-abuse treatment. *Criminal Justice and Behavior, 17*(1), 71–92.

Wexler, H. K., Falkin, G. P., Lipton, D. S., & Rosenblum, A. B. (1992). Outcome evaluation of a prison therapeutic community for substance-abuse treatment. In C. G. Leukefeld & F. M. Tims (Eds.), *Drug abuse treatment in prisons and jails* (NIDA Monograph No. 118, pp. 156–175). Rockville, MD: National Institute on Drug Abuse.

Wexler, H. K., & Lipton, D. S. (1993). From reform to recovery: Advances in prison drug treatment. In J. Inciardi (Ed.), *Drug treatment and criminal justice* (pp. 209–227). Newbury Park, CA: Sage Publications.

Wexler, H. K., Lipton, D. S., & Johnson, B. D. (1988). *A criminal justice system strategy for treating cocaine-heroin abusing offenders in custody.* Issues and practices paper in Criminal Justice. Washington, DC: U.S. Department of Justice.

Wexler, H. K., Magura, S., Beardsley, M. M., & Josepher, H. (1994). ARRIVE: An AIDS education/relapse prevention model for high-risk parolees. *International Journal of the Addictions, 29*, 361–386.

Wexler, H. K., Melnick, G., Lowe, L., & Peters, J. (1999). Three-year reincarceration outcomes for Amity in-prison therapeutic community and aftercare in California. *Prison Journal, 79*(3), 320–336.

Wexler, H. K., & Williams, R. (1986). The "Stay'n Out" therapeutic community: Prison treatment for substance abusers. *Journal of Psychoactive Drugs, 18,* 221–230.

Whillhite, S. A., & O'Connell, J. P. (1998). *The Delaware drug court: A baseline evaluation.* Dover, DE: Anova Associates and State of Delaware Statistical Analysis Center.

White, J. L., Moffitt, T. E., Caspi, A., Bartusch, D. J., Needles, D. J., & Stouthamer-Loeber, M. (1994). Measuring impulsivity and examining its relationship to delinquency. *Journal of Abnormal Psychology, 103,* 192–205.

White, W. L. (1998). *Slaying the dragon—The history of addiction treatment and recovery in America.* Bloomington, IL: Chestnut Health Systems.

Winick, C. (1962). Maturing out of narcotic addiction. *Bulletin on Narcotics, 14,* 1–7.

Winick, C. (1988). Some policy implications of the New York State civil commitment program. *Journal of Drug Issues, 18,* 561–574.

Winifred, M. (1996). Vocational and technical programs for women in prison. *Corrections Today, 58,* 168–170.

Winters, K. C. (1998, November). *Substance abuse and juvenile offenders.* University of Minnesota. Paper presented at the Physicians Leadership for National Drug Policy Conference, Washington, DC.

Winters, K. C. (1999). *Treatment of adolescents with substance use disorders.* Rockville, MD: Center for Substance-Abuse Treatment.

Wish, E. D. (1988). Identifying drug-abusing criminals. In C. G. Leukefeld & F. M. Tims (Eds.), *Compulsory treatment of drug abuse: Research and clinical practice* (NIDA Research Monograph 86, ADM 94-3713). Washington, DC: U.S. Government Printing Office.

Wish, E. D., & O'Neil, J. A. (1989). *Drug use forecasting (DUF).* National Institute of Justice Research Report. Washington, DC: U.S. Department of Justice.

Wish, E. D., O'Neil, J., & Baldau, V. (1990). Lost opportunity to combat AIDS: Drug abusers in the criminal justice system. In C. G. Leukefeld & R. J. Battjes (Eds.), *AIDS and intravenous drug use: Future directions for community-based prevention research* (NIDA Research Monograph Series 93, pp. 187–209). Rockville, MD: National Institute on Drug Abuse.

Withurn, D. J. (1993). *High HIV prevalence among female and male entrants to US correctional facilities (1989–1992): Implications for prevention and treatment strategies.* Proceedings of the 121st Annual Meeting of the American Public Health Association, Oct. 24–26. San Francisco, CA: American Public Health Association.

World Health Organization. (1993). *Global programme on AIDS: WHO Guidelines on HIV infection and AIDS in prisons.* Geneva, Switzerland: WHO/Global Programme on AIDS.

Yochelson, S., & Samenow, S. E. (1976). *The criminal personality* (Vol. 1). New York: Jason Aronson.

Young, D. (1996). *Retaining offenders in mandatory drug treatment programs: The role of perceived legal pressure.* New York: Vera Institute of Justice.

Zuckerman, B. (1996). Drug effects: A search for outcomes. In C. L. Wetherington, V. L. Smeriglio, & L. P. Finnegan (Eds.), *Behavioral studies of drug-exposed offspring: Methodological issues in human and animal research* (NIDA Research Monograph 164, pp. 277–287). Rockville, MD: U.S. Department of Health and Human Services.

Index

437

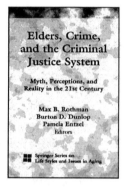